Decision Making

Edited by

GERARDO R. UNGSON, University of Oregon

DANIEL N. BRAUNSTEIN, Oakland University

Decision Making:

An Interdisciplinary Inquiry

KENT PUBLISHING COMPANY

A DIVISION OF WADSWORTH, INC.
BOSTON, MASSACHUSETTS

KENT PUBLISHING COMPANY
A Division of Wadsworth, Inc.

Editor: Jack McHugh
Production Editor: Michael Paladini
Designer: Carol Rose
Production Coordinator: Linda Siegrist

Printed in the United States of America

1 2 3 4 5 6 7 8 9 — 86 85 84 83 82

LIBRARY OF CONGRESS CATALOGING IN PUBLICATION DATA
Main entry under title:

Decision Making
"Based on a conference *New Directions in Decision Making: An Interdisciplinary Approach to the Study of Organizations,* sponsored by the Office of Naval Research, and the Graduate School of Management, University of Oregon . . . held at Eugene, Oregon on March 1–3, 1981."

Bibliography: pp. 337–357

Includes indexes.

1. Decision making — Congresses.   I. Ungson, Gerardo R.   II. Braunstein, Daniel N.   III. United States. Office of Naval Research.   IV. University of Oregon. Graduate School of Management.   V. Conference on Decision Making (1981 : University of Oregon).
HD30.23.D38   658.4'03   82-15253
ISBN 0-534-01161-6   AACR2

TO OUR PARENTS . . .

Decision Making:
An Interdisciplinary Inquiry

Editors:

Gerardo R. Ungson, University of Oregon
Daniel N. Braunstein, Oakland University

Contributors and Commentators:

Marinus J. Bouwman
Robert W. Chestnut
Terry Connolly
Larry L. Cummings
Ward Edwards
Hillel J. Einhorn
Baruch Fischhoff
Donald Gerwin
John R. Hayes
Robin M. Hogarth
George P. Huber
Jacob Jacoby
Daniel Kahneman
Howard Kunreuther

Arie Y. Lewin
Sarah Lichtenstein
Kenneth R. MacCrimmon
James G. March
Henry Mintzberg
John Payne
Louis R. Pondy
Michael I. Posner
Paul J. H. Schoemaker
Zur Shapira
John W. Slocum, Jr.
Ronald N. Taylor
Francis D. Tuggle
Amos Tversky
Karl E. Weick

Based on a conference "New Directions in Decision Making: An Interdisciplinary Approach to Study of Organizations" sponsored by the Office of Naval Research, and the Graduate School of Management, University of Oregon. The conference was held at Eugene, Oregon on March 1–3, 1981.

Preface

The Conference on Decision Making, held in March 1981, brought together prominent researchers from Behavioral Decision Making, Human Problem Solving, and Organizational Decision Making to compare their theoretical positions, methods, and applications. The conference was organized with the expectation that dialogue between these researchers would be fruitful in clarifying fundamental conceptual questions, research strategies, and assumptions that would eventually lead to integrative or convergent research.

For three days, conference participants presented "state-of-the-art" papers, provided critiques and commentaries, presented rebuttals to commentaries, and discussed many applications of theoretical ideas in the areas of business policy and strategy, accounting and finance, public policy, organizational design, and decision support systems. The lively and stimulating exchange of ideas, as well as points of tangency, agreement, and conflict are highlighted in nine position papers, ten commentaries, and six meta-commentaries that encompass a full range of issues on contemporary decision-making research. The results, published in this conference book, present a significantly authoritative book not only for researchers in these areas but to all those interested in the understanding and improvement of decision making.

As always, there are numerous persons who were instrumental in making the conference a successful one. We sincerely thank Richard M. Steers of the Graduate School of Management, University of Oregon, for his overall guidance, assistance, and encouragement throughout the entire project. To David Stonner of the U.S. Office of Naval Research, we offer our appreciation for his belief in and support of the conference. We also acknowledge the support of the T. O. Yntema Fund of the School of Economics and Management of Oakland University. Paul Slovic and Baruch Fischhoff of Decision Research were particularly helpful in providing both direction and critique of the conference design. James Reinmuth, Dean of the Graduate School of Management, University of Oregon, and Ron Horowitz, Dean of the School of Management and Economics, Oakland University, were understanding of our escalating long distance telephone calls, and were helpful in providing graduate student help and support for the conference.

During the course of the conference, Harry Waters provided invaluable help in ensuring that logistical arrangements were in order. David Dilts made sure that all conference proceedings were tape-recorded. Angeline McArthur, in addition to assisting in conference administrative chores, also proofread the entire manuscript and provided critical comments and important editorial suggestions in the process. We wish to thank Carol Heid and Tracy McElhinney for their patience in transcribing the tapes and in typing various parts of the manuscript. Thanks are also due to Dan Valentine and Jill Palmiere of Valentine Travel, who were particularly helpful in arranging travel schedules and "Oregon Coast Trips" for the participants.

Finally, we need to acknowledge the efforts made by the authors in developing papers for this conference. Many of the authors were already overcommitted to a number of other projects at the time they were contacted, yet they made a special effort to write papers for this particular conference. To them, and to all other conference attendees who contributed to discussions, we owe our special thanks. Finally, we are indebted to Dorothy Wynkoop of the Graduate School of Management, University of Oregon, whose day-to-day encouragements and good humor made this project an enjoyable experience.

Gerardo R. Ungson
Daniel N. Braunstein
May 1982

Contents

Decision Making

1 Introduction to Decision Making: An Interdisciplinary Inquiry

Gerardo R. Ungson, University of Oregon
Daniel N. Braunstein, Oakland University

After several decades of research activity, what can researchers from behavioral decision making, human problem solving, and organizational decision making learn from one another? In March of 1981 a group of more than sixty prominent researchers, including leading authorities from these three research fields and an interdisciplinary mix of representatives from accounting and finance, consumer behavior, organizational theory, and business policy and strategy, met to compare their theoretical positions and their research strategies, assumptions, and applications.

The conference was organized in the hope that the dialogue would encourage integrative or convergent research. The need for dialogue is evident when one considers the diversity of research disciplines used in the study of decision making. Through the years, scholars from such fields as psychology, economics, mathematics, statistics, organizational behavior, and management have done research in decision making. Though university courses and curricula, professional associations, and research journals devote singular attention to the study of decision making, it is commonly acknowledged that the scholars and practitioners involved in decision making differ significantly in their concepts, approaches, methods, and applications. The proliferation of labels, for example, behavioral decision making, decision theory, human information processing, and social judgment theory, is testimony of the growing divergence and complexity of decision-making research.

The attempt at the lofty goal of integrating numerous research disciplines is not a novel effort; efforts have been made by others through conferences and review papers (see Hammond, McClelland, and Mumpower 1980). These efforts, however, have emphasized only one level of analysis: individual, small group, or organizational.

We were trained in organizational behavior, and we were interested in relating work developed at the individual level to that on the organizational level. Our interest was not in extending the level of analysis *per se*, but in depicting how the interaction between individual and organizational decision making might improve the picture of real-world, managerial decision making. We argue that extant research of the individual level in the areas of behavioral decision making and human problem solving attends to simplified representations of real-world problems in order to create highly controlled experimental situations. Experimental control, however, is often attained at the expense of losing the context of real world decisions. On the other hand, research in organizational decision making focuses on contextual relationships underlying decision making in groups and organizations, but lacks the experimental controls necessary to rigorously examine those relationships. Awareness of points common to individual and organizational analysis could aid in a better understanding of real-world decisions.

Yet there is little cross-referencing in the research literature among researchers of behavioral decision making, human problem solving, and organizational decision making. This lack of integration is not surprising, as the

3

research fields are clearly differentiated in methodology, levels of analysis, and epistemology. However, there are compelling arguments that dialogue should take place among the research fields. First, all of the researchers are interested in study and improvement of decisional processes. For behavioral decision theorists particularly, the interest in improving decision making in applied settings has led to an examination of context effects and task-environmental elements. Second, notable parallels exist between individual and organizational decision making, particularly in learning, modeling, and conflict. Third, emerging work on decision aids and support systems emphasizes both the individual decision maker and the organizational context of these systems. Finally, some commentators (Hammond, McClelland, and Mumpower 1980) have suggested that there are "kinship ties" between the disciplines that warrant further exploration.

These calls for dialogue need to be carefully examined by the different fields comprising decision-making research, rather than by a single field where they would get a more sympathetic hearing. The dialogue should lead to a better understanding of theories on mutually shared concepts, further elaboration of kinship ties, and an exploration of possible points of synthesis in the future. This effort, represented by the conference, is premised on the belief that once there is an awareness of similarities and differences, research leading to integration will commence.

Framework for Dialogue

We envisaged the central theme of the conference to be the contrast between individual and organizational decision making. To provide perspective on some of the issues of mutual interest to individual and organizational decision theorists, we have defined three issues as an initial framework for dialogue. These issues relate to: (1) context effects in individual decision making, (2) cognitive processes by which individuals use information to solve problems, and (3) prescriptive implications for improving decision making in applied settings. Our intention at this point is not to present a comprehensive research agenda, but simply to highlight pivotal issues that would provide framework for dialogue.[1]

Context Effects in Decision Making

Problems have been typically described in terms of well-structured and ill-structured phenomena. The former is characterized by the completeness, specificity, and familiarity of problem-related information, for example, rules, transformation states, and desired outcomes, to the problem solver (MacCrimmon and Taylor 1976, Gerwin and Tuggle 1978). Some examples include cryptarithmetic and chess problems, more commonly associated with Simon and his associates (for example, Newell and Simon 1972), comparisons of multiattribute dimensions associated with studies of human judgment and

---

1. The following sections are based on G Ungson, D. Braunstein, and P. Hall, "Managerial Information Processing: A Research Review," *Administrative Science Quarterly* 1981 26:116–134. Used by permission.

choice (for example, Hammond, Hursh, and Todd 1964), consumer behavior (for example, Wright 1975, Jacoby 1975a), and probabilistic tasks associated with studies of judgmental heuristics (for example, Tversky and Kahneman 1974).

Interest in how individuals perceive or internally represent a problem led some researchers to examine what they termed *ill-structured problems*, defined by Simon and Hayes (1976a, p. 277) as those problems to which the problem solver contributes definition and resolution, using information generated from initial unsuccessful attempts at a solution. They also noted that ill-structured problems could result from the ambiguity or incompleteness of informational inputs. These concepts are consistent with more recent formulations of problems in managerial decision-making contexts (Mintzberg 1973, Mitroff and Emshoff 1979, Lyles and Mitroff 1980). Some examples include open-ended financial analysis, developing strategic decisions, and analyzing a turbulent environment.

We argue that conceptions about problem solving and decision making are to some extent determined by context effects. That persons go through successive steps of acquiring information, evaluating alternatives, and making choices may be an adequate representation of problem solving in well-structured problems. This representation, however, may be drastically different when a problem solver is faced with a messy, fluid, and contingent decision-making context, as in typical cases of ill-structured problems. By attending to the nature of contextual influences on decision making, we may develop different conceptions of how decisions are framed, and of the underlying cognitive processes that are used in making decisions.

Cognitive Processes in Decision-Making Contexts

After reviewing the development of decision aids, Simon (1965) made the comment that these aids to human thinking are developed without understanding the thought process itself. To a great extent, this comment has motivated researchers to study cognitive processes endemic to decision making in a variety of settings (see Slovic, Fischhoff, and Lichtenstein 1977). The concepts of judgmental heuristics (Tversky and Kahneman 1974), paramorphic representations (Hammond, Hursh, and Todd 1964), or problem-solving styles (Lyles and Mitroff 1980) describe various models of the cognitive process. Other heuristics and cognitive processes have been described (Fischhoff 1975; Payne 1976; Slovic, et al. 1977). In general, cognitive processes have been described as simple; serial and sequential; bounded, in terms of problem orientation; and familiar or anchored to previous problem experience. Most of these heuristics and cognitive processes were developed from analyzing well-structured problems.

We think, however, that such a focus is too limited when seeking to understand the types of cognitive processes occurring in managerial decision-making contexts. Given the time dimension in which organizational decisions are evoked, programmed, and recalled, it seems appealing to describe cognitive processes in terms of causal scripts (Abelson 1976), or tacit models (Langer 1976). Scripts are developed by individuals from previous experience, and are used in contexts in which they are perceived as applicable.

Under certain conditions, scripts can be invoked without prior activation or reflection (Langer 1976). It is this context in which persons are said to act before they think. Studies in organizational decision making (March and Olsen 1976, Starbuck and Hedberg 1976), in which organizations generate potential actions without stimulus of specific problems, are consistent with the above formulation.

The determination of what cognitive processes are used cannot be made independently of the research methods employed to describe these processes. The methods used have generic strengths and weaknesses. For example, protocols are rich in detail, but have been questioned as an adequate representation of the thought process (Nisbett and Wilson 1977). Another concern is whether protocols substantially change the nature and course of thought processes by limiting them to the main sequence (Neisser 1963). If such concerns are valid, then other processing modes, for example, multiple processing, might not be as well studied.

Other methods for studying cognitive processes such as model-fitting approaches (correlational, regressional, and functional measurement) have been generally criticized as inadequate descriptions of the underlying processes of decision-making behavior, since these approaches do not map the details of successive stages in the decision-making process (Payne, Braunstein, and Carroll 1978; Svenson 1979). Despite the criticisms, these approaches are used extensively in representing judgmental processes, as evidenced by the success reported in bootstrapping studies, that is, where a mathematical model based on cognitive processes of a problem solver was substituted for the problem solver's actual decisions (Dawes 1979).

Improving Decision Making

An interest in correcting judgmental biases has led to the development of decision aids to improve individual decision making (Phelps and Shanteau 1978, Lichtenstein and Fischhoff 1980). It has been noted, however, that decision aids, applied largely to well-structured problems, may not be as applicable to ill-structured problems (Connolly 1977; Mintzberg, Raisinghani, and Theoret 1976; Lyles and Mitroff 1980). It remains unclear that these aids that work well for individuals in experimental settings will prove as effective when environmental or context effects are taken into account. The challenge for decision theorists, therefore, is to extend the efficacy of decision aids to individuals in an organizational context.

The difficulty in developing decision aids for individuals in an organizational context is that the concept of a correct decision is not clear. A decision that appears functional, and therefore correct, in the short run may be dysfunctional in the long run, and vice versa. In addition, the lack of a clear analogue for a utility function at the organizational level makes both measurement and interpretation of any measurement very difficult. One way of gauging the success of organizational problem-solving methods would be to measure the extent of their institutionalization. Institutionalization, however, may impede the solution of newer, more novel problems (Cohen and March 1974, March and Olsen 1976).

An interesting development in the area of decision aids is the growing popularity of decision support systems (Keen and Morton 1978). Perhaps integration between the research fields will come about when both individual and organizational decision theorists work together in designing these systems.

Structure of the Book

Guided by these issues of context-inclusion, cognitive processes, and prescriptive measures, we invited participants to review major developments or to present empirical applications in behavioral decision making, human problem solving, and organizational decision making research. In addition, commentators were selected to critique and build on some of the issues presented in the review (state-of-the-art) and application papers. Finally, representatives from each of these research fields were asked to present some directions for integrating the three research areas. Taken together, there were twenty-five papers which we have grouped into six sections of related papers. There are three state-of-the-art papers, six application papers, ten commentaries, and six meta-commentaries. Specific headings, authors, and commentators are presented in the table below.

TABLE 1

SECTION	TOPIC	AUTHOR	COMMENTATORS
1	INTRODUCTION	Gerardo Ungson and Daniel Braunstein	
2	BEHAVIORAL DECISION THEORY	Hillel Einhorn and Robin Hogarth	Terry Connolly Kenneth MacCrimmon
3	HUMAN PROBLEM SOLVING	John Hayes	Michael Posner Sarah Lichtenstein
4	ORGANIZATIONAL DECISION MAKING THEORY	James March and Zur Shapira	Baruch Fischhoff Daniel Kahneman
5	APPLICATIONS, I		
	A. Financial Diagnosis	Marinus Bouwman	John Payne Ronald Taylor
	B. Model of Intrafirm Dynamics	Francis Tuggle and Donald Gerwin	
	C. Economics of Protection	Howard Kunreuther	

TABLE 1   (Continued)

SECTION	TOPIC	AUTHOR	COMMENTATORS
6	APPLICATIONS, II		
	A. Behavioral Process Research	Robert Chestnut and Jacob Jacoby	Henry Mintzberg John Slocum
	B. Decision Support Systems	George Huber	
	C. Decision Analysis	Howard Kunreuther and Paul Schoemaker	
7	META-COMMENTARIES		
	A. Framework for Decision Analysis and Critique	Larry Cummings	
	B. On Real Decisions	Lou Pondy	
	C. State-of-the-Art of Decision Research	Arie Lewin	
	D. View from a Barefoot Decision Analyst	Ward Edwards	
	E. Remarks on the Study of Decision Making	Amos Tversky	
	F. Rethinking Research on Decision Making	Karl Weick	
8	EPILOGUE	Gerardo Ungson and Daniel Braunstein	

While the papers generally deal with the issues of context-inclusion, cognitive processes, and prescriptive measures, a strict partitioning of the papers in terms of these three themes was not attempted. In developing their main arguments, many of the papers presented different perspectives on these themes, thus making such a partitioning difficult. Instead, we organized the initial sections (2–4) by presenting the three state-of-the-art papers, each followed by two commentaries, and an ensuing response to these commentaries. Subsequent sections (5 and 6) have a similar format using application papers instead of state-of-the-art papers. The six meta-commentaries are presented in a single section (7). Our contribution consists of this introduction and an epilogue, as well as introductions for each section, in which we present our own views on accomodating integration within these research fields. In adopting this particular approach, we wish to emphasize the process of dialogue that characterized the formulation of these papers.

Overview of Papers

The twenty-five papers resonate with the three issues of context-inclusion, cognitive processes, and prescriptive measures. As we said, a partitioning of the papers in terms of these issues was not attempted, as the different perspectives of these themes are subsumed under the main theme of each paper. We will describe the papers in terms of their main themes. A more detailed discussion of the papers is presented in the introduction to each chapter.

The first state-of-the-art paper, "Behavioral Decision Theory: Processes of Judgment and Choice," by Hillel Einhorn and Robin Hogarth, avoids the encyclopedic review characteristic of previous ones (see Slovic, Fischhoff, and Lichtenstein 1977a), and focuses on their conceptions of rationality of judgment and the implications of these conceptions on information acquisition, evaluation, action, and feedback learning in behavioral decision research.

Commentaries by Kenneth MacCrimmon and Terry Connolly critically question the relevance of behavioral decision-making research to real-world decisions. MacCrimmon argues that extant behavioral decision theory reveals little about decisions and behavior, and consequently it provides little guidance on how to solve real-world problems. Connolly argues that both the overfrequency of success and the preponderance of thoughtless action may undermine traditional characterizations of decision-making as represented by behavioral theory. In response, Einhorn and Hogarth remind us of how the study of judgment and choice is ultimately evaluated by its validity, that is, the degree to which it can be justified to oneself and others, and of how this concern, together with the limitations of laboratory studies, might not presently meet the full demands for relevance and utility.

In the second state-of-the-art paper, "Issues in Protocol Analysis," John R. Hayes explains why protocol analysis may have been misunderstood in the past, and he presents some distinctive advantages of the method. Posner acknowledges that protocol analysis has served as a useful coding device to study mental processes, but he cautions us on the limitations of the technique, particularly on how the thought process may change in the course of verbalization. Similarly, Lichtenstein states that the incompleteness of protocols constitutes a problem in interpreting them. In response, Hayes refers to Ericsson and Simon's (1980) classification of protocols, which suggests that different types of protocols (think-aloud, retrospective, introspective) reflect different types of thought processes, and that the criticisms of Posner and Lichtenstein are consistent with the predictions of the Ericsson and Simon classification.

The third state-of-the-art paper, "Behavioral Decision Making and Organizational Decision Making" by James March and Zur Shapira, attends to the similarities and differences between the two research fields. In his commentary, Baruch Fischhoff discusses how the "smartness" of organizational decisional behavior might be viewed as irrational if taken superficially. Dan Kahneman speaks to the importance of introducing the context effects to decision making and relates properties of organizations with properties of the mind. In a response, Shapira discusses further similarities and differences between individual and organizational behavior.

The application papers provide a vast array of conceptual questions, theoretical sources, levels of analysis, and research methods. Using protocol analysis, Marinus Bouwman presents differences on how novices and experts interpret financial statements. Francis Tuggle and Donald Gerwin present the results of their computer simulation of business policy decisions. Howard Kunreuther discusses the adjustment processes used by consumer and firms in cases where low probability events are perceived. Robert Chestnut and Jacob Jacoby elaborate on the developments and potential of "behavioral process research" in consumer behavior research. George Huber discusses the development and potential of decision support systems in improving decision making in organizations. Finally, Howard Kunreuther and Paul Schoemaker present a framework to incorporate descriptive and prescriptive components in the context of flood insurance cases.

The difficult task of critiquing and integrating all these papers was accepted in earnest by four commentators: Ronald Taylor, John Payne, Henry Mintzberg, and John Slocum. Taylor differentiates the papers by level of analysis and theoretical sources, and discusses the potential of the papers in improving decision making. Payne elaborates on the contributions and limitations of each of the papers. Similarly, Mintzberg critiques the papers, particularly in terms of their adequacy in representing real-world decisions. Finally, Slocum implores the need to include organizational variables, such as strategy and structure, in examining individual decisional processes and decision support systems.

The final task of providing meta-commentaries was given to Larry Cummings, Lou Pondy, Arie Lewin, Ward Edwards, Amos Tversky, and Karl Weick. Larry Cummings, Lou Pondy, and Arie Lewin develop different tracks in attempting to integrate the state-of-the-art papers and their respective commentaries. Cummings systematically classifies each of the papers into level of analysis and states of decision analysis, and presents some unresolved issues. Pondy focuses on six characteristics of what he calls "real decisions." Lewin suggests a forum, for example, decision engineering, in which behavioral and organizational decision theorists may take integrating roles. In a highly provocative paper, Edwards presents his perplexity at the term "rationality," particularly when applied to some conceptions made by organizational decision theorists. Tversky discusses some future directions for behavioral decision theory, citing the need for all researchers to reconsider accepted conceptions of rationality. Finally, Weick vividly portrays a number of themes made in the conference through a cartoon on soup sampling, and discusses directions in which accommodations for eventual integration may take place.

2 Behavioral Decision Theory

Behavioral Decision Theory: Processes of Judgment and Choice

Hillel J. Einhorn, *University of Chicago*
Robin M. Hogarth, *University of Chicago*

Commentaries:

On Taking Action Seriously: Cognitive Fixation in Behavioral Decision Theory

Terry Connolly, *Georgia Institute of Technology*

On Lincoln's Doctor's Dog, or Where Are We in Behavioral Decision Theory?

Kenneth MacCrimmon, *Northwestern University and University of British Columbia*

Reply to Commentaries:

Einhorn and Hogarth

Over the past decades, the term *behavioral decision theory* has been applied to the study of information utilization in judgment and choice, to the development of mathematical representations of decisional behavior, and, recently, to the examination of a subjects' deviations from normative models of judgment and choice. The prototypical research study involves attempts to expose research subjects to some controlled input stimulation, to observe the resulting output behavior, and to infer something about the nature of the cognitive process which mediates input and output behavior. Most of these studies were conducted in highly controlled experimental settings.

In the Einhorn and Hogarth paper which follows, the problem of using optimal models is considered in light of issues of rationality of judgment and of implications drawn for behavioral decision research. These implications focus upon the need to better understand the role of the intuitive processes that are a part of decision making. Research bearing upon these processes is reviewed in four areas: information acquisition, evaluation, action, and feedback/learning. The findings are examined for their potential contributions to a more complete psychological theory of decision making that includes the actual task structure, the representation of the task in the mind of the decision maker, and the information processing capabilities of the individual.

The literature cited in the Einhorn and Hogarth article is quite extensive, and covers a wide variety of research hypotheses, controls, and instrumentation. Yet there are those who wish us to consider such research incomplete. That is, despite experimentation by hundreds of researchers, there may be, according to these critics, something about the experimental situations, or the nature of the tasks or the dependent variables, which does not capture the essence of the decision process as it occurs in real life. The two critiques which follow the Einhorn and Hogarth paper support this contention.

Connolly prefaces his discussion with two questions: (1) if problem solvers are indeed the type of intellectual cripples portrayed in some theories of decision making, why do they make good decisions? and (2) why is there a constant assumption that prior thinking is the primary, or only, guide to effective action? Using a series of examples, Connolly argues that action may supplement, or even be an alternative to, reflection in complex problem solving. He invokes the term *microadaptive,* as opposed to *macroadaptive,* rationality to explain situations in which success is achieved via a series of small, incremental adjustments within the structure of a single task. Finally, he presents rudimentary notions of temporal sequencing and interactive decisional behavior to position "behavior" more firmly into behavioral decision theory.

MacCrimmon wonders if the past 30 years of research in behavioral decision theory have increased our understanding of the breadth of behavior involved, if the research has tuned us into what happens in actual decisions, and helped to develop more sophisticated theory. Could the research of the 1970s have been done as well in the 1940s? If so, what have we learned in the past three decades?

By focusing on some of the basic characteristics of the Einhorn and Hogarth paper, MacCrimmon probes further into the current contribution of behavioral decision theory. But in examining what he considers to be strengths in their paper, he also finds qualities which indicate some inherent weaknesses of the field. The advantage of using cognitive psychology to deal with the mental processes surrounding decisions can become a liability if it omits the mental representation of group and organizational influences. The interplay between decision and judgment is important only if decision making is attended to by the researchers along with judgmental processes. Analysis of the deviation of actual behavior from optimal models is only useful when the optimal model is adequately characterized. Finally, the dynamics of the relationship between decision processes and learning require more comprehensive treatment.

In suggesting some directions for behavioral decision theory, MacCrimmon reiterates the need to examine more broadly the influences in the decision process which can be traced to group, organizational, economic, and political conditions. He suggests that behavioral decision theorists should focus on real, rather than contrived, laboratory conditions. Finally, he argues for the building of more systematic and falsifiable theories.

In their response, Einhorn and Hogarth remind us that the study of judgment and choice is ultimately evaluated by its validity, that is, the degree to which the study can be justified to oneself and others. Validity, in turn, can be related to truth and accuracy. By *truth* they mean that the decision process should have a logical, deducible structure. In contrast, *accuracy* is criterion-referenced, that is, it refers to the ability of the decision to match or predict some external outcome.

Yet truth and accuracy can conflict, in spite of the fact that both are highly related to validity. The implications of these statements for psychological experiments are then discussed, particularly how such experiments are lacking in terms of providing feedback and structure for Connolly's microadaptive behavior.

Acknowledging then that psychological experiments have not provided the full context for testing real-world decisions, Einhorn and Hogarth implore researchers to provide richer descriptions of decisions to improve the experimentation process. In order to do this, they agree that experimental designs must better examine the action—outcome—feedback process, since it has been neglected in behavioral decision research, and that more redundancy should be built into experimental environments so that they become more representative of real-world conditions.

The papers examine the methodological and conceptual boundaries that differentiate behavioral decision theory from the other domains of decision-making research. While clarifying these boundaries, the papers also raise more questions. In their quest for greater validity, do experimenters constantly trade too much truth, as it subjectively exists in decision-making subjects, in favor of experimenter-determined accuracy? When should considerations of the comparative advantage of cognitive research give way to pressing concerns for more relevant variables? Finally, what will behavioral decision theorists do when they face the challenge of validating their theories in terms of truth, rather than in terms of accuracy? The ultimate challenge faced by behavioral decision theorists may come when the need for validation of theories in terms of truth outweighs the need for validation in terms of accuracy.

Behavioral Decision Theory: Processes of Judgment and Choice

Hillel J. Einhorn, *University of Chicago*
Robin M. Hogarth, *University of Chicago*

Why are normative theories so prevalent in the study of judgment and choice, yet virtually absent in other branches of science? For example, imagine that atoms and molecules failed to follow the laws supposed to describe their behavior. Few would call such behavior irrational or suboptimal. However, if people violate expected utility axioms or do not revise probabilities in accord with Bayes's theorem, such behavior is considered suboptimal and perhaps irrational. What is the difference, if any, between the two situations? In the latter we implicitly assume that behavior is purposive and goal-directed, while this is less obvious (if at all) in the former. (It is problematic how one might treat plant and animal behavior according to a descriptive-normative dichotomy.) Therefore, if one grants that behavior is goal-directed, it seems reasonable to assume that some ways of getting to the goal are better, in the sense of taking less time, making fewer errors, and so on, than others. Indeed, much of decision research concerns evaluating and developing ways for improving behavior, thereby reflecting a strong engineering orientation (Keeney and Raiffa 1976; Edwards 1977; Hammond, Mumpower, and Smith 1977). Moreover, comparison of actual behavior with normative models has been important in focusing attention on the discrepancies between them, and this attention in turn has raised important questions about the causes of such discrepancies.

Central to normative theories are the concepts of rationality and optimality. Recently, Simon (1978a) has argued for different types of rationality, distinguishing between the narrow economic meaning, that is, maximizing behavior, and its more general dictionary definition of "being sensible, agreeable to reason, and intelligent." Moreover, the broader definition itself rests on the assumption that behavior is functional. That is,

> Behaviors are functional if they contribute to certain goals, where these goals may be the pleasure or satisfaction of an individual or the guarantee of food or shelter for the members of society. . . . It is not necessary or implied that the adaptation of institutions or behavior patterns to goals be conscious or intended. . . . As in economics, evolutionary arguments are often adduced to explain the persistence and survival of functional patterns and to avoid assumptions of deliberate calculation in explaining them (pp. 3–4).

Accordingly, Simon's concept of "bounded rationality," which has provided the conceptual foundation for much behavioral decision research, is itself based on functional and evolutionary arguments. However, although one may agree that evolution is nature's way of doing cost/benefit analysis, it does not follow that all behavior is cost/benefit efficient in some way. We discuss this later with regard to misconceptions of evolution, but note that this view: (1) is unfalsifiable (see Lewontin 1979, on "imaginative reconstructions"); (2) renders the concept of an "error" vacuous; and (3) obviates the distinction between normative and descriptive theories. Thus, while it has been argued that the difference between bounded and economic rationality is one of degree, not kind, we disagree.

The previous review of this field (Slovic, Fischhoff, and Lichtenstein 1977) described a long list of human judgmental biases, deficiencies, and cognitive illusions. In the intervening period this list has both increased in size and influenced other areas of psychology (Bettman 1979, Mischel 1979, Nisbett and Ross 1980). Moreover, in addition to cataloging the types of errors induced by the manner in which people make judgments and choices, concern has now centered on explaining the causes of both the existence and persistence of such errors. This is exemplified by examination of a basic assumption upon which adaptive and functional arguments rest, namely the ability to learn (Einhorn and Hogarth 1978, Hammond 1978a, Brehmer 1980). However, if the ability to learn is seriously deficient, then dysfunctional behavior can not only exist but persist, thus violating the very notion of functionality. It is therefore essential to delimit the conditions under which this can occur. Indeed, the *general* importance of considering the effects of specific conditions on judgment and choice is emphasized by the following irony: the picture of human judgment and choice that emerges from the literature is characterized by extensive biases and violations of normative models whereas the opposite view emerges from work on lower animals. That is, in the latter, much choice behavior seems consistent with optimizing principles (for example, Killeen 1978, Rachlin and Burkhard 1978, Staddon and Motheral 1978). The danger of such pictures is that they are often painted to be interesting rather than complete. In the next section we consider the complexities involved in evaluating discrepancies between optimal models and human responses, and how persistent dysfunctional behavior is consistent with evolutionary concepts.

Are Optimal Decisions Reasonable?

How are discrepancies between the outputs of optimal models and human responses to be evaluated? First, consider the human responses to be generated through a cognitive model of the task, and note the different possibilities: (1) both models could inadequately represent the task, but in different ways; (2) the optimal model is a more adequate representation than the person, indeed, this is the assumption upon which most decision research is predicated; and (3) the person's model is more appropriate than the optimal model — a hypothesis suggested by March (1978). Furthermore, in the absence of discrepancies, neither model could be appropriate if it misrepresented the environment in similar ways. Therefore, before one compares discrepancies between optimal models and human judgments, it is important to compare each with the environment.

Task Versus Optimal Model of Task

We begin by offering a definition of optimality, namely, decisions or judgments that maximize some explicit and measurable criterion (for example, profits, errors, and time) *conditional on certain environmental assumptions and a specified time horizon.* The importance of this definition is that it stresses the conditional nature of optimality. For example, Simon (1979b) points out that because of the complexity of the environment, one has but two alternatives: to build optimal models by making simplifying environmental assumptions, or to build heuristic models that maintain greater environmental realism (see also Wimsatt 1980). Unfortunately, the conditional nature of optimal models has not been appreciated and too few researchers have considered their limitations. For instance, it has been found that people are insufficiently regressive in their predictions (Kahneman and Tversky 1973). While this is no doubt true in stable situations, extreme predictions are not suboptimal in nonstationary processes. In fact, given a changing process, regressive predictions are suboptimal. The problem is that extreme responses can occur at random *or* they can signal changes in the underlying process. For example, if you think that Chrysler's recent large losses are being generated by a stable process you should predict that profits will regress up to their mean level. However, if you take the large losses as indicating a deteriorating quality of management and worsening market conditions, you should be predicting even more extreme losses. Therefore, the optimal prediction is conditional on which hypothesis you hold.

The above is not an isolated case. For example, Lopes (1980a) points out that the conclusion that people have erroneous conceptions of randomness (for example, Slovic, Kunreuther, and White 1974), rests on the assumption that well-defined criteria of randomness exist. She convincingly demonstrates that this is not the case. Or, consider the work on probability revision within the Bayesian framework (for example, Slovic and Lichtenstein 1971). Much of this work makes assumptions (conditional independence, perfectly reliable data, well-defined sample spaces), that may not characterize the natural environment. Moreover, alternative normative models for making probabilistic inferences have been developed based on assumptions different from those held by Bayesians (Schaeffer 1976, Cohen 1977, see also Schum 1979, for a discussion of Cohen). In fact, Cohen's model rests on a radically different system that obeys rules quite different from the standard probability calculus. Competing normative models complicate the definition of what is a "bias" in probability judgment and have already led to one debate (Cohen 1979, Kahneman and Tversky 1979b). Such debate is useful if for no other reason than it focuses attention on the conditionality of normative models. To consider human judgment as suboptimal without discussion of the limitations of optimal models is naive. On the other hand, we do not imply that inappropriate optimal models always, or even usually, account for observed discrepancies.

The definition of optimality offered above deals with a single criterion or goal. However, actual judgments and choices are typically based on multiple goals or criteria. When such goals conflict, as when they are negatively correlated (for example, quantity and quality of merchandise, see Coombs and Avrunin 1977), there can be no optimal solution in the same sense as the single criterion case (Shepard 1964). That is, the most one can do is to execute the trade-offs or compromises between the goals that reflect one's values. Therefore, the imposition of subjective values for resolving conflicts leads to rejecting "objective" optimality and replacing it with the criterion of consistency with one's goals and values. Furthermore, even the single goal situation is transformed into a multiple goal case when judgments and choices are considered over time. For example, consider the single goal of maximizing profits. Conflicts between short-run and longer-run strategies can exist even with a single well-defined criterion. Therefore, unless a time horizon is specified, optimality can also be problematic in what might seem to be simple solutions.

Environment Versus Problem Space

The importance to behavior of the cognitive representation of the task, that is, "problem space," has been emphasized by Newell and Simon (1972). It is now clear that the process of representation and the factors that affect it are of major importance in judgment and choice. For example, work on estimating probabilities via fault trees (Fischhoff, Slovic, and Lichtenstein 1978); response mode effects inducing preference reversals (Grether and Plott 1979); coding processes in risky choice (Kahneman and Tversky 1979a); "problem isomorphs" in problem solving (Simon and Hayes 1976); context effects in choice (Aschenbrenner 1978; Tversky and Sattath 1979) and agenda setting (Plott and Levine 1978); purchasing behavior (Russo 1977); and causal schemas in probability judgments (Tversky and Kahneman 1980a) illustrate the effects of problem representation on behavior.

It is essential to emphasize that the cognitive approach has been primarily concerned with *how* tasks are represented. The issue of *why* tasks are represented in particular ways has not yet been addressed. However, given functional arguments, this is a crucial issue in view of the way minor contextual changes can lead to the violation of the most intuitively appealing normative principles, for example, transitivity.

The reconciliation of persistent errors and biases with functional arguments has taken two forms. First, it has been claimed that such effects can be overcome by increasing incentives (through higher payoffs and/or punishments). In one sense, this argument is irrefutable since it can always be claimed that the incentive wasn't high enough. However, direct evidence shows that increased payoffs do not necessarily decrease extreme overconfidence (Fischhoff, Slovic, and Lichtenstein 1977) nor prevent preference reversals (Grether and Plott 1979). Furthermore, the indirect evidence from clinical judgment studies in naturally occurring settings, where payoffs are presumably high enough to be motivating, continues to indicate low validity and inferiority to statistical models (Dawes 1979). In addition, claims that people will seek aids and/or experts when the stakes are high (Edwards 1975) are predicated on the assumptions that people know that they don't know, and they know or believe that others do know. On the other hand, it is foolish to deny that payoffs, and thus motivation, have no effect on processes of judgment and choice. Indeed, one only needs to recall the fundamental insight of signal detection theory (Green and Swets 1966), namely, that both cognitive and motivational components affect judgment (see also Killeen 1978).

A second way of reconciling biases with functional arguments involves enlarging the context in which performance is evaluated. This has taken four forms:

1. One view of evolutionary theory (as espoused by the sociobiologists, for example, Wilson 1978) could lead to the belief that the human system represents the optimal design for a complex environment. Heuristics exist because they serve useful functions and their benefits outweigh their costs. While this view is often espoused, there is surprisingly little evidence to support it. An important exception is the simulation study by Thorngate (1980), where it was shown how heuristics can often pick the best of several alternatives across a range of tasks. No study that we are aware of, however, has ever considered the distribution of tasks in the natural environment in which heuristics would work well or poorly.

2. Hogarth (1980a) has argued that most judgments and choices occur sequentially and that many biases reflect response tendencies functional in dynamic environments. Furthermore, the static tasks typically investigated reflect a preoccupation with those relatively simple situations for which optimal models can be constructed.

3. Toda (1962) has claimed that it is the coordination of behavior that reflects an organism's efficiency, not individual and thus isolated actions. Furthermore, coordination between functions requires trade-offs and these can be facilitated by limitations (for example, a limited memory facilitates efficient forgetting of needless detail).

4. Cost/benefit analyses can be expanded to include "the cost of thinking" (Shugan 1980), which seems compatible with notions of bounded rationality.

While there is much merit in the above arguments, care must be taken since they can easily become tautological; that is, costs and benefits can be defined *post hoc* in accord with a presumption of optimality. However, can there be actual dysfunctional behavior, rather than seeming dysfunctional behavior, that persists, and if so, by what mechanism(s)?

Since functional arguments rest on evolutionary theory, it is easy to overlook the fact that nonadaptive behavior can also be compatible with principles of natural selection:

1. Biological evolution is directly related to the amount of variance in the genotype (Lewontin 1979). For example, the development of wings could be functional for humans on many occasions. However, without an appropriate mutation, the chance of which is miniscule, such evolution cannot take place. While it is evident that physical limitations preclude certain types of behavior regardless of incentives to the contrary, biological limitations can also preclude certain cognitive operations (Russo 1978a). For example, the study of memory indicates limitations on short-term storage and retrieval. Furthermore, Seligman (1970) has explicated biological limitations in the learning process itself. Cognitive limitations can therefore

persist and be dysfunctional (relative to given goals) for the same reasons that account for physical limitations.

2. The time frame of human biological evolution is such that it can be considered constant over many generations. It is thus difficult to determine whether any current trait or mechanism is becoming more or less adaptive, or if it is a vestige without apparent function (for example, the human appendix; see also Skinner 1966). Therefore, without denying general cost/benefit considerations over the very long run, dysfunctional behaviors may persist for extremely long periods by human standards. The demise of the dinosaur, for example, is popularly cited as an example of the effectiveness of natural selection. It is easy to forget, however, that dinosaurs existed for about 160 million years. So far, humans are a mere 2.5 million years old (Sagan 1977).

3. Humans adapt the environment to suit their own needs as well as adapting to the environment. For example, poor eyesight is certainly dysfunctional, yet a major judgment aid, eyeglasses, has been invented to deal with this problem. Note that this aid actually works against natural selection; that is, those with poor vision will not be selected against since their survival chances become equal to those without the need for glasses. In fact, if poor eyesight were correlated with higher reproductive rates, there would be an increase in the aggregate level of this deficiency.

4. The analogy has been drawn between learning and evolution (for example, Campbell 1960). The attempt, however, to link individual learning with species level survival is problematic (Lewontin 1979). For example, consider whether response competition within an organism can be viewed as identical to competition between organisms. While the latter can and has been analyzed via game theoretic ideas of zero-sum payoffs and conflicting interests, such an approach seems foreign to intra-individual response competition.

Intuitive Responses and Optimal Models. The above arguments leave us on the horns of a dilemma. Given the complexity of the environment, it is uncertain whether human responses or optimal models are more appropriate. Furthermore, we know of no theory or set of principles which would resolve this issue. Indeed, the optimal–intuitive comparison presents the following paradox: Optimal models have been suggested to overcome intuitive shortcomings. In the final analysis, however, the outputs of optimal models are evaluated by judgment, that is, do we like the outcomes, do we believe the axioms to be reasonable, and should we be coherent?

If the assessment of rationality ultimately rests on judgment, what are its components? Imagine being a juror in a trial and having to decide whether someone who has committed a heinous crime acted rationally. The prosecution argues that the crime was meticulously planned and carried out, thus demonstrating that the person was in complete control of what he or she was doing. Note that this argument defines rationality by the efficiency with which means are used to attain ends. Moreover, this manner of defining rationality is exactly what decision theorists have stressed, namely, given one's goals, what is the best way of attaining them? The defense, however, argues that the goal of committing such a crime is itself evidence of irrationality. That is, rationality is to be judged by the goals themselves. Moreover, the argument is made that the deliberative way such despicable goals were reached is itself an indication of irrationality. Finally, the defense argues that when one understands the oppressed social or familial background of the defendant, the irrational goals are, in fact, reasonable. This last point emphasizes that goals can only be understood within the person's task representation. Moreover, this argument highlights a crucial problem; that is, to what extent *should* one be responsible for one's task representation? (See Brown 1978.)

What are the implications of the above for behavioral decision theory? First, judgments of rationality can be conceptualized as forming a continuum that can be dichotomized by imposing a cut-off when actions must be taken. This idea has been advanced by Lopes (1980) with respect to judging randomness. She suggests that the placement of the cut-off can be viewed within a signal-detection framework; that is, payoffs and costs are reflected by the cut-off point. Second, judged rationality is a mixture of the efficiency of means to ends (called *instrumental rationality,* Tribe 1973) and the "goodness" of the goals themselves (see Brown 1978). While the former is familiar to decision theorists, the latter is the concern of moral philosophers, theologians, and the like. Still, on a practical level it is of concern to all. In fact, it may well be that the efficacy of decision aids comes from structuring tasks, so that the nature of one's goals is clarified (Humphreys and McFadden 1980). Third, the importance of *behavioral* decision theory lies in the fact that even if one were willing to accept instrumental rationality as the sole criterion for evaluating decisions, knowledge of how tasks are represented is crucial, since people's goals form part of their models of the world. Moreover, their task representation may be of more importance in defining errors than the rules they use within that representation. For example, imagine a paranoic who processes information and acts with remarkable coherence and consistency. Such coherence of beliefs and actions is likely to be far greater than in so-called normal people. When does coherence become rigidity? Thus, the representation of the world as a place where others persecute one is the source of difficulty — not necessarily the incorrect or inconsistent use of inferential rules or decision strategies.

Strategies and Mechanisms of Judgment and Choice

The inescapable role of intuitive judgment in decision making underscores the importance of descriptive research concerned with how and why processes operate as they do. Moreover, the most important empirical results in the period under review have shown the sensitivity of judgment and choice to seemingly minor changes in tasks. Such results illustrate the importance of context to refer to *both* the formal structure and the content of a task. On the other hand, normative models gain their generality and power by ignoring content in favor of structure and thus, they treat problems out of context. Content, however, gives meaning to tasks, a fact that should not be ignored in trying to predict and evaluate behavior. For example, consider the logical error of denying the antecedent; that is, "if A, then B," does not imply "not A, then not *B*." However, as discussed by Harris and Monaco (1978), the statement "If you mow the lawn (*A*), I'll give you $5 (*B*)," does not imply that if you don't mow the lawn (not *A*) you won't get the $5 (not *B*). Or, consider a choice between a sure loss of $25 and a gamble with 3 to 1 odds in favor of losing $100 versus $0. Compare this with the decision to buy or not to buy an insurance policy for a $25 premium to protect you against a 75-percent chance of losing $100. Although the two situations are structurally identical, it is possible for the same person to prefer the gamble in the first case yet prefer the insurance policy in the second. For experimental results, see Hershey and Schoemaker 1980a. Such behavior can be explained in different ways: The person may not perceive the tasks as identical since content can hide structure (Einhorn 1980), and even if the two situations are seen as having identical structure, their differing content could make their meaning quite different. For example, buying insurance may be seen as the purchase of protection (which is good) against the uncertainties of nature, while being forced to choose between two painful alternatives is viewed as a no-win situation.

While context has typically been defined in terms of task variables, it is clear from the above examples that it is also a function of what the person brings to the task in the way of prior learning experience, and biological limitations on attention, memory, and the like, that affect learning. Therefore, the elements of psychological theory in decision making must include a concern for task structure, the representation of the task, and the information processing capabilities of the organism.

In order to discuss specific findings in the literature, we artificially decompose processes of judgment and choice into several subprocesses: information acquisition, evaluation, action, and feedback learning. We are well aware that these subprocesses interact and that their interaction is of great importance in the organization and coordination of decision making. Accordingly, we will consider these issues in the appropriate subsections.

The Role of Acquisition in Evaluation

Much work in judgment and choice involves the development and testing of algebraic models that represent strategies for evaluating and combining information (Slovic and Lichtenstein 1971). Although work in this tradition continues (for example, Anderson 1979), it has been accompanied by increasing dissatisfaction in that processes are treated in a static manner; that is, judgments and choices are considered to be formed on the basis of given information. In contrast, the process of information search and acquisition should also be considered (see Elstein, Shulman, and Sprafka 1978) since evaluation and search strategies proposed in the literature imply various search processes either explicitly (for example, Tversky and Sattath 1979) or implicitly (Payne 1976). Of great importance is the fact that the concern for how information is acquired raises questions about the role of attention and memory in decision making that have received relatively little concern (see Hogarth 1980b, Rothbart, in press). Furthermore, concern for the dynamics of information search has necessitated the use of different methodologies; for example, process-tracing approaches such as verbal protocols and eye movements, as well as information display boards (Payne 1976). However, these methods need not replace more general modeling efforts, and they may in fact be complementary to them (Payne, Braunstein, and Carroll 1978; Einhorn, Kleinmuntz, and Kleinmuntz 1979).

The importance of considering the interdependence of evaluation and acquisition can be seen in considering the issue of whether people lack insight into the relative importance they attach to cues in their judgment policies. The literature contains conflicting evidence and interpretations (Nisbett and Wilson 1977, Schmitt and Levine 1977). However, the use of weights in models as reflecting differential cue importance ignores the importance of attention in subjective weight estimates, and it illustrates our emphasis on understanding persons and tasks. Correspondence between subjective and statistical weights requires that people attend to and evaluate cues, *and* that such cues contain both variance and low intercorrelations. Disagreement between subjective and statistical weights can thus occur for three reasons: (1) people lack insight; (2) people attend to, but cannot use, cues that lack variance (Einhorn, Kleinmuntz, and Kleinmuntz 1979); and (3) cues to which attention is not paid are correlated with others such that the nonattended cues receive inappropriate statistical weights. Both process-tracing methods and statistical modeling are necessary to untangle these competing interpretations.

Acquisition

Acquisition concerns the processes of information search and storage — both in memory and the external environment. Central to acquisition is the role of attention, since this necessarily precedes the use and storage of information. We discuss attention by using an analogy with the concept of figure-ground, noting that, as in perception, the cognitive decomposition of stimuli can be achieved in many ways. Accordingly, different decompositions may lead to different task representations (see Kahneman and Tversky 1979b). Indeed, context can be thought of as the meaning of figure in relation to ground.

In an extraordinary article, Tversky (1977) analyzed the psychological basis of similarity judgments and, in so doing, emphasized the importance of context and selective attention in judgmental processes. He first noted that our knowledge of any particular object

> is generally rich in content and complex form. It includes appearance, function, relation to other objects, and any other property of the object that can be deduced from our general knowledge of the world (p. 329).

Thus, the process of representing an object or alternative by a number of attributes or features depends on prior processes of selective attention and cue achievement. Once features are achieved, the similarity between objects a and b, $s(a,b)$, is defined in terms of feature sets denoted by A and B, respectively. Thus,

$$s(a,b) = \theta f(A \Omega B) - \alpha f(A-B) - \beta f(B-A) \qquad \text{Eq. 1}$$

where, $A \Omega B$ = features that a and b have in common; $A-B, B-A$ = distinctive features of a and b, respectively; f = salience of features; and θ, α, and β are parameters. Note that Eq. 1 expresses $s(a,b)$ as a weighted linear function of three variables, thereby implying a compensatory combining rule. The importance of Eq. 1 lies in the concept of salience (f) and the role of the parameters. Tversky first defines salience as the intensity, frequency, familiarity, or more generally, the signal-to-noise ratio of the features. Thereafter, the way in which the f scale and the parameters depend on context are discussed. We consider three important effects: asymmetry and focus, similarity versus difference, and diagnosticity and extension.

Asymmetry and Focus. Asymmetry in similarity judgments refers to the fact that the judged similarity of a to b may not be equal to the similarity of b to a. This can occur when attention is focused on one object as subject and the other as referent. For example, consider the statements, *a man is like a tree* and *a tree is like a man.* It is possible to judge that a man is more like a tree than vice versa, thus violating symmetry and metric representations of similarity. The explanation is that in evaluating $s(a,b)$ versus $s(b,a)$, $\alpha > \beta$ in Eq. 1; that is, the distinct features of the subject are weighted more heavily than those of the referent. Hence, the focusing of attention results in differential weighting of features such that symmetry is violated.

Similarity Versus Difference. The similarity/difference occurs when $\alpha = \beta$ and $s(a,b) = s(b,a)$. In judging similarity, people attend more to common features, while in judging difference, they attend more to distinctive features. This leads to the effect in which

> a pair of objects with many common and many distinctive features may be perceived as both more similar and more different than another pair of objects with fewer common and fewer distinctive features (Tversky 1977, p. 340).

Diagnosticity and Extension. The first effect results from a shift in attention due to focusing on an anchoring point, the subject. The second is caused by a shift in attention induced by different response modes. The third effect, diagnosticity and extension, involves changes in the salience of the features in an object due to the specific object set being considered. For example, consider the feature "four wheels" in American cars. Such a feature is not salient since all American cars have four wheels. However, a European car with three wheels on an American road would be highly salient. Therefore, salience is a joint function of intensity and what Tversky calls *diagnosticity,* which is related to the variability of a feature in a particular set (see Einhorn and McCoach 1977). An important implication of diagnosticity is that the similarity between objects can be changed by adding to or subtracting from the set. For example, consider the similarity between Coca-Cola and Pepsi-Cola. Now add 7-Up to the new set and note the increased similarity of the colas.

Although Tversky's paper is of great importance for judgment and choice, it has not been linked to earlier concepts such as representativeness, anchoring and adjusting, or availability. However, the question of context and the figure-ground issues which underlie similarity would seem to be of great importance in understanding these heuristics and their concomitant biases as well as a wide range of phenomena in the literature. To illustrate, we first discuss work on base rates.

Earlier work (reviewed in Slovic, Fischhoff, and Lichtenstein, 1977) indicated that subjects ignore base rates, and it was postulated that this resulted from use of the representativeness heuristic and/or the apparent salience of concrete or vivid information (Nisbett et al. 1976). A base rate, however, can only be defined conditional on some population, or sample space. Whereas many might agree that the base rates defined by experimenters in laboratory tasks make the sample space clear, the definition of the population against which judgments should be normalized in the natural ecology is unclear. Consider an inference concerning whether someone has a particular propensity to heart disease. What is the relevant population to which this person should be compared? The population of people in the same age group? The population of the United States? Of Mexico? There is no generally accepted normative way of defining the appropriate population. Thus, for naturally occurring phenomena, it is neither clear whether people do or do not ignore base rates, nor whether they should ignore them (see also Goldsmith 1980, Russell 1948).

Even in the laboratory, base rates are not always ignored. Indeed, Tversky and Kahneman (1980) have argued that base rates will be used to the extent that they can be causally linked to target events. Their data supported this hypothesis and Ajzen (1977) independently reached similar results and conclusions. A further implication of causal thinking concerns asymmetries in the use of information; that is, information that receives a causal interpretation is weighted more heavily in judgment than information that is diagnostic, although probability theory accords equal weight to both. Whether such judgments are biased or not depends on whether one believes that causality should be ignored in a normative theory of inference, as is the case in standard probability theory (see Cohen 1977, 1979 for a different view).

Bar-Hillel (1980) further explicated the conditions under which base rates are used. She argued that people order information by its perceived degree of relevance to the target event, with high relevant dominating low relevant information. Causality, Bar-Hillel argued, is but one way of inducing relevance; it is sufficient but not necessary. Relevance can also be induced by making target information more specific, which is tantamount to changing the figure-ground relationship between targets and populations. We believe that further elucidation of the role of causality in judgment is needed (Mowrey, Doherty, and Keeley 1979), and we note that the notion of causality, like probability, is conditional on the definition of a background, or "causal field" (Mackie 1965).

Central to the distinction between figure and ground is the concept of cue redundancy. As Garner (1970) has stated, "good patterns have few alternatives," that is, cue redundancy helps achievement of the object and thus sharpens figure from ground. Tversky (1977) makes the point that for familiar, integral objects there is little contextual ambiguity, but this is not the case for artificial, separable stimuli. For example, consider the differential effects of acquiring information from intact or decomposed stimuli (the former being more representative of the natural ecology, the latter of experimental tasks). Phelps and Shanteau (1978) have shown that when expert livestock judges are presented with information in the form of eleven decomposed, orthogonal attributes of sows, they are capable of using all information in forming their judgment; however, when presented with intact stimuli (photographs), their judgments can be modeled by a few cues. These results illustrate that people can handle more information than previously thought; moreover, the results can be interpreted as indicating that cue redundancy in the natural ecology reduces the need for attending to and evaluating large numbers of cues. Redundancy in the natural ecology also implies that cues can indicate the presence of other cues and can thus lead one to expect cue co-occurrences. For example, in a study of dating choice, Shanteau and Nagy (1979) showed that subjects used cues not presented by the experimenters. That is, when choosing between potential dates from photographs, subjects' choices were influenced by the probability that their dates would be accepted even though this cue was not explicitly given.

The importance of redundancy in acquisition has been discussed by Einhorn, Kleinmuntz, and Kleinmuntz (1979), who note the following benefits:

> (1) Information search is limited without large losses in predictive accuracy; (2) attention is highly selective; (3) dimensionality of the information space is reduced, thereby preventing information overload; (4) intersubstitutability of cues is facilitated; and (5) unreliability of cues is alleviated by having multiple measures of the same cue variable (p. 466).

Studies and models that fail to consider cue redundancy in search processes are thus incomplete. For example, consider risky choice in the natural ecology versus the laboratory. (For reviews of risk, see Libby and Fishburn 1977, Vlek and Stallen 1980). In the former, probabilities are typically not explicit and must be judged by whatever environmental cues are available. A particularly salient cue is likely to be the size of the payoff itself, especially if people have beliefs about the co-occurrence of uncertainty and reward (for example, large payoffs occur with small probabilities). Thus, payoff size can be used as a cue to probability (see Shanteau and Nagy 1979). Moreover, the degree of perceived redundancy may also be important in understanding issues of ambiguity in decision making (see Yates and Zukowski 1976). That is, one's uncertainty about a probability estimate (so-called second order probability) may be related to a variety of cues, including payoff size. In fact, Pearson (1897) noted that although means and variances of distributions are usually treated as independent, in the natural ecology they tend to be correlated and can thus be used as cues to each other. The analogy to means and variances of payoff distributions from gambles seems useful.

The temporal order of information acquisition can also affect salience, by creating both shifts in figure-ground relations and differential demands on attention and memory. Consider as an example the effects of simultaneous versus sequential information display. In a study of supermarket shopping, Russo (1977) found that when unit prices were presented to shoppers in organized lists (ordered by relative size of unit prices, hence simultaneous presentation), purchasing behavior was changed relative to the situation where shoppers either did not have unit price information, or such information was simply indicated next to products on the shelves, the latter implying sequential acquisition. An interesting aspect of this study is that it represents a form of decision aiding quite different from those proposed in earlier work. That is, instead of helping people to evaluate information that has already been acquired (for example, through bootstrapping or multiattribute models), one eases strain on memory and attention by aiding the acquisition process itself. However, that greater understanding of attention and memory processes is necessary for the success of this approach was underscored in a study by Fischhoff, Slovic, and Lichtenstein (1978) on the use of *fault trees*. Fault trees are diagnostic check lists represented in treelike form. The task studied by Fischhoff, Slovic, and Lichtenstein involved automobile malfunction and had experts (automobile mechanics) and novices as subjects. The results indicated that the apparently comprehensive format of the fault tree blinded both expert and novice subjects to the possibility of missing causes of malfunction.

Since information is normally acquired in both intact form and across time, or sequentially, determining the manner and amount of information to be presented in acquisition aids is a subject of great importance. It raises issues of both how external stimuli cue memory and the organization of memory itself (Broadbent, Cooper, and Broadbent 1978; Estes 1980). Different ways of organizing information, for example, by attributes or by alternatives in a choice situation, could have implications for task representation. In addition, several recent studies of the "availability" heuristic (Tversky and Kahneman 1973) have further emphasized how ease of recall from memory has important effects on judgment (Kubovy 1977). Moreover, experimenters should be aware that subjects interpret stimuli rather than respond to them. For example, Tversky and Kahneman (1980a) show that when information is presented in a manner involving an ambiguous time sequence, intuitive interpretations may reflect a reordering of that information to conform to the time dependence of naturally occurring phenomena.

That figure-ground relation at a particular point in time affects judgment and choice has been demonstrated in a number of studies. A particularly compelling example is given by Tversky and Kahneman (1981). It is expected that a certain flu will kill 600 people this year and you are faced with two options: option 1 will save about 200 people; option 2 will save about 600 people with probability of 1 to 3 and no people with probability of 2 to 3. Now consider a rewording of the alternatives: option 1 will result in about 400 people dying; option 2 gives a 1 to 3 probability that none will die and a 2 to 3 chance that about 600 will die. By a simple change in the reference point induced by formulating the same problem in terms of lives lost or saved, cognitive figure and ground are reversed, as were the choices of a majority of subjects. Similar preference reversals can be obtained through the isolation effect, where sequential presentation of information can isolate and hence highlight the common components of choice alternatives. Aspects common to alternatives are canceled out, and the choice process is determined by comparing the distinctive features of the alternatives.

Payne, Laughhunn, and Crum (1979) have linked reference effects to the dynamic concept of aspiration level and have further illustrated how this linkage affects the encoding of outcomes as losses or gains relative to a standard (rather than considering the overall wealth position implied by different end states). Sequential effects in choice have also been demonstrated by Levine and Plott (1977) and Plott and Levine (1978) in both field and laboratory studies. The structure of an agenda was shown to affect the outcomes of group choice by sequencing the comparisons of particular subsets of alternatives. Tversky and Sattath (1979) have further considered implications of these effects within individuals when sequential elimination strategies of choice are used. That judgment should be affected in a relative manner by momentary reference points should, however, come as no surprise (see Slovic and Fischhoff 1977). Weber's law predicts this, and the prevalence of "adjustment and anchoring" strategies in dynamic judgmental tasks is congruent with these findings (Hogarth, 1980a).

Cognitive figure-ground relations vary considerably on the ease with which they can be reversed. On the one hand, the tendency not to seek information that could disconfirm one's hypotheses (Mynatt, Doherty, and Tweney 1977, 1978) illustrates strong figure-ground relations where confirming evidence is attracted to the figure, and possible disconfirming evidence remains in the ground. Consider also the difficulty of reformulating problem spaces in creative efforts where inversion of figure and ground is precisely what is required. On the other hand, situations also arise where figure and ground can invert themselves with minor fluctuations in attention, as in the case of "reversible figures" in perception. Whereas the analogy one could draw between "preference reversals" and "reversible figures" is possibly tenuous, both do emphasize the role of attention. In particular, the fluctuating nature of attention implies that for certain types of stimulus configurations, task representations can be unstable. Both choice and the application of judgmental rules have often been stated to be inherently inconsistent and hence probabilistic (Brehmer 1978, Tversky and Sattath 1979). However, the effects of fluctuating attention in producing such inconsistencies has not been explored.

Lest it be thought that the importance of attention in acquisition is limited to descriptive research, Suppes (1966) has stated: "What I would like to emphasize . . . is the difficulty of expressing in systematic form the mechanisms of attention a rationally operating organism should use" (p. 64). Furthermore, Schneider and Shiffrin (1977) have raised the possibility that attention is not completely under conscious control. Thus the normative problem posed by Suppes becomes more difficult.

Evaluation /Action

Imagine that you are faced with a set of alternatives and have at your disposal the following evaluation strategies: conjunctive, disjunctive, lexicographic, elimination by aspects, additive, additive difference, multiplicative, majority of confirming instances, or random. Furthermore, you could also use combinations of any number of the above. How do you choose? The wide range of strategies one can use in any given situation poses important questions about how one decides to choose (Beach and Mitchell 1978, Svenson 1979, Wallsten 1980). For example, what environmental cues "trigger" particular strategies? What affects the switching of rules? Are strategies organized in some way (for example, hierarchically), and if so, according to what principles? Although there has been concern for meta-strategies, most notably in Abelson's "script" theory (1976), the need for general principles is acute. This can be illustrated in the following way. Each evaluation strategy can be conceptualized as a multidimensional object containing such attributes as speed of execution, demands on memory (for example, storage and retrieval), computational effort, chance of making errors, and the like. Each strategy, however, could also be considered as a meta-strategy for evaluating itself and others. For example, an elimination-by-aspects meta-strategy would work by eliminating strategies sequentially by distinctive attributes. The choice of a meta-strategy, however, would imply a still higher level choice process, thereby leading to an infinite regress.

The above emphasized the need for finding principles underlying choice processes at all levels. One appealing possibility suggested by Christensen-Szalanski (1978, 1980) is that of an overriding cost/benefit analysis, which can induce suboptimal behavior in particular circumstances. This possibility raises several issues:

1. The meaning of costs and benefits is necessarily dependent on task representation, and thus, context. For example, a tax cut can be viewed as a gain *or* a reduced loss (Kahneman and Tversky 1979b, see also Thaler 1980, for an illuminating discussion of how this affects economic behavior).
2. Cost/benefit "explanations" can always be applied after the fact and thus become tautological (see the earlier discussion, p. 19).
3. The very notion of balancing costs and benefits indicates that conflict is inherent in judgment and choice. For instance, consider our earlier example of the options of insuring against a possible loss versus facing a no-win situation. The former can be conceptualized as an approach–avoidance conflict, the latter as an avoidance–avoidance conflict.

In fact, Payne, Laughhunn, and Crum (1979) have demonstrated the importance of considering the perceived conflict in choice in the following way: Subjects first made choices between pairs of gambles. A constant amount of money was then added or subtracted from the payoffs such that, for example, an approach–avoidance gamble was changed to an approach–approach situation. With gambles altered in this manner, systematic preference reversals were found. Hence, while the structure of the gambles remained unchanged, the nature of the conflict and the choices did not.

The importance of conflict in choice has been emphasized by Coombs and Avrunin (1977), who considered the joint effects of task structure and the nature of pleasure and pain. They begin by noting the prevalence of single-peaked preference functions (that is, nonmonotonic functions relating stimulus magnitude to preference) in a wide variety of situations. For example, consider the usual belief that more money is always preferred to less. While this violates single-peakedness, note that great wealth increases the risk of being kidnapped, of social responsibility to spend wisely, of lack of privacy, and so on. Thus, if one also considered these factors, it may be that there is some optimal level beyond which more money is not worth the increased trouble. Hence, there is an approach–avoidance conflict between the "utility for the good" and the "utility for the bad." The nature of this conflict eventuates in a single-peaked function given the behavioral assumption that, "Good things satiate and bad things escalate" (Coombs and Avrunin 1977, p. 224). Therefore, at some point, the bad becomes greater than the good and overall utility decreases. In the single-object case, it is not central that the bad escalate — only that it satiate at a slower rate than the good.

The theory becomes more complex when objects are characterized on multiple dimensions. For example, consider a number of alternatives that vary on price and quality, and suppose that some are both higher in price and lower in quality than others. Such dominated alternatives would seem to be quickly eliminated from further consideration. Indeed, the second principle in the theory is just this: dominated options are ignored. Hence, the alternatives that remain form a Pareto optimal set. While single-peakedness requires stronger conditions than this, from our perspective the important point is that the remaining set of alternatives highlights the basic conflict; namely, higher quality can only be obtained at a higher cost.

While the role of conflict in choice has received earlier attention (Miller 1959), its usefulness for elucidating psychological issues in decision making has not been fully exploited (however, see Janis and Mann 1977). We consider some of these issues by examining the role of conflict in, respectively, judgments of worth or value, deterministic predictions, and probabilistic judgments. Conflict in taking action is now discussed.

Conflict in Judgment

Consider the conflict between subgoals or attributes when one is judging overall value or worth. If dominated alternatives are eliminated, this elimination will result in negative correlations between the attributes of objects in the nondominated set, thereby insuring that one has to give up something to obtain something else. The resolution of the conflict can take several forms, the most familiar being the use of compensatory strategies, usually of additive form, although multiplicative models have also been used (see Anderson 1979). Psychologically, this approach can be thought of as conflict "confronting" since conflict is faced and resolution is achieved through compromise. Of crucial concern in executing one's compromise strategy is the issue of judgmental inconsistency (Hammond and Summers 1972). While the origin of such inconsistency is not well understood (see Brehmer 1978), it has often been considered as reflecting environmental uncertainty (Brehmer 1976). Inconsistency, however, may exist in the absence of environmental uncertainty. For example, price and quality can each be perfectly correlated with overall worth, yet one could argue that this correlation highlights the conflict and thus contributes to inconsistency. Although the theoretical status of conflict and inconsistency needs further development, it should be noted that methods for aiding people to both recognize and reduce conflict through compensatory compromise have been developed, and several applications are particularly noteworthy (Hammond and Adelman 1976; Hammond, Mumpower, and Smith 1977).

Alternatively, conflict in judging overall worth can be resolved by avoiding direct confrontation and compromise. Specifically, noncompensatory strategies allow evaluation to proceed without the difficulties (computational *and* emotional) of making trade-offs. As indicated above, the conditions in both task and person that control strategy selection remain relatively unchartered. However, in addition to the error/effort trade-offs thought to influence such decisions (Russo 1978a), the existence of conflict per se and the need to take it into account makes this issue problematic.

The evaluation of information in making predictions from multiple cues raises further questions concerning conflict in judgment. In particular, when a criterion is available for comparison one can consider conflict and uncertainty to arise from several sources: uncertainty in the environment due to equivocal cue–criterion relations; inconsistency in applying one's information-combination strategy; and, uncertainty regarding the weighting of cues appropriate to their predictiveness. These three aspects and their effects on judgmental accuracy have been considered in great detail within the lens model framework (Hammond et al. 1975). Moreover, the integration of uncertain and contradictory evidence, which is at the heart of prediction, can be seen as an attempt to establish "compensatory balance in the face of comparative chaos in the physical environment" (Brunswik 1943, p. 257). Brunswik called this integrative process "vicarious functioning," and Einhorn, Kleinmuntz, and Kleinmuntz (1979) have expanded on this to show that the compensatory process captured in linear models can also be seen in the fine detail of process-tracing models developed from verbal protocols. Furthermore, they argued that linear models represent cognitively complex and sophisticated strategies for information integration. The continued predictive superiority of bootstrapping, however, and even of equal-weight linear models over clinical judgment (Dawes 1979), attests to the difficulty of establishing the *correct* compensatory balance. (See also Armstrong 1978a, 1978b; and Dawes 1977, for further work on the statistical versus clinical prediction controversy.)

The basic issues involved in studying deterministic predictive judgment also underlie interest in probability judgment. That is, both are concerned with the making of inferences from uncertain and conflicting data/evidence. However, the different terminologies used in each approach reflect different historical antecedents: the psychology of inference on the one hand, and a formal theory of evidence (de Finetti and Savage 1954), on the other. Formal approaches are concerned with developing general structures for inferential tasks independent of specific content. However, as noted previously, the psychology of inference is intimately concerned with both content and structure. This distinction is central for understanding the discrepancies between the outputs of formal models and intuitive processes found in recent research. To illustrate, whereas causality has no role in probability theory, it is important in human inference (Tversky and Kahneman 1980a). Moreover, the existence of causal schemas can lead to the reinforcement of a person's cognitive model after receiving contradictory evidence, rather than its revision. Schum (1980) has demonstrated the enormous statistical intricacies involved in the Bayesian modeling of inferences made from unreliable data. Indeed one interpretation of this work is that a purely formal approach cannot handle the evaluation of evidence in any relatively complex task, such as a trial. The role of content, however, in simplifying these tasks has not been explored. For example, the use of a heuristic such as representativeness, which depends on content via similarity, takes on added importance in a *normative* sense (see Cohen 1979). That is, in the face of great complexity, the use of heuristics and content may be necessary to induce structure.

The importance of heuristics in making inferences has long been recognized (Polya 1941, 1954) and current interest in them seems well justified. However, their present psychological status requires more specification (see Olson 1976). For example, the use of the same heuristic can lead to opposite predictions. (For an example concerning "availability," see Einhorn 1980.) In addition, the ease with which heuristics can be brought to mind to explain phenomena can lead to their nonfalsifiability. For example, if representativeness accounts for the nonregressiveness of extreme predictions, can adjustment and anchoring explain predictions that are too regressive?

As with deterministic predictions, there has been much concern with the accuracy of probabilistic judgment. Measurement of accuracy, however, raises issues of defining criteria and of the adequacy of samples. Moreover, in the Bayesian framework subjective probabilities represent statements of personal belief and therefore have no objective referent. Nonetheless, Bayesian researchers have borrowed relative frequency concepts to measure how well probabilistic judgment is calibrated, that is, the degree to which probability judgments match empirical relative frequencies (Lichtenstein, Fischhoff, and Phillips 1977) and what variables affect calibration (Lichtenstein and Fischhoff 1977). Calibration has therefore become the accuracy criterion for probabilistic judgment similar to the achievement index in the lens model. Moreover, the research findings in the two paradigms are also similar; namely, most people are poorly calibrated, and even the effectiveness of training is limited for generalizing to other tasks (Lichtenstein and Fischhoff 1980).

Judgment = Choice?

Is judgment synonymous with choice? The normative model treats them as equivalent in that alternative x will be chosen over y if and only if $u(x) > u(y)$; that is, evaluation is necessary and sufficient for choice. However, from a psychological viewpoint, it may be more accurate to say that while judgment is generally an aid to choice, it is neither necessary nor sufficient for choice. That is, judgments serve to reduce the uncertainty and conflict in choice by processes of deliberative reasoning and evaluation of evidence. Moreover, taking action engenders its own sources of conflict (see the following section, "Conflict in Action") so that judgment may only take one so far; indeed, at the choice point, judgment can be ignored. The distinction between judgment and choice, which is blurred in the normative model, is exemplified in common language. For example, one can choose in spite of one's better judgment whereas the reverse makes little sense.

The distinction made between judgment and choice should not be construed to mean that judgment and choice are unrelated. In many situations they are inseparable. For example, consider diagnostic and prognostic judgments and the choice of treatment in clinical situations. It seems unthinkable that choice of treatment could proceed without prior diagnosis and prognosis. More generally, this example illustrates several additional points:

1. Since judgment is deliberative, there must be sufficient time for its formation.
2. Deliberation can itself be affected by the size of payoffs; for example, people may invest in judgment to insure against accusations of irresponsibility in the event of poor outcomes (for example, malpractice — from others and from oneself, see Hogarth 1980b).
3. When alternatives are ordered on some continuum, a quantitative judgment may be necessary to aid choice, as when choosing a therapy that varies in intensity.

These examples point to the importance of considering the conditions under which judgment and choice are similar or different, a crucial question that has barely been posed.

Conflict in Action

The conflict inherent in taking action, as distinct from conflict in judgment, occurs because action implies greater commitment (see Beach and Mitchell 1978; Janis and Mann 1977). Such commitment induces conflict in several ways:

1. Whereas the existence of alternatives implies freedom to choose, the act of choice restricts that very freedom. Hence, keeping one's options open is in direct conflict with the need to take action.
2. Given a set of nondominated alternatives, Shepard (1964) has stated,

   . . . at the moment when a decision is required the fact that each alternative has both advantages and disadvantages poses an impediment to the attainment of the most immediate subgoal; namely, escape from the unpleasant state of conflict induced by the decision problem itself (p. 277).

   Thus, conflict is inherent in choice as an attribute of the choice situation.
3. Unlike judgments, actions are intimately tied to notions of regret and responsibility. For example, consider the decision faced by career women of whether to have children. An important component in this choice may involve imagining the regret associated with both alternatives later on in life. Or, imagine the conflict involved in choosing a place to live and work where responsibilities to oneself and to one's family do not coincide.

As with the resolution of conflict in judgment, conflict resolution in action can involve either avoidance or confrontation. One important form of avoidance is not to choose. Corbin (1980) has recognized the importance of the no-choice option noting that it can take three forms: refusal, delay and inattention. Moreover, she notes that attraction to the status quo has two advantages: it involves less uncertainty, and there may be "less responsibility associated with the effects of 'doing nothing' than with some conscious choice." Toda (1980a) points out that people often make "meta-decisions" (for example, to smoke), to avoid the conflict of having to decide on future occasions. Thaler and Shiffrin (1980) further point out the importance of developing and enforcing self-imposed rules, rather than allowing oneself discretion, in avoiding the conflicts of self-control problems.

Although choice involves considerable conflict, the mode of resolution typically considered in the literature is a confronting, compensatory strategy embodied in the expected utility model. This model is based on the following tenets:

1. The expected utility, $E(U)$, of a gamble whose payoffs are x and y with probabilities p and q $(p + q = 1.0)$, is given by $E(U) = p\,u(x) + q\,u(y)$. Note from the formulation that: (a) the rule says that the evaluation of a gamble is a weighted average of future pleasures and pains, where the weights are the probabilities of attaining these outcomes; (b) the evaluation is solely a function of utility and probability, there being no utility or disutility for gambling per se; (c) the rule assumes that payoffs are independent of probabilities; that is, wishful thinking (optimism) or pessimism are not admissible; (d) there is no inconsistency or error in executing the rule. Thus, although the rule specifically deals with the uncertainty of future events, it does not consider the evaluation process itself to be probabilistic (however, see Luce 1977). Moreover, choice is assumed to follow evaluation by picking the alternative with the highest $E(U)$.

2. The theory assumes that the utility of payoffs is integrated into one's current asset position. Hence, final asset positions determine choice, not gains and/or losses.

3. Although not central to $E(U)$, it is generally assumed that people are risk averse; that is, utility is marginally decreasing with payoff size.

Whereas the $E(U)$ model has been proposed as a prescriptive theory, much confusion exists in that it has been extensively used to both explain and predict behavior. However, while the descriptive adequacy of $E(U)$ has been challenged repeatedly (see Slovic, Fischhoff, and Lichtenstein 1977), Kahneman and Tversky's "prospect theory" (1979b) is the first comprehensive attempt at an alternative formulation. Since elements of this theory are discussed throughout this review, we only consider the proposed evaluation model. Prospect theory superficially resembles the $E(U)$ model in that the components involve a value function, v; decision weight, $\pi(p)$; and a compensatory combining rule. However, the value function differs from utility in that:

1. It is defined on deviations from a reference point (where $v(0) = 0$) rather than being defined over total assets. Furthermore, the reference point may be either identical to or different from the asset position depending on a number of factors, somewhat akin to Helson's adaptation level.

2. It is concave for gains but convex for losses inducing "reflection effects" via risk aversion for gains and risk seeking for losses. For example, consider the choice between $3000 and a 50-percent chance at $6000 or 0. While many would prefer the sure gain of $3000 to the gamble, exhibiting risk aversion, if the sign of the payoff is changed, for example, −$3000 or a 50-percent chance at −$6000 or 0, they might prefer the gamble to the sure loss. Note that the reflection effect contradicts the widely held belief that people generally abhor and seek to avoid uncertainty (Hogarth 1975, Langer 1977).

3. It is steeper for losses than for gains; that is, the pain of losing is greater than the pleasure of winning an equal amount.

Although decision weights are not subjective probabilities as such, they reflect the impact of uncertainty on the evaluation of prospects (gambles), and they are transformations of probabilities. They have several interesting properties; for example, the sum of complementary decision weights does not sum to one (subcertainty), and small probabilities are overweighted. These properties, when combined with those of the value function in bilinear form, induce *inter alia*, overweighting of certainty (thus resolving Allais's paradox), violations of the substitution axiom, and avoidance of probabilistic insurance. Karmarkar (1978, 1979) was also able to explain many similar violations of the $E(U)$ model by transforming probabilities into weights (using a single parameter) and then incorporating them into what he called a subjectively weighted utility model.

Although the above models are an important step in analyzing choice behavior, March (1978) has made a penetrating analysis of the deficiencies in conceptualizing tastes/preferences in such models. He points out that people are often unsure about their preferences (see also Fischhoff, Slovic, and Lichtenstein 1980a) and that uncertainty concerning future preferences complicates the modeling of choice. For example, how does one model the knowledge that one's tastes will change over time, but in unpredictable ways? Moreover, although instability and ambiguity of preferences are treated as deficiencies to be corrected in normative approaches and as random error in descriptive models, March (1978) points out that

> . . . goal ambiguity, like limited rationality, is not necessarily a fault in human choice to be corrected but often a form of intelligence to be refined by the technology of choice rather than ignored by it (p. 598).

The management of conflict induced by unstable preferences over time is also central to self-control (Thaler 1980). The recognition that one's tastes can change, and that such changes are undesirable, leads to precommitment strategies to prevent the harm that follows such changes. For example, consider saving money in Christmas clubs which pay no interest but which restrict the freedom to withdraw money before Christmas in order to protect one against one's self. The behavior of a member of such a club is difficult to explain without resorting to a multiple-self model (Freud 1923, Sagan 1977, Toda, in press). Conceptualizing decision conflict as the clash between multiple selves is a potentially rich area of investigation and could provide useful conceptual links between phenomena of individual and group behavior. For example, individual irrationality might be seen as similar to the various voting paradoxes found in group decision making (Plott 1976).

Feedback Learning

The beginning of this review indicated a questioning of the basic assumption upon which functional and adaptive arguments rest, namely, the ability to learn. We now consider this in light of our discussion of heuristic and other rule-based behavior. For example, how are rules tested and maintained (or not) in the face of experience? Under what conditions do we fail to learn about their quality? Are we aware of our own rules?

Hammond (1978a) and Brehmer (1980) have discussed a number of important issues bearing on the ability to learn from experience. The former paper considers six "modes of thought" for learning relations between variables which include: true experiments, quasi-experiments, aided judgment, and unaided intuitive judgment. These modes vary on six factors, including the degree to which variables can be manipulated and controlled, feasibility of use, and covertness of the cognitive activity involved in each. Hammond points out that the most powerful modes, involving experimentation, are least feasible and thus not likely to be implemented. Unfortunately, the least powerful modes are most feasible and hence most common. Thus, correct learning will be exceptionally difficult since it will be prey to a wide variety of judgmental biases (Campbell 1959). The seriousness of this difficulty is further emphasized by the seeming lack of awareness of the inadequacy of unaided judgment. Brehmer (1980) has further considered the difficulties inherent in learning from experience by contrasting such learning with laboratory studies and formal learning through teaching. The former is far more difficult in that: (1) We don't necessarily know that there *is* something to be learned; (2) if we do know that there is something to be learned it is not clear *what* is to be learned; and (3) there is often much ambiguity in judging *whether* we have learned (for example, what, if anything, did the United States learn from the Vietnam war?).

The general difficulties of learning from experience have also been demonstrated in specific areas. For example, Shweder (1977) has analyzed the ability of adults to learn environmental contingencies and points out that:

1. Whereas adults are capable of correlational reasoning, they frequently use cognitive strategies that can result in the genesis and perpetuation of myths, magic, and superstitious behavior.
2. Judgments of contingency are frequently based on likeness and similarity. For example, the treatment of ringworm with fowl excrement in primitive societies is based on the similarity of symptoms to "cure."
3. Contingencies provide the links in structuring experience by implying meaning through context. For example, "the trip was not delayed because the bottle shattered" can be understood when speaking of "launching a ship."

The learning of contingencies between actions and outcomes is obviously central for survival. Moreover, contiguity of actions and outcomes is an important cue for inferring causality (Michotte 1963) and thus, for organizing events into "causal schemas" (Tversky and Kahneman 1980a). A particularly important type of contingent learning that has received little attention involves the learning and changing of tastes and preferences. For example, consider the unpleasant affect felt by a child after eating a particular vegetable, and the ensuing negative utility so learned; or, imagine the changes in the same child's taste for members of the opposite sex as he or she grows older. Concern with the normative model, in which tastes are fixed, has obscured important psychological questions about the nature of tastes/preferences (see March 1978).

The learning of action–outcome connections illustrates an obvious but essential point; that is, learning occurs through outcome feedback (see Powers 1973). Since multiple actions must be taken over time, judgment is often required to predict which actions will lead to specified outcomes. Thus, feedback from outcomes is used to evaluate both judgments and actions. This assumes that the quality of decisions can be assessed by observing outcomes. Nonetheless, decision theorists have pointed out that outcomes also depend on factors that people cannot control; hence, decisions should be evaluated by the *process* of deciding. While there is much merit in this argument, the distinction between good/bad decisions and good/bad outcomes is strongly counterintuitive and may reflect several factors: (1) People have a lifetime of experience in learning from outcomes; (2) whereas process evaluation is complex, outcomes are visible, available, and often unambiguous; and (3) evaluation of process is conditional upon an appropriate representation of the task (see above). People cannot ignore outcomes in evaluating decisions.

The role of outcome feedback has been extensively studied within a number of probability learning paradigms. Estes (1976a, b), however, has emphasized the importance of considering what is learned in such tasks. In a series of experiments using simulated public opinion polls, he found that subjects coded outcomes as frequencies rather than probabilities. Indeed, as the history of probability indicates, the notion of probability was late in developing, a key difficulty being the specification of the sample space (such problems persist — see Bar-Hillel and Falk 1980). Einhorn and Hogarth (1978) note that the transformation of frequency into probability requires paying attention to nonoccurrences of the event of interest as well as the event itself. This added burden on attention and memory may thus favor the coding of outcomes as frequencies rather than probabilities. Moreover, the tendency to ignore nonoccurrences is intimately related to the lack of search for disconfirming evidence (Wason and Johnson-Laird 1972; Mynatt, Doherty, and Tweney 1977, 1978). Furthermore, attempts to alter this tendency have been generally unsuccessful, although Tweney et al. (1980) have reported some success. Whether or not this tendency can be modified, we note that it is not limited to scientific inference; for example, how many people seek disconfirming evidence to test their political, religious, and other beliefs, by reading newspapers and books opposed to their own views?

The implications of the above for learning from experience were explored by Einhorn and Hogarth (1978). They specifically considered how confidence in judgment is learned and maintained despite low, and/or even no, judgmental validity. The tasks analyzed are those in which actions are based on an overall evaluative judgment, and outcome feedback is subsequently used to assess judgmental accuracy. The structure of this task makes learning difficult in that:

1. When judgment is *assumed* to be valid, outcomes that follow action based on negative judgment cannot typically be observed. For example, how is one to assess the performance of rejected job applicants?
2. Given limited feedback (which can also result from a lack of search for disconfirming evidence), various task variables, such as base rates, selection ratios, and the self-fulfilling treatment effects of taking action per se, can combine to produce reinforcement through positive outcome feedback. Thus, one can receive positive feedback in spite of, rather than because of, one's judgmental ability. A formal model of this process was

developed in which outcomes were generated by combining various task variables with the validity of judgment. The results indicated a wide range of conditions where overconfidence in poor judgment can be learned and maintained.

Of great importance to the issue of learning from experience is awareness of the task factors that can influence outcomes. Such factors include the probabilistic nature of the task itself (see Brehmer 1980), as well as other task variables discussed in multiple-cue probability learning studies (Hammond et al. 1975). Einhorn (1980) has discussed this issue within the concept of outcome-irrelevant-learning-structures (OILS). OILS refers to the fact that in certain tasks, positive outcome feedback can be irrelevant or even harmful for correcting poor judgment when knowledge of task structure is missing or seriously in error. The concept is obviously similar to the notion of "superstitious" behavior (Skinner 1948, Staddon and Simmelhag 1971). However, the concept of OILS raises a consumer who uses a conjunctive rule when purchasing a wide range of products. It could be argued that positive outcomes following purchases reinforce the use of the rule, the specific behaviors, or both. The issue is complex and would seem to depend on the extent to which people are aware of their own judgmental rules (Hayek 1962, Nisbett and Wilson 1977, Smith and Miller 1978). That is, to what extent are judgmental rules reinforced without awareness, and can inappropriate rules be *un*learned? The importance of this question is that it raises the issue of whether, or to what extent, procedures for correcting judgmental deficiencies can be developed.

It is important to stress that awareness of task structure does not necessarily lead to learning (see Castellan 1977). Furthermore, it is possible to choose not to learn. For example, consider a waiter in a busy restaurant who believes he can predict those customers most likely to leave generous tips; the quality of his service reflects this prediction. If the quality of service has a treatment effect on the size of the tip, the outcomes confirm the prediction. With awareness of the task structure, the waiter could perform an experiment to disentangle the treatment effects of quality of service from his predictions; that is, he could give poor service to some of those judged to leave good tips and good service to some of those judged to leave poor tips. Note that the waiter must be willing to risk the possible loss of income *if* his judgment is accurate, against learning that his judgment is poor. Therefore, there is conflict between short-run strategies for action that result in reasonably good outcomes versus long-run strategies for learning that have potential short-run costs. That is, would you be willing to risk loss of income by doing a real experiment in order to learn? This dilemma is quite frequent, yet it is not clear that awareness of it would lead to the choice to learn.

Methodological Concerns

The substantive matters discussed in this review raise various issues regarding the methodology of decision research. We consider some of these by posing the following questions: (1) How can we know whether applications of decision aids improve the quality of decisions? (2) how prevalent are judgmental biases in the natural environment? and (3) what methods are most likely to provide insight into decision processes?

The review by Slovic, Fischhoff, and Lichtenstein (1977) reported a growing number of applications of decision aids in a wide variety of fields, and this growth continues (see Jungermann 1980, and references). However, it is appropriate to ask whether such applications work and how one can know if they work. While care in applying basic principles of experimental design involving consideration of threats to internal and external validity are recognized in some applications (see Russo 1977), many more can be characterized as one-shot case studies where the experimental treatment is the decision aid or procedure. Although painful, it might be remembered that such a design is scientifically useless for assessing treatment efficacy. The fact that clients are likely to seek aid from decision analysts (broadly defined) when things are not going well, renders evaluation of pretest–posttest designs lacking control groups particularly susceptible to regression effects.

The difficulties of evaluating decision aids have been noted by Fischhoff (1980), who draws an analogy between decision analysis and psychotherapy. He writes that,

> like psychotherapy, decision analysis is advocated because the theory is persuasive, because many clients say that it helps them, because many practitioners are extremely talented, and because the alternative seems to be to sink back into an abyss (seat-of-the-pants decision making).

Indeed, we note that decision analysis might be called "rational therapy" if that term were not similar to one already in use (see Ellis 1977 on "rational-emotive therapy"). The importance of Fischhoff's analogy is twofold: it raises basic questions regarding the evaluation of decision aids, and it provides some necessary, if not sufficient, motivation to do something about it.

The issue concerning the prevalence of judgmental biases in the natural environment raises familiar questions of external validity (Brunswik 1956). Ebbesen and Konečni (1980) have studied several judgment tasks within laboratory and natural settings (for example, setting of bail, driving a car) and have found major differences in results. In reviewing these and other studies they conclude:

> There is considerable evidence to suggest that the external validity of decision-making research that relies on laboratory simulations of real-world decision problems is low. Seemingly insignificant features of the decision task and measures cause people to alter their decision strategies. The context in which the decision problem is presented, the salience of alternatives, the number of cues, the concreteness of the information, the order of presentation, the similarity of cue to alternative, the nature of the decomposition, the form of the measures, and so on, seem to affect the decisions that subjects make.

Given the above, the issue of external validity is not liable to be resolved without recourse to theory that attempts to answer how tasks vary between the laboratory and the natural environment and what kinds of effects can be expected from such differences. Howell and Burnett (1978) have taken a first step in this direction by proposing a cognitive taxonomy based on task variables and response demands that affect judgments of uncertainty. However, greater concern with how people's experience influences their judgment is needed. For example, Bar-Hillel (1979) has pointed out that although people ignore sample size in certain laboratory studies, they seem to judge sample accuracy by the *ratio* of sample size to population. Furthermore, she emphasizes that such a rule can be justified in the natural environment, since one typically samples without replacement. For example,

> When dining out, one samples, without replacement, some dishes from a menu and generalizes about the restaurant's quality. When shopping in a new store, one samples, without replacement, the price of several items and judges how expensive the store is (p. 250).

Lacking theoretical guidance, one has no recourse but to judge the prevalence of judgmental biases. There are two extreme views. The most optimistic asserts that biases are limited to laboratory situations which are unrepresentative of the natural ecology. However, Slovic, Fischhoff, and Lichtenstein (1977) point out that in a rapidly changing world it is unclear what the relevant natural ecology will be. Thus, although the laboratory may be an unfamiliar environment, lack of ability to perform well in unfamiliar situations takes on added importance. The pessimistic viewpoint is that people suffer from "cognitive conceit" (Dawes 1976); that is, our limited cognitive capacity is such that it prevents us from being aware of its limited nature. Even in a less pessimistic form, this view is highly disturbing and emphasizes the importance of further research on the factors which foster or impede awareness of the quality of one's judgmental rules.

Both of the above positions presuppose the internal validity of the experimental evidence concerning judgmental biases. However, Hammond (1978b) has criticized much of this research by pointing out the inadequacy of exclusive reliance on between-subjects designs for studying cognition. For example, he notes that many experimental demonstrations of "illusory correlation" rest on the incorrect specification of the sampling unit; that is, the sampling unit should be defined by the stimuli judged within each person, not by the people doing the judging. Thus, while group data may indicate large effects, unless sufficient stimuli are sampled, no single individual can be shown to exhibit the bias (see also Hershey and Schoemaker 1980b). Within-subjects designs, however, can also be problematic in that effects due to memory when responding to stimuli across time (for example, anchoring and carry-over), may distort the phenomenon being studied (Greenwald 1976). This is particularly important when considering possible biases in judgment made in unique circumstances. Hence, the temporal spacing between administration of stimuli is a crucial variable in within-subjects designs, and its effects also need to be studied.

While controversy exists regarding the appropriateness of different experimental designs for studying decision processes, the need for multimethod approaches is generally acknowledged (Payne, Braunstein, and Carroll 1978). Such approaches, which can use methods as diverse as statistical modeling and verbal protocols or eye movements, not only provide much needed evidence on convergent validity, but may also be necessary to discriminate between strategies that can result in identical outcomes (Einhorn, Kleinmuntz, and Kleinmuntz 1979; Tversky and Sattath 1979). Furthermore, in addition to positive scientific effects, multimethod approaches may have the salutory effect of convincing researchers that "truth" can be shared.

Conclusion

Decision making is a province claimed by many disciplines, for example, economics, statistics, management science, and philosophy. What should be the role of psychology? We believe this can be best illustrated by the economic concept of comparative advantage. For example, how much typing should the only lawyer in a small town perform (Samuelson 1948)? Even if the lawyer is an excellent typist, it is to his or her and the town's advantage to concentrate on law, provided that typing is not a rare skill. Similarly, we believe that psychologists can best contribute to decision research by elucidating the basic psychological processes underlying judgment and choice. Indeed, this review has tried to place behavioral decision theory within a broad psychological context and by doing so, has emphasized the importance of attention, memory, cognitive representation, conflict, learning, and feedback. Moreover, the interdependence and coordination of these processes suggest important challenges for understanding complex decision making. In order to meet these challenges, future research must adopt a broader perspective (see Carroll 1980) by investigating the topics discussed here and also those not usually treated in decision literature (for example, creativity, problem solving, and concept formation). Given the ubiquity and importance of judgment and choice, no less of a perspective will do.

ACKNOWLEDGMENT

Reproduced with permission from the *Annual Review of Psychology,* Volume 32, © 1981, by Annual Reviews, Inc. The authors wish to thank Jay Russo for his many incisive comments on draft of this review. They also wish to thank the following people for their suggestions and support: Nick Dopuch, Ed Joyce, John Payne, and Paul Schoemaker. The superb abilities of Charlesetta Nowels in the preparation of this chapter are gratefully acknowledged.

On Taking Action Seriously: Cognitive Fixation in Behavioral Decision Theory

Terry Connolly, *Georgia Institute of Technology*

An invitation to comment on a major review paper allows one a clear choice: to focus either on the review itself or on the subject matter being reviewed. I shall take the second course. The first is essentially foreclosed, unless one were to quibble about this inclusion or exclusion, this summary too strong, that too weak, this area covered in too much detail, that in too little. On such matters the reader would do well to prefer Einhorn and Hogarth's judgments to mine (fallible though both must be). Their paper is clearly an outstanding summary and synthesis of what we have accomplished in the last three years — an intellectual tower from which we can survey the area and gain some perspective on the territory we have explored, and what we might usefully explore next.

So: What of the view? Where is behavioral decision theory in 1982? Without denying the progress and excitement of the discipline, I must confess that my primary reaction is a feeling of perplexity. My puzzlement has two rather distinct focuses, but I suspect that these may be merely blurred images of the same issue. I shall first outline the two matters I find puzzling, and then explore the possibility of their interconnection.

Some Questions on Behavioral Decision Theory

The first object of my perplexity is what I referred to recently as "The Decision Competence Paradox" (Connolly 1980a), a notion caught far more pithily in a colleague's comment on Nisbett and Ross's first eight chapters: "If we're so dumb, how come we made it to the moon?" (Nisbett and Ross 1980). In either phrasing, the issue is much the same. We have now amassed a startling body of evidence attesting to the fallibility of human judgment and inference, and there is no reason to suppose that the catalog malfunctions is now complete. How, then, are we to account for quite common appearance of human competence in complex tasks to which sound judgment would appear crucial: moon landings, management of complex organizations, conduct of our daily lives, and, indeed, good research on human inference. If we truly are as dumb as the research suggests, the source of wonder is not that we can go to the moon, but that we can make it to work on an average day.

The point should not be pressed too hard. There is no strict paradox, either logical or empirical. As Einhorn and Hogarth (above, p. 16) point out, the picture of inferential failure is "often painted to be interesting rather than complete," emphasizing possibly unusual failures over possibly commonplace successes. Similarly,

> . . . there is no logical contradiction between the assertion that people can be very impressively intelligent on some occasions or in some domains and the assertion that they can make howling inferential errors on other occasions or in other domains (Nisbett and Ross 1980, p. 250).

It may be, in short, that our decisional batting average is compatible with our inferential error rate. Lacking data, I can report only my sense of uneasiness, "If we're so dumb. . . ."

The second object of my perplexity is hazy but persistent, taking on sharpness only when I try to convey the implications of a specific finding to a class of pragmatic engineers. A comment from one such engineering student, referring to the subjects in one series of experiments, captures it nicely: "These dudes don't seem to *do* much, they just think and fill out questionnaires." The comment is not merely routine philistine attack on laboratory science, but a serious question about a crucial assumption of behavioral decision theory research: prior thinking is the primary, or only, guide to effective action; ineffective thinking must lead to a high probability of ineffective action.

The *reflection first, action later* model does run deeply through our approach to decision problems. Though Einhorn and Hogarth note the artificiality of the decomposition, their review structure of information acquisition, evaluation, action, and feedback learning does mirror the field's areas of specialization. We are thus struck by a sense of ingenious heresy when Weick (1977) discusses "enactment" processes, or when March (1978) speaks of "posterior rationality," discovering intentions in the interpretation of past actions rather than using them as guides to the future. Though such processes certainly appear familiar, they have an air of impropriety to them. One wants to say that this is not real decision making, but merely a misuse of its apparatus for other purposes. Real decision making demands that action occur only at the termination of, and guided by, some period of reflection. Faulty reflection leads to faulty action.

This neat partition and temporal sequence of cognition and action is far from universal in the natural ecology. Action and thought often seem intimately intertwined in everyday problem solving and decision making — perhaps in ways that raise the effectiveness of the whole process. If action and thought were intertwined in everyday problem solving, both of my perplexities might be on the road to resolution. Perhaps one of the reasons our laboratory subjects reflect so poorly is that we artificially remove them from their ecologically familiar, and helpful, interaction with the problem environment.

An example I have discussed elsewhere (Connolly 1980b) might help to clarify the argument. Consider a householder confronting the problem of an overgrown hedge. Our normal research approach might formulate the problem as: How does the householder decide where to cut each limb? (assuming reflection is required before action can be taken). We might then present a series of pictures of limbs of varying thickness, angle, weight, and so on, and ask the subjects to indicate where they would cut each. Perhaps we would then regress height of cut on branch characteristics, and compare the subjects' decisions with those of an "optimum cutting model" developed in conjunction with a friendly colleague in the mechanical engineering department. No doubt we would find systematic nonoptimalities in the subjects' decisions.

The trouble is that no sane person actually tries to solve the hedge-clipping problem in this reflection-first way. What we do is take a few modest snips, inspect the results, snip a little more, inspect again, and so on, until the hedge is acceptably neat. The acceptability of the solution is far less dependent on the correctness of the initial judgment and far more dependent on the iteration with the problem itself than would be captured in the laboratory study parodied above. In short, action may be a supplement, or even an alternative, to reflection, not merely a result of it, in complex problem solving. As shown in classic sensorimotor experiments (Held and Freedman 1963), depriving the subject of active involvement with the problem seriously impedes performance.

Macroadaptive and Microadaptive Rationality

The emphasis on action rather than reflection is already embodied in notions of *adaptive rationality* (March 1978, Cyert and March 1963). The emphasis there, however, is on what could be called *macroadaptive rationality*, the long-term achievement of sensible action that comes from learning in a series of task repetitions. The present emphasis is on a more *microadaptive* rationality, where success is achieved by a series of modest nibbles and adjustments within the structure of a single task. As March (1978) notes, macroadaptive rationality requires that "the world and preferences are stable and the experience prolonged enough" for actual and optimal behavior to converge. Microadaptive rationality requires tasks that are tolerant of multiple small nibbles, accessible to repeated inspection, and an actor with some rough sense of how large a first cut to make. Note also that the macroadaptive process would produce hedge clippers who might do quite well in our imaginary laboratory study, though unable to articulate their wisdom. The microadapter produces only a well-clipped hedge, with no necessary wisdom to pass on to beginners, or to demonstrate to experimenters.

Microadapters enjoy a number of advantages over "proper" (reflection-first) problem solvers, and thus may be able to get by with cruder cognitive equipment. They do not need strongly predictive theories of the problem structure, and they are thus spared both the need to load their general theories with particularistic data and the vulnerability to errors and oversimplifications that comes from imperfections in that theory. (See Einhorn and Hogarth 1980, p. 56, on the "conditionality of normative models," and p. 57–59 and elsewhere on the difficulties of matching the external problem to the internally represented "problem space.") Short-term memory requirements are greatly eased, since both initial problem representation and the results of partial solution attempts are stored in the problem itself, not in the solver's memory. Such external storage of partial solutions also makes the solver less vulnerable to interruptions. (See Simon 1962, on the relative vulnerability of the watch-makers Hora and Tempus.) Finally, microadapters may be less prone to difficult trade-offs between conflicting goals, since the problem may allow sequential, rather than simultaneous, attention to different objectives.

A microadaptive strategy may also enjoy advantages when we move from the individualistic focus of our laboratory studies to the multiperson, multi-problem chaos of much real-world problem solving. In such realistic environments, taking action may have a number of benefits, quite apart from the possibility of solving a particular problem. It may, for example, solve the real problem directly, as when the underlying problem is a spouse's demand to "do something about the yard." Any of a wide range of visible strenuous activities, not only hedge clipping, will solve this problem adequately. The visibility of action may similarly serve as a signal to other participants, as yet unknown. Neighbors may come forward with advice on technique or reminders of community rules on permissible hedge heights. Solution benefits may be brought forward in time: the hedge is quickly, if imperfectly, clipped, so that payoffs need not await the clipper's completion of graduate studies in the cantilever properties of cut limbs.

It is not difficult to suggest classes of problems for which microadaptive approaches will fail. Nuclear wars and childbearing decisions are poor settings for a strategy of "try a little one and see how it goes"; and parachute packers who boast of never having had any complaints might do well to read Einhorn and Hogarth (1980) on the restaurant waiter's outcome-irrelevant learning structure. The argument here is not that microadaptive strategies are universally superior to prior rationality, simply that they often may be. If this superiority is in fact common, then it seems likely that our individual and collective approaches to solving problems and making decisions will tend to be of this form. We may thus open at least a beachhead on the perplexing problem of the persistence of dysfunctional behavior — in this case, leaping before we look. The microadaptive argument suggests that leaping is often an attractive, cognitively efficient alternative to extended looking. It is dysfunctional only from the perspective of our strong implicit commitment to prior rationality, echoing again Einhorn and Hogarth's (1980, pp. 55–57) discussion of the "conditionality of normative models."

This is not the place for an extended review of literatures suggesting action as a useful and widely used problem-solving device, but three quick supportive lines of argument can be quickly sketched. First, models such as those of Simon (1956) or Toda (1962) suggest how well cognitively limited decision makers can do in difficult environments if they are allowed to act, not just think. Second, the managerial world portrayed by Mintzberg (1973) and others suggests the hectic, much interrupted environment in which decisions are often made. Microadaptiveness may be the best that one can hope for in such a setting — and, as argued here, it may be quite good. Finally, the virtues of a disjointed-incremental or "muddling through" strategy in dealing with immensely complex social problems have been persuasively argued by Lindblom (1965) on several of the same grounds as suggested here.

On Taking Action Seriously

The two perplexities with which I started these comments — the appearance of overfrequent decisional success, and the research focus on pure thinking — may thus be linked to the same underlying issue. We have focused too tightly on the thinking aspects of decision making, depriving our subjects of what may be a crucial decision aid: the iterative taking of action, monitoring of progress, and adapting of action to problem response. We have placed the focus of rationality solely in the mind of the human, when it might be better placed in the interaction of actor-plus-environment. We have, in short, become cognitively fixated, in a twofold sense.

How might we move to "take action seriously" in our research? How might we put the "behavior" more emphatically in "behavioral decision theory"? I have neither wit nor space to outline any detailed research agenda here, but at least two directions for enriching our current paradigm seem worth exploring: temporal sequence and interactive shaping of decision behavior. We have made striking progress in capturing at least some aspects of how a physician draws inferences from a set of diagnostic data. We have made initial forays into understanding how he or she decides on which, and how many, laboratory tests to acquire, finding once again that human performance is less than overwhelming (see Zieve 1966). But this still treats the initial diagnosis as terminal (which, in the other sense, it too often promises to be). If the disease in question is one for which the only available treatment is a one-pass, kill-or-cure intervention, such a research focus is appropriate. But are there not many diseases, for which our hedge-clipping analogy is more appropriate, for which even a wildly wrong initial diagnosis can be, and routinely would be, corrected in the normal course of monitoring and adjusting treatment? In such cases, research interest expands beyond the accuracy of the initial diagnosis to the convergence of diagnosis and treatment over time. At intermediate points in the convergence, the treatment prescribed might be examined for its diagnostic as well as its remediative benefits. The decision strategy suggested here is closely parallel to that driving Campbell's (1969) "experimenting society." I'm not entirely comfortable being treated by an "experimenting physician" — but if that is, in fact, the decision strategy my physician is using, I hope our research could help him or her to use it well.

On the laboratory side, we have already made useful inroads into treating thought and action within the same framework. The growing body of work on information-search processes (see Einhorn and Hogarth 1981a, pp. 62–63) and the related work on fault trees (Fischhoff, Slovic, and Lichtenstein 1978) treats inference as a sequential, active process, though still focused on the single terminal decision. Perhaps even closer to the orientation suggested here is the work within the decision escalation paradigm (for example, Staw and Ross, 1978), in which consequences of inference and action at one time affect inference and action at a later time. It seems likely that further development along these lines will be greatly facilitated by the development of computer-interactive games that allow the subject extended sequences of search, inference, and action. I have suggested elsewhere that such development might usefully involve collaboration between behavioral decision theorists and computer systems designers working with decision support systems.

Conclusion

My original hope in preparing these comments was that, with the advantage of Einhorn and Hogarth's excellent review, I would be able to propose some modest new insight or promising direction. Rereading my draft after only a couple of weeks, I find less novelty than I had hoped. Casually reviewing a 1978 collection of papers on judgment and public policy (Hammond 1978a), I find myself multiply anticipated. In this one short volume, Hammond (1978a, pp. 15–20) reminds us of the superiority of inquiring systems that allow active intervention in the target system. Einhorn (1978, p. 163) argues that one "extremely important factor that is often overlooked is the feedback effect that the outcomes of decisions at one time can have on behavior at a later time," and he proposes that "this topic needs much more careful study." Even my pet phrases are scooped. While delighted to find Boulding (1978) comment that "it is amazing that any human process ever goes from bad to better, as it surprisingly often does," I am chagrined that he refers to this state of affairs as the "paradox of decision." I suspect that a more scholarly rereading of Egon Brunswik would find my entire argument pithily presented in a sentence or two. Clearly, it is somewhat short of total novelty.

And yet the two perplexities remain. Real humans in their real ecologies do appear to act more, and err less, than do our laboratory subjects. Perhaps the two contrasts are related, and action, in the forms of tinkering, nibbling, and incremental microadaptiveness, provides a sometimes crucial decision aid. Certainly, we have adequate theoretical justification for exploring the possibility, and the methodological problems of both laboratory and field studies do not appear insuperable. Perhaps when the next review of behavioral decision theory appears we will be able to point more clearly to its consideration of behavior, as well as of cognition. Perhaps, in short, it's time to take "action" seriously.

On Lincoln's Doctor's Dog, or Where Are We in Behavioral Decision Theory?

Kenneth R. MacCrimmon, *Northwestern University and University of British Columbia*

In reflecting on the Einhorn and Hogarth paper and the field of behavioral decision theory, I'm reminded of the old joke about the scholar who writes an academic treatise on slavery. He wants it to be a best-seller so he asks his publisher what he should do. His publisher tells him that books on Lincoln, on doctors, and on dogs sell particularly well. So our colleague calls his book, *Lincoln's Doctor's Dog*. Unfortunately, the reader, although learning something about Lincoln, has difficulty seeing his relevance to doctors and dogs.

In relating this story to our current context, I would conjecture that the reader of the Einhorn and Hogarth paper, although learning something about behavior, will have difficulty seeing its relevance to decisions or theory. I will focus on behavior, decision, and theory, and will organize my comments into three categories:

1. Assuming that the Einhorn and Hogarth paper is an adequate reflection of the field, how would we appraise the current progress in behavioral decision theory?
2. Is the Einhorn and Hogarth paper an adequate reflection of the state of the field? What are the strengths and weaknesses of the paper?
3. Where should the field be headed? What are the promising new directions?

Progress in Behavioral Decision Theory as Reflected in the Einhorn-Hogarth Paper

In assessing the progress in behavioral decision theory, I find it useful to adopt two perspectives. Consider the following exercise. First, suppose we subtract thirty years from all the dates in the paper and give the paper, a newly discovered 1951 survey, to colleagues in related areas of psychology or social science. In examining this survey, would they be surprised at the pre-1950 state of advancement in knowledge? Readers are invited to make their own appraisal, and in doing so note that the second paragraph of the paper would contain the sentence: "Recently, Simon (1947) has argued for different types of rationality. . . ." Other parts of the translation would be similarly unsurprising. You can try it yourself or on your colleagues and form your own conclusions.

As an alternative perspective, instead of the strategy "translate," try the strategy "match." Drop all dates from the Einhorn and Hogarth paper and from Edwards's 1961 review article, and invite someone in a related area to judge which article appeared twenty years after the other.

These exercises are not meant to suggest that the references in the Einhorn and Hogarth paper are outdated. Indeed, their up-to-dateness necessitated obscuring the dates. The point of the exercises, obviously, was to question whether we have made much progress in behavioral decision theory over the past twenty or thirty years. Certainly a number of behavioral studies have been conducted, but have they contributed significantly to our understanding of real decisions or to our development of real theory? A reasonable case could be made that the earlier review paper exhibited work that covered a wider range of the behavioral sciences, that it was directed more toward actual decisions, and that it had more concern for theory.

Strengths and Weaknesses of the Einhorn-Hogarth Paper

I shall state some of the virtues of the paper and consider any qualifications.

1. The principle of comparative advantage is invoked — psychologists should focus on psychological aspects. This makes a great deal of sense. If psychologists become too concerned with economic or engineering concerns, then psychological factors will not be studied. If psychologists focus excessively on psychological aspects, however, it could lead, as shown by this paper, to an inward approach that does not take advantage of connections with other disciplines. Also of concern is that behavioral decision theory may get implicitly defined even narrowly within psychology. Although a short survey cannot be expected to cover all areas, the almost total absence of any reference to group and organizational influences is noteworthy. It is difficult to think of many real decisions for which such factors are absent.

2. The paper does not attempt to provide an elaborate survey but it is concerned with raising some fundamental issues. From the outset, the paper tackles key questions, such as descriptive versus normative approaches and context effects. The paper is more thought-provoking than the usual survey, which limits its usefulness as a survey. Even on the topic of linear models, in which the authors have made key contributions, there is no systematic compilation of current results. When research results are presented, they are treated uncritically. For a more traditional survey the reader can refer to the excellent paper by Slovic, Fischhoff, and Lichtenstein (1977). Einhorn and Hogarth's treatment of basic issues is more successful on psychological topics, such as figure-ground, than on philosophical topics, such as causality.

3. The paper intertwines the discussion of decision and judgment. The dividing line between decision and judgment is unclear and it is useful to treat the two together. The work on one can then have relevance for the other (for example, modeling similarity judgments). An unfortunate consequence of the joint treatment, however, is that little emphasis is placed on decision making per se. There are fewer than twenty examples in the

paper; most consist of only a line or two, and of these, no more than two or three, if that, deal with decisions. For example, even though many important decisions were involved in Chrysler's recent difficulties and in government support considerations, Chrysler is mentioned only with regard to profits — a totally nondecision focus. The same is true of other examples dealing with mowing lawns, tax cuts, ringworm, and waiters. Would a real decision maker recognize that the paper deals with decision making?

4. The paper provides a useful focus on the deviation of actual behavior from the optimal model. In studying actual decisions, Einhorn and Hogarth emphasize the usefulness of having a benchmark from which to observe and understand deviations. While a fair amount of discussion is devoted to this perspective, we are not told precisely what the "optimal model" or "normative theory" is. Presumably it is usually expected utility theory, or is it?

5. The paper stresses dynamic aspects in the form of evolutionary concerns and learning. Insightful discussions are presented on change, learning, feedback, etc. It would have been helpful if this concern had been carried through to the current state of dynamic models of decision, as in the review by Rapoport and Wallsten (1972). The paper makes a variety of other contributions, including raising key questions about research methods, attempting to reconcile choice and process approaches, and cautiously arguing these approaches.

In making an overall appraisal, it is important to keep in mind the primary objective of behavioral decision theory, which is to help us describe, explain, and predict how decisions are made. How does the Einhorn and Hogarth paper help us in doing these things? Let us consider the questions in the conceptual and the applied senses. On the conceptual level, we might ask how much more we now know about how decision situations are perceived and represented, how information is acquired and processed, how conflicting objectives are reconciled, and how uncertainty and risks are handled. The answer to the first item listed is more positive than to the other ones. The paper's main contribution is linking perceptual and learning processes with the decision process. The paper's weakest conceptual area is a lack of concern with the more standard topics in decision and choice.

On the applied level, we need to ask whether one can now better explain decisions such as why Iran released the American hostages when they did, why American automobile firms did not respond more quickly to the demand for small cars, and why one accepts or rejects a new job. Unfortunately, the paper does not provide much help in addressing such questions, or even simpler ones.

Too much work in behavioral decision theory has deemphasized the broader aspects of behavior, decisions, and theory.

Directions for Behavioral Decision Theory

The earlier discussion suggests the need for broader decision focus, attention to real decisions, and development of systematic, falsifiable theories. A few remarks on each of these areas would be an appropriate way to conclude my commentary.

Broader Aspects of Behavior

Tying decision making to basic individual psychology is important. This integration, however, should not obscure the need to consider group and organizational influences (for example, Janis 1972 and Weick 1979). We also need to improve our efforts to integrate work in artificial intelligence and related problem-solving studies (for example, Raphael 1976, Newell and Simon 1972). We should not forget the bridges built to decision theory in economics, statistics, political science, philosophy, and so forth. Such connections were a highlight of earlier reviews, and we should not lose sight of important work made possible by the interaction of such disciplines. Recent candidates for inclusion here are Schelling's *Micromotives and Macrobehavior* (1978), Green and Laffont's *Incentives in Public Decision Making* (1978), and Leibenstein's *Beyond Economic Man* (1976).

Real Decisions

Decision making encompasses most important human behavior, ranging from individuals purchasing insurance to nations dealing with crisis. Studies linking actual decisions with existing concepts and theories are particularly valuable. For instance, Kunreuther and his associates (1978) have studied individuals in floodplains and earthquake regions by relating their perceptions and insurance decisions to optimizing and satisficing models. Allison (1971) has provided insights into the decisions taken in the United States and in Russia during the Cuban missile crisis by viewing the events in terms of three different models. Although lab studies can be useful, when they take advantage of their inherent control, it is not always apparent what natural environment is being simulated. In interpreting any empirical results, as well as any conceptual developments, you might keep in mind a standard set of situations (for example, individuals deciding among goods or careers, or organizations deciding among factors of production or handling clients). Research that is not relative to some real decision may be good research but hardly behavioral *decision* theory.

Theory Construction and Testing

Our task as social *scientists* is to describe, explain, and predict decisions. These activities require that we understand the particular circumstances surrounding a decision, and that we formulate the appropriate behavioral law connecting the circumstances with the decision taken. In most social sciences, emphasis is placed on studying the circumstances of a decision, such as the social context or the environmental uncertainty, rather than the development of behavioral laws. If, however, any attention is to be given to the construction of useful generalizations, it is the responsibility of the psychologists studying decision making. Even if one does not take a completely reductionist view, it is hard to conceive of general laws not primarily psychological in content. Real laws are very difficult to formulate, but their difficulty in formulation does not imply that we should ignore the task of conceptualizing some kind of covering laws.

By explicitly stating and keeping in mind the conditions and laws required to explain decision behavior, we assure a higher likelihood of pursuing the best paths of research investigation.

In studying major decisions, it may be useful to use a modification of the Dray-Hempel covering law model of explanation. In our adaptation (Mac-Crimmon 1976) of this approach the law model takes roughly the following form:

> There is a belief premise: Agent *A* perceives the situation as type *S*. There is a goal premise: *A* wants to attain goal *G*. There is a disposition premise: *A* is disposed to act in manner *D*. There is a resource premise: *A* is able to consider alternatives, including action *X*. The covering law then would be of the form: An agent *A* in a situation perceived as type *S*, striving to attain *G*, will, if disposed to act in manner *D*, do *X*. The expanation is: *A* did *X*.

At a minimum, this model can serve to structure the conditions of relevance to a decision. More ambitiously, though, we are led to ask how we can form the basis for the covering laws themselves.

Although little progress seems to have been made in establishing decision laws, there are various theories of particular aspects of decision behavior. In many cases, however, these models amount to little more than *post hoc* ways of classifying data. Many researchers find the need to develop their own specialized model or language rather than striving for commonality. When some new data does not fit the model, then a new model is developed. Given the fluidity of the model development, it is difficult to conceive of empirical observations that could falsify it.

One interesting variant, though, has been the development of provocative and challenging models. The purpose of these studies has been to force us to change our usual way of thinking about decision making. The work on garbage can models (Cohen, March, and Olson 1972), groupthink (Janis 1972), and editing operations (Kahneman and Tversky 1979b) are good examples. The inability to falsify these models, or in some cases even to specify them clearly, is not a major concern. By changing the way we think about decision making, they contribute to both theory development and testing.

More effort should be devoted to constructing carefully specified theories. Decision making, in contrast to much of social science, already has the advantage of existing axiomatic theories, particularly those of von Neumann, Morgenstern, and Savage. Over the years, attention has been paid to testing them and making them operational. To the extent that there are gaps between the predictions of the theory and actual decisions, it is desirable to strive for modifications in the theories while retaining their clear specification and falsifiable form.

Theory development is a slow process and we have a long way to go, but the first step is to renew attention to real theory.

We conclude with a quote from that famous decision maker, Hamlet: "The cat will mew and the dog will have his day."

Reply to Commentaries

Hillel J. Einhorn, *University of Chicago*
Robin M. Hogarth, *University of Chicago*

Jacob Bronowski (1978, pp. 78–79) tells the following story about Bertrand Russell, who is reputed once to have said at a dinner party:

> "Oh, it is useless talking about inconsistent things, from an inconsistent proposition you can prove anything you like!". . . Someone at the dinner table said, "Oh, come on!" He said, "Well, name an inconsistent proposition" and the man said, "Well, what shall we say, 2 = 1." "All right," said Russell, "what do you want me to prove?" The man said, "I want you to prove that you are the pope." "Why," said Russell, "the pope and I are two, but two equals one, therefore the pope and I are one."

Now consider the following from Emerson's essay, "Self-reliance":

> A foolish consistency is the hobgoblin of little minds, adored by little statesmen and philosophers and divines. With consistency a great soul has simply nothing to do. (1883, p. 58.)

The above passages reflect the conflict that lies at the heart of current research in behavioral decision theory — namely, the importance of consistency in following rules, axioms, and the like, versus abandoning rules in particular cases when judgments and choices seem to imply a "foolish consistency." The present addendum to our review of behavioral decision theory considers this issue briefly (for more details, see Einhorn and Hogarth 1981b). We begin by examining one example of the recent work on "cognitive illusions" (Tversky and Kahneman 1981).

Imagine that the following rule was presented to you as a way to be consistent in your choices: If you prefer A to B ($A > B$), then you should prefer a gamble in which you win A with probability p (and zero with probability $1-p$) to B with probability p (and zero with probability $1-p$). Stated formally, if $A > B$, then $(A, p) > (B, p)$. This seems quite sensible since the inclusion of a common probability in both A and B should not change the order of preference. Kahneman and Tversky (1979b), however, have shown that when subjects choose between $A =$ a sure \$3000 versus $B =$ \$4000 with $p = 0.8$, most prefer A; but, when asked to choose between $C =$ \$3000 with $p = 0.25$ versus $D =$ \$4000 with $p = 0.20$, most prefer D. Note that $C = (A, 0.25)$ and $D = (B, 0.25)$. Therefore, although the formal rule seems sensible in general, it is violated by many people in specific situations. When people recognize the inconsistency of their choices with a rule they wish to follow, they experience confusion, bewilderment, and conflict. The resolution of the conflict is particularly difficult since there are no higher principles to which one can appeal. To resolve the conflict one must rely on the very intuitions that were not trusted in the first place, otherwise, why have a formal rule? This example clearly illustrates the conflict between the importance of being consistent (Russell 1948) and the fear that consistency is foolish if it leads to outcomes and results that are intuitively unacceptable (Emerson 1883). Furthermore, although some people change their choices to maintain consistency after extensive discussion, many others do not (Slovic and Tversky 1974). Therefore, it is not ignorance of the importance of maintaining consistency that explains the adherence to inconsistent choices.

The above example, as well as others in the literature, illustrates the following basic point: Choices, inferences, judgments, and the like, are ultimately evaluated by their validity, by which is meant the degree to which they can be justified to oneself and others. The degree of validity or justifiability is itself based on two general factors, neither of which is perfectly related to it. These factors are: (1) the logical deductibility or consistency of statements, hereafter called *truth*; and (2) the accuracy with which the content of particular statements, choices, and so on, matches or predicts what we consider to be reality. Therefore, we posit that

$$\text{Validity} = f \text{ (truth, accuracy)} \qquad \text{Eq. 1.}$$

The concept of truth, as defined here, is wholly structural. Thus, a syllogistic conclusion appropriately derived from incorrect (that is, inaccurate) premises is *true* regardless of how inaccurate it is vis-à-vis one's world knowledge. Formal systems must have *truth* since, as the Russell story illustrates, the presence of any inconsistency in the system means that anything can be proved (that is, deduced). Accuracy, on the other hand, refers to the degree to which judgments, inferences, etc., match or predict some external criterion or standard. The distinction can perhaps be made clearer by considering the difference between proving theorems (a favorite pastime in formal systems) and proving theories in science. In the former, truth/consistency is paramount; that is, do the results follow from the premises and the set of permissible operations? In the latter, accuracy is crucial; does the theory explain and predict empirical phenomena? Whereas there is no disagreement on the feasibility of proving theorems, philosophers of science have disagreed on whether theories can be proved; for example, recall Popper's views (1959) that theories can only be disproved, never proved. In dealing with specific cases and empirical phenomena, however, cues to accuracy are invariably involved and can conflict with logical truth.

That truth and accuracy can conflict is surprising to many since both are highly related to validity. However, although this does imply that they are themselves highly correlated, the less-than-perfect relationship means that there will be situations where one is high and the other is low. The earlier example involving choices between gambles is one such case; that is, the cues related to the sure thing in the first set of gambles and the small probability differences in the second set lead to choices that are inconsistent with the rule.

Cases of low truth and high accuracy are also possible. For example, the winner of a recent Spanish lottery told a journalist that he picked the winning ticket because it ended in the number 48. His reason involved the fact that he dreamed of the number 7 for seven nights in a row and $7 \times 7 = 48$. As Braine (1978) has pointed out,

> We confuse truth with validity or justifiability. Validity has to do with the quality of the reasons that make a rule suitable as a premise. The pragmatically useful evaluation of an inference rule is almost always a validity judgment . . . people . . . are not aware that there is a truth judgment that can be made that is not a validity judgment.

The distinction between truth and accuracy in determining validity has several important implications that bear on the appropriateness of various normative standards typically used in decision research. We briefly consider three such implications. (See Einhorn and Hogarth 1981b for more details.)

1. Statements and conclusions drawn from formal systems (for example, probability theory, axiomatic choice theory) while logically consistent (high truth), are nevertheless judged as to their validity. For example, the accuracy of the premises can be judged, and if found wanting, the conclusions are not accepted. At another level, one can tentatively accept conclusions; however, to the extent that people are aware that the entailments of those premises are not fully known to themselves, they may wait to judge the validity of the conclusions in particular cases. One is reminded of the Socratic dialogues in this regard; that is, by agreeing with a set of seemingly harmless assumptions, Socrates leads his protagonist to absurd conclusions. When engaged in similar discussions, many of us will wait to hear the conclusions before giving full support to the assumptions/axioms, regardless of how reasonable they sound in the abstract. Note that in specific situations the content, and thus the meaning of information, calls forth cues to accuracy that may conflict with truth. Indeed, much work on inference and choice has shown large context effects, including various violations of normative rules. However, normative rules are contentless and thus concerned solely with truth. When truth conflicts with accuracy of content, it is not an easy matter to determine what is the "right" answer. In fact, the determination of what constitutes an error in judgment and choice is the topic of much current debate (Cohen, in press; Einhorn and Hogarth, in press; Hogarth, in press; March 1978).

   This point can be illustrated by considering the results of several psychological experiments which show that people are suboptimal or irrational decision makers. When experimenters adopt normative standards as yardsticks for performance, many forget Savage's (1954) admonition that those models are appropriate for "small worlds" which embody various simplifying assumptions. Indeed, psychological experiments can be considered "small worlds"; they have not as yet captured the larger world in two important respects. First, subjects rarely receive continuous feedback about their judgments and thus cannot apply habitual, incremental strategies in which feedback can reduce both task complexity and the commitment implied by specific actions (see Connolly, this volume; Hogarth, in press). Indeed, understanding decision making as sequences of action–outcome–feedback loops is an important dimension missing from most current research. Second, experimental environments do not contain much redundancy and often serve to demonstrate the skills of experimenters to get subjects to use imperfect single cues in inappropriate ways. That is, subjects are prevented from taking advantage of the redundancies they typically encounter in natural ecologies where they use multiple, intersubstitutable cues and processes (Brunswik 1952).

2. As pointed out by Einhorn and Hogarth (1981b):

> The relationship between truth and validity is not static. For example, consider Bernoulli's initial advocacy of maximizing expected value as a rational strategy of choice (Schoemaker 1980a; Lopes, in press). Such a rule could not account for people refusing to buy the St. Petersburg lottery, which has an infinite expected value, nor the persistent buying of insurance, which has a negative expected value. Faced with these inconsistencies, Bernoulli proposed the concept of utility rather than value. Many years later, von Neumann and Morgenstern (1947) provided the axiom system and proof (logical deduction) that maximizing expected utility follows from acceptance of the axioms. Note that what is now considered by some to be a normative model of rational choice is a consequence of rationalizing behavior that used cues that were thought to be valid (marginally decreasing utility) but not yet incorporated in a formal model.

3. The distinction between truth and accuracy in determining validity bears directly on the inherent limitations of deductive systems for providing guidelines to appropriate behavior in given situations. Such limitations arise because the need to maintain perfect consistency in a formal system necessarily results in narrowing its domain of application. Indeed, this problem has been famous in mathematics ever since Gödel proved his impossibility theorem (see Nagel and Newman 1958) showing that

> there is an endless number of true arithmetical statements which cannot be formally deduced from any given set of axioms by a closed set of rules of inference.

Thus, incompleteness is an essential component of formal systems. Indeed, such incompleteness may lie at the heart of the uneasiness one may feel at following axioms and rules that lead to conclusions, choices, and inferences that are intuitively unacceptable. However, one should not thereby conclude that logical truth and formal systems are irrelevant in determining validity. Both truth *and* accuracy are important. The challenging task for future research is to improve our normative models by enlarging the context in which they have been used. This will involve incorporating better descriptions of what people are doing and why they are doing it. If, as Goldman (1978) has put it, "Ought implies can," understanding the psychological and biological limits and capabilities of the organism *ought* to be our first priority.

3 Human Problem Solving

In reviewing the development of decision aids, Herbert Simon (1965) made the comment that these aids to human thinking were developed without understanding the process they sought to aid — the thought process itself. Accordingly, Simon's research and that of his colleagues (see review in Ericsson and Simon 1978, 1979) have attempted to detail the thought processes underlying human problem solving. The essence of this approach is to develop a model of individual cognitive process based on the subject's verbalizations (protocols) of various tasks and problems. The approach also entails the extraction of decision-making rules from protocols and formalizing these rules into a computer algorithm (Clarkson 1962, Bettman 1971, Kleinmuntz 1975, Bouwman 1978b, Svenson 1979). Most of these studies attempted to infer some characteristics of elementary information-processing activities, such as storage and retrieval from short-term memory, scanning lists in memory, and the use of certain basic processing rules for the recognition of stimulus patterns. Eventually, applications moved from chess problems, cryptarithmetic, and simple algebraic problems to more complex problems in consumer behavior, financial diagnosis, and language comprehension (Bettman 1974, Payne 1976, Just and Carpenter 1977, Svenson 1979).

While these process-tracing methods might provide more specific insights into the information-processing strategies used by individuals, there is a debate over whether the data collected in the verbalizations are isomorphic with the actual cognitive processes (Nisbett and Wilson 1977; Simon 1978c; Ericsson and Simon 1978, 1979, 1980). In general, the experimental controls under which the protocols are generated, as well as the underlying inferences, have become subjects of controversy.

In the state-of-the-art paper for this section, Hayes deals with these issues, especially the considerations of protocol-coder reliability, independence of coder judgment from the theories tested, and relating the protocol-data to alternative models. He does this in light of criticisms made by Nisbett and Wilson (1977) that the task of verbalizing may significantly distort the thought process of the subjects. Hayes cites evidence to refute this argument, and argues that protocols can enable us to understand the more complete picture of problem solving despite their incompleteness. He suggests that when the results from the more traditional input–output experiments are used to help interpret the protocol data, the most reasonable interpretation of the data can be made.

In their commentaries, Posner and Lichtenstein deal with these issues in different ways. Posner acknowledges the value of protocol analysis in studying the thought process, but questions the assumption that protocols provide a full and undistorted record of the underlying processes in which problems are solved. Two specific problems are discussed. First, participant behavior (for example, step-by-step deliberation of hypothesis) may suppress spectator behavior (for example, accumulated impressions associated with prototypical instances) by altering the performance of problem solvers. Two studies, one by

59

Bruner and Potter (1964) and another by Hislop (1970), are presented to sub-stantiate this claim. The second problem is that a substantial part of thought processes is unconscious in nature, making measurement from verbal and eye-movement protocols difficult.

Relatedly, Lichtenstein focuses on how the incompleteness of protocols leads to difficult interpretational problems. Incompleteness is particularly acute for expert subjects, as in the case of those who have performed the task so many times that their performance has become routinized, and are not prone to verbalize details. Lichtenstein also discusses how experimental demands may lead subjects to change their cognitive processes. Finally, she challenges Hayes's claim that coding in protocol analysis can be made independent of the theory being tested. She argues that theory guides protocol construction and analysis, and that "true" independence, while being a laudable goal, is unat-tainable in practice.

Responding to these issues, Hayes frames the studies in contention, for example, Hislop's study (1970) and Bruner and Potter (1964), in terms of Ericsson and Simon's (1980) three levels of verbal reports. Hayes argues that "level three" verbalizations, defined as "articulation after scanning, filtering, and inference have modified available information," may, in fact, change the reported processes in ways discussed by Posner and Lichtenstein. Thus, the Hislop, and the Bruner and Potter studies do not violate the Ericsson and Simon (1980) model, and are, in fact, consistent with the predictions of the model. Moreover, Hayes acknowledges that protocols are generally incom-plete. However, as protocols are more complete than any other data from other methods, a concern for completeness should lead to an adoption of protocol analysis, rather than its rejection.

In summary, the papers highlight the controversial elements of protocol analysis. Given the present debate on the use of protocols, the commentaries have provided us a timely and appropriate discussion of internal validity issues. Given our interest in the individual–organizational linkage, however, the extension of this debate should likewise cover issues of external validity. That is, how might protocol analysis be used to study ill-structured problems characteristic of managerial decision making? If managerial decision making is indeed as unstructured and as fragile as Mintzberg (1973) suggests, what would the underlying "traces" of such decisions developed from protocol analysis indicate? Relatedly, how serious a concern would the suppression or incompleteness of protocols be (see, for example, criticisms raised by Posner and Lichtenstein) if the point of interest is what managers express (as opposed to repress)? Perhaps the concerns correctly raised by Posner, Lichtenstein, and others might be ultimately resolved in the application of protocol analysis to problem-solving contexts in which both internal and external validity may be adequately examined.

Issues in Protocol Analysis

John R. Hayes, *Carnegie-Mellon University*

Protocol analysis is a very powerful tool for identifying psychological processes, but it has been woefully underemployed. I believe that there are two major reasons for its lack of popularity. First, there have been widespread doubts about its validity — doubts which have arisen in part because protocol analysis has been confused with other methods, such as introspection. Second, protocol analysis is a nonstandard technique for which there are as yet no readily available primers or instruction manuals. Researchers who might consider using protocol analysis may decide against it because of uncertainties about how to proceed.

In this paper, I will discuss evidence on the validity of protocol analysis and say a bit about how to do it. The result, I hope, will be to convince a few people to try it, and thus make protocol analysis a bit more popular as a method.

Input–Output Analysis and Process-Tracing Techniques

In the behaviorist tradition the most acceptable way to analyze task performance was to correlate input and output. In learning studies, for example, a typical experiment might involve varying the properties of the material to be learned and measuring the resulting changes in learning time and errors. Typically, researchers did not observe what went on during learning — that is, they did not try to see "how the learner did it." Indeed, some, like Skinner, felt it was unscientific to make inferences about unseen processes intervening between input and output.

Information processing psychology had diverged radically from this earlier tradition by focusing directly on the analysis of these unseen processes. Data for the analysis is derived not only from the traditional input–output measures — that is, error rates and response times — but also from a variety of process tracing techniques. We will describe three such techniques here: motor protocols, eye-movement protocols, and verbal protocols. All three kinds have proven to be very useful for describing psychological processes.

Motor Protocols

To obtain motor protocols, we observe the obvious physical activities of our subjects — activities such as walking, picking things up, reaching, etc. The following motor protocol, collected by Köhler (1925, p. 174), describes the activities of Sultan (an ape) as he solved a simple problem.

(March 26th): Sultan is squatting at the bars, but cannot reach the fruit, which lies outside, by means of his only available short stick. A longer stick is deposited outside the bars, about two metres on one side of the objective, and parallel with the grating. It can not be grasped with the hand, but it can be pulled within reach by means of the small stick (see Figure 1). Sultan tries to reach the fruit with the smaller of the two sticks. Not succeeding, he tears at a piece of wire that projects from the netting of his cage, but that, too, is in vain. Then he gazes about him; (there are always in the course of these tests some long pauses, during which the animals scrutinize the whole visible area). He suddenly picks up the little stick once more, goes up to the bars directly opposite to the long stick, scratches it towards him with the "auxiliary," seizes it, and goes with it to the point opposite the objective, which he secures. From the moment that his eyes fall upon the long stick, his procedure forms one consecutive whole, without hiatus. . . .

Köhler used the observation that the solution occurred suddenly to argue that Sultan's solution process involved "insight." Further, Köhler used the observation that the solution ran off smoothly and continuously to argue that Sultan "knew what he was doing" from the moment of insight.

Motor protocols are especially valuable for use with subjects who have limited language abilities — for example, children and animals.

Eye-Movement Protocols

An eye-movement protocol is a record of the places in a scene where the subjects fix their gaze (that is, their eye fixations) as they perform a task. In some cases, we can obtain sufficiently accurate information about eye

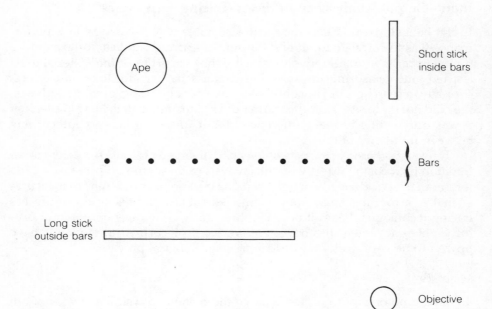

FIGURE 1   Köhler's experimental arrangement of two sticks (from Köhler 1925).

movements just by looking at the subjects (as Fantz, 1961, has done), to see if they are looking left or right. In other cases, we must use sophisticated equipment such as an eye-movement camera (Mackworth and Thomas 1962) to obtain precise eye positions.

Figure 2 shows the eye movements of an expert chess player during the first five seconds of examining the chess position shown in Figure 3 (Tichomirov and Poznyanskaya 1966). Using these data, Simon and Barenfeld (1969) have argued that what the chess expert was doing was examining attack and defense relationships among the pieces. Eye-movement protocols have also been used to study tasks such as reading (Carpenter and Just 1978) and solving number puzzles (Winikoff 1966).

Verbal Protocols

To collect a verbal or "thinking aloud" protocol, subjects are asked to say aloud everything that crosses their minds while they are performing the task, no matter how trivial the thought may be. When we collect writing protocols, for example, we instruct the subjects as follows: "If you read anything, read it

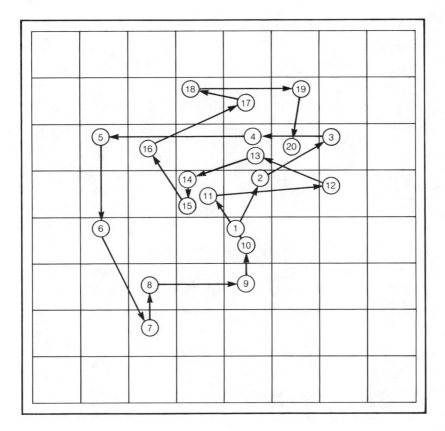

FIGURE 2   Record of eye movements for the first 5 seconds (from Tichomirov and Poznyanskaya 1966).

aloud; if you write anything, say what you are writing; if you think anything, say it aloud, even if it is only swearing." Even with such explicit instructions, however, subjects may forget and fall silent — completely absorbed in the task. At such times the experimenter will say, "Remember, tell me everything you are thinking."

When the subject has been given the thinking-aloud instructions, we turn on the tape recorder and present the task which the subject is to perform, for example, to write about abortion for a teenage audience. The data collected consist of the transcribed tape recording together with all of the notes and written output the subject may produce.

Figure 4 shows a typical thinking-aloud protocol for a subject solving a water-jug problem. We will analyze this protocol in greater detail later.

Process Tracing and Input–Output Methods

Figure 5 shows the relations we assume among input, output, psychological processes, and the data obtained by process tracing methods. Notice that we do not assume that psychological processes are observed directly. Rather, we

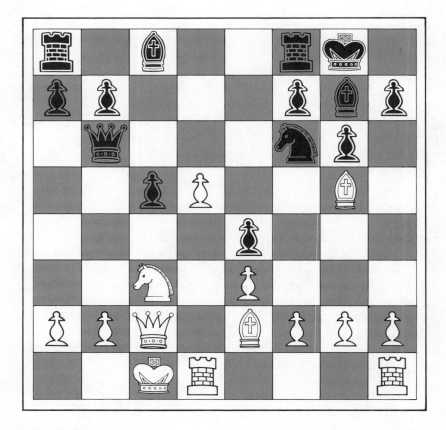

FIGURE 3   Middle game position used by Tichomirov and Poznyanskaya (black to
            play).

Water-Jug Problem: Given Jug A which contains 9 quarts; Jug B, 42 quarts; and Jug C, 6 quarts, measure out exactly 21 quarts.

Protocol

1. Uh, the first thing that's apparent is half of B is, is the uh, the
2. amount that you want.
3. *Exp.*: Uh huh.
4. Um, you can't get 21 from just multiplying up A or C.
5. You get 18 and 18 respectively, that's as close as you can get,
6. I guess. Um, so I'll try to think of the different combinations that
7. might . . . come up with a surplus . . . or deficit of the 21 quarts . . . and
8. 9 and 6 are, 15 . . . if you took two 9s and two 6s, you'd have 30 which
9. would leave you . . . and pour them into the 42 container, you'd have a,
10. an open space of a, 12, which means nothing. How about . . . see . . . now I'm
11. trying to think of how close to 42 you can get with a 9 and the 6 quantities.
12. You can get . . . I forget the 7 table. It's been a long time since I've
13. had to multiply or anything so you'll have to give me some time. Um,
14. 9 times 5 is 45 . . . hm, 6 times 7 is 42, I think. Is that right?
15. *Exp.*: Uh huh.
16. OK, so you can, uh . . . fill B with C, evenly . . .
17. *Exp.*: You could . . .
18. So, . . . if you were to take . . . 36 . . . hm, oh, uh, 6 times 4 is 24 . . . and if you, uh,
19. What I'm trying to get rid of is, is, 3 quarts there . . .
20. *Exp.*: Good.
21. So if you were to, um . . . still 24. I, I was trying to think possibly,
22. some way, of . . . the difference between the 6 and the 9 is 3 quarts. I
23. was trying to think of . . . a way to uh . . . oh, how about . . . you put the 3, 6
24. quart quantity into the 42 bottle, which is 18, then the runoff, from
25. pouring a 9 into a 6 which is 3 and 18 is 21.
26. *Exp.*: Good.

FIGURE 4   Protocol of a water-jug problem.

assume that these processes trigger observable events which we do observe. These events are used to infer the occurrence of the underlying processes and the order in which they occur. For example, suppose that we are tracing the eye movements of a subject who is solving the cryptarithmetic problem shown in Figure 6. The sequence of eye movements can be taken as a reasonable indication that the subject has first processed column 1 and then column 6.

Process tracing methods differ from traditional methods in that they make use of information about processes intervening between input and output. Notice, though, that to interpret process tracing data we must take inputs and outputs into account. To understand what Sultan was doing we had to understand his input — that is, the problem situation he faced. To interpret the chess player's eye movements, we had to know the placement of the pieces on the board. Knowing the input, then, is essential in protocol analysis. Knowing the output is important, too. Suppose that by analyzing the eye movements in Figure 2, we decided that the chess player was considering taking black's pawn with his knight. We would be very remiss if we failed to find out what move was actually made. Inferences from process tracing data should be cross-validated whenever possible.

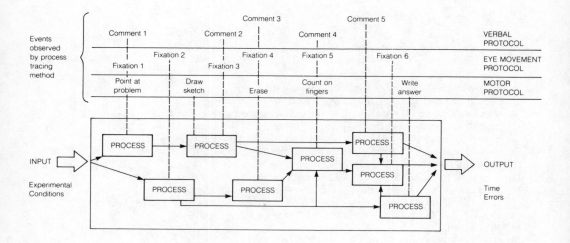

FIGURE 5   Inputs, outputs, and processes.

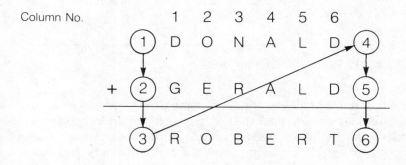
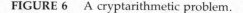

FIGURE 6   A cryptarithmetic problem.

Evaluating the Validity of Verbal Protocols

While motor and eye-movement protocols have generally been accepted as valid sources of scientific data, many have questioned the validity of verbal protocols. Three major issues have been raised:

1. Subjects may not be able to report accurately on their own mental processes. On the basis of a selective review of the literature, Nisbett and Wilson (1977) concluded that subjects are generally not aware of their own processes. Rather, when they are asked to describe their mental processes,

they describe what they believe their mental states should have been — not what they actually were.

2. Even if subjects could report accurately on their mental processes, the act of reporting may distort those processes. Clearly, the potential for such distortion exists. For example, suppose that we were to ask subjects who were doing long division problems to report every time they noticed an odd number. Such a reporting procedure would certainly change the way the subjects attended to the division task and would very likely interfere in a serious way with the computations.

3. Because verbal protocols are extremely complex, one may wonder whether an analysis of a protocol is objective and factual or simply the projection of the analyst's biases. Without some assurance of objectivity, it would be foolish to use protocol analysis to establish or test a scientific theory.

In a careful review of the literature, Ericsson and Simon (1980) have examined the first two issues and have presented a model of verbal reporting which accounts for the known facts. Figure 7, which outlines the processes of protocol collection and analysis, is consistent with the model.

Ericsson and Simon (1980) postulate that when subjects perform a task such as mental multiplication in their usual way, some of the information involved in performing the task, but typically not all of it, is attended to and enters short-term memory.

If subjects give a concurrent verbal report of their mental processes — that is, if they try to say how they are performing the task *while they are performing it* — the consequences will depend on the nature of the task and on the nature of the report.

1. If the subject is reporting memory traces which are verbal, then reporting appears neither to change nor to slow down task performance.
2. If the subject is reporting nonverbal memory traces, then reporting may slow task performance but does not appear to change its course or structure.
3. If the subject is asked to report information which would normally not be attended to while performing the task, for example, tell me every time you think of an odd number, then reporting may modify the usual sequence of mental processes involved in performing the task.

If subjects try to report retrospectively, that is, *after they have performed the task,* much of the relevant information may be lost from short-term memory. The longer the interval between task performance and report, of course, the larger the amount of information likely to be lost.

The Ericsson and Simon model not only accounts for the literature they surveyed, but also for the literature surveyed by Nisbett and Wilson. Most of the studies cited in the Nisbett and Wilson review either involve retrospective reports or ask the subjects to report information which they would not normally attend to in the course of performing the task. Accurate reports of mental processes would not be expected in such studies. In fact, none of the studies reported by Nisbett and Wilson violates the predictions of the Ericsson and Simon model.

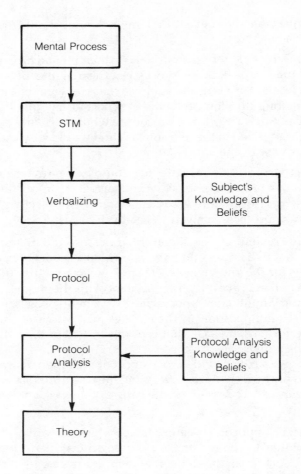

FIGURE 7   Processes of protocol collection and analysis.

What does the Ericsson and Simon model predict about verbal protocols? Verbal protocols are concurrent reports which do not require subjects to attend to anything they would not normally attend to in performing the task. The model predicts that such reports will not change the course or structure of task performance although they may slow it down. In the case of verbal tasks such as writing and reading, the model predicts that protocols may not even slow task performance.

The third issue, the objectivity of protocol analysis, is a complex one. We will discuss it under three headings — coder reliability, independence of observation and theory, and differentiating alternative theories.

Coder Reliability. Any study in which protocols are analyzed by only one coder is subject to criticism on the ground that the coder reliability has not been established and that, until it is, the claimed observations cannot be credited as objective (publicly observable) facts.

There is nothing intrinsic in the protocol analysis method which prevents researchers from obtaining measures of coder reliability. In a recent study of processes in written composition (Hayes and Flower 1980), we measured coder reliabilities for several aspects of protocol coding. In the simpler coding tasks, reliabilities were quite high — on the order of 90–95 percent agreement between independent raters. By simple coding tasks I mean tasks such as: (1) identifying protocol segments which correspond to processes of reading written material or writing sentences on paper; (2) differentiating notes from formed text; and (3) differentiating metacomments, that is, comments about the writing process from content statements, which are comments about the topic.

Of greater concern theoretically are the reliabilities of judgments in which coders are trying to relate protocols to process models. Our model of composition specified four major processes: generating ideas, organizing, writing sentences, and editing. The judges' task was to associate each content statement in the protocol with one of the four processes which they believed was most likely to have generated it. The agreement between judges was 84.7 percent.

Independence. When we analyze protocols, we want to be sure that the coders' judgments are independent of the theory being tested. If coders make judgments in the context of a complete protocol, theory may influence coders' judgments through contextual cues. For example, a coder may tend to classify a statement as an instance of idea generation if it occurs very early in the protocol, but as sentence writing if it occurs later.

To determine if consistent judgments about writing processes can be made in the absence of context, Flower and I (Hayes and Flower 1980) conducted the following study.

We selected 51 content statements from a protocol and typed them on cards. The cards were then shuffled and presented for judgment by independent coders. The average agreement among the coders was 72 percent. Most of the disagreements (16 out of 22) involved judgments of editing. Many segments that some coders attributed to editing other coders attributed to generating ideas. Editing may be especially difficult to identify out of context because "edits" often present a comment on the previous segment or represent a change in a previous segment. It is difficult, for example, to see that segment 87, "I guess all elements are low level," indicates editing for redundancy unless one also sees segment 86, "even low-level elements of writing." If we ignore the editing judgments, average agreement among coders is 86 percent. Good agreement can be achieved in coding protocols, then, even in the absence of context.

Recently, Ericsson and Simon (1980) have developed a computer-controlled system for presenting protocol segments in random order to the coders.

Differentiating Among Alternative Theories. Suppose that a researcher has a model of intelligent problem solving in some area and reports that in a protocol study the model accounts for, say, 80 percent of the subject's choices. Suppose, further, that we believe him. How much credit do the data reflect on the model?

As one approach to answering this question, we might ask if the subject's behavior differs significantly from chance in the direction predicted by the model. Finding that it did, however, would be a rather weak recommendation of the model. It is likely that any reasonable model, for example, hill climbing, or means–ends analysis, would do better than chance. The real question is, "Do other reasonable models do as well as 80 percent?" If the researchers don't tell us how other reasonable models fit their data, then, alas, we have difficulty in determining whether our 80 percent fit is remarkable or not. Since complete protocols are not usually provided in research reports, we typically can't do the comparison ourselves.

Recently, R. Neches (1978) has implemented a computer system which makes it easy to match a protocol segment successively to several models of the behavior. The experience of using such a system is chastening. After matching a pretty good model to the data, one can be convinced, despite a few vaguenesses, that the current model is quite adequate. When this model is followed by a really good model, one is horrified by one's credulity. The vagueness in the previous interpretation now turns into clear clues that the new model is correct and the earlier one wrong. Comparison of the models side by side is clearly helpful in differentiating between the models. Studies in which the data are matched only to one model may leave us wondering how well other reasonable models might have done.

Doubts about the validity of protocol analysis undoubtedly discourage many from using it as a research technique. I suspect that even more people are discouraged from using it because they feel they don't know how to analyze a protocol. I am often asked, "How do you do protocol analysis?" I wish I could answer by providing a definitive procedure as for finding a square root. Unfortunately, this question is only a little less general than the question, "How do you analyze data?" A complete answer has to depend on a knowledge of the particular task, the subjects, and what you are trying to find out, as well as general principles. Fortunately, there are some principles and some heuristics which can be very helpful.

1. Protocols may be very complex. Don't be discouraged if you find them very confusing on first reading. In fact, they may require many hours of study before they become reasonably clear. Segmenting the protocol into smaller, more manageable units can make the task of analysis easier because it divides the judgmental task into parts and clearly specifies the boundaries of the parts to be judged. Figure 8 shows a portion of a writing protocol segmented to aid analysis for content statements and metacomments.

2. In analyzing a protocol, you are trying to understand the behavior of a single subject. In the worst case, you may require a different model to describe the behavior of each subject. Generally it is perilous to average across subjects. A model based on averaged data may describe none of the subjects.

3. The analyst's purpose is the major factor which determines how a protocol analysis ought to be carried out. If the purpose is simply to explore, then establishing coder reliability and independence of coder judgment from theory may be unimportant. Figure 9 is a section of a protocol in which we were exploring for difficulties which poor writers might have in writing

55   56   57
(Fortunately – times have changed) – (opportunities no longer) . . . (um) – (let's

58   59
not be wholly optimistic.) (Opportunities are seldom any longer restricted

60   61
by sexual stereotypes.) (Will a) – (Will a ten-year-old know what that means?) –

62
(I'll put it down for now but I think I'll change it.) . . . (This means for

63   64   65
you that you can choose your life work) – (a) – (to correspond to your special

66
gifts as a person) – (and you don't have to – be afraid that people won't

67
understand or accept your choice.) (It's easier to write kids' themes.) . . .

68
(Thinking now about titles since I'm supposed to write about a woman's role.)

69   70   71   72
(Um) – (thinking about something like – be glad) (or some) – (I don't know) –

73   74
(anyway) – (all right let's see)

FIGURE 8   A segmented portion of a writing protocol.

Oh, what can I say? — Drat, I broke the pencil point again — keep on breaking the pencil

point — *I also have to* — i-e- drop the e — *to do what is called a - quote - back-up - dash - semi-colon* —

This is a way of storing — -g- looks like an -f- on top — *of storing* — uh — *the computer* — Oh, drat —

broke it again — *for information* — uh — *to a roll of magnetic tape* — My -c- looks like an -e- at the

end of magnetic — I have to change that — Let me get the eraser out here — put it up on my

pencil — um — Okay — Here we go — Okay, where am I at?

FIGURE 9   A poor writer attempting to construct a sentence.

sentences. In this case, a number of difficulties is quite evident. Unfortunately discovery isn't always this easy. If the analyst's purpose is to test
hypotheses, then establishing coder reliability and independence of coder
judgment from theory is essential.
4.   The most important aid in analyzing a protocol is knowledge of what the
task demands and knowledge of the resources and limitations which

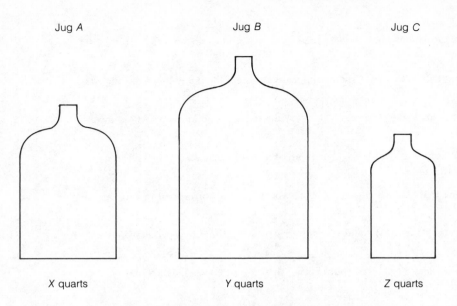

FIGURE 10   Noncalibrated jugs used to solve the water-jug problem.

humans bring to the task. Such knowledge can be derived from task analyses and from psychology journals, but it is wise to get firsthand experience by doing the task yourself before trying to analyze protocols of other people.

An Example of Protocol Analysis

To illustrate the application of these principles, let's examine the protocol in Figure 4 in detail and try to make some reasonable guesses about what the subject was doing.

Water-jug problems require the subject to measure out a specified quantity of water using three jugs, as shown in Figure 10. None of the jugs has calibration marks. That is, there are no marks indicating a one-quart level, a two-quart level, etc. The subject is told only how much each jug will hold when it is full.

In his first sentence, the subject mentions something which appears to be irrelevant to solving the problem. He mentions the fact that the desired amount (21 quarts) is just half the quantity contained in Jug B. Now, division is a very useful operation in many algebra problems. In this problem, if we could divide Jug B in half, the problem would be solved. But alas! There is no division operation in water-jug problems. All we can do is add and subtract the quantities in Jugs A, B, and C. Why, then, does the subject notice that the desired quantity is half of B? The simplest answer seems to be that he is confusing water-jug problems (perhaps because he isn't thoroughly familiar with them) with the more general class of algebra problems. If this answer is correct, we would expect that the subject would stop noticing division relations as he gains more experience with water-jug problems. In fact, that is what happened.

In line 3, the experimenter (Exp.) does just what the experimenter is supposed to do — that is, he is noncommital. In general, the experimenter should answer only essential questions and remind the subject to keep talking.

From lines 4 and 5, we can guess that the subject has successively added 9s to get 9, 18, 27 . . . and 6s to get 6, 12, 18, 24 . . . and realized that neither sequence includes 21. From lines 6 through 10, we can see that the subject begins to consider combinations of 9s and 6s which may be added together to obtain interesting sums, or subtracted from the 42-quart container to obtain interesting differences. While considering sums, the subject fails to notice that the sum 6 + 6 + 9 solves the problem.

In lines 11 through 14, the subject tries to find out if 42 quarts can be obtained by adding 9s and 6s. The answer is "yes," but it doesn't help the subject to find a solution. It appears to be a "blind alley." In this section, the subject indicates several times that he doesn't feel confident about multiplication.

In lines 15 and 17, the experimenter provides the subject with a small amount of information by confirming his uneasy suspicion that 6 times 7 equals 42. On occasion, the experimenter must decide whether or not to provide information the subject requests. In this case, since the experimenter was really interested in water jug problems rather than in arithmetic, he decided to supply an arithmetic fact.

In lines 18 and 19, the subject realizes that if he had a way to subtract 3 quarts from 24 quarts, he could solve the problem. In line 20, the experimenter appears to slip by providing the subject with approval, when he would better have remained silent. In line 21, the subject is still thinking of working from 24 quarts. In line 22, he discovers a way to add (rather than subtract) 3 quarts by pouring A into C and catching the overflow. In lines 23 and 24, he decides to work from 18 quarts rather than 24 quarts and then (on line 25) immediately solves the problem.

Now, let's stand back from the details of the protocol to see if we can characterize the whole problem-solving process that the subject engaged in. Before reading further, review the discussion of the protocol and then try to characterize the problem-solving process yourself.

One way to characterize the problem-solving process is to describe it as a search for an operator or a combination of operators to solve the problem. (In this case, the operators are arithmetic procedures such as division and subtraction.) In Figure 11, where we have diagrammed this search process, we can see that search proceeds, generally, from simple to complex — that is, from single operators to complex combinations of operators.

Up until line 18, the subject's search for a solution could have been guided by the problem statement above. That is, by reading the problem statement, the subject could have decided that what was needed to solve the problem was some combination of algebraic operators. Up to line 18, he could simply be trying one combination after another. We call this sort of search *forward search*, that is, it is search suggested by the problem statement alone. In lines 18 and 19, however, the subject formulates a goal on the basis of his difficulties in solving the problem. He notes that he hasn't been able to get closer than three quarts to the answer and attempts to find an operator that will subtract three quarts. This

LINES IN PROTOCOL	OPERATOR APPLIED	OUTCOME	COMMENT
1–2	Divide by 2	Fail	Operator not available
4–5	Add 9s	Fail	
4–5	Add 6s	Fail	The subject apparently doesn't try all combinations because he fails to notice that $6 + 6 + 9 = 21$
6–8	Add 9s and 6s	Fail	
7–10	Add 9s and 6s and subtract from 42	Fail	
18–19	Notice difficulty	Succeed	The subject notices the operators above got him no closer to 21 than 24; he sets the goal of finding an operator to subtract 3
22	Overflow 9 into 6	Fail	
23–25	Add 6 three times and overflow 9 into 6	Succeed	

Forward Search — rows 1–2 through 7–10

Means–ends Analysis — rows 18–19 through 23–25

FIGURE 11   The search process used for solving the problem.

goal depends not just on the problem statement but also on the subject's experience in trying to solve the problem—that is, on his distance from the goal. It is a form of means–ends analysis in which the subject attempts to find a means to the end of reducing his distance from the goal.

The whole solution process then consists of (1) an initial phase of forward search through an increasingly complex sequence of operators, followed by (2) a phase of means–ends analysis in which the subject succeeds in finding a solution.

In analyzing a protocol, we attempt to describe the psychological processes which a subject uses to perform a task. To do this, it is useful to be familiar both with the properties of the task and with the problem solver's component psychological processes. In analyzing the water-jug protocol above, knowing that the task required algebraic operators and that human problem solvers often use processes of forward search and means–ends analysis helped us to recognize how the subject had organized these processes in his search for a solution. In the same way, when we analyze other protocols, knowledge of other tasks and of other psychological properties will be useful. This is not to say that we must already understand a performance before we can analyze it. It is just that when we do understand some things about the performance, we can use them very profitably to learn other things.

In analyzing the water-jug protocol in Figure 4, knowledge of the psychological phenomenon of set is very helpful. The problem used in this protocol can be solved in either of two ways. It can be solved by the procedure B − A − 2C, or it can be solved by the simpler procedure: A− C. Just before solving this problem, the subject worked a series of six problems, all of which required the procedure B − A − 2C for solution. As a result, we would expect the subject to show a set to use the B − A − 2C procedure. As lines 6 through 9 show, the subject actually solves the problem by the A − C procedure. However, if we look back to lines 3 and 4, we see that the subject's first problem-solving attempt was to subtract A from B. This suggests that he started to use the B − A − 2C procedure even though he didn't carry it through. Clearly, analyzing the protocol gives us evidence about the subject's solution process that we can't get just by looking at the answer.

The protocol of the age problem (shown in Figure 12) illustrates again the usefulness of knowledge of task demands and component psychological processes for understanding human performance. As in many problems, part of the difficulty of age problems lies in keeping track of relevant information. Unless problem solvers are very careful in labeling information, they are likely to confuse a person's age at one time with the same person's age at a different time. For example, problem solvers who have only a single label which they use both for "Mary's age now" and "Mary's age then" — let us say "Mary" or "M" — are very likely to confuse Mary's age now with Mary's age then. This is just what happens in this age problem protocol.

John is now twice as old as he was when Mary was three years older

than he is now, but he is only half as old as Mary is at present.

Now how old are they?

1. Um, um, John is now twice as old as he was when Mary was

2. three years older than he is now. But he is only half as old as Mary

3. at present. Um, um, three years older is the only number supplied,

4. so I'm going to start working from there. I guess, and uh, . . .

5. *Exp.*: What are you thinking?

6. I get absolutely nothing from those questions.

7. I am drawing a blank at the moment, um, I am trying to sort out John

8. and Mary, I guess, here, because, the words don't lend themselves to

9. be deciphered into, like, two neat little John and Mary columns, um,

10. and it's hard. Okay. John is twice as old . . now . . than when he was when

11. Mary was three years older than him . . Oh wow! Um, but he is only half

12. as old as Mary at present . . . So, um, John equals, hm, now I'm trying

13. to think of a . . I don't know why it just occurred to me that maybe if

14. I plugged John and Mary and the information into little, little, you

15. know, John equals Mary plus three, or something like that, you know,

16. Little *x, y*?

17. *Exp.*: Uh huh.

18. I don't know what you call them.

19. *Exp.*: Equations.

20. Equations. Okay. Got to warn you, I flunked math in sixth grade. So um,

21. um, ah . . . John is now twice as old as he was when Mary was three years

22. older than he is now. . , Okay, so John equals . . um, Mary and three . . . , which

23. doesn't do me any good, and he is only half as old as Mary at present,

24. so I have to know how much John is worth first, here, and, uh, . . Mary is

25. three years older than he is . . , and half as old as Mary at present. Um,

26. Mary is three years older than he is now, but he is only half as old as

27. Mary at present. . . So he has to be, hm . . . Mary is three years older than

28. he is now . . . and Mary is twice his age. Then he's got to be three years

29. old.

30. *Exp.*: All right.

FIGURE 12   An age protocol.

Analysis of the Problem

To solve this problem, it is necessary to distinguish four quantities — John's age now, JN; John's age then, JT; Mary's age now, MN; and Mary's age then, MT. Three equations can be derived from the problem statement.

$JN = 2 JT$ that is, John is twice as old now as he was then.

$MT = JN + 3$ that is, Mary then was three years older than John is now.

$JN = \frac{1}{2} MN$ that is, John now is half as old as Mary now.

In addition, because we know that John and Mary age at the same rate, we can derive a fourth equation:

$JN - JT = MN - MT$ that is, the difference between John's age now and John's age then is the same as the difference between Mary's age now and Mary's age then.

Armed with these equations, those adept at algebra can determine that John's age now is 6 and Mary's age now is 12.

Now, let's see what our subject has done. From lines 15 through 29, she frequently confuses John's and Mary's ages now with John's and Mary's ages then. In fact, nowhere in the protocol is there any evidence that she ever makes the now–then distinction. In lines 27 and 28, she derives two equations:

$$\text{Mary} = \text{John} + 3, \text{ and}$$

$$\text{Mary} = 2 \times \text{John}$$

The second one is correct, but the first is not because it confuses Mary's age then with Mary's age now. The subject then solves these equations and concludes, incorrectly, that John's age now is 3.

Protocols Are Incomplete

Typically, protocols are incomplete. Many processes occur during the performance of a task which the subject can't or doesn't report. The psychologist's task in analyzing a protocol is to take the incomplete record which the protocol provides, together with his knowledge of human capabilities, and to infer from these a model of the underlying psychological processes by which the subject performs the task.

Analyzing a protocol is like following the tracks of a porpoise. Occasionally, the porpoise reveals itself by breaking the surface of the sea. Its brief surfacings are like the glimpses which the protocol affords us of underlying mental process. Between surfacings, the mental process, like the porpoise, runs deep and silent. Our task is to infer the course of the process from these brief traces.

Protocol Analysis and Human Cognition

Michael I. Posner, *University of Oregon*

Extensions in the Use of Protocol Analysis

In psychology it is not unusual for methods to be imported from one area to another, often without recognition of the similarity. As Hayes correctly points out, protocol analysis is an underused tool in the study of human cognition, but it has a long and important tradition in other areas of psychological research. For example, much of the work on ethnology, ecological approaches to human behavior, and developmental psychology has relied on systematic coding of observations. These observational codes yield a kind of protocol which is a systematic description of the observed behavior of the organism under consideration. Indeed, observational coding is such an important aspect of quite different areas of psychology that we teach this form of protocol analysis to our undergraduate students as a basic part of their methods course. Many of the issues of reliability, sampling, and combining data across subjects to which Hayes alludes have also arisen in the area of behavioral coding (Sackett 1978).

What is novel in the form of protocol analysis represented by Hayes, and what runs afoul of the behaviorist traditions, is not the systematic observations that yield the protocol, nor even the use of verbalization as their basis, but the claim that the protocol can be used to trace the underlying covert processes by which subjects solve problems. Pure behaviorists do not accept the notion that a hidden covert process is necessary to describe overt behavior. It is, of course, one of the contributions of Simon and the information processing tradition that owes so much to him, that such covert processes have become important parts of psychological theory and investigation.

As a psychologist interested in the study of human cognition, I can't help but be enthusiastic about the use of protocol analysis to extend the range of investigation of human mental activity. The somewhat cumbersome experimental method of manipulating independent variables in an attempt to isolate underlying mental operations is a slow process. No doubt it can never be extended to any but a small range of the various mental tasks of which the human is capable. Exploration of vast territories of complex mental activity, such as chess playing and complex decision making, by protocol analysis foreshadows its use by other forms of experimental investigation.

There are, however, problems in the assumption that the verbal protocol of the subject gives a full and undistorted record of the underlying processes by which a problem is solved. Many of these reservations, I think, are implicit in Hayes's presentation and more completely explored in Ericsson and Simon's

(1980) recent paper, but some of them are not made sufficiently explicit. I would like to take a few moments to raise some cautions about the use of protocol analysis as a means of tracing the mental processes used in the solution of problems.

Problems in the Application of Protocol Analysis to Human Cognition

Suppression of Spectator Behavior by Participant Behavior

The human nervous system is capable of abstracting from input information and accumulating a broad range of impressions. These impressions often are amenable to verbal analysis, but sometimes they are not. For example, consider the case of expert diagnosticians. When presented with an interesting case, experts may diagnose it rapidly and correctly. Later, asked how they arrived at the diagnosis they might reply simply, "X looked like a person who had Y disease."[1] Like successful clinical diagnosticians, many of our natural concepts, life decisions, and problem solutions are based on accumulated impressions that create concepts with prototypical instances and fuzzy boundaries (Rosch and Lloyd 1978). Solution of problems based on such concepts has been called by Heidbreder (1946) *spectator behavior.* Solutions based on step-by-step deliberate hypotheses were called by Heidbreder *participant behavior* but are now widely referred to as "hypothesis testing." "Hypothesis testing" is a highly serial, often purely verbal process. Hypotheses shape the information we remember about the world. In much psychological thinking, hypothesis and spectator behavior have been contrasted as two approaches to the understanding of problem solving. The former is often associated with cognitive psychologists, while the latter is associated with behaviorist or learning theory approaches. Both spectator and hypothesis behavior, however, may alter performance by interfering with spectator behavior. This possibility has been explored in several experiments.

In one classic study (Bruner and Potter 1964), subjects are shown pictures of complicated objects or scenes out of focus. The pictures were slowly focused until a position was obtained clear enough for subjects to respond correctly. It was found that exposing subjects to the out-of-focus picture caused them to hypothesize about the picture and reduced performance relative to subjects who did not see the picture until it was more in focus. Earlier exposure produced poorer performance.

Another study illustrates more directly the important effects, not only of verbalization itself, but even of the timing of the verbalization on problem solving (Hislop 1970, as cited in Brooks 1978). Subjects were given concept formation problems varying in the number of relevant dimensions from 1 through 7. In one group of subjects a verbal rule had to be stated prior to each successive classification of an instance. Another group first classified the present instance and only then stated a verbal rule. As the number of relevant dimensions increased, the advantage of the classification-first group became

---

1. I would like to thank Dr. Jerome B. Posner for this example.

quite marked. The differences between the groups were not only quantitative but the strategies they used to solve the problem also differed. The author concluded that the group verbalizing first tended to let their behavior be influenced by a strict hypothesis and adopted a win-stay, lose-shift strategy. The classification group-accumulated impressions of the feature is common among correct instances. With complex evidence this method led to superior performance.

In their *Psychological Review* paper, Ericsson and Simon (1980) allow for the possibility that verbal protocols will seriously alter problem solution in situations where the problem involves visual encodings. They say:

> Our model predicts that this additional processing may have three kinds of effects: It may slow down performance on the main task, it may change the structure and course of performance of the main task, and it may influence what is remembered about the task and is later available to retrospective verbalization.

Hayes, however, only cautions us about the first of these changes, suggesting that if information is in nonverbal form verbalization may slow the performance. Perhaps Hayes reduces the caution because Ericsson and Simon do not review any studies showing qualitative changes in their paper. I think the preceding studies cited suggest that the original caution is in order. I would also submit that the caution applies more broadly than just to cases where visual encoding is involved. Spectator behavior may occur whenever information must be accumulated from complex sources that provide it in a form other than explicit verbal hypotheses. In my view, that includes almost all of the interesting situations where problem solving occurs in the real world.

Conscious and Unconscious Processes

An even broader problem with verbal protocols is when a substantial part of the internal processes are unconscious. Fortunately, modern work in cognitive psychology has given us some means for investigating such processes, at least in limited experimental situations. While these methods are not presently developed to produce protocols for process tracing, they might on occasion illuminate the interpretation of such protocols.

It has long been known that many processes that go on within the mind are unconscious. No one would suppose that neurophysiological processes such as the depolarization of membranes are available directly to awareness. It is the contribution of the last 20 years of cognitive psychology to indicate that even very complex semantic processes may go on in the mind without awareness.

It may be this intuition that leads Hayes to advocate that we supplement verbal protocol with eye-movement protocols. It has often been supposed in cognitive psychology that the direction of the eyes is an indicator of where the subject is attending. But there is a problem with the use of eye movements as a measure of the subject's current attention. My colleagues and I have shown (Posner 1980) that even visual attention can be dissociated from the current position of the eyes. The ability to attend one place and look another is probably limited and may not represent a very strong objection to the general use of eye-movement protocols. A more serious problem is that whenever the eyes are open they must be pointed someplace. If the subject is attending to information in memory or from another modality, the eyes may be looking at a place that does not represent the current direction of the subject's attention.

The assumption that some peripheral output like verbal behavior or the position of the eyes reliably and invariably informs us about the current status of complex mental processing has been challenged seriously by the data from split-brain subjects. Information presented to the right hemisphere may undergo sufficiently complex processing for the subject to be able to pick out the item indicated by the word with their left hand, even though they are unable to say anything about the experience verbally. Indeed, there is some evidence that the right hemisphere is capable of such complex phenomena as self-recognition, political opinions, and ideas about future career choices (Gazzaniga and LeDoux 1977). In the mind of the split-brain subject, these complex events can be dissociated from verbalization.

It might be argued that the exciting results on the split brain, or those reported by Weiskrantz (1977) in the case of visual scotoma, or by Hilgard (1977) on hypnosis are very special cases in which complex mental activity is dissociated from the person's own awareness. Many studies in cognitive psychology, however, suggest that the same dissociations occur in the mind of normal individuals.

Consider the widely accepted view that activation of a given mode or concept in semantic memory spreads automatically to related concepts (Collins and Loftus 1975). This activation is often not available to consciousness. When a new item occurs that shares aspects of the concepts that have already been activated, it has more ready access to awareness. If one reports verbally the things that come to consciousness, the context which may have caused that particular idea out of the many potential ideas may be left out. In the example of spreading of activation, the word that initiates the spread is available to consciousness. One might argue that a verbal protocol would allow one to infer the spreading attention based on the succession of ideas that comes to mind. However, recent results (Marcel 1981) suggest that even the initiating item may be unavailable to the subject's awareness. Marcel has studied conditions under which an item is so heavily masked that the subject is unable to discriminate its presence, but it still primes items that follow it. In that case, the initiating event is completely unavailable to the subject's consciousness and would not appear in his verbal protocol, but that initiating would even determine the selection of other ideas that follow it.

It has always been known to lay people that one is not conscious of all events that occur in the mind. What is revolutionary in the work of modern psychology is that very complex mental events such as the elaboration of the semantics of words may go on without the awareness of the person in whose mind they are taking place and, even more, that the consequences of these unconscious activities can have reliable and observable effects upon the events that follow them. It is a disturbing finding of cognitive psychology that the window of consciousness is only a relatively narrow and fleeting one. Much of what we do is predetermined by previous learning, and is not under the control of our current intentions. I do not conclude from this that the window of consciousness as evidenced in verbal reports is unimportant. However, the abundance of unconscious mental events, and the evidence that the formation of verbal hypotheses tend to suppress these unconscious events, raise serious cautions with the kinds of theory developed entirely from an analysis of verbal or eye-movement protocols.

Herbert Simon, John Hayes, and their associates have made a substantial contribution to the literature of cognition by adapting protocol methods to the job of process tracing in problem solving and decision making. It is a powerful tool and one that can be very helpful as an adjunct to the study of cognitive life. But there are reservations. Perhaps Hayes has put it best: "Analyzing the protocol is like following the tracks of a porpoise." If activity is below the surface of the subject's own awareness and thus below the surface of his verbal behavior, one must entice the porpoise to the surface where he can be easily observed. As a consequence, one may reduce important subsurface activity and thus miss many of the facts of human problem solving. Although the porpoise may run deep and silent, we do have techniques available in cognitive psychology for probing the subsurface. These methods may not be easily adapted for handling aspects of complex decision making and problem solving, but they should be taken into consideration when one attempts to interpret how likely it is that the verbal protocol is the full story of the cognitive processes involved in the solution.

ACKNOWLEDGMENT

I would like to thank Mary K. Rothbart for her help in relating protocol analysis to other forms of coding and for a critical analysis of this discussion.

Commentary on Hayes's Paper

Sarah Lichtenstein, *Decision Research*

Hayes's paper has provided us with a short course on verbal protocol analysis to persuade us to use it more often in decision-making research. I find myself deeply sympathetic to this appeal. In the relatively short history of research in decision making, there has been a gradual change from an emphasis on optimal models — do people make decisions as they ought? — to an emphasis on process models — how do people make decisions? I believe that this is a healthy shift and that protocol analysis can be valuable in facilitating the change. Nonetheless, I can't help feeling that Hayes has glossed over some problems with verbal protocol analysis that need to be examined in order to make the technique most useful.

Hayes acknowledges that verbal protocols are necessarily incomplete. I would have hoped for guidance about when this problem is most severe. It may be that experts, that is, people who have performed a task so many times that their performance has become routinized, are least able to verbalize their thought processes, whereas beginners will find their thoughts more available. If so, are we doomed to develop a decision-process theory based on naiveté?

Then, how does the experimenter train subjects to minimize incompleteness? We are firmly trained, all our lives, *not* to report out loud everything that we think. For example, when I see an old friend whom I haven't seen for some time, my first thoughts are along the lines of, "Oh my God, what's his name?" and "What a ghastly tie he's wearing!" But I don't say these things out loud. After that first moment of panic, I recover his name and say, "Hello, John, how are you?" Our habit of not saying what we think is strong and deep. What is the best way to overcome that habit?

I believe that Hayes has gone too far in rejecting the criticism that the act of reporting distorts the processes being studied. Perhaps this is only a natural reaction to the extreme views of Nisbett and Wilson (1977), who seem to want to throw the baby out with the bath water. But is it reasonable to suppose that, even in the best possible circumstances (that is, when the subject is asked to report verbal memory traces of a verbal task), *no* changes occur because of the act of reporting? I find this claim astounding. I would have been more convinced of the value of protocol analysis had Hayes acknowledged the possibility of being misled and instructed us on the art of minimizing disruptive or biasing effects. Two biasing effects concern me here.

First, to what extent do the experimental demands involved in asking subjects to think aloud lead them to change their strategies? Subjects may adopt whatever strategy they think the experimenter expects, or a strategy designed to make them look less the fool and more the careful, logical decision maker. Perhaps not: I have often been impressed by my own subjects' willingness to be utterly honest, even when that meant they looked quite foolish.

Then, too, I wonder if Hayes's subjects ever think about their thoughts. I do. The request, "A penny for your thoughts," sometimes leads me not only to notice what I'm thinking, but to think about noticing what I'm thinking, and so forth, even to the point of thinking about the infinite regress involved in thinking about thinking. I may be atypical in this, but I doubt if I'm unique. Such second- and third-order thoughts, when they occur, surely disrupt the process the experimenter is interested in.

The second problem Hayes glosses over arises from his insistence that coding be independent of the theory being tested. Although this appears to be a worthy goal, it is unattainable. Indeed, it's a "catch 22." If you have no theory when you look at a protocol, you won't know how to segment it or what codes to attach to the segments. It is precisely your theory that tells you what to look for in the protocol. Thus there is no way of keeping your theory from impinging on your coding. Of course, such a link between theory and analysis is not limited to protocol analysis; it is with us whenever we analyze data of any kind. Recognizing it, we can take steps to minimize its impact. The danger lies in denying that the dependence exists, and in insisting that in this sense our analyses are "objective."

One is tempted to infer from Hayes's paper the belief that concurrent reporting is valid and valuable, whereas retrospective reporting has less worth or is more flawed. My own view is that both techniques have value and both have flaws. With both techniques, one worries that the data obtained may provide not only an incomplete view of the thinking process, but perhaps an altered view. Concurrent reports may be altered by the disruptions due to the reporting itself. Retrospective reports may be altered by inaccurate reconstruction of partially forgotten material. It seems reasonable to suppose that these two kinds of changes will have quite different effects. Thus we should use both techniques, hoping that by viewing the mind through two lenses with different flaws we can more readily see what is really there.

Reply to Commentaries

John R. Hayes, *Carnegie-Mellon University*

I find myself in very general agreement with the two commentators. In responding I will make just a few comments on matters of emphasis and detail.

Ericsson and Simon (1980, p. 227) distinguish three situations in which subjects give concurrent verbal reports:

> The verbalizations involve either direct articulation of information stored in a language (verbal) code (Level 1 verbalization); articulation or verbal recoding of non-propositional information without additional processing (Level 2 verbalization); or articulation after scanning, filtering, inference, or generative processes have modified the information available (Level 3 verbalization).

According to Ericsson and Simon, their model predicts that Level 1 verbalizations will not change the course of the reported cognitive processes, nor slow them down; Level 2 verbalizations may slow the reported processes, but will not change their course. Level 3 verbalizations, on the other hand, may change the reported processes in important ways, especially if subjects are asked to report information they would not normally attend to in the performance of the task.

In my paper, I described three reporting tasks which I hoped would exemplify Ericsson and Simon's three levels of verbalization. Posner's comments made me realize that I had not described these tasks carefully enough. In particular, I should have described my second task as one in which the subject is reporting nonverbal memory traces *without additional processing.* An example of such a task would be a task involving images of numbers and letters — images which have very familiar names and are easy to report without additional processing. A task which required the subject to describe unfamiliar pictures would involve Level 3 verbalization.

The Hislop study described by Posner (Hislop 1970, as cited in Brooks 1978) also appears to involve Level 3 verbalization. Asking the subjects to report a rule prior to classifying instances may well have forced subjects to attend to information which they would not normally have heeded in performing the task. The results of the Hislop study, then, do not violate the predictions of the Ericsson–Simon model.

When we use protocol analysis as a research tool, it is important for us to know that protocols are incomplete. When we construct theories from clues provided by protocols, we must know that there *are* psychological processes which are never conscious or are only intermittently conscious. We have to assume that the processes which are visible "on stage" are supported and accompanied by many other processes "off stage." Our theories will often require us to make inferences about the "off stage" processes.

The fact that protocols are incomplete, however, shouldn't discourage us from using protocol analysis when we are choosing among experimental methods. While protocols *are* incomplete, we must recognize that they are *less* incomplete than nearly any other method available to us. A concern with completeness, then, should lead us to favor protocol analysis rather than to avoid it.

Processes sometimes disappear from consciousness with practice. We have observed, for example, that when moderately experienced writers are asked to write for children, they devote considerable attention to their audience. We were surprised, however, that a protocol from our most experienced writer showed very little conscious attention to the audience, even though the test which this writer produced was very well adapted to young readers. When we questioned him afterward, he told us that he had written three children's books, and that the processes of adapting to a young audience had become quite automatic to him.

Protocols, then, provide a shifting window onto thought processes. As a person becomes more skillful in performing a task, we can expect that some processes will disappear from the window, and others — perhaps very high-level planning processes — will appear. Perhaps it will be possible to gauge a person's skill at a task by noting those processes which appear in the protocol and those which do not.

The difficulties which subjects experience in giving protocols vary considerably. Some people say that they talk to themselves while they work anyway, so that giving a protocol doesn't seriously change their normal practice. Others may experience awkwardness only for the first few minutes. Subjects who give more than one protocol say that the procedure becomes much more comfortable with practice.

I do hope that some of the readers of this volume will try generating protocols themselves. The mysteries of protocols seem much less deep when you have experienced the method yourself.

4 *Organizational Decision Making*

Behavioral Decision Theory and Organizational Decision Theory

James G. March, Stanford University
Zur Shapira, Hebrew University

Commentaries:

Latitude and Platitudes: How Much Credit Do People Deserve?

Baruch Fischhoff, Decision Research

Bureaucracies, Minds, and the Human Engineering of Decisions

Daniel Kahneman, University of British Columbia

Reply to Commentaries

Zur Shapira, Hebrew University

Organizational decision theory has developed from diverse sources. Political science and sociology can be contrasted with normative decision theory and the economic theory of the firm in examining their influences on theories of decision making in organizations. The former examines the contextual influences upon the decision process, while the latter examines the conditions promoting rational behavior. In the state-of-the-art paper by James March and Zur Shapira, they argue that although roots of organizational decision theory are diverse, the theory is an elaboration of a basic conception of human action in which alternatives are constantly being evaluated in terms of their future consequences for prior preferences.

How then, can organizational decision theory be compared and contrasted with the behavioral decision theory illustrated in Einhorn and Hogarth? March and Shapira acknowledge that there is a natural kinship between the two, in that they both examine deviations from rational models of choice. However, they also point out that there are considerable distinctions between the two in terms of theoretical focus and research method. Behavioral decision theory is essentially cognitive and generally uses experimental methods; organization decision theory is primarily theoretical and naturalistically oriented, examining rather conspicuous individual and social phenomena. The most salient distinction between the two may be found in the characteristic picture of the decision maker which emerges from the research.

The decision maker, as seen by some behavioral decision theorists, is portrayed as constantly deviating from normative models provided by statistical decision theory. In contrast, organizational decision theory pictures the decision maker purposefully participating in a messy world of bounded rationality, intentional nondecisions, convenient inconsistencies, and legitimated biases. Two themes which emphasize this view in the March and Shapira paper are the adaptiveness of "foolishness" and the intentional ordering of disorder.

The adaptiveness of foolishness is a result of typical organizational experiences. As optimizing the survival of organizations may perhaps be distinct from optimizing the survival of individual members, organizations are encouraged not to "bother with forecasts of dramatic changes, and not to make decisions in an analytically sensible way." From the point of view of individual decision makers, the organization may be dealing irrationally with the decision alternatives. But from the point of view of the organization, the story is quite different. Similarly, there seems to be a form of order in the ways a decision is enacted by an organization, but it is not the conventional order which normative decision theory suggests ought to be imposed.

If this picture is accurate, then the decision-making process itself becomes significant as a symbol of important aspects of organizational life. According to March and Shapira the symbolic aspect of the decision process may have two important consequences. The first is instrumental. That is, it serves to establish legitimacy, both of decision making and decision makers. The second is broadly interpretive: the process gives meaning to many organizational demands upon individual members.

March and Shapira conclude that behavioral decision theory and organizational decision theory ought to jointly examine three issues arising from descriptive studies of actual behavior: preference development, alternatives to standard "wisdom," and design of better decision procedures, or "decision engineering."

In their critique, both Baruch Fischhoff and Dan Kahneman suggest that the findings of organizational decision theory may have some implications for our understanding of the structure of individual decision-making behavior. Fischhoff points out that although the picture painted by some cognitive researchers is that of fallible people deviating from rationality to create fallible organizations, the reverse picture may be just as valid. "Smart" organizations may be creating "savvy" decision makers whose behavior approaches rationality much closer than we tend to give them credit for. Extrapolating from the March and Shapira paper, Fischhoff summarizes a number of what he considers speculations about the smartness of organizations, behaviors which can be misunderstood as irrational if viewed superficially. He then goes on to present a similar analysis for individuals. He states that the difficulty in this analysis is when our imaginations become substitutes for valid explanations.

Kahneman, in his analysis of the potential relations between properties of organizations and properties of the mind, considers four issues: the use of symbols, psychic costs, inconsistencies that have utility, and predictive frameworks. Although it is problematic how to make the jump from organizational to individual levels of analysis and back again, the exercise may help us sharpen our perspective at each end of the line. Kahneman considers an end product of this activity to be the improved design of organizational frameworks to fit the decision limitations of individuals.

A specific area of design might include the appropriate scheduling of information exposure to avoid the contamination of decisions based upon facts by premature hardening of opinions. Whether or not this might work could be the subject of much developmental research. Such research would be profoundly affected by the model of organization used. Kahneman alludes to the organization as a kind of factual decision-making "machine." His view may be in contrast with models suggested by organizational decision theory as discussed by March and Shapira that are based upon decision-making ideologies.

In response, Shapira discusses the correspondence between individual decision making and organizational decision making, but he clarifies how an information processing model of an organization is different from the cognitive model of individuals. For example, the ways in which memories are stored and represented, and how relevant information is gathered and stored, may be different in individuals and organizations. Furthermore, the treatment of organizational decision making as an aggregate of individuals making decisions is troublesome, particularly in cases of choice reversals. Shapira concludes that the relationship between individual and organizational decision making may be better assessed when questions about generalizing experimental laboratory data to real-life situations are resolved.

Perhaps one of the most distinctive contributions of organizational decision theory will be in the area of what Simon (1976) refers to as premises based upon values, as contrasted with premises based upon facts. If the organization is managed by ideology, rather than by information, then decisions become based mainly upon value premises, and many of the characteristics which March and Shapira view as endemic to disorderly decision making can be considered as quite rational and adaptive. Whether they are less so in the case of organizations emphasizing the management of information becomes an empirical question.

In any case, all sides seem to agree that we need to pay more attention to the nature of the organizational structure in relation to the nature of the decision, especially in the elaboration of alternatives. March and Shapira suggest that some major unfinished business for organizational decision theory concerns the development of a more comprehensive theory of search, with special emphasis on clarifying the notions of satisficing and attention. They also direct us towards a further examination of the process of decision simplification as a better way to understand how inferences are made under highly uncertain circumstances. If organizational decision theory could provide some important clues in these areas, our understanding of decision making would certainly be richer.

Behavioral Decision Theory and Organizational Decision Theory

James G. March, *Stanford University*
Zur Shapira, *Hebrew University*

Theories of Decision Making

We wish to explore some relations between two different fields of decision-making research. The first is research and theory focusing on individual choice behavior. For simplicity, we will call that field behavioral decision theory. It has its roots in statistical decision theory and economic theories of rational behavior, but most of the recent work has been carried out by experimental cognitive psychologists (Slovic, Fischhoff, and Lichtenstein 1977; Einhorn and Hogarth 1981a). The second field is research and theory focusing on organizational decision making. For simplicity, we will call that field organizational decision theory. It has roots in decision theory (including game theory) and economic theories of the firm, but most of the recent work has been carried out by behavioral students of organizations (March 1981a, Nelson and Winter 1981, Pfeffer 1981a, Scott 1981). The two fields are different but they have a history of conspicuous cross-pollination. Some of the early work in organizational decision theory was, in a very general way, an effort to represent decision making in organizations as intendedly rational, but subject to rather severe cognitive constraints, and some of the early work in behavioral decision theory was affected by speculations about organizations. In fact, students of human choice move rather easily back and forth from discussions of individual decision making to discussions of organizational decision making, using many of the same concepts for both.

This history of promiscuity is a natural result of their kinship. To a substantial extent, students of individual and organizational choice share intellectual roots. These intellectual roots are the progeny of rational models of choice, familiar to most of the behavioral social sciences but best known in their statistical decision theory or theory of the firm forms. Rational models see decisions as being made by the evaluation of alternatives in terms of their future consequences for prior preferences. A large portion of the theoretical developments in the analysis of choice behavior — both at the individual and the organizational level — is some form of elaboration of that underlying vision of willful human action. Both in studies of individuals and in studies of organizations, there is a persistent fascination with the extent to which decision making reflects processes and produces outcomes familiar to the modern decision scientists.

Despite their shared heritage, studies of organizational and individual decision making have distinct differences in methods and emphases, reflecting some combination of differences between individuals and organizations and the fortuitous meanderings of intellectual enthusiasms. The differences in methods are clear. Cognitive research on individuals is characteristically experimental. Typically, it is part of an effort to identify some regularities of inference or information processing that can be captured by a small set of propositions. On the other hand, although built on empirical observations and attempts to describe behavior, organizational decision theory is primarily theoretical rather than empirical. For the most part, the theory is a collection of simple ideas and metaphors intended to help make some sense of the naturally occuring events of organizational life. The ideas concern conspicuous phenomena, not those that demand subtle research design and suitable samples. Many of the key observations are close to everyday knowledge. The problem is not so much to identify phenomena as it is to provide a plausible interpretation of them, particularly when they seem peculiar from the perspective of rational choice. The search for interpretations of relatively conspicuous but apparently anomalous behavior makes the work and style of research on organizational decision making often close to that of a classical ethnographer, historian, or novelist. There is a tendency to see organizational events as being embedded in a rich texture of social, ideological, historical, political, and personal contexts.

The methodological differences are important, but they are probably less significant than the substantive differences. In the development of ideas in both behavioral decision theory and organizational decision theory somewhat different intellectual traditions and theoretical tastes have led to different emphases. Consider five different frames for interpreting human-choice behavior:

1. *Anticipatory choice.* It is possible to see individuals or organizations as acting on the basis of some conception of the future consequences of present action for preferences currently held. In this vision, we assume that we can identify such things as expectations, estimates, tastes, and probabilities in a way that is recognizable as some variant on conventional single-person decision theory. There is *a* preference, *an* expectation, *a* probability estimate that can be associated with the organization or individual, and those preferences, expectations, and probability estimates are reasonably orderly.

2. *Conflict.* It is possible to see individuals or organizations as being subject to unresolved internal conflict. There are unreconciled preferences, expectations, and beliefs, and yet, decisions are made. This view of decision making seems to fit an organizational setting, where different individuals can be seen as acting willfully and strategically on behalf of irreducibly conflicting individual preferences. In such a case, the organization must act through some process, most commonly bargaining or politics, that does not presume agreement on purpose. Such a vision is, however, also possible as a view of individual behavior. There is no profound *a priori* reason for attributing an integration within individuals adequate to escape intra-individual strategic action. Individuals cope with internal conflict through the use of personally imposed deadlines, moral strictures, and binding commitments.

3. *Learning.* It is possible to see individuals or organizations as learning from their experience. Rather than being oriented to expectations about the future, current behavior can be seen as reflecting the lessons of the past. The experiences of a particular history are transformed into propensities to act in ways that will be sensible if the experiences are correctly understood and the world is stable. Changes in behavior tend to be incremental modifications of past behavior, and a decision maker learns from the apparent consequences of each small step before undertaking the next.

4. *Rules and roles.* It is possible to see individuals or organizations as acting on the basis of rules. The immediate criterion of action is the *appropriateness* of a particular rule to a particular situation, not its anticipated consequences for current tastes. The terminology is one of obligations, roles, and duties, but it extends beyond such moralistic terms to a view of intelligence from the way a history of experience is stored in them (irretrievably) through the differential survival and growth of organizations, cultures, and individuals that follow them.

5. *Disorderly action.* It is possible to see individuals or organizations as acting in any of the four ways suggested above, but under conditions in which the "noise" swamps the "signal." Goals may be ambiguous, attention problematic, memory incomplete, causality confusing. As a result, action, however oriented to making choices in a way consistent with expectations, desire, or experience, may become dominated by the buzzing confusion in which it occurs. Order of presentation effects become important, and focus of attention becomes important. Decisions become collections of problems and solutions linked by simultaneity more than by causal association.

Most recent work in behavioral decision theory adopts the perspective of anticipatory action. The studies are prototypically examinations of the extent to which individuals treat preference, expectations, probabilities, and information in the ways we would expect from a proper decision theorist. Although it is difficult to assess the frequency of their occurrence in natural environments, there appear to be numerous conditions in which we can find intelligent individuals acting like incompetent decision theorists. There appear to be conditions in which individuals are effective "intuitive scientists." The vision of action underlying the studies is willful and anticipatory. Decisions are seen as being based on preferences and expectations. Recent work on organizations, on the other hand, is less focused on a view of action as some variation of willful problem solving. Although ideas about bounded rationality and problemistic search are standard, recent work emphasizes the ubiquity and significance of unresolved conflict in organizations, the ways in which action is based on rules, a picture of organizations as reacting to experience rather than anticipating the future, and the ambiguities underlying organizational actions. Notions of loose coupling, disorderliness, nondecisions, problematic attentions, learning, and garbage-can decision processes are frequent themes.

These differences between behavioral decision theory and organizational decision theory combine with their similarities in intellectual base and tradition to provide a reason for the remainder of this paper. We do not intend to make a complete review of either domain of research. Our objectives are more modest.

Assuming a general awareness of the major themes of behavioral decision theory, we compare some of those themes with some recent themes in organizational decision theory. The comparison proceeds from, and to some extent documents, two general arguments. The first is that behavioral decision theory and organizational decision theory cover different domains with different central concerns. Neither is a special case, nor an application of the other. The second argument is that, such differences notwithstanding, behavioral and organizational decision theorists are working on related problems with similar ideas.

Behavioral Decision Theory

Since there are several reviews of behavioral decision theory readily available (Edwards 1954, 1961; Becker and McClintock 1967; Rapoport and Wallsten 1972; Slovic, Fischhoff, and Lichtenstein 1977; Einhorn and Hogarth 1981a), we will not attempt to provide another. It may, however, be appropriate to summarize a few of the findings that will be used to illustrate possible linkages with theories of organizational decision making.

Early studies of individual choice showed that human subjects were likely to overestimate low probabilities, underestimate high probabilities, and to be somewhat more conservative estimators than would be expected if they were proper Bayesians (see the reviews cited above). More recent work has identified a handful of key judgmental heuristics that are often used in forming estimates involved in making choices under risk (Tversky and Kahneman 1974). The likelihood of an event is overestimated if it is easy to recall or imagine relevant instances (Tversky and Kahneman 1973, Nisbett and Ross 1980). Since this "availability" is affected by factors such as recency and saliency, it may lead to systematic bias in estimating frequencies. Individuals appear to be insensitive to the sample size of their observations and to base-rate information in making posterior probability estimates (Tversky and Kahneman 1973; Kahneman and Tversky 1973). Small samples are treated as though they were as representative of the populations from which they are drawn as would be larger samples. Individuals adjust their first approximations to an estimate on the basis of additional evidence. However, the adjustment heuristic used may lead to errors in assessing the probability of disjunctive and conjunctive events and to assigning too-narrow confidence limits on the estimates (Tversky and Kahneman 1974). Individuals tend to be overconfident of their ability to estimate the probability of an uncertain event (Lichtenstein and Fischhoff 1977), and this overconfidence is not easily challenged (Fischhoff, Slovic, and Lichtenstein 1977). Individuals tend to overestimate the probability of events that actually occur, as well as the extent to which they or others would have been able to predict past events had they been asked to do so (Fischhoff, 1975).

These studies of estimation have been increasingly supplemented with studies that examine the ways in which individuals simplify choices in order to make them. Incomplete data, incommensurable data dimensions, and multiple alternatives have been shown to encourage the use of simplifying strategies (Payne 1976, Slovic and MacPhillamy 1974). In particular, there is a tendency to compare pairs of alternatives rather than the whole list (Russo and Rosen 1975) and to minimize reliance on explicit trade-offs or the use of other numerical computations (Slovic, Fischhoff, and Lichtenstein 1977). Presumably as a result of such simplifications, individuals exhibit choices that are sometimes inconsistent (Lichtenstein and Slovic 1971, Kahneman and Tversky 1979a, Grether and Plott 1979, Shapira 1981) and intransitive (Tversky 1969).

The best elaborated of these simplifications are those discussed by Tversky and Kahneman. Tversky's (1972) original model describes choice as a sequential elimination process. Alternatives are viewed as a set of aspects (for example, houses described by price, size, location, etc.). At each stage in the choice process one aspect is selected, the order being determined probabilistically with more important aspects having a higher probability of being considered early. Any alternative that fails to meet an aspiration level with respect to the considered aspect is eliminated. The process continues until all alternatives but one are eliminated. A description of that process in terms of a preference tree has recently been suggested (Tversky and Sattath 1979). This elimination-by-aspects model identifies a procedure that permits individuals to cope with the complications of multiple attributes of value. Subsequently, Kahneman and Tversky have looked particularly at the ways single-attribute risky choices are made. In prospect theory (Kahneman and Tversky 1979b) they provide an interpretation of some frequently observed anomalies in individual choice between pairs of alternatives that are equivalent from the point of view of decision theory. They specify a critical reference point (for example, where expected value equals zero), a utility function that is concave above that point and convex below it, and a weighting function that transforms the probability of an event into an alternative weight to form "expectations." This weighting function has properties (for example, low probabilities are overweighted) that make choices between alternatives that are indistinguishable from a decision theory perspective dependent on the way in which the choices are "framed" (Tversky and Kahneman 1981).

These results are examples of numerous others that reflect similar concerns with the ways in which individuals process information about the probable consequences of their actions in situations involving risk. The emphasis in the examples, as in the field as a whole, is on identifying behavioral biases — ways in which observed estimations and choices deviate from what would be expected if the experimental subjects saw the decision situation clearly (that is, as the experimenter sees it) and acted consistently according to the principles of statistical decision theory. The general result is that human subjects often behave in a way that is not predicted by the assumption that they are proper decision theorists with well-behaved objective functions.

Organizational Decision Theory

Organizational decision theory is a cognitive interpretation of organizations, how they make decisions and deal more or less deliberately with questions of information, control, choice, and management. The research domain for studies of organizations is a mundane world. The prototypic cognitive structure is an accounting system, the prototypic research protocol is a manual of standard operating procedures, and the prototypic research question is: How do organizations survive when the xerox machine breaks down? Thinking of organizational "cognition" is appropriately suspect. The study of cognition is primarily a study of individuals; individuals in a social setting without doubt, and influenced by their social context, but nevertheless a study of individuals. Students of cognition are understandably uncomfortable with discussions of the "cognitive behavior" of institutions. It seems natural to impute thinking, consciousness, and intentionality to individuals, somewhat less natural to use the same metaphors with regard to complex combinations of individuals.

Such purities may be honorable, but they are not completely honored in the study of choice. Students of organizations have a long tradition of moving rather cavalierly from theories of individual cognition and choice to theories of organizational cognitions and choice (March and Simon 1958, Weick 1979). This is not primarily because organizational decisions are made by individuals. Organizational decisions are no more made by individuals than the choices of individuals are made by the hands that sign the papers. Theories of individual decision making are potentially interesting for students of organizations because they describe the ways a relatively complicated system processes information, organizes confusions, and comprehends and affects its external and internal worlds. For similar reasons, theories of organizational decision making have something useful to say about individual choice behavior. One misleading feature of some ideas about individuals is our tendency to exaggerate individual coherence. For many purposes, individuals are better seen as organizations, than vice versa (Kahneman, pp. 121–125).

To illustrate the spirit of recent work on decision making in organization, we propose to touch briefly on five domains. These are (1) the way information is used in organizations, (2) the ways organizations change, (3) the way disorder is ordered in organizational decision processes, (4) the way preferences are processed, and (5) the way the ritual and symbolic elements of decision making affect the decision process. A more detailed introduction can be obtained from the references attached to these comments.

Information in Organizations

According to standard rational theories of information, organizations will invest in information up to the point at which the marginal expected return from the information equals the marginal expected cost. The value of information is measured by the contribution it makes to effective discrimination among alternative choices. But when we observe actual organizations, what we see is usually something that looks quite different. They gather information and don't use it. Ask for more, and ignore it. Make decisions first and look for the relevant information afterwards. In fact, organizations seem to gather a great deal of information that has little or no decision relevance, information that, from a decision theory point of view, is simply gossip. Were one to ask why organizations treat information in these ways, it would be possible to reply that they are poorly designed, badly managed, or ill informed. To some extent, many certainly are. It is not difficult to find incompetence in organizations. But the pervasiveness of the phenomena suggests that perhaps it is not the organizations that are inadequate, but our conceptions of information. For example, March and Feldman (1981) argue that there are several sensible reasons why organizations deal with information the way they do.

First, organizations operate in a surveillance mode more than they do in a problem-solving mode. In contrast to a theory of information that assumes that information is gathered to resolve a choice among alternatives, organizations scan their environments for surprises and solutions. They monitor what is going on. Management in organizations involves decision making and problem solving, but those activities are only a small part of management. Management also includes overseeing the functioning of the organization, looking for breakdowns, and maintaining control. Such activities call for gathering a great deal of information that appears irrelevant to decisions. Moreover, insofar as organizations deal with problems, their procedures are systematically different from those anticipated in standard decision theory. Organizations characteristically do not solve problems; they copy solutions from others. Indeed, they often do not recognize a "problem" until they have a "solution."

Second, organizational participants seem to know, or at least sense, that most information is tainted by the process by which it is generated. On the one hand, information is socially constructed. The social construction of reality makes it difficult to assess the independence of repeated observations. It is typically quite hard to disaggregate social belief into its bases. As a result, the confidence generally expressed in socially validated facts, including those reporting expert judgment, may be considerably greater than a judicious decision maker or organization should place in them. The social process by which confidence in judgment is developed and shared is not overly sensitive to the quality of judgment. Moreover, most of the information presented in organizations is subject to strategic misrepresentation. It is likely to be presented by someone who is, for personal or subgroup reasons, trying to persuade the organization to do something. Our theories of information-based decision making (for example, statistical decision theory) are, for the most part, theories of decision making with innocent information. Organizational information is rarely innocent, and thus is rarely as reliable as an innocent would expect. Theories of agency (Hirschleifer and Riley 1978) suggest some of the complications in devising information structures that are insensitive to conflict of interest.

Third, highly regarded advice is often bad advice. Organizations are often criticized for ignoring good advice. It is easy to contemplate organizational histories and find instances in which good advice and good information were ignored. It is a common occurrence. Consequently, we tend to see organizations as perversely resistant to advice and information. In fact, most highly regarded advice is probably bad advice, and much generally accepted information is misleading. Even where conflict of interest between advice givers and advice takers is a minor problem, advice givers typically exaggerate the quality of their advice, and information providers typically exaggerate the quality of their information. It would be remarkable if they did not. Organizations seem to act in a way that recognizes the limitations of good advice and reliable information.

Fourth, information in organizations is a signal and symbol of competence in decision making. Gathering and presenting information symbolizes and demonstrates the ability and legitimacy of decision makers. In complex organizations, it is not easy to measure directly the contribution of participants to the outcomes for the organization. As a result, evaluation of the quality of performance is tied to process measures. A good decision maker is one who makes decisions in a proper way; a good organization is one that functions in a modern, well-informed manner, one that exhibits expertise and uses generally accepted information. Organizations and decision makers compete for reputations, and this competition stimulates the overproduction of information.

As a result of such considerations, information plays both a larger and a smaller role than is anticipated in decision theory-related theories of organizational information. It is larger in the sense that it contributes not only to the making of decisions but to the execution of other managerial tasks and to the broad symbolic activities of the organization. It is smaller in the sense that the information used in an organization is less reliable and more strategic than is conventionally assumed, and is treated as less important.

Organizational Change

Most discussions of change in organizations grow out of a concern for making them do what we want them to do. As a result, many theories of change in organizations emphasize planned, intentional, anticipatory change. They imagine situations in which individuals or groups choose future directions and then try to lead an organization. Observations of actual organizations indicate that such a script for change is unusual. Efforts to change organizations are often frustrated, even when the individuals and groups involved appear powerful. Often organizations fail to accept recommendations for change, fail to have planned for dramatic change in their environments, and are slow to innovate.

March (1981b) argues that these observations may lead us to confuse organizational resistance to change with organizational resistance to *arbitrary* change. In fact, organizations adapt routinely and easily to their experience, though they rarely do exactly what they are told to do by proper authorities or managers. They change as a result of the mundane processes of learning, selection, regeneration, conflict, problem solving, and contagion. They follow rules that are contingent on the environment, and track that environment in such a way as to produce large changes without great difficulty. Most changes that occur are probably sensible from the point of view of the survival of an organization. But since adaptation occurs at several levels simultaneously and in a confusing and changing world, sensible adaptive processes sometimes produce surprises. As a result, understanding organizational change may be not so much a matter of looking for unique change processes as one of looking for the ways in which routine procedures and ordinary behavior both facilitate easy adaptation and result in occasional surprises.

It is possible to find numerous elaborations of this theme. We will limit ourselves to a few. First, it is possible to see technological change in an organization as a result of a simple adaptive process in which organizations learn and modify search investment decisions (Levinthal and March 1981). Suppose organizations learn what return to expect from their search decisions, that is, they learn to have a reasonable level of aspiration. At the same time, suppose they learn competence in search through experience at it. The more they search in a particular way, the higher the expected return from that kind of search. Finally, suppose they learn how to allocate effort to different search alternatives as a consequence of experience with the outcomes of past allocations. Explorations of such learning processes indicate that organizations are sensitive to the relative speed of the three kinds of learning and to the fortuitous outcomes of probabilistic events. Thus, very similar processes operating in probabilistically identical environments can produce considerable variation in organizational change.

It is also possible to view organizational change as occurring through a process of selection. By building on observations of the importance of standard operating procedures and decision rules (Cyert and March 1963, Padgett 1980a), we can portray organizations as evolving collections of invariant rules (Winter 1975, Nelson and Winter 1981). The mix of rules observed in a family of existing organizations reflects the differential growth and survival of organizations that follow different rules in a particular environment. A similar perspective, but focusing on selection of organizational forms rather than rules, is found in Hannan and Freeman (1977). Conceptions of organizations as evolving mixes of inexplicably sensible rules and structures have been appealing to students of organizations who would like to assume that organizations act in an optimal way even though the processes they use seem far from rational calculation. Information about past experience is stored, irretrievably, in the rules and forms that survive. The argument is an interesting one, and we will return to a version of it again later. Still, it assumes that selection processes are rapid enough or general enough to be insensitive to rates of change in the environment. Under such conditions, the equilibrium properties of the processes are of considerable interest. Behavioral students of organizations have generally been less interested in emphasizing the equilibria of adaptive processes than they have been in describing the timepaths of movement under conditions of environmental instability and uncertainty, and in identifying some of the conditions under which the information content of rules or organizational forms will be less or greater than the information content of explicitly rational procedures. The latter issue is, of course, a classic one in the ideology of social change.

A theme that runs through several treatments of organizational change as an adaptive process is the problem of foolishness in organizations (Winter 1971; Cohen and March 1974; Weick 1979; Hedberg, Nystrom, and Starbuck 1976; Pondy and Mitroff 1979). The discussion of foolishness has emphasized two main concerns. On the one hand, organizations that focus too narrowly on achieving present objectives reduce their chances for inadvertant discovery of alternative goals through experience. In a world in which preferences are discovered through action, there is some need for experimenting with actions that cannot presently be justified. On the other hand, organizations are systems that are adapting at several levels, and actions that are optimal from the perspective of one level are unlikely to be optimal from the perspective of another. It is likely, for example, that optimizing on the survival prospects of an organization will be inconsistent with optimizing at the individual level. Of greater interest in recent work, however, has been the potential for conflict between the survival needs of individual organizations and the needs of larger systems of organizations. For example, suppose that a business organization learns from its experience. It will learn that most innovative ideas are bad ones, that most advice is bad advice, that most forecasts of dramatic future changes are wrong, and that if you make decisions in an analytically sensible way you will usually be disappointed. As a result, an organization will learn not to innovate, not to take most advice, not to bother with forecasts of dramatic changes, and not to make decisions in an analytically sensible way. But it is clear that some potential innovations are very good, some advice is very good, some dramatic changes will certainly occur in the future, and some of the best decisions are made analytically. Generally, it is wiser for any individual organization to wait for another organization to experiment with innovations and then adopt those that seem to work. But since that is true of every organization, there is a system problem of producing the "foolishness" that sometimes leads to new discoveries. On average, such foolishness is dumb. It has a negative expected value. What we require, therefore, is a process of decision that, in effect, reduces the likelihood of survival for the individual organization making the decision, but makes the conditions for other organizations more benign.

The organizational processes that have evolved are not conscious strategies by which organizations enter into contracts to share the costs and benefits of risky innovative adventures. Rather, they are rules of behavior within organizations that stimulate, or tolerate, foolishness. These include responses to organizational slack. Under favorable conditions, organizations systematically reduce the tightness of controls over subgroups and individuals. As a consequence, they encourage activities that are justified on the suborganizational level but are probably suboptimal at the organizational level. Similarly, organizations encourage or are led to accept rules of professional conduct that are, from the organization's point of view, foolish. For example, managers are encouraged to "make their marks," to make changes. It is doubtful that the expected value of a change is positive. So, most efforts by managers to leave some sign of their existence are probably mistakes. But the rule encourages the kind of experimentation that, at some cost to the organization, leads to occasional discovery of practices that are generally useful. Since individual organizations are probably somewhat more enamored of individual organizational survival than would be optimal for the system of organizations, these "unconscious" rules protect sensible system-wide behavior from the predations of rational organizational analysis.

The Ordering of Disorder

Making decisions ordinarily presumes an ordering of the confusions of life. The classic ideas of order in organizations involve two closely related concepts. First, it is assumed that events and activities can be ordered in chains of ends and means. We associate action with its consequences, and participate in making decisions in order to produce intended outcomes. Thus, consequential relevance arranges the relation between solutions and problems and the participation of decision makers. Second, it is assumed that organizations are hierarchies in which higher levels control lower levels and in which policies control implementation. Observations of actual organizations suggest a more confusing picture. Actions in one part of an organization appear only loosely coupled to actions in another. Solutions seem to have only a vague connection to problems. Policies aren't implemented. And decision makers seem to wander in and out of decision arenas. The whole process has been described as a kind of funny soccer game (March and Romelaer 1976, p. 276):

> Consider a round, sloped, multi-goal soccer field on which individuals play soccer. Many different people (but not everyone) can join the game (or leave it) at different times. Some people can throw balls into the game or remove them. Individuals, while they are in the game, try to kick whatever ball comes near them in the direction of goals they like and away from goals they wish to avoid.

Disorderliness in organizations has led some people to argue that there is very little order to organizational decision making. A more conservative position, however, is that the ways in which organizations bring order to disorder is less hierarchical and less a collection of means–ends chains than is anticipated by conventional theories. There is order, but it is not the conventional order. In particular, it is argued that any decision process involves a collection of individuals and groups who are simultaneously involved in other things. Understanding decisions in one arena requires an understanding of how those decisions fit into the lives of participants. The logic of order is temporal. Problems, solutions, and decision makers fit together because they are available at the same time. Thus, decisions depend on an ecology of attention, and important elements of the distribution of attention are exogenous to any specific decision process.

From this point of view, the loose coupling that is observed in a particular organization is a consequence of a shifting intermeshing of the demands on the attention and lives of the whole array of actors. It is possible to examine any particular decision as the seemingly fortuitous consequence of combining different moments of different lives, and some efforts have been made to describe organizations in something like that cross-sectional detail (Krieger 1979). A more limited version of the same fundamental idea focuses on the allocation of attention. The idea is simple. Individuals attend to some things, and therefore they do not attend to others. The attention devoted to a particular decision by a particular potential participant depends not only on the attributes of the decision but also on alternative claims on attention. Since those alternative claims are not homogeneous across participants, and since they change over time, the attention any particular decision receives can be both quite unstable and remarkably independent of the properties of the decision. The same decision will attract much attention, or little, depending on the other things that participants might be doing. The apparent erratic character of attention is made somewhat more explicable by placing it in the context of multiple, changing claims on attention.

Such ideas have been used to deal with flows of solutions and problems, as well as participants. In a garbage-can decision process (Cohen, March, and Olsen 1972; Padgett 1980b), choice opportunities are seen as connecting solutions, problems, and decision makers not only in terms of rules of access that might reflect beliefs about the causal connections among problems and solutions and the legitimacy of decision-maker participation, but also in terms of their simultaneous availability. In the model, it is assumed that there are exogenous, time-dependent arrivals of choices, problems, solutions, and decision makers. Problems and solutions are attached to choices, and thus to each other, not because of their inherent connections in a means–ends sense but in terms of their temporal proximity. The specific collection of decision makers, problems, and solutions that comes to be associated with a particular choice opportunity is orderly — but the logic of the ordering is temporal and con-textual rather than hierarchical or consequential. At the limit, almost any solution can be associated with almost any problem — provided they are contemporaries.

Preference Processing

Theories of decision making in organizations generally recognize that the consequences of organizational actions are often highly uncertain. Much of the modern development of theories of choice can be described as the elaboration of ways to deal with incomplete information about the consequences of action. Thus, we have game-theory treatments of the uncertainties surrounding con-sequences that depend on the actions of strategic actors, and statistical decision-theory treatments of consequences known only up to a probability distribution. Theories of choice are characteristically much less concerned with the possibility of uncertainty about preferences.

But observations of organizations suggest that preferences are more prob-lematic than we would expect. Organizations do not appear to have preference functions much like those anticipated by the theory. It has long been observed that organizations often use preference rules which establish acceptable levels of performance or accomplishment, rather than optimizing rules (Simon 1947, 1957; March and Simon 1958; Cyert and March 1963; Winter 1971; March 1981a). Such a view transforms a theory of choice to a theory of search, and it has been used effectively to understand some features of organizational be-havior. But such a conception of preferences is only a small part of the more recent picture. Organizational preferences seem often to be imprecise. When they are precise, they often seem inconsistent. Preferences that are expressed are often not followed. Preferences change, often endogenously as a result of a choice. The differences between organizational preferences as we experience them, and organizational preferences as they appear in most theories, are large enough to argue that there is a rather fundamental mismatch between concep-tions of intelligent choice and the behavior of complex organizations.

It should not be surprising that organizations fail to achieve well-behaved coherent preference functions. The cognitive limitations that stimulated a theory of bounded rationality undoubtedly extend to preference processing as well as to other forms of information processing in decision making. Thus, it is possible to view the curiosities of organizational preferences as symptoms of limitations that might be overcome. Such a view, however, probably attributes too much of organizational behavior to cognitive limits. At least, it is possible to argue that the ambiguous preferences used by organizations are not so much a case of reluctant adaptation to the information-processing limitations of or-ganizations as they are intelligent approaches to other fundamental problems of choice. Perhaps organizations are smarter than theories of choice recognize.

Since the argument has been elaborated in more detail elsewhere (March 1978), we will simply note here some of the reasons for imagining that am-biguity in preferences may have some advantages over more classical criterion functions. The argument is old (Mill 1838). First, ambiguity allows preferences to develop. An organization undoubtedly needs to reflect present preferences in present action, but it must also be conscious of the fact that preferences develop through experience, that one of the purposes of action is to explore alternatives. By doing things for no good reason, organizations discover preferences which they subsequently recognize as better. Ambiguity in preferences treats this process of change in a more direct manner — and probably in a more efficient manner — than does an emphasis on precision and consistency. Coherence and consistency limit learning of new purpose.

Second, ambiguity about preferences is an implicit acknowledgment of the difficulty of guessing future desires. Action taken today will have consequences realized in the future. Thus, the relevant preferences for current action are not the preferences we have today, but the preferences we will have in the future when the consequences are realized. Guessing those preferences would be difficult — even if it were not complicated by the endogenous character of the changes to come. An ambiguous taste is a family of hypotheses about possible future preferences. Since the individual members of the family cannot be specified, future preference hypotheses are better described poetically than as a probability distribution over the alternatives.

Third, organizations, like individuals, are coalitions of inconsistent preferences, some of them inappropriate. We want things that we know we shouldn't want, would like to give up but know we can't. These powerful desires or interests cannot simply be told to go away. They won't. As a result, organizations seem to function better by allowing conflict among contending interests rather than by trying to establish explicit trade-offs or by reducing them to some overall criterion. A commitment to morality is sustained by recognizing human weakness. Inconsistent and irreconcilable demands are met by creative obfuscation and sequential attention. The process is not guaranteed to be effective, and sometimes leads to seemingly endless cycles of choice that are unedifying. It is, however, a minor manifestation of the classic human awareness of the limits to coherence.

Fourth, organizations may prefer ambiguity in preferences because of an awareness of the political nature of rational argumentation and analysis. Any form of argument or analysis is a potential political instrument in the hands of those who are good at it. Rational argument is powerful and useful, thus it is subject to corruption. At the heart of efficiency in rational analysis is the organization of information so that it identifies a choice consistent with the preferences of the actor. In order for that analysis to be maximally efficient, the preferences need to be known with precision, so that only information necessary to a choice is gathered. But the precision that improves the efficiency of the analysis simultaneously increases vulnerability to manipulation through rational argument. Ambiguity and conflict in preferences reduce organizational vulnerability — though at some cost.

Myths, Symbols, and Ritual

Most theories of choice assume that a decision process is to be understood in terms of its outcomes, that decision makers enter the process in order to affect outcomes, and that the point of life is choice. The emphasis is instrumental, and the central conceit is the notion of decision significance. Studies of organizations, on the other hand, seem often to describe a set of processes that make little sense in such terms. As has already been noted above, information that is ostensibly gathered for a decision is often ignored. Individuals fight for the right to participate in a decision process, but then do not exercise that right. Studies of managerial time persistently indicate that very little time is spent in making decisions. Rather, managers seem to spend time meeting people and making managerial performances (Mintzberg 1973). Contentiousness over the policies of an organization is often followed by apparent indifference about their implementation.

These anomalous observations appear to reflect, at least in part, the extent to which organizational decision processes are only partly — and often almost incidentally — concerned with making decisions. March and Olsen (1976, pp. 11–12) observe:

> Indeed, the activities within a choice situation may be explicable only if we recognize the other major things that take place within the same arena at the same time. A choice process provides an occasion for a number of other things, most notably:
>
> an occasion for executing standard operating procedures, and fulfilling role-expectations, duties, or earlier commitments;
>
> an occasion for defining virtue and truth, during which the organization discovers or interprets what has happened to it, what it has been doing, what it is going to do, and what justifies its actions;
>
> an occasion for distributing glory or blame for what has happened in the organization, and thus, an occasion for exercising, challenging or reaffirming friendship or trust relationships, antagonisms, power or status relationships;
>
> an occasion for expressing and discovering "self-interest" and "group interest," for socialization, and for recruiting (to organizational positions, or to informal groups);
>
> an occasion for having a good time, for enjoying the pleasures connected to taking part in a choice situation.
>
> The several activities are neither mutually exclusive nor mutually inconsistent. They are aspects of most choice situations and illustrate their complexity. Decisions are a stage for many dramas.

In short, decision making is an arena for symbolic action, for developing and enjoying an interpretation of life and one's position in it. The rituals of choice infuse organizations with an appreciation of the sensibility of organizational arrangements and behavior. They tie routine organizational events to beliefs about the nature of things. The rituals give meaning, and meaning informs life. From this point of view, understanding organizational decision making involves recognizing that decision outcomes may often be less significant than the ways in which the process provides meaning in an ambiguous world. The meanings involved may be as grand as the central ideology of a society committed to reason and participation. Or they may be as local as the ego needs of individuals or groups within the organization.

Symbols in organizations are sometimes treated as perversions of organizational decision processes. They are portrayed as ways in which the gullible are misled into acquiescence. In such a portrayal, the witch doctors of symbols use their tricks to confuse the innocent, and the symbolic features of choice are viewed as simple opiates. Although there is no question that symbolic action is often taken strategically, few students of organizations accept such an heroic picture. Effective decision making in organizations depends critically on the legitimacy of the processes of choice and their outcomes, and such legitimacy is consistently problematic in a confusing, ambiguous world. Confidence in the legitimacy and adequacy of decisions is part of the context of organizations that work. And that confidence cannot be assumed to be automatic.

As a consequence, organizations need to orchestrate the process of choice in a way that legitimizes the choices, the choosers, and the organization. In most cases, the orchestration tries to assure an audience of two essential things. First, that the choice has been made intelligently, that it reflects planning, thinking, analysis, and the systematic use of information. Organizations plan, gather information, develop analyses, consult authorities, and prepare reports partly in order to discover the correct choice. But those performances are also the means by which an organization reassures itself, and its audiences, that it is a proper organization making proper decisions. Second, the orchestration is an assurance that the choice is sensitive to the concerns of relevant people, and that the right people have been influential in the process. Who the right people are is, of course, itself a complicated issue, partly affected by the orchestration of decision. For example, part of the drama of decision is used to reinforce the idea that managers and managerial decisions affect the performance of organizations. Such a belief is, in fact, difficult to confirm using the kinds of data routinely generated by a confusing world. Yet such a belief is important to the functioning of a hierarchical system. Executive compensation schemes and the mythology of executive advancement are used to reassure executives and others that an organization *is* appropriately controlled by its leadership.

Still, to see the symbolic structure of decision making as serving an important instrumental function in establishing the legitimacy of decisions and decision makers is to see organizational ritual in a subordinate way. It becomes a possibly necessary limitation on the purity of life. Some students of organizational choice would make a stronger claim. Life is not primarily choice. It is interpretation. Outcomes *are* generally less significant than process. It is the process that gives meaning to life, and meaning is the core of life. Organizations and the people in them devote so much time to symbols, myths, and rituals because they care a great deal about them. From this point of view, choice is a mythic construction justified by its elegance, and organizational decision making should be understood and described in approximately the same way we would understand and describe a painting, a poem, or a sculpture.

The perspective is too grand for ordinary research, but it leads to a few mundane implications. In particular, we should observe that the study of choice in organizations is concerned with events that will often not be as central to the organization as they are to the scholars who study them. The cognitive processes involved in relatively unimportant activities may be different from the processes involved in more central activities. The distribution of attention becomes more critical, and explicit decision outcomes become less paramount. In particular, the theater of decision becomes an appropriate research concern, not as a perversion of the process or as a constraint on the outcomes, but as a major focus. Trying to understand decision making as a way of making decisions may be analogous to trying to understand a religious ceremony as a way of communicating with a deity. Both characterizations are correct but both are misleading.

Some Implications

When we examine these recent developments in theories of organizational decision making and compare them with recent developments in behavioral decision theory, they form a mosaic of overlapping but separate concerns. They are different fields with different perspectives. They are appropriately specialized. But they may occasionally profit from a little attention to one another.

Implications for Organizational Decision Theory

It is possible to see the experimental results from behavioral decision theory as a series of findings to be replicated or not in an organizational setting. Organizations provide a natural place to examine how much individual behavior as it is observed in relatively simple experiments persists in the real world. Such efforts to examine the generality of experimental results are clearly important to the behavioral understanding of choice, but we wish to emphasize a somewhat different perspective on the way in which studies of individual choice may have implications for organizational decision theory. They are a basis for elaborating and refining the theory.

Modern theories of organizational decision making trace a heritage from Barnard (1938), Simon (1947), March and Simon (1958), and Cyert and March (1963). Within that heritage, organizational behavior is seen as boundedly rational, as limited by the information processing capabilities of human actors. Simon (1957, p. 198) observed:

> . . . the first consequence of the principle of bounded rationality is that the intended rationality of an actor requires him to construct a simplified model of the real situation in order to deal with it. He behaves rationally with respect to this model, and such behavior is not even approximately optimal with respect to the real world. To predict his behavior we must understand the way in which this simplified model is constructed, and its construction will certainly be related to his psychological properties as a perceiving, thinking, and learning animal.

This link between the individual psychology of human decision makers and the choice behavior of organizations has continued to be important in organizational decision theory (Steinbruner 1974, MacCrimmon and Taylor 1976, Connolly 1977, Staw 1980a), but its preeminence as the focus of that theory began to disappear with Cyert and March (1963). Some of the best known of recent works in the field (for example, March and Olsen 1976, Pfeffer and Salancik 1978, Weick 1979), while attentive to the ideas of bounded rationality, are more concerned with other things. As a result, the theoretical links between students of individual choice and students of organizational choice have become less rich than they might be. We will mention three links (a) aspiration levels, prospect theory, and satisficing, (b) attention and search, and (c) decision simplification, that might be made between recent concerns of behavioral decision theory and some of the presumptions of theories of organizations.

Aspiration Levels, Prospect Theory, and Satisficing. Consider the following assertions.

1. Organizations and individuals have two-valued preference functions; they distinguish alternatives having good enough outcomes from those that do not; they respond to situations in which no alternative has good enough outcomes by searching for additional alternatives.
2. Under conditions of uncertainty, organizations and individuals make choices that maximize the probability of attaining outcomes that are good enough.
3. Organizations and individuals are averse to risks when the expected value is above a target, and seek risks when the expected value is below the target.

These statements — or some very close to them — can be found in discussions of organization theory (March and Simon 1958), economic theory (Radner 1975), and behavioral decision theory (Tversky and Kahneman 1981). They are closely related, but their precise relations have not really been explored.

For example, the original satisficing idea was essentially a theory of search, not of choice. The key feature of the theory was the notion that alternatives were evaluated sequentially and that the central question then was whether to search further or accept the alternative available. Variations in search produced variations in both organizational slack and performance smoothing over a series of situations. In effect, those theories ignored the possibility that the expectations about the value of an alternative might not be completely captured by the expected value. Subsequent developments both in economics and behavioral decision theory first speculated and then confirmed, to some extent, a plausible sensitivity of satisficing choice to the variance of the probability distribution over consequences, that is, to risk. These developments have not found their way back into organizational decision theory in as rich a way as might be hoped. In particular, it is only recently that it has been noted that *if* organizations that are failing become risk-seeking, they simultaneously maximize their chances of surviving and reduce their life expectancies.

The implications of such ideas for the study of innovations and life-histories of organizations have not completely escaped attention. At the same time, however, that attention has suggested a caution. The original aspiration level search model led to a simple prediction: organizations would innovate when they were in trouble. The comparable prediction from the newer theory would be that organizations would accept riskier alternatives when in trouble. Both predictions are plausible, but neither seems strongly supported by research on organizations. As has been noted a number of times (Cyert and March 1963, Daft and Becker 1978, Kay 1979, March 1981a), innovation and risk-taking in organizations is not reliably predicted by such simple models. There is more to be done, but largely because of the work in behavioral decision theory, the models can now be specified in new ways that might make some of the relations a bit clearer.

Attention and Search. The acquisition, storage, and retrieval of information are major focuses for work on behavioral decision theory (for example, Slovic,

Fischhoff, and Lichtenstein 1977; Nisbett and Ross 1980; Einhorn and Hogarth 1981a). Factors such as *framing, concreteness,* and *imaginability* are understood better in the literature on individual choice than comparable ideas are in the literature on organizational choice. This is true despite the fact that most modern theories of decisions in organizations place considerable emphasis on attention as a major factor in determining the flow of events (see March and Olsen 1976). Not all information is attended to, not all problems are noticed, not all solutions are discovered, not all potential participants are involved (Mintzberg 1973, Padgett 1980b).

These issues are central to several theories, but the empirical understanding of attention and search processes in organizations is limited. It has been speculated (Cyert and March 1963) that organizations search in the *neighborhood* of current solutions, but the idea of a neighborhood has rarely become more refined than a simple form of incrementalism on numerically represented actions (for example, prices, budget allocations). It has been speculated (Cohen, March, and Olsen 1972) that solutions and problems are connected primarily by their simultaneity rather than by their causal linkage, but the determinants of simultaneity have not been discussed to any significant extent. It has been speculated (Cyert and March 1963) that organizational action is based on standard operating procedures, and that organizations apply appropriate rules to situations, but there is little understanding of the processes by which particular rules are evoked in particular situations. It has been noted (Mintzberg 1973) that managers attend to only a few sources of information, but the ways in which organizational actors secure information are not extensively studied.

There is no guarantee that the processes of attention and search that are found among individuals will be germane to organizational action, and even less, that those processes will capture adequately the special features of parallelism that are conspicuous in organizations. But if recent ideas about organizational choice are near the mark, then the behavioral decision-theory emphasis on information acquisition, storage, and recall offers fortuitous potential benefit to organizational decision theory.

Decision Simplification. Individuals and organizations do not solve (explicitly) the full decision problems they face. Not all alternatives are considered, not all relevant information is gathered, not all values are introduced into the choice. Organizational decision theory has emphasized a small number of theoretically crucial simplifications. These include a simplification of preferences to two-value functions, a simplification of uncertainty to uncertainty avoidance, and a simplification of causal inference to ideas of executive responsibility and correlation. These ideas can be illuminated by recent work in behavioral decision theory on closely related themes. For example, elimination by aspects (Tversky 1972) and preference trees (Tversky and Sattath 1979) can be seen as elaborations of organizational notions of sequential attention to goals. They introduce additional complexity to the more primitive ideas found in the organizational literature. In a similar way, ideas of "framing" and "pseudocertainty" in behavioral decision theory may be connected to efforts to understand the ways in which organizations simplify complex decision situations, as may investigations of human causal inference. Since much organizational action depends on making inferences or guesses under highly uncertain circumstances, the research on individual inference is likely to say something about what happens in an organization. For example, the tendency of individuals to exaggerate, after the fact, the probability of an unlikely event that happened to occur (Fischhoff 1975) is identical to less systematically verified observation about organizational inference (March and Olsen 1976). And the insensitivity of individuals to sample size in establishing confidence in parameter estimates (Tversky and Kahneman 1974) has been used (March and March 1978) in developing a model of organizational performance sampling, evaluation, and promotion.

The three examples of potential links between behavioral and organizational decision theory which we have chosen are not exhaustive. But they illustrate some possible areas in which organizational decision theory might profitably work with results already familiar to behavioral decision theory, or likely to be developed in the near future. They are examples of situations in which research findings and ideas drawn from behavioral decision theory might provide a texture and elaboration for some familiar speculations in the study of organizations.

Implications for Behavioral Decision Theory

The study of organizations includes both the study of individual behavior as it is embedded in, and affected by, an organizational context, and the study of how a relatively coherent system functions in a relatively difficult world. Thus, the contribution of organizational decision theory to behavioral decision theory — if there is one — is both a set of observations of how individual choice behavior fits into, and is influenced by, a real nonexperimental setting, and the suggestion of some system-level phenomena of organizational choice that might have individual analogues. We will make two ordinary conjectures. The first is that some individual behavior that seems relatively inexplicable in experimental settings would become more understandable if we thought of it as stemming from heuristics developed for surviving in the kinds of organizations in which individuals spend much of their lives. The second conjecture is that a single individual may be better imagined to be an organization than our language suggests. For most purposes that means that decision processes used by a system in which there is unresolved conflict, parallel processing, less-than-perfect coordination, and considerable loose coupling may be a part of individual decision making, as they are of organizational decision making (Kahneman, pp. 121–125). As a result, it may be useful for behavioral decision theory to consider the ways in which organizations deal with (1) conflict, (2) the accumulation of history into standard rules, and (3) the characteristics of decision making under conditions of ambiguous preferences.

Conflict.   Important features of organizational decision behavior depend on the existence of significant unresolved conflict. The fact that preferences are not shared makes it problematic to assume an objective function for an organization. Students of individual choice behavior might want to consider the possibility that individual behavior embedded in a system of conflict may be systematically different from that anticipated by decision theory (Einhorn and Hogarth 1981a). Consider, for example, attempts to understand mistakes individuals make in handling information. It has been observed that individuals do not always treat information in quite the way that would be expected from intelligent decision theorists. But almost all of the discussion of such deviations in the behavioral decision-theory tradition treat information as innocent, as some kind of neutral input to an estimation procedure. If an individual lives in a world in which conflict of interest is the usual situation, information-processing rules are likely to represent solutions to a somewhat different estimation problem, one in which most information is provided by others whose interests are not identical to those of the person using the information.

In addition, it is possible that conflict models of choice may come closer to describing individual behavior under some circumstances than do models that assume greater precision and consistency in tastes. Individuals seem to function with considerable unresolved conflict in goals, and this conflict is not generally resolved before a choice is made. As a result, some of the organizational procedures for decision making in the absence of goal agreement may have analogues in individual choice. These include classical devices such as bargaining and logrolling, and somewhat more recently noted procedures that exploit limitations in attention to produce a pseudoconsensus. For example, organizations have been noted to attend to conflicting goals sequentially, doing one thing one day and another thing the next as they face a changing mix of demands (Cyert and March 1963). Sequential attention allows the organization to avoid having to make explicit trade-offs that are difficult to determine. In addition, organizations buffer conflicting goals by delegation and organizational structure, by organizational slack, and by loose coupling between policies and their implementation. Similar phenomena (for example, the separation of attitudes and behavior) have been studied at the individual level, but it is probably fair to say that behavioral decision theory has focused too heavily on a conception of tastes derived from statistical decision theory to be much concerned with the possibility that inconsistent preference functions are not unfortunate accidents or symptoms of poor training but fundamental features of individual life.

History-Dependent Processes. It is a minor curiosity of work on decision making that behavioral decision theorists, though primarily psychologists, have had only modest interest in history-dependent decision processes (but see Einhorn and Hogarth 1981a). A decision-theory frame interprets behavior as a result of anticipations currently held. Students of organizational decision making are somewhat more interested in ideas that make behavior a reflection of past experience. Organizations are often seen as modifying their behaviors as the result of a history of action and subsequent outcomes. In the usual form, these modifications are stored as rules for action, and we examine the ways in which organizational rules change as a result of either direct experience (experiential learning) or the differential survival and growth of organizations following particular rules (evolutionary selection). The models of learning and selection found in theories of organizational choice are quite crude, but they combine a history-dependent perspective with a concern for the rationality of adaptive processes. In the typical case, it is possible to show how a simple set of adaptive rules will permit the organization to find optimal, or near optimal, choices *if* experience is prolonged enough, the environment and organizational tastes are stable enough, and the search terrain is orderly enough. In such situations, learning and selection become comparatively powerful tools of the intendedly rational organization or individual. The interest for students of behavioral decision theory in this perspective might lie both in the linkage it makes between the intelligence of calculation and the intelligence of adaptation, and in the opportunities for exploring the results of adaptive processes where experience is relatively brief, the environment and tastes are changing, and the search terrain is filled with local optima. Individuals, like organizations, might be seen as learning in a changing, ambiguous environment that can make the lessons they learn misleading.

Considerations such as these have led students of organizational decision making to examine some of the consequences of trying to learn in a confusing and changing environment; how organizations adapt when different parts of the system are simultaneously learning different things from different perspectives; the ways in which the experience from which we learn is constructed as a social belief; and the ways in which populations of practices evolve through natural selection when the environment is changing and relatively disorganized. This perspective on adaptation can be characterized simply: organizational decision theorists see learning and selection as simple processes that are pervasive. The processes are simple, but their consequences are varied, and sometimes surprising, when applied to the confounded and confusing world in which decisions are made. Such a perspective might not be entirely inappropriate for a similar investigation of history-dependent decision processes in individuals.

Preferences. Within a decision-theory paradigm, choice depends on two critical guesses. The first is a guess of the uncertain future consequences of current action. The second is a guess of the uncertain future preferences for those consequences when they are realized. Within decision theory, the second guess is treated as derived from choices. Thus, we talk about the preference for one choice over another, and of objective functions revealed by choices. This perspective is carried over into behavioral decision theory. When Tversky and Kahneman (1981) speak of the dependence of "preferences" on frames, or of "preference reversals," they refer to the way in which a subject's choice between two gambles changes without a change in the objective consequences of the alternatives offered. The usual interpretation is that framing results in a cognitive misunderstanding of the objective probabilities, that is, that the first guess is affected by the way in which the information is presented. The inclination is to treat inconsistent choices as a reflection of confusion about risk. An individual's wants are taken as not problematic. Inconsistent choices result from human limitations in making the first guess, not the second.

This emphasis has recently been questioned by Fischhoff, Slovic, and Lichtenstein (1980). As they observe, decision theory has consciously avoided treating ambiguity and uncertainty in preferences as lying within the domain of interest. Yet it is difficult to see how one can do so indefinitely if one is interested in understanding intentional behavior. On the whole, organizational decision theory has been more inclined to treat the uncertainties about future preferences explicitly. Rather than beginning with the revealed preference vision, theories of organizations are inclined to start with some rudimentary notion of organizational goals, tastes, wants, objectives, or preferences. Normally, only a somewhat conscious articulation of a set of desires by which future outcomes can be assessed is assumed. The study of preference processing in organizations is the study of how beliefs about objectives are developed and brought to bear on decisions. The preferences are typically inconsistent, often in contradiction to one another. They are often ambiguous. They change over time, often endogenously. They do not much resemble the precise, stable, consistent tastes of decision theory. It is possible that the classical view of economics is correct — that wants are stable and that a theory of individual choice is basically a theory of the first guess. But if that view is sometimes inadequate, the study of decision making will have to be attentive to the complexities of preference processing as well as to those of subjective probabilities about future consequences.

These three examples of conflict, history-dependent processes, and preferences are no more exhaustive than were the earlier examples of possible implications for organizational decision theory. They are intended to suggest some possibilities for moving from ideas about organizations as decision makers to ideas about individuals. Organizational decision theory does not translate immediately into implications for behavioral decision theory, but as we move toward perspectives on individual cognitive structures that emphasize the inconsistencies, parallelisms, and indeterminacies of individual information processing, ideas from organization theory may become more relevant.

Implications for Decision Engineering

Decision theory is a normative theory. It purports to provide a set of rules by which an intelligent person or organization might act. Behavioral decision theory and organizational decision theory are behavioral theories. They purport to describe some features of how actual individuals and organizations do, in fact, act. Decision engineering is a loose name for a collection of efforts to bring how people act and how we believe they ought to act somewhat closer together. Some students of choice see behavioral deviations from the canons of rationality as correctable faults. They look for ways to improve the rules that individuals and organizations follow, and to eliminate biases and mistakes in inference, for example. Other students of choice argue that the same deviations of behavior from decision theory may show an intelligence different from, but not consistently inferior to, the rational catechism. They look for ways to modify ideas of intelligence to accommodate the special advantages of adaptation, rules, disorderliness, and conflict. As a general rule, students who fit their analyses within the frames of consequential action or strategic action appear to be systematically more inclined to look for ways to make individuals and organizations behave like proper decision theorists than are students of choice behavior who emphasize adaptation, rules, or disorderliness. Although there are numerous counterexamples, this means that behavioral decision theorists tend to view the possibilities for decision engineering somewhat more optimistically than do organizational decision theorists. For the former, the engineering problem is one of teaching individuals how to avoid some pitfalls in decision analysis. They try to modify behavior. For the latter, the engineering problem is one of understanding and using forms of implicit intelligence. Behavioral decision theorists are likely to imagine reducing the discrepancy between observed behavior and canons of intelligence by changing the behavior. Organizational decision theorists are somewhat more likely to try to reduce the discrepancy by changing the canons.

In pure form, neither strategy makes sense. The first is unduly arrogant about the perspicacity of our models. The second is overly sanguine about the information content of traditional action. But it is hard to look at the enthusiasms of students of choice without being concerned that they may impute greater sagacity to decision theory than its record justifies. Such concerns lead to an interpretive vision for theories of choice. In such a vision, we recognize that ordinary actors know a good deal about decision making. They have rules, habits, and "instincts" that they use successfully. Those pragmatic procedures are often difficult to reconcile with the intellectual model of choice that ordinary actors accept. They live pragmatically, talk theoretically, and contemplate the disparity between the life and the talk. The tension between the two is useful, certainly not to be eliminated. But assuming that differences between observed behavior and theoretically proper behavior are necessarily manifestations of ignorance is probably a mistake. Clearly, decision makers are not always sensible. They make mistakes. They behave in perverse ways. But it is often useful to ask whether there are intelligent interpretations of decision behavior that make the observed behavior sensible. Such an approach uses behavioral decision theory and organizational decision theory as bases for improving standard normative models of choice.

Good theories, of course, like good consultants or good poets, do not try to replace the knowledge and judgment of experienced actors but to increase the *joint* product of wisdom and analysis. Thus, what a good theory should do is not to maximize the total explained variance (or any similar thing) but to maximize the contribution on the margin to the intelligence we have. And to do that, theories, like consultants and poets, often best perform their role if they articulate the ways in which what everybody knows is not quite right. As a result, both behavioral decision theory and organizational decision theory may have some possible minor contribution to make to decision engineering.

In developing that contribution, we suspect that behavioral decision theory and organizational decision theory jointly might focus on three natural issues arising from research on actual decision behavior.

1. The issue of preferences. The way in which preferences appear in conventional decision theory is sufficiently distant from the way in which we observe them in individuals and organizations that it is easy to find many significant decisions for which decision theory is clearly incomplete.

2. The issue of alternative wisdoms. Rational calculation of expected consequences of action is a form of intelligence. It is, however, not the only form

of intelligence. In particular, history-dependent choice exhibits intelligence that can be demonstrated to be greater under some circumstances. Decision theory needs an appropriate modesty with respect to its vision of intelligence.

3. The issue of engineering design. Decision theory is a decision procedure provided to individuals and organizations. It is a *good* decision procedure if the consequences of it being used by ordinary individuals and organizations are good. Any procedure may be misused, but it is poor engineering to design a procedure that is particularly prone to misuse. Decision theory as a form of engineering must be assessed in terms of its actual, and not its hypothetical, consequences.

It would, of course, be nice to be able to say something definitive about one or more of these issues. We cannot. But in the honored tradition of final words, we invite behavioral decision theorists and organizational decision theorists interested in decision engineering to consider how what we know about human choice can suggest some changes in what we believe about sensible decision procedures.

ACKNOWLEDGMENT

This paper is based on research supported by grants from the Spencer Foundation, the Hoover Institution, and the Stanford Graduate School of Business. We are grateful for the comments of Baruch Fischhoff, Daniel Kahneman, and Amos Tversky.

Latitude and Platitudes: How Much Credit Do People Deserve?

Baruch Fischhoff, *Decision Research*

The central conundrum of research on decision making is that it is extraordinarily difficult to study simultaneously the form of decision-making rules that people use and the substantive considerations incorporated in them. The obvious interim solutions are to assume that one knows in advance either the substance or the rules. Researchers who adopt the former strategy often conduct studies in which all the information needed to make rational decisions is available. They observe how recipients of that information encode and combine it. Because those people are being compared with the absolute standard of optimal behavior, results in such studies are typically interpreted as departures from that standard. The contrasting research strategy is to assume that one knows the rules that people use and try to divine the substantive considerations that they choose to operate those rules on. Because the assumed rule of choice is typically some form of rationality, participants in these studies are often found to be quite savvy. With enough creativity one can generally find something that may have been optimized in the light of some conceivable interpretation of the available data. Thus, depending on the degree of preference for granting either the substantive information or the pertinent rules, a continuum exists ranging from unforgiving to all-forgiving research strategies.

All-Forgiving Research

Smart Organizations

The provocative paper by March and Shapira clearly falls on the upbeat end of the continuum running from unforgiving to all-forgiving. Looking at organizations as corporate decision makers, the authors advance a variety of reasons why organizations may be smarter than they seem when they stray from the tenets embodied in normative models of decision making or reject outright those tenets and the prophets of rationality who bear them. Consider the following suggestions from the March and Shapira paper.

> When organizations seem to be ignoring information, they may be: (1) really taking it all in, in a surveillance mode that emits only intermittent observable signs; (2) discounting its importance because the vehemence with which it was advanced does not seem justified; (3) doing the opposite of what the information would suggest if taken at face value, because they

mistrust the messenger who brought it; or (4) showing the inevitable omissions that arise from a sophisticated scheme of dividing attention.

When organizations seem to be poking along and resisting change, they may actually be poking around in order to: (1) gather more information before acting; (2) work through the higher-order implications of taking what seems to be the logical action; or (3) learn about their situation and capabilities through the deliberate hesitancy of trial-and-error actions.

When organizations seem to be inconsistent, the observer might just be seeing: (1) how their preferences evolve over time; (2) how they experiment with experiences designed to help them learn what they want when their preferences are initially vague; or (3) how they refuse to resolve by fiat internal contradictions that are part and parcel of the richness or ambiguity of life and the human condition.

Finally, when organizations seem to be wasting time on chatter, they may actually be: (1) raising the probability that a proposed action will be implemented by building support for it; (2) producing a consensual symbolic interpretation of events, actions, and outcomes, thereby making the organization a corporate actor for a particular decision; or (3) maximizing the satisfaction of group members, thereby ensuring long-term organizational stability.

In fact, we may have here what might be called an exercise in forgiveness, an exercise that might be usefully exploited, as I will suggest.

Savvy Individuals

One ought to note first, though, that even if the comparable arguments for individual decision makers are somewhat less developed by March and Shapira, still almost all of the speculations about organizations that are offered in their paper, or summarized above, could be read as speculations about individuals, following the necessary anthropomorphizing. Indeed, performing that transformation suggests that something akin to March and Shapira's model of organizational function might be the result if one tried to "organizomorphize" many models of individual behavior. Freud, Murray, and White are just a few of the old names in psychology who viewed individual behavior as a messy process of continually learning by doing, dividing attention, sustaining action, and resolving internal disputes about what is really important.

Indeed, a legitimate research strategy, at least for the sake of hypothesis generation, might be to assume deliberately that there is nothing true about organizations that is not also true about people, and vice versa. That is, work the metaphor for all it's worth. Doing so might lead one to ask, on a descriptive level, how these similar people and organizations create one another — whatever one's view of their respective capabilities is. How do fallible people create fallible organizations, and vice versa (for example, by restricting one another's ability to learn from experience or to recognize and use good advice)? How do savvy individuals create savvy organizations and vice versa (for example, by providing codified rules of action and opportunities for modeling behavior)?

On a prescriptive level, one might ask how to design savvy organizations that muted, rather than magnified, the foibles of their members or how to prepare people to survive and prosper in fumbling organizations.

If one adopts the all-forgiving position, observation of individual behavior would seem to provide many ways to find method in apparent madness whose analogues might be sought profitably in organizational settings. Consider, as before, the following examples.

> People have been berated for "part–whole inconsistency" when they endorse a general principle, but not a specific principle that seems, to the observer, to flow from it. They might favor integration but not want it to happen on their block, or they might express an attitude, but not exhibit a corresponding behavior. In most cases, however, closer examination reveals that it takes not just one principle but a set of principles to infer a corollary, and that the logical force of observers' inferences rests on some additional empirical or moral assumptions.

> Lay people are regularly berated by technical experts for having different, that is, irrational, views about the magnitude of the risks that technologies pose. Some of these disagreements, however, may be traced to differing definitions of the term *risk*, whereas others are due to disagreements about the catastrophic potential of technologies, an aspect of risk that is often quite arguable.

> Participants in public debates often tend to view their opponents as being unreasonable for failing to stick to the topic. Some of this irrational behavior may represent the rational pursuit of officially unreasonable objectives. Consider, for example, an individual who is opposed to increased energy consumption but is asked only about which energy source to adopt or where to site a proposed facility. Because the answers to these narrow questions provide a *de facto* answer to the broader question of growth, such an individual may have little choice but to fight dirty by trying to sabotage the proceedings.

> Drivers are often maligned for their failure to wear seat belts. However, their formulation of the problem might be quite different from that of the safety expert. The latter sees the tens of thousands of lives that might be saved from the small statistical reduction in each trip's probability of ending in death. Individual drivers may see that probability as minute and rationally view the inconvenience or discomfort of buckling up as too great to justify the benefits perceived as small in such a low-probability situation.

Seemingly unreasonable behavior may appear less unreasonable from the vantage of a different perspective. The perspective, in any situation, may need to be more thoroughly explored before conclusions can be drawn about what is really transpiring in an individual's behavior.

The Role of Imagination in Research

Yet the tricky part of such explorations is, of course, that imagination may become a substitute for explanation. Economists have often been faulted for rationality grubbing, in assuming that people are maximizing something and searching relentlessly until they find out what that something is. Their refusal to take chaos for an answer has led them to create — and get quite a bit of mileage out of — such semistructured notions as transaction costs and the second-guessing of fiscal policy. Perhaps it becomes free-play time when we extend the range of considerations to include such goals as learning, legitimation, and achieving symbolic consensus. If errors can be good because they tell us about properties of the environment, we may find ourselves in the position of the Jules Feiffer character who summarizes lessons he has learned from frustrated romances as having made him the Renaissance Man of the Rejects. Does anything go?

Three purposes come to mind for exploiting such exercises in imagination and forgiveness. Each offers somewhat different opportunities for, and challenges to, these putative explanations. Each embodies a somewhat different notion of bounded irrationality.

Position I (The Descriptive Position)

In this case, one is in the business of describing how people or organizations actually make decisions. To this end, there are no *a priori* bounds on the kinds of variables that might be relevant. But there are a number of empirical questions that one might ask in trying to discipline the kind of speculations offered in the March and Shapira paper. Are there any unambiguous signs of people showing any sensitivity to the variables we are touting (as opposed to ambiguous signs of their showing great sensitivity)? Is there consistency in the variables to which people attend, across situations, individuals, or organizations? (Logically, there needn't be, but that would be a troubling finding.) If asked to do so, can people *deliberately* execute the schemes that we are attributing to them? And can we identify life experiences that would have shaped the behavior patterns we claim to have observed?

Position II (The Normative Position)

Here, the rules of behavior we are describing represent how people either behave or should want to behave. Support for such claims might come from:

1. theoretical analyses of how it could, in fact, make one happy to follow these rules in at least some situations (or, more modestly, that the adherent of such rules should be able to get through life);
2. testimonials from decision makers to the effect that these rules represent a codification of how they either try to behave or would try to behave in some of the more satisfactory of all possible worlds;
3. empirical evidence indicating that those who follow the rules are more successful than some comparison groups or some base rate (for example, do organizations with a rich consensual symbolic life file for bankruptcy less often than those without it?).

Position III (The Fall-Back Position)

Here, one is in the insight business, wherein the goal is to provide a richer understanding of decision situations. There are as few tests for wisdom as there are substitutes. More specific goals that one might be trying to achieve are offered here.

1. Developing a richer set of concepts with which to describe behavior and the possible influences upon it, concepts which might serve as the basis of controlled studies or as part of the tool kit used in decision-making ethnography.
2. Offering a richer set of perspectives for those acting as decision consultants. These perspectives may enable them to expand the set of decision alternatives, understand implicit constraints, ease implementation, or communicate better with their clients.
3. Clarifying the assumptions and constraints of our respective research methodologies and the environments we choose to study. Such clarification should help us to improve the mesh between research emerging from different traditions, to resolve apparent contradictions between studies by revealing the differential visibility of different phenomena from various perspectives, and to generalize our results more responsibly by virtue of understanding better the match between the situations we have studied and those we are interested in.
4. Discouraging categorical statements about what life or people are like. Neither is like anything in twenty-five words or less.

These may be old questions. Even if that is the case, March and Shapira's paper has given us some new grist for the old mill — and heightened the importance of grinding away.

Bureaucracies, Minds, and the Human Engineering of Decisions

Daniel Kahneman, *University of British Columbia*

It is a pleasure to comment on the excellent paper by Jim March and Zur Shapira, which considers two topics I have been thinking about recently. I am just back from Israel, where I gave a workshop called "Human Engineering of Decision Making." Since then, I have been working on a paper on the psychology of attention, which has a section that we title, with tongue-in-cheek, "Toward a Bureaucratic Model of the Mind." The two topics, of course, are quite closely related to the theme of the present paper — a lucky accident for me. I shall comment briefly on both.

Bureaucracies and Minds

The essay by March and Shapira makes the organizational metaphor very appealing to the psychologist interested in individual decision making. Many of the properties ascribed to organizations in that paper are excellent hypotheses about what might also be true for individuals. Some questions that arise in describing organizations turn out to be illuminating in thinking about persons as well. The model of the person as a collection of persons has often been used to describe motivational conflict, but it is no less applicable in the purely cognitive domain. For example, there are many situations in which an individual simultaneously appears to know something and to be ignorant of the same thing. It is quite common for some parts of an organization to have knowledge that other parts of the organization do not share, but an interesting question arises: When can we say that a complex organization such as the CIA or General Motors knows or understands something? And is the situation really different when we wish to say that an individual knows or understands something? It turns out to be almost as difficult to apply these words sensibly to individuals as to organizations. As the discussion of protocols by Hayes (pp. 61–77) brought out, it seems likely that there are units of the bureaucratic organizations inside our heads that simply do not know what other units are doing. In the case of individuals as well as organizations, it is difficult to pin down who *I* am: the knower, the understander, the decider.

Some ideas that March and Shapira develop in their discussion of organizations are directly applicable to individuals. For example, March and Shapira analyze performance in organizations so as to emphasize the important role of symbolic values. Much of what happens within an organization is motivated by symbolic needs and controlled by the utilities of symbols, but I would not be surprised if this were equally true of individuals. Under the influence of the economic model of human beings, we have acquired the professional habit of thinking that people act mainly in order to get things, but this emphasis on tangible goods is probably exaggerated. In many contexts, the manner in which we get things is what matters. I could easily write out a long list of goods that I would love to have but would not lift a finger to get, and there are many that I would gladly accept if offered, but would never ask for. Our utilities for ways of getting things are normally much greater than our utilities for the things themselves.

The matter cannot be dismissed by assuming that the utilities of goods dominate decisions when we act within the bounds of accepted norms. Even within these bounds, the psychic costs and benefits associated with the manner of action can vary greatly, with large effects on overall utility. The significance of these costs and benefits can be appreciated by asking how much of what people do is intended to achieve tangible objectives, and how much is done to avoid embarrassment, guilt, or shame. Indeed, the common emphasis on tangible rewards and punishments may even lead us to exaggerate the importance of shame and the public aspects of embarrassment. The accounts we keep with ourselves are not concerned mainly with tangible things, or with crude anticipations or reconstructions of social rewards and punishments. The currency of our internal economy consists in large part of self-administered symbolic side-payments.

An important property of social organizations is that their values often cannot be given a coherent description. Nor can those of individuals. It used to be thought that inconsistencies of individual choices and opinions arise from error or confusion, but recent literature tends to question the very existence of systematic, internally consistent preferences, at the individual as well as on the organizational level.

The difficulty of achieving coherence arises both at any moment of time and over the course of time. I touch here on a theme that March (1978) developed in an earlier essay, concerning the predictive character of utilities. The question is as simple as it is fundamental: When people decide to take action in order to achieve certain objectives, do they really know whether they are going to like what they get when they get it? How good are people at predicting the hedonic consequences of their actions? Clearly, any theory concerned with the rationality of action must be concerned with this problem, but I know of no research that has dealt specifically with people's ability to predict how much they will enjoy later what they want now.

I can report here a preliminary study with four subjects, students in a course, required by me this year to have a large helping of their favorite ice cream every day for a week, and to keep a diary of what happened to them. Before starting on this rather pleasant experimental task, each participant predicted the effect of the treatment on his or her appetite for ice cream. The results of this casual experiment were as follows. Two of the participants reported signs of addiction. One described a moment of panic after she discovered that she might run out of ice cream when the store would be closed.

Another described her sadness at the close of the experiment. Two others had developed a distinct aversion for the stuff by the end of the week. The most interesting finding was that, in this sample of four, there was no correlation between prior expectations and the actual changes of attitude toward the ice cream. In fact, one of the two participants who showed signs of addiction had predicted aversion, and one of those who developed aversion had predicted addiction. These tentative observations support a suspicion I have had for some time, that people know very little about how they function as pleasure machines. After all, it is difficult to conceive of a more elementary exercise in self-prediction than the one I assigned my students. Yet, in more significant decisions, including those pertinent to marriage and employment, there is usually uncertainty about the stability of the object, as well as about the stability of the attitude. I think that determining what rationality might mean for people who might be ignorant of their own properties, such as how pleasure is best experienced, would be an interesting and important endeavor.

Human Engineering of Decision Making

Let me now turn to the second theme of my remarks, the human engineering of decision making. The discipline of human engineering developed in World War II, when the war made it necessary to mass-produce military equipment and to acquire personnel skilled in operating that equipment. It was vital to devise airplanes that pilots could be trained to fly in a short period, and which they could then be trusted to fly in the stress and confusion of combat without making fatal mistakes. The guiding idea of human engineering, then, is to fit the machine to the limitations of the human operator. For example, since it is easier for the operator of an airplane to brake by a pulling motion rather than by a pushing one, it is the task of the expert in human engineering to impose the appropriate constraint on the design of such brakes.

To apply the metaphor of human engineering to the present context, we must view the organization as a machine. One of the functions of this machine, although not the only one, is to make decisions. The people involved can be seen as operators. And the question is: How do we fit the machine to the limitations of the operators? To answer this question we must break it into two others: What limitations of those participants in the effort of decision making most seriously affect the quality of decisions? And what institutional arrangements and standard operating procedures are most likely to minimize the impact of the operators' limitations? The hope is that it may be possible to suggest changes in the institutional arrangements and procedures of a particular organization by jointly considering its specific functions and the limitations of its operators. Here I shall hint at a few examples.

Michael Posner, in his paper "Protocol Analysis and Human Cognition," (pp. 78–82) refers to the classic Bruner-and-Potter study, which demonstrated that observers were hampered in identifying images of familiar objects by initial exposures to very blurred versions of these images. They were worse off than other observers who were simply not given these exposures. The conclusion was that people may be slow to discover the truth if they are blinded by incorrect hypotheses, which they developed when exposed initially to information of low validity. A recommendation about the structuring of information systems could be derived from these observations. Specifically, they suggest that experts who have been following the gradual accumulation of intelligence about a particular problem are not always the best judges of its significance. It may be useful to have other experts in the organization, who are not exposed to the same flow of information, and who are given the relevant material only after a substantial amount of it has accumulated.

In addition to the interpretation of information, there is a question of the institutional arrangements and procedures most likely to produce unbiased estimates and predictions. How can we ensure that the best information available to the organization will be brought to bear on a decision? How can we ensure that raw information is appropriately combined into the highly digested form of estimates and predictions that are normally used in decision-making deliberations? Some ways of collecting data and forecasts are better than others (Fischhoff 1982, Kahneman and Tversky 1979a). A particularly critical task for the human engineering of decisions is to provide arrangements that separate issues of values from issues of beliefs. One of the observations I find most frightening among significant social debates is the high correlation between the values that people have and their beliefs about matters of fact. For example, it seems perfectly legitimate for someone to feel that there is an too much welfare, and that the virtues of self-reliance should be restored. It is equally legitimate to argue for the importance of charity. These are value judgments. But the observed correlation between the positions people take on these issues of value and their beliefs in economic propositions about the relation between income and the propensity to save somehow seems too high to be reasonable.

There is a need for procedures designed to reduce the contamination of factual beliefs and predictions by wishes and values. One way to do this may be to ask experts for opinions about specific details rather than global evaluations, which are more likely to be contaminated by beliefs about what the organization should do (which in turn are likely to be contaminated by the values attached to outcomes). Some years ago, for example, in the context of an experiment about the collection and dissemination of expert information in strategic decision making, Zvi Lanir, Ruth Beyth-Marom, and I interviewed many leading political experts in Israel about the possible developments from Henry Kissinger's shuttle diplomacy following the 1973 war. Many of these experts had views of their own about what should be done. Some were doves, others were hawks, and any meeting between them always elicited sharp differences of opinion. Much to our surprise, differences appeared to vanish when these experts were asked to assign numerical probabilities to specific designated events, perhaps because the mode of questioning promoted objectivity, but perhaps even more because it separated judgment from recommendation more sharply than other methods of eliciting expert opinion.

The structuring and scheduling of the information delivered to decision makers is one of the most significant tasks in the human engineering of decisions. Decision makers are limited in their ability to process information. They are also prone to the Bruner-and-Potter effect I mentioned earlier: the effects of exposure to invalid information persist after that information has been discredited. Social psychologists have studied this phenomenon under the label of a "debriefing" effect. Even the most explicit debunking of previously believed information commonly leaves a substantial residue of belief (Ross and Lepper 1980). Thus, we should ask: How can the flow of information to the decision maker be planned for maximal effectiveness? How can the decision maker be screened from information likely to be invalid or uselessly redundant? In what ways can we maximize the impact of new information? Is the preparation of thick reports for executives to take home at night always the best way? It seems obvious that a preliminary sensitivity analysis can be very helpful in isolating the uncertainties on which the ultimate decision should mainly depend. Focusing the attention of information gatherers, experts, and decision makers on these areas may help in optimizing the use of precious and severely limited resources: the time and processing capacity of overworked decision makers. Human engineers of decision making will not deride the high executive who wants to make crucial decisions on the basis of a page of facts and predictions. They will only insist on a very careful design of that one essential page.

Finally, I will mention just a few other areas in which a human engineering approach could prove fruitful. An especially important set of questions concerns the correspondence between the interests of the people who make the decisions and the interests of the institution on behalf of which the decisions are made. What are the institutional arrangements that minimize possible conflicts? For example, does an emphasis on individual accountability increase or decrease the rationality of the decisions that are made within an organization, and the correspondence between the motives of the individuals and the objectives of the institution? Another set of problems concerns attitudes to risk, and the selection of arrangements to promote the desirable degree of risk taking by individual decision makers within the organization. The significant technical point in this regard is that people appear to be, to a first approximation, proportionately risk-averse. That is, they take the same risk premium (as a percentage of the stake) in small gambles and in large ones. But suppose that the management of a large firm, in which many decisions are made in decentralized manner, wants to impose a certain global level of risk taking. How should they go about it? The surprising result is that the individual decision makers within the organization should be encouraged to be proportionately *more* risk-taking than the organization as a whole wishes to be, because risks are reduced statistically in the pooling of many (relatively) small decisions. Such a conclusion certainly runs against the grain, and against the practice in many organizations, which pay lip service to "initiative" at all levels, but reserve risk-taking for the higher echelons. When it has been determined that risk-taking should be promoted actively, it is a task for the human engineer of decisions to devise arrangements that can achieve this goal.

Response to Commentaries

Zur Shapira, *Hebrew University*

The main issue that arises out of Baruch Fischhoff's and Danny Kahneman's commentaries concerns the relationships between individual and organizational decision making. In Fischhoff's words, "Is there anything like organizational decision making? . . . Or, are there only individuals who are making decisions within organizations?" Professor March and I have suggested that organizational decision theory is a cognitive interpretation of organizations, and we have devoted some effort toward explaining this view, since it may seem unnatural to impute thinking and consciousness to organizations. Our paper addresses itself to the relationships between behavioral decision theory and organizational decision theory in an attempt to examine the relevance of findings in one area to those in the other. I would like to discuss these relationships a bit more.

Since organizations consist of individuals, we should expect some correspondence between individual decision making and organizational decision making; yet, an information processing model of an organization is quite different from the cognitive model of people. For example, the ways in which information is represented and stored in an individual's memory may not be particularly relevant to the way organizations store information. Actually, there are no limits to organizational memory since an organization can decide to store its information in a variety of ways, a privilege that human memory does not have. Yet an important feature of organizational memory from the perspective of decision making is how relevant information is gathered on the one hand and retrieved on the other. Despite these differences, it seems that the heuristics of human information processing and judgment, such as availability, would be relevant to organizational decision making. Mintzberg's studies of managerial behavior may serve as an example in this regard. Similarly, organizational decision theory may be relevant to individual decision making, as is suggested by Kahneman's notion of the bureaucratic model of the mind.

The relationships between behavioral and organizational decision theory can be divided into a number of categories. If a single organizational decision maker, such as a department head, is the subject of analysis, the relations are obvious. If, on the other hand, we are interested in organizational decision making and are focusing on the group level, for example, the board of directors, the relevance is not so clear. If all the members of the decision-making group have similar preference functions, similar information-processing capabilities, and the same information, it would be interesting to compare, for example, the ways in which they would frame decisions as individuals and as a group. If, however, all group members do not share the assumed attributes, we find ourselves in a different situation in which conflict, strategic use of information, and the like, will be the major variables. In such a case, it would be very difficult to attribute choice reversals in organizational decision making to differential framing rather than to conflicting interests (due to different utility functions) that are competing in a dynamic process. In this respect, a view of organizational decision making as a mere aggregation of individual decision making may be troublesome. While the individual–aggregate view of organizational decision making is incomplete, a related approach has proven useful and is employed here. This approach, with its roots in the writings of Cyert, March, and Simon, posits that organizations make decisions in an analogous way to individuals. There are differences between the two, but the paradigm is basically the same.

Blending organizational and behavioral theories of decision making is conceptually sound, and serves the important purpose of cross-pollination as well. Each field asks different questions. In behavioral decision theory, preference reversals are one of the most researched phenomena. In organizational decision theory, on the other hand, preferences serve in many cases as an independent variable, as, for example, in the garbage can model where problematic preferences are taken as an input rather than as the output of the decision process.

Before the relationship between individual and organizational decision making can be accurately assessed, questions as to the generalizability of experimental lab data to real-life situations must be resolved. Studying decision making in the lab eliminates many important variables, such as the strategic characteristics of information. While there have been attempts to conduct studies of decision making outside the lab (for example, Fischhoff et al. 1978, Kunreuther et al. 1978a), more studies that investigate the pervasiveness of heuristics in situations of natural decision making are needed to determine the relevance of behavioral decision theory findings to organizational decision making. At the same time, bringing into the lab several characteristics of decision situations in organizations, such as conflict, may help clarify the role that heuristics and differential framing of decision problems play in actual decision situations. Although a definitive answer as to the relationship between organizational and individual decision making awaits advances in research methodology, analogies between the two would seem to offer benefits for research in both of these fields.

5 Applications of Information-Processing and Decision-Making Research, I

The Use of Accounting Information: Expert Versus Novice Behavior

Marinus Bouwman, University of Oregon

An Information-Processing Model of Intrafirm Dynamics and Their Effects Upon Organizational Perceptions, Strategies, and Choices

Francis Tuggle, Rice University
Donald Gerwin, University of Wisconsin-Milwaukee

The Economics of Protection Against Low Probability Events

Howard Kunreuther, University of Pennsylvania

Commentaries:

On Improving Applied Decision Making: Comments on the Bouwman, Tuggle and Gerwin, and Kunreuther Papers

Ronald Taylor, University of British Columbia

Applications of Information-Processing and Decision Theories: A Discussion

John W. Payne, Duke University

The three state-of-the-art review papers presented in the initial part of this book are followed by a series of applications papers which elaborate upon, extend through examples, and otherwise amplify the concepts contained in the state-of-the-art papers. Six such applications papers are presented in groups of three, each group followed by two short discussions of their contrasting content areas and methodologies. For perspective, the papers are presented in two separate chapters (Chapters 5 and 6).

These papers can be better understood if we place them along several dimensions relative to the three state-of-the-art papers. The dimensions are (1) the level of analysis, (2) the predominant theoretical sources, and (3) the typical methodology. By placing them so, we are enabled to build a perspective of how some theoretical problems in behavioral decision theory and organizational decision theory can be resolved through application.

The first group of papers focuses on (1) use of accounting information, (2) management strategy in response to perceptions of the environment, and (3) perceptions of low probability events by consumers and firms in the insurance industry. These papers address the issue of information search and processing, but they use three distinct levels of analysis: intra-individual, intrafirm, and interfirm, respectively. The theoretical sources and methodologies employed are quite diverse.

The initial paper by Marinus Bouwman studies the process by which a financial statement is examined, with emphasis on differentiating between expert and novice behavior. The task of examining accounting information contained in financial statements is viewed as similar to that of a medical doctor examining a patient's symptoms for indications of a disease. That is, the firm's financial condition, the disease, constitutes an underlying conceptual system which the financial analyst does not directly see, but rather infers from observable accounting data, the symptoms.

The theoretical basis for this study is the theory of human problem solving developed by Newell and Simon (1972) that postulates that problem solving takes place in a problem space, defined as the subject's internal representation of the problem, the task environment, and the general environment in which the problem is solved. The research method, known as protocol analysis, is designed to elicit a better understanding of the internal processes by which novices and experts build a problem space. The data consist of the verbalizations of subjects in the course of interpreting financial reports.

The second paper, by Tuggle and Gerwin, also deals with the processing of alternative interpretations of information, but in contrast with Bouwman, the unit of analysis is the entire firm. A model is built which considers the impact of various forms of organizational coalitions upon a firm's perceptions, strategies, and choices. In this model, the representation of the task environment is considerably different from that of human problem solving, particularly in terms of the values, preferences, goals of the dominant coalition, and environmental factors perceived by that coalition. Finally, the representation of the

131

task environment is modified by strengths and weaknesses of the firm relative to other marketplace competitors.

Tuggle and Gerwin's use of the information-processing (IP) framework is an attempt to integrate the finer points of organizational theory and business policy and strategy. Specifically, their framework allows for the development of precise and testable theory on the interplay of organizational decisions, strategy formulation, and environmental factors. In order to treat all the components of their complex model adequately, Tuggle and Gerwin resort to a computer simulation methodology. They formulate a system of programs which they call EPASP1 and EPASP2 in order to deal with both well-structured as well as unstructured choice procedures in the firm. Using this approach, they present situations in which coalitions affect perception and strategy formulation, and consider how these may affect actions by the chief executive officer.

In the third paper, by Kunreuther, the unit of analysis is interfirm; that is, the dynamics of different firms operating in a common market are examined. The adjustment processes of both consumers and firms are specifically studied in the insurance industry where low probability events are perceived. In effect, the firm is treated as if it were an individual actor making decisions in the market environment. A probability distribution of events is altered by the perceptual processes of consumers and firms, which are, in turn, influenced by the impact of pricing structure, type of loss information available, the nature of decision rules used, and the firm's perceptions of consumer behavior. The outcomes are examined by Kunreuther in a framework encompassing supply–demand equilibriums.

The theoretical sources of his paper come from normative economic theory and behavioral decision theory. The research method is that of supply–demand analysis from classical economics. However, the results of experiments in behavioral decision making are a central part of his analysis. Key issues dealt with include a threshold model of individual consumer choice, a sequentially made price/loss perception, and instances of consumer "regret."

Ron Taylor's critique follows, focusing on the implications of the cognitive phenomena of human judgment and choice for applied decision making in organizational contexts. Three issues are advanced regarding (1) advances in theory development, (2) reevaluation of research methods, and (3) strategies for applied decision making. Taylor suggests a need for a more general theory to guide research, rather than restricted theories to account for specific judgmental behaviors. In this regard, he acknowledges the contribution of the Bouwman and Kunreuther papers for addressing the area in which problems are recognized and formulated — an area which has received little attention in the research literature.

In regard to methodology, Taylor argues that too much applied research is based on research paradigms that emphasize sophisticated measurement and objective norms. Taylor points out that we should be concerned with the reactions of our subjects in the experimental setting, and with the extent to which our results are artifacts of experimental situations. In general, he suggests that research problems should not be constrained by available methods, but that other, newer methods be examined for use in studying interesting problems. For example, present efforts to improve decision making can be expanded to investigate possible correspondence between the amount of information required for making effective decisions and the information processing capabilities of decision makers.

Taylor proposes three strategies for achieving such a correspondence: (1) decision makers with high information-processing can be selected; (2) decision makers can be trained to overcome informational limitations and biases; and (3) the informational demands of a decision problem can be reduced by applying appropriate decision aids. In conclusion, Taylor implores the need for alternative organizational decision-making models that more accurately reflect the psychological, social, and organizational influences on choices. More models of the process of decision making should be investigated to meet the full demands of improving applied decision making.

John Payne then notes the emphasis of research in decision making shifting from basic research (for example, testing the power of our theories) to applied research (for example, improving problem solving and decision behavior). In this context, he acknowledges the contributions made by Bouwman, Tuggle and Gerwin, and Kunreuther. He recognizes, however, that our present understanding of decisional behavior by individuals faced with simple tasks in the laboratory is far from complete. Moreover, he recognizes that there is an applied value of understanding responses to laboratory decision tests such as simple gambles.

Commenting on the research method employed by Bouwman, Payne suggests that protocol analysis serves a highly useful function in exploratory research. However, he raises concerns about the lack of summary measures of behavior that would allow the reader to make some inferences regarding the generalizability of the results obtained. Such a concern leads to additional questions on the utility of protocol analysis for applied research.

Regarding Tuggle and Gerwin, Payne states that computer simulation may provide the best way of handling complex interactions. Yet the very complexity of the simulation also leads to problems of interpretation. In addition, there is concern regarding the method of validation when results are compared with business policy cases. Then, in a final comment on the Kunreuther paper, Payne discusses the value of an integrated approach employing sources from economics, psychology, and behavioral decision making.

The three applications papers represent the ways in which research in decision making can be differentiated by level of analysis, predominant theoretical sources, and methodology. While Taylor and Payne acknowledge the value of integrated research, they also specify some conceptual and methodological problems that underlie such an effort. Indeed, much more integrated research will have to be done to meet the full demands of improving applied decision making. At a minimum, however, the papers can provide the base for interdisciplinary studies aimed at understanding the complexities of both individual and organizational decision making.

The Use of Accounting Information: Expert Versus Novice Behavior

Marinus J. Bouwman, *University of Oregon*

The objective of this paper is to explore the differences between expert and novice behavior. Interest in this topic is a direct result of attempts to teach novices how to become experts. Setting out to accomplish this task, one is quickly confronted with the question: What exactly differentiates the expert from the novice? In other words, what are the operational teaching objectives one wishes to achieve? Unfortunately, despite a long history of teaching, answers to these questions are still hard to formulate. For example, in the teaching of medical diagnosis, one of the oldest and most formalized examples of education, the following statement is characteristic of the feeling of frustration experienced by educators: "After many years of formal training in diagnosis, a prospective diagnostician's behavior is characterized by a stereotyped, inefficient, and frequently unsuccessful diagnostic strategy." (Leaper et al. 1973). A large part of diagnostic training is left to the process of gaining experience, whatever that may be.

One of the major reasons for this situation is the expert's inability to describe his or her own diagnostic process in detailed and operational terms. In fact, it appears that experts may teach students one diagnostic method while they themselves use an entirely different method, without even being aware of this inconsistency. This paper is part of a larger effort to use the increasingly more powerful techniques of information-processing psychology to study the differences between expert and novice behavior (Simon and Simon 1977, Larkin 1977). The objective of these studies is to develop detailed, operational models of problem-solving behavior — frequently formulated as computer programs — of both the expert and the novice. Although these models do not describe the learning process as such, they do define in operational terms, that is, in terms of strategies of decision making, processes, and specific knowledge, the differences between expert and novice behavior that the educational process is trying to overcome.

This paper will present and compare the decision-making behavior — in terms of verbal protocols — of an expert and a novice on a particular accounting task, the analysis of financial statements. The basis of the comparison will be a model (computer program) of financial analysis which has been used successfully to describe completely the decision-making behavior of a novice (Bouwman 1978a). The concentration on only two subjects is deliberate, as this allows an in-depth analysis of individual behavior. The discussion of the subjects' behavior will be preceded by a description of the precise accounting task and the experimental design. In addition, a formal task analysis will be presented, providing the theoretical framework for the comparison of subjects' behavior.

Financial Analysis

The accounting task studied is the analysis of financial statements. Provided with a set of financial statements describing the performance of a certain company over a number of years, a financial analyst is asked to evaluate this information. The result of the analysis is a judgment of the position of the company.

The analysis of financial statements is, from a methodological point of view, a diagnostic process. The analyst goes through a considerable amount of data looking for clues (the symptoms) which may help locate possible problems (or diseases) from which the company (the patient) is suffering. It is an attempt to identify the state of an underlying system, given a set of observable symptoms. There are two important aspects of the diagnostic task that clearly differentiate it from the "game tasks" generally studied in information-processing psychology. First of all, the objective of the diagnosis is not well defined. It is not clear at the outset what constitutes an acceptable solution: This will have to be specified during the diagnostic process. Second, it is not possible to solve the diagnostic task by simply applying general problem-solving methods. Rather, the problem solver must also command a considerable amount of specific knowledge dealing with the particular task.

Task Analysis

A first step in the study of decision-making behavior is an exhaustive and detailed analysis of the task. What are the characteristic aspects of the task, what intermediate decisions must be made, what information must minimally be available, and so forth? Clearly, no analysis of this kind will determine what the financial analyst *must* do. On the other hand, outlining the environment in which the financial analysis takes place is a prerequisite for examining how the analyst proceeds through this environment.

There are several information sources which help outline this environment. The first one is a *logical task analysis.* If the final solution requires the presence of "statement A," for instance, one might logically be able to determine that therefore "statements $B_1,...,B_n$" must have been arrived at. And that, in turn, each of those statements requires that certain other knowledge, and processes to generate that knowledge, must have been available to the problem solver. There is nothing assumed here about the subject's financial analysis behavior. It may even be entirely illogical. However, the "logically minimal knowledge and processes" provide a baseline for the analysis of observed behavior.

A second information source about the task itself is the *professional literature* in the various diagnostic fields (for example, in medicine, industrial process control, computer program debugging, and financial analysis). In medicine, particularly, a large amount of literature is available dealing with the teaching of diagnosis. And although much of that literature deals with medical knowledge as such, with diseases and symptoms and their complex interrelations, an increasingly larger portion focuses on the mechanics, the thought processes, of making a diagnosis. Examples of such studies are: (1) DeDombal (1971), Feinstein (1973a, 1973b, 1974), and Hull (1972), which describe the thought processes of the expert physician as viewed by physicians; (2) Rimoldi (1961) and Andrew (1972), which try to establish a model of diagnosis as a basis for education; and (3) Kleinmuntz (1968), Wortman (1972), and Pople (1977), which study diagnosis from a cognitive-psychology point of view. The most crucial research, however, is the work by Newell and Simon (1972), who developed the concept of task analysis as it is used here. Their work, consolidated in their comprehensive theory of human problem solving, provides the basis for this research.

Problem Space

Newell and Simon argue that problem solving takes place in a problem space. A problem space is the subject's internal representation of his or her task environment, which includes the problem to be solved, as well as the environment in which it takes place. This internal representation can contain only part of what is potentially available in the task environment, and, moreover, it is not unique, as there generally are many different ways to represent the same task environment. The particular problem space used by a subject determines entirely what information is available during the problem-solving process, and conversely, any information used during problem solving must be part of the problem space. Although Newell and Simon admit that they cannot prove that all problem-solving behavior necessarily takes place in a problem space, they do consider the existence of a problem space to be "a major invariant of problem-solving behavior that holds across tasks and across subjects" (Newell and Simon 1972).

Problem-solving behavior can be viewed as a path through the problem space. The path consists of a sequence of nodes, called knowledge states, each representing the total dynamic knowledge about the problem available at that point. The nodes are connected by a series of links, called operators, representing the processes that generate one knowledge state from the other. Since problem-solving behavior may vary greatly from one problem space to another, due to differences in information and available operators, a detailed study of the protocols of each individual subject would therefore be required to determine what problem space or spaces are used by that particular subject. The research of Newell and Simon demonstrated, however, that the variety in problem spaces actually used by a group of subjects is quite small. There usually are only a few problem spaces which are used by most of the subjects, and these problem spaces appear to depend much more on the task than on the individual subject's characteristics.

In order to provide a basis for the comparison of expert and novice behavior, a general problem space for the task of financial analysis will be defined.

This problem space is based on a logical analysis of the financial diagnostic task, and a survey of the relevant professional literature. The first step in defining the problem space is to specify the contents of the *knowledge state* (Newell and Simon 1972): Exactly what information is stored at a node? Since this information represents the dynamic, current knowledge at that point of the analysis, a knowledge state is defined as consisting of a collection (that is, a list) of facts (or symptoms), along with relations between those facts, problem—hypotheses, and leads. This is a minimal definition, as every diagnostic reasoning process must select at least some symptoms or facts, relate these facts to each other, and formulate some kind of problem—hypotheses. The formulation of leads (for confirmation of problem—hypotheses) is not strictly necessary, but seems intuitively a reasonable *a priori* candidate for inclusion. (Obviously, there are many more, and much more sophisticated information structures than these simple lists of items. Other candidates are structures like a mental model of the firm under consideration, modified according to the observed symptoms, presenting at each knowledge state a complete picture of the firm's position.) Clearly, the information available at a knowledge state will be one of the crucial aspects of the analysis of problem-solving behavior.

Two particularly interesting knowledge states are the initial and the final states: the beginning and the end of the subject's problem-solving path. The initial state can be defined as a collection of empty lists: The company is a new one for the subject, so there is no reason to assume prior knowledge. The final state is a regular knowledge state but with one addition: the identification of a particular problem—hypothesis as the final diagnosis.

The second aspect of the problem space is the *operators* which allow problem solving to proceed from one knowledge state to another. Considering the cumulative, descriptive type of knowledge state proposed here (Newell and Simon 1972), the set of operators will at least have to contain: (1) processes that create elements (symptoms, relations, hypotheses, etc.); (2) processes that add elements to memory; and (3) processes that select, rank order, or delete elements in order to arrive at a final conclusion. Figure 1, which presents the problem space described here, contains a set of such operators. This set represents the kinds of operators that one logically would expect to observe in the diagnostic reasoning process, and that is generally accepted in the professional literature. The exact formulation of these operators, however, can no longer be based on a purely theoretical analysis. A theoretical analysis can tell us what to look for in general terms, but the specifics can only be determined by actually examining problem-solving (protocol) data.

A final aspect of the problem space is the *background information* (in addition to the temporary, dynamic information contained in the present knowledge state) that is available during the problem-solving process. First, one would expect some kind of path information about how the present knowledge state was reached. Also, one would expect various kinds of reference information: (1) some kind of task-specific (economic/accounting) knowledge that links symptoms to problems and vice versa; (2) some knowledge about the functioning of a firm describing how various symptoms, states, and variables interact with each other; and (3) a set of typical symptom patterns identifying typical problems. Furthermore, the financial statement information remains available

KNOWLEDGE STATE:
   List of significant facts (symptoms), plus list of relations, plus list of problem−hypotheses, plus list of leads.

OPERATORS:	CHANGE IN KNOWLEDGE STATE:
Select financial item for analysis	−
Examine financial item	−
Remember symptom	Add
Match symptoms against typical patterns	Add
Formulate relation between symptoms	Add/rank-order
Formulate problem−hypothesis	Add/rank-order
Confirm	Add/delete/rank-order
Select final problem−hypothesis (diagnosis)	Rank-order

INITIAL STATE:
   Empty lists

FINAL STATE:
   Knowledge state plus final problem−hypothesis

FIGURE 1   The Diagnostic Problem Space

during the entire analysis, and may function as an additional *external memory*. Clearly, not all types of information need to be available to all subjects. However, the availability of at least some of this information is an essential prerequisite for diagnostic reasoning behavior.

General Diagnostic Program

In assessing the feasibility and completeness of the diagnostic problem space, the discussion so far has used mainly arguments based on a theoretical analysis of the diagnostic process. The only real test of the feasibility of a problem space is, however, the existence of a program able to make a diagnosis while operating within this space. Figure 2 presents the outlines of such a program, phrased in terms of the elements and operators of the diagnostic problem space. The program has a "generalized production format" (Newell and Simon 1972); that is, it consists of a number of modules (productions), each consisting of a "test-part" and an "action-part." During execution the test-part of a module is examined, and if the conditions are "true," the corresponding action-part is executed.

    The basic control mechanism of the diagnostic program is the selection of a next piece of financial information, followed by a testing of the conditions, and the activation of one or several processes operating on this information. The first process to be activated will generally be the examination of the financial figures, including an evaluation of the significance of the results. However, this is not always necessary. For example, if the financial information item had been selected in order to confirm a proposed problem−hypothesis, a direct comparison may be made. The program, being a general model of the diagnostic process, is not very specific with respect to what conditions are tested and

DIAGNOSE COMPANY (financial data) (→diagnosis):

1. Select next item (financial data) (→item),
        If success,
2.   Test conditions for general examination,
              if true,
                  examine (item) (→symptom);
                    if result is "significant,"
                        remember symptom (→list of significant facts);
3.   Test conditions for problem confirmation (list of leads),
              if true,
                  confirm lead (item) (→list of significant facts,
                      list of relations, list of problem−hypotheses);
4.   Test conditions for diagnosis recognition,
              if true,
                  match list of significant facts against list of
                      typical symptom patterns (→diagnosis);
                  if success, report diagnosis and stop.
5.   Test conditions for symptom integration,
              if true,
                  formulate relation (symptom, list of significant facts)
                      (→list of relations, list of leads);
6.   Test conditions for problem formulation,
              if true,
                  formulate problem−hypothesis (list of significant facts,
                      list of relations) (→list of problem−hypotheses,
                      list of leads);
7.   Continue selecting next item;
8.   If fail,
          Report "end of data";
          Select final diagnosis (list of problem−hypotheses, list of
              relations, list of significant facts)
              (→diagnosis);
          Report diagnosis and stop.

FIGURE 2   General Diagnostic Program

when, neither is it specific about exactly what follow-up actions take place. Clearly, this is a matter of individual behavior. The program provides the general framework; the following analyses of individual behavior will operationalize this for two specific cases.

The Experimental Design

A detailed comparison of individual decision-making behavior requires an experimental design that generates detailed behavioral process information on a continuing basis. A methodology that provides that information is the collection of thinking-aloud protocols: observing subjects who think aloud while performing a particular task, and recording on tape a literal transcript of their behavior. The subjects studied here were given a set of financial statements that consisted of five pages of information containing balance sheets, income statements, financial ratios, sales figures, and production data, covering the past three years of operation of the firm (see Appendix A on page 156 for an example of such a set). The subjects were asked to "make a quick evaluation of the position of the firm" and to indicate the underlying problem areas, if any. Each subject analyzed four different cases (sets of statements) during a single session. The first case was used for training to familiarize the subjects with the task and the thinking-aloud requirements. Three of the cases each contained one particular main problem, and one case showed a company without any major problems. The subjects were asked to complete their evaluation within ten to fifteen minutes. Actual times ranged from six to twenty-five minutes.

The Student Subject

A total of fifteen students participated in the experiment, divided into a beginners group (eight students, two courses in accounting), and an advanced group (seven students, five courses in accounting). The students were working towards their masters degree in industrial engineering, and had selected a major in managerial accounting. The subject selected for discussion here, S9, is a typical example for the advanced student group. "Typical" means that S9's protocol was similar in appearance to those of the other subjects with respect to the *relative frequencies* of the coded protocol lines, and the *problem behavior graph*.

The behavior of S9 (see protocol in Appendix B) has been studied in great detail in a previous paper (Bouwman 1978a). The information provided here is a summary of that previous study. In addition, the descriptions of S9's behavior have been tested by translating them into operational computer programs, and simulating these programs on the same financial cases. The results of these simulations closely matched the observed behavior of S9, from the initial examination of the information to the formulation of a final evaluation.

A program that describes the overall diagnostic behavior of S9 is presented in Figure 3. The program has the same format as the general diagnostic program of Figure 2, and is expressed in the same "diagnostic operators," though not using all of them. Also, it is considerably simplified in a number of respects. As before, the basic control mechanism is the selection of a next piece of financial information, followed by the execution of various follow-up activities. But now the program makes explicit exactly when and under what conditions each major diagnostic operator is executed. It no longer states, for example, to "test conditions for examination," but instead specifies that S9 as a rule starts with the examination process. It states that an attempt to find a relation between observed facts is only made after a new significant fact has been discovered. Before further examining the implications of this program, the major diagnostic operators reported in the program must be discussed in more detail.

EXAM – The Examination of Information. The information is presented in quantitative form, though none of the student subjects analyzing the information dealt with it in those terms. Each subject had his own way of extracting certain features from those numbers. *Examination* is defined as the process of analyzing the presented information and translating it into more convenient qualitative terms. Examination also screens the information, selecting only those data which promise to be particularly relevant in the formulation of a diagnosis.

DIAGNOSE COMPANY (financial data) (→diagnosis):

1. Select next item (financial data) (→item),
    if success,
2.   Examine (item) (→symptom);
      if result is "significant,"
        remember symptom (→list of significant facts);
3.   Test if item is marked "lead" (list of leads),
     if true,
        confirm lead (item) (→list of significant facts,
          list of relations, list of problem−hypotheses);
4.   Test if new symptom has been added to list of significant facts,
     if true,
        formulate relation (symptom, list of significant facts)
          (→list of relations, list of leads);
5.   Test if "problem" available,
      if false,
        formulate problem (list of relations)
          (→problem, list of leads);
6.   Continue selecting next item;
7.   If fail,
    Report "end of data";
    Select final diagnosis (problem) (→diagnosis);
    Report diagnosis and stop.

FIGURE 3   The Student's Diagnostic Program

In order to translate the quantitative information into qualitative terms, subjects have at their disposal a set of so-called basic operators. The most frequently used basic operators are:

INCR: the determination of a simple time trend or *incr*ement (for example, "inventories are up," "demand declined");

TREND: the determination of a more complex time *trend* (for example, "demand is back to the level of 1976");

CA: the *c*omparison with general industry *a*verages (for example, "profit margin is below average");

C: the *c*omparison with other items (for example, "the demand estimate is way above the actual demand");

CI: the *c*omparison with *i*nternal standards (that is, rules of thumb like "net income ought to be positive").

Not all operators are used with the same frequency. S9, like most students, strongly prefers the CA and the INCR operators. The use of CA is limited, as industry information is not always available. Table 1 gives the relative frequencies of basic operator application for S9. (Data on a different subject — S14 — are also provided, but a discussion of this aspect is deferred until later.)

The result of the examination process is a qualitative characterization of financial information. This qualitative characterization is then judged for its expected significance for the overall evaluation of the company. Only information that is judged potentially significant is remembered by S9 (as indicated by a

TABLE 1   Distribution of Examination Operators

| | BASIC EXAMINATION OPERATOR | | | | | |
	INCR	TREND	CA	C	CI	TOTAL
S9/Case 1	23	5	5	3	4	40
S9/average, all cases	23	4	8	3	3	41
S14/Case 1	2	16	5	5	7	35

REMember operator in the program). And only information that is remembered will be available for subsequent diagnostic evaluation.

RELATE – The Formulation of Relations. The essence of S9's diagnostic reasoning is the integration of detected (significant) facts into a consistent structure. As a matter of fact, this integration process virtually determines the diagnosis. Protocol analysis indicates that this integration process is one of "linking together facts that explain each other." For example, if S9 observes that "sales are down" and "inventory is up," he concludes that "sales down explains inventory up." Linking together these facts — defined as the process of formulating a relation (RELATE) — serves two purposes. First, it removes "inventory up" from the list of possible causes of the problem, since it is now explained by another fact. Secondly, it increases the importance of "sales down" as something to check further. This process of formulating relations does not need to be restricted to two facts: Elaborate chains involving many facts may be generated. On the other hand, it is not likely that all observed significant facts will fit into the same relation chain. Facts may simply not be directly related to each other, or they may be inconsistent. Consequently, several relation chains may be developed, each internally consistent but not necessarily consistent with the others. Table 2 shows some examples of the kinds of relations generated by S9.

PROB – The Selection of the Problem. The chains of relations provide the basis for the formulation of a final diagnosis. Contrary to what one would logically expect, S9 (and all other student subjects, for that matter) does not appear to generate any formal hypothesized causes of these significant facts. Instead, S9 appears to look solely for the observed significant fact that explains most others. Moreover, once such a fact, called the problem, has been found, S9 appears to be very selective in his use of additional information. Once a problem has been found, S9 appears to be interested only in information that confirms, or directly contradicts the problem. Information that might modify or improve the problem is not really wanted. Finally, when all information has been examined, it is the problem that is reported as his final diagnosis.

TABLE 2   Examples of Relations Formulated by S9

RELATION	SOURCE (Protocol line)
Capacity increase explains why depreciation expenses are up a lot.	Lines 16–17, 63–64 Free recall text
Demand large decrease explains why the demand estimate is too high.	Lines 38–39
Depreciation expenses up explains why the net income is negative.	Free recall text
Demand increase explains why capacity is up.	Line 63

The Problem Behavior Graph. Since the diagnostic program that describes S9's behavior is a simplified version of the general diagnostic program, it follows that the problem space used by S9 is a subset of the general problem space defined earlier. For if other kinds of information had been used by S9, this would necessarily have been evidenced in his program in the form of an additional operator, or the modification of an existing one. Consequently, one can describe S9's diagnostic process as a path through this general problem space, a path starting from the initial knowledge state, progressing from one knowledge state to another though the application of diagnostic operators, and finally reaching or not reaching the knowledge-state goal: the formulation of a diagnosis. Analysis of this path and comparison of the paths of different subjects on the same case will clearly answer questions like: When is what process used? What information flows from one process to another? And how is the diagnosis gradually developed?

In order to facilitate analysis and comparison of these problem-solving paths, a visual representation has been developed, called the Problem Behavior Graph (PBG). Figure 4 presents an example of such a graph, and the corresponding construction rules. As the construction rules indicate, knowledge states are represented by nodes, and operators are represented by connecting lines. A list of operators used is provided in Table 3. An operator abbreviation above the line specifies what operator is applied. Due to space limitations, it is not feasible to list the complete knowledge state at each node, so only the additions and eliminations relative to the previous knowledge state are listed. In order to present the PBG in a visually convenient format, every recurrence of "reading new financial figures for examination" (READ) — a process which implies the end of a present line of thought — starts a new line of the graph.

The PBG of S9/Case 1. Figure 5 presents the PBG of S9's analysis of Case 1. The PBG shows S9's behavior as ten relatively short sequences, each starting

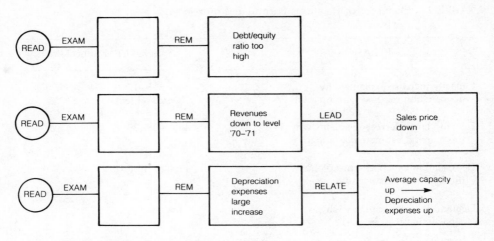

A state of knowledge is represented by a block.

An occurrence of reading financial information is represented by a circle.

The application of an operator to a state of knowledge is represented by a horizontal line leading to the right. The result is the node at the end of the line.

Each reading for examination incidence starts a new line.

Time runs to the right, then down.

FIGURE 4   Construction Rules for the Problem Behavior Graph

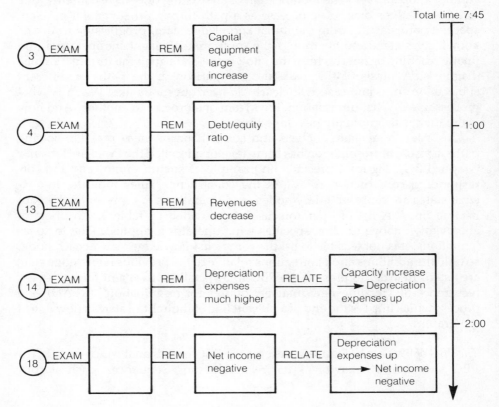

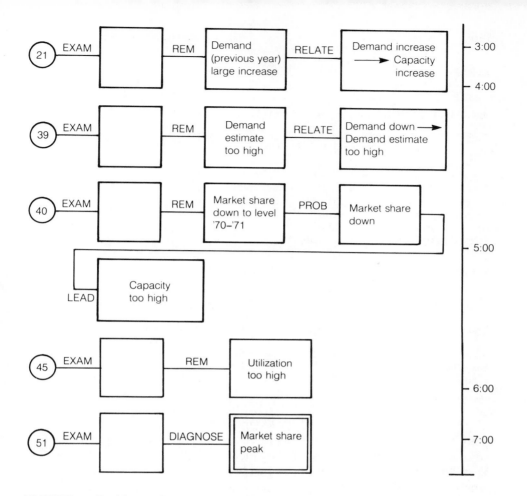

FIGURE 5   Problem Behavior Graph of Subject S9/Case 1

TABLE 3   Operators Used in the Problem Behavior Graph

DIAGNOSTIC OPERATORS (Used by both subjects)

NAME	ABBREVIATION	DESCRIPTION
Examine	EXAM	Examine financial item
Remember	REM	Remember symptom (fact)
Formulate relation	RELATE	Formulate relation between symptoms
Formulate problem	PROB	Select symptom as *the* problem
Formulate lead	LEAD	First stage of confirmation attempt
Select diagnosis	DIAGNOSE	Select/formulate final diagnosis

ADDITIONAL DIAGNOSTIC OPERATORS (Used exclusively by S14)

Company type	TYPE	Characterization of general company behavior
Search	SEARCH	Local, in-depth examination of financial information
Summarize	SUM	Summarize findings
Formulate hypothesis	HYP	Formulate problem—hypothesis
Confirm lead	CONF	Second stage of confirmation attempt

with examination behavior, followed by up to three other operators. The amount of examination represented by each EXAM operator may vary greatly, as is illustrated by the line numbers inside the "READ" boxes which indicate where in the protocol each particular examination sequence started. This variation, however, is not relevant here, because the results of the examination process per se do not cause any changes in the existing knowledge state, but rather provide the conditions for the application of other operators. The operator that usually follows the EXAM operator is the REM operator, which adds a new fact to the list of significant facts (which is part of the knowledge state). And the operator most frequently following the REM operator, if any, is the RELATE operator.

The picture of S9's diagnostic process that is presented by the PBG is a rather simple one. S9 sequentially examines information and stores significant findings (facts) in memory. Those facts are checked for relationships which might link them together and, if successful, these relations are added to memory as well. The subject appears to restrict himself to a mere collecting of relevant data, postponing a possible problem formulation almost until the very end.

S9's first and only attempt to formulate a problem finally occurs as he is examining the sales information (protocol lines 40 and following). Apparently, S9 now has collected enough facts that can be explained by a "declining market share" so that this is promoted as the "real problem." At this point a critical change takes place in S9's diagnostic objectives. From here on S9 appears to be very satisfied that he has found the problem, and he is consequently no longer interested in looking further. He still identifies one additional significant fact, and he probably also confirms his previously formulated problem-lead. The decision, however, seems to have been made, and it is this formulated problem that, barring a subsequent direct contradiction, is to be reported as his final diagnosis.

The Expert Subject

In addition to the students, three professional accountants (CPAs) participated in the experiment. They were provided the same information and given identical instructions as the students. Although the differences in behavior among the three accountants were more significant than the differences among the students, the differences in behavior between the accountants as a group and the students as a group were of an even larger magnitude. In order to highlight the differences between student and expert behavior, the behavior of student S9 will be contrasted with the behavior of one of the accountants, subject S14.

The PBG of S14/Case 1. The protocol of S14 on Case 1 (listed in Appendix B) presents, at first sight, a familiar picture. This is to be expected because there are a number of processes that need to be performed in any diagnostic evaluation, regardless of its complexity. No diagnosis can be formulated without some means of examining information, of selecting relevant findings, of identifying or hypothesizing a problem, and so on. Figure 6, presenting the PBG for S14 clearly illustrates this, since the expert employs each process of decision making that is used by the student.

While there is a similarity in the kinds of operators employed, there is no such similarity in the "operator mix." Entirely absent from the professional's behavior is the dominance of the EXAM-REM and EXAM-REM-RELATE operator sequences, characteristic of the student's behavior. S14 employs, and employs regularly, the entire variety of operators. Particularly noticeable is the frequent use of "search" and "confirmation" operators, which were largely absent among the students.

Strongly related to the operator mix is the diagnostic strategy. As the PBG illustrates, there is no trace left of the passive student strategy of "collect data and see what happens." If S14 notices something significant, he immediately searches for an explanation or for possible consequences. And as soon as S14 is able to formulate a problem–hypothesis, he does so. Moreover, he uses these hypotheses, through the formulation of leads, to actively direct the continuing analysis. Another important strategy difference, to be further substantiated in the following pages, is that S14 is not after a single problem but after the *total picture*. S14 insists on developing a total picture where all detected significant facts can take their place. A final diagnosis is only formulated after a satisfactory picture has been developed.

Expert and Novice Diagnostic Operators Compared

The comparison of PGBs, however, needs to be complemented by an in-depth analysis of the individual diagnostic operators. Although these operators are functionally equivalent, do they actually represent the same behavior? The following sections, on EXAM, RELATE, and diagnostic reasoning, will focus more on this issue.

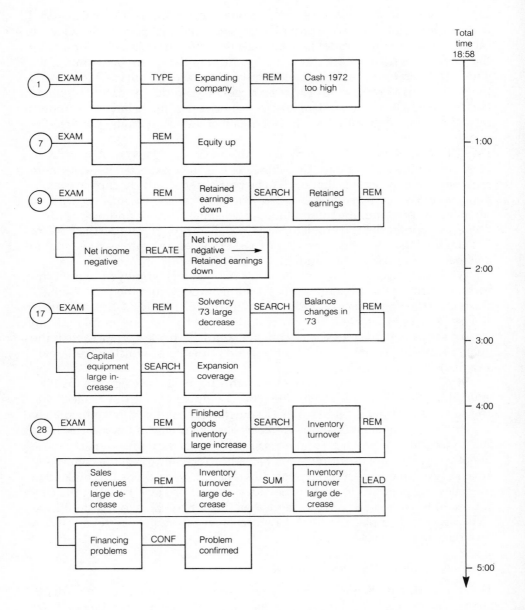

FIGURE 6. Problem Behavior Graph of Subject S14/Case 1

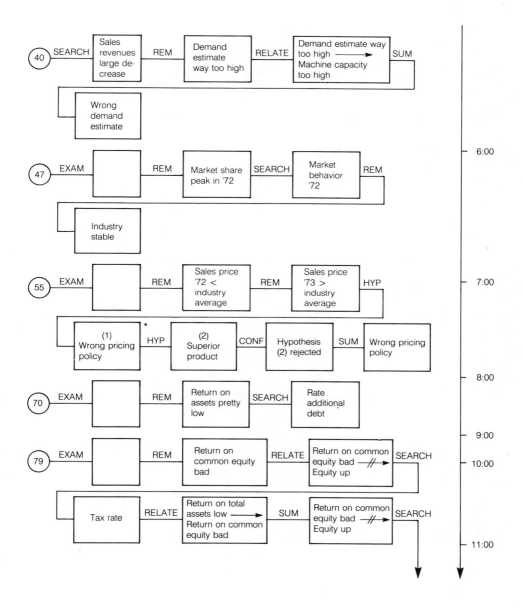

FIGURE 6 (Continued)

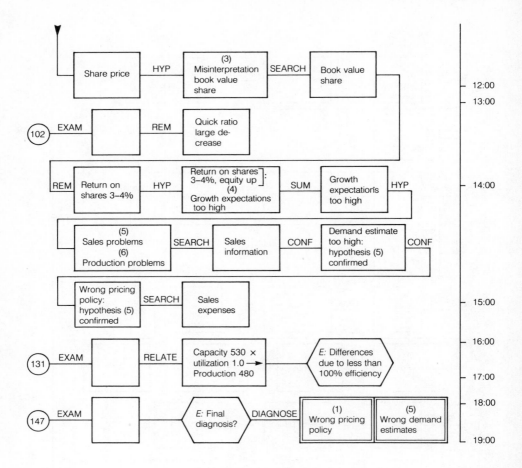

* In contrast to the previous conventions, the HYP box here contains the generated problem–
  hypothesis as reported by the subject. The number inside the box is the PBG hypothesis
  identification number.

FIGURE 6   (Continued)

The Examination of Information. There are two main aspects of the process of examination: (1) the available basic examination operators, and (2) the examination strategy. The following discussion will deal with each aspect in turn.

Figure 7 presents the first seventeen lines of the protocol of S14. As these lines illustrate, S14 seems to employ similar basic examination operators to the student: S14 develops qualitative characterizations of the available figures, and employs processes like the evaluation of a trend (lines 2 and 10) and the comparison with various kinds of norms (lines 5 and 14). However, there are also some important differences between this professional and the student. First, S14 does not restrict his evaluation to the most recent year(s). And second, S14 does not completely forget about the actual figures, but remembers a selected few in addition to the qualitative characterizations.

As might be expected, the differences are much more striking with respect to the "operator mix." As an illustration, Table 1 (p. 142) presents the relative basic operator frequencies for S14 on Case 1. Relative to S9, there is a noticeable shift away from the simple INCRement operator towards the more complex TREND operator. Also, there are many more comparisons against an internal norm or rule of thumb.

Closely related to this examination behavior is the "company type" operator, TYPE, which produces a general background against which the individual

1. I am looking at the balance sheet totals, . . .
2. and there I see, ... quite a bit of growth . . from eh 70 to 71, . . 72 stable, and then a substantial jump *again* going to 73 . . eh.
3. Are there . . any components which are not company tied? . .
4. In process inventory, . . (0.30) finished goods, accounts receivable, *no* . .
5. The cash policy, . . it does kind of hit me . . that at the end of 72 they suddenly had a whole lot of cash . .
6. It looks to me a bit excessive to have so much money available, but it could very well be . .
7. Capital stock . . from 3000 to 6000, + so a stock issue . . eh 60,000 . .
8. And *another* issue over here . .
9. We see the same thing in the premium on capital stock . . . . .
10. The retained earnings are also increasing regularly . .
11. Wait a minute, . . it goes . . 160, 164, 172, . . and then dives to 126 . . .
12. *Well,* in that case we get hold of the income statement, ... the income statement . .
13. Production, sales information, financial information . . ah, here . . .
14. Ah, they indeed really run into losses in 73 . .
15. Yes, so that means, that then is the decrease of the retained earnings . . .
16. Nice for those shareholders who had then bought these shares . . .
17. Long-term debt . .

FIGURE 7   Protocol of Subject S14/Case 1 (Lines 1–17)

observations can be compared. In the first lines of the protocol, for example, S14 is not so much examining specific items, but instead is looking at some general figures in order to get an impression of what is going on in the company. And it is not until S14 notices an obvious violation of this "expanding" company impression that the first in-depth examination behavior is initiated (lines 10–12). With respect to the actual realization of the TYPE operator, this protocol does not contain enough information. The protocol suggests that the company impression is based on an initial few arbitrary financial items. On the other hand, the use of one or more selected trend-setting items cannot be ruled out.

Returning to the process of examination, the second major aspect is the examination strategy. S9, as a typical student, employed a *sequential* strategy — a mere following of the order in which the information was presented. In contrast, the examination of S14 seems to be directed by a rather extensive *checklist* — a structured list of questions, partly standard, partly conditional — that is part of S14's permanent financial knowledge. The "standard" questions of the checklist are those questions asked automatically, irrespective of the actual values involved. Two examples of such questions are presented in (1) lines 3–4, where S14, as a matter of course, scans the balance sheet for one particular type of information, and (2) in lines 18–22, where S14 computes the debt/equity ratio and the solvency. "Conditional" questions, on the other hand, are only asked if certain conditions (that is, the presence or absence of certain values of certain items) have been met. Illustrative examples are (1) line 25, where the observed "capital equipment increase" (=condition) is followed by the question "What has the financing been?" and (2) line 75, where the observed "meager return on assets" prompts the question "What have the consequences been for the company's borrowing capacity?"

In summary, the use of a checklist appears to characterize S14's examination behavior. Although its real impact clearly cannot be evaluated on the basis of a single protocol, it is implicitly referred to many times. Moreover, additional protocols on other cases are available elsewhere (Bouwman 1978b), and while not discussed in this paper, do further support the checklist concept.

The Formulation of Relations. The second major diagnostic process, RELATE, is the linking together of observed, significant facts in "relations." S14's RELATE process does not seem to differ much from that of the student. The formulated relations are essentially qualitative and, at this level of analysis, these relations do not appear to require any radically different processes than those proposed in the general model of diagnosis. Nevertheless, there is a crucial difference in strategy as is illustrated in the expert's protocol, lines 79–81. Here S14 is not linking two facts together because one provides an explanation for the other, which is the usual way of formulating relations and the only way used by the student subject. Instead, S14 relates those two facts because they seem to contradict each other!

Focus on apparent contradictions is actually an efficient way of linking facts together. It is logically much more expedient to look for problems by searching for contradictions rather than for consistencies. Indeed, S14 uses the contradic-

Case 1 protocol.) In contrast, the student S9 never used it. Moreover, out of five advanced students who analyzed all three cases, there was only one incidence of a student reporting an apparent contradiction between two observed facts. And even then, he merely reported it: it never played a role in his further diagnostic analysis. The protocols do not provide any clues about the reasons why students fail to explore contradictions. Task analysis does suggest, however, that focusing on contradictions is a more ambiguous and less structured activity than focusing on consistencies. Possibly, one needs a certain level of expertise to be able to do this efficiently. On the other hand, it may just be a matter of strategy. Students may have never been told to consider the contradictions.

Diagnostic Reasoning. For students, these processes of examination and formulation of relations virtually determine their entire behavior. Formulating a diagnosis merely becomes a matter of identifying one of the observed facts as the problem. However, for expert S14, the real process of diagnostic reasoning begins here. Rather than merely identifying a single problem, S14 attempts to synthesize a complete picture of the company's functioning, including its problems. Clearly, S14 must have tools to perform this task. The main tools used are (1) the application of "summary" statements, (2) the availability of a "list of common diseases," and (3) the generation of problem–hypotheses. In the remainder of this paper, these tools will be further described.

Consider the following behavior. In line 28, S14 notices the strongly increasing finished goods inventory. This evidently does not look right, as S14 decides to investigate this inventory further by relating it to the sales revenues. The sales revenues are strongly decreasing. These two facts lead S14 to conclude that the company is virtually "producing for inventory." This statement, however, is more than just another significant fact. It is a fact that explains, and summarizes, part of the observed behavior, in this particular case, the behavior of the inventory in relation to the revenues.

These summaries are S14's extension of the student's problem concept. A summary statement represents, or summarizes, a related group of findings. And, as S14 is interested in the whole picture, rather than in a single problem, it becomes irrelevant whether these findings actually are problem indicators or not. The introduction of the summary concept serves several purposes. A summary terminates a certain line of exploration in a meaningful way. It may also guide the further analysis, as its identification frequently generates new leads. And finally, since a summary groups a number of findings into a single statement, it further reduces the subject's memory load. The PBG shows various examples of summary statements (identified by the SUMmarize operator). In addition to the above example, S14 formulates the summaries "wrong demand estimate" (lines 43–46), "wrong pricing policy" (lines 63–64), "unlikely stock issue" (lines 80–81), and "wrong growth expectations" (lines 111–112). Not all of these summaries are observed significant facts. The "unlikely stock issue," for example, is the result of the formulation of a relation, and the "wrong growth expectations" is the result of a problem–hypothesis generation.

Although some summaries may replace or include others, S14's basic strategy is to generate a list of summaries that covers the various areas of the company's operations. The term "list," however, should not be taken too literally here. S14's protocol behavior, without providing concrete proof, certainly does suggest a more sophisticated means of storing this information than the simple lists discussed so far. Instead, S14 may actually use a model of the firm — not a general model of a typical firm, but a specific model describing this particular firm — to integrally store this information.

The summary statement is the first of S14's diagnostic reasoning tools. Its power is considerably increased by the second tool: the "list of common (financial) diseases." As the reader may have noticed in the above discussion, a rather crucial jump was made in S14's behavior from the combined statements "finished goods inventory strongly increasing" and "sales revenues strongly decreasing" to the summary statement "producing for inventory." This jump may seem logical, but it is by no means trivial. One explanation for what happens here, based on an analogy with medical diagnostic reasoning, is that S14, through experience, has developed a list of frequently occurring problems, or "diseases." The problem of "producing for inventory," for instance, is a rather common phenomenon, which any expert undoubtedly will have encountered many times. And so is the "misrepresentation of the book value per share," which S14 generates (lines 90–91) as an apparently typical reason for an unlikely but successful stock issue. These and other examples strongly suggest the existence of a list of financial problems, where a *problem* is defined as a typical combination of significant facts. The existence of such a list facilitates S14's analysis in a number of ways: it transfers part of diagnostic reasoning to diagnostic recognition; it expresses the diagnostic process in more generally used, and therefore more accessible terms; and finally, it generates additional leads for further confirmation and evaluation.

A final element of S14's diagnostic reasoning is the formulation of problem–hypotheses: the process of inferring possible causes for a given fact. Although this process is generally assumed to be one of the most essential diagnostic processes, analysis of the students' behavior has shown this not necessarily the case, since there was no trace of such behavior in their protocols. S14, on the other hand, indeed does use this process. A typical example is presented in lines 58–64 of the protocol. In line 58, S14 notices that the sales price was below average in 1972 and above average in 1973. S14 immediately follows this observation with two possible hypothesized causes: (1) the company may have a superior product which warrants such a higher price, or (2) they may have been unsuccessful with their pricing policy. Although the first cause is immediately rejected, it does clearly illustrate the process of hypothesis generation.

The formulation of hypotheses concludes our discussion of the diagnostic processes observed in S14's behavior. Although the formulation of the final evaluation (diagnosis) has not yet been specified, it does not require any additional processes. After generating summaries, common problems, and/or problem–hypotheses, the formulation of a final evaluation becomes merely a process of selecting the most explanatory elements from this wealth of information. A simple selection rule (that is, select the first fact that explains at least three other basic facts) worked very well in the computer program that simulated S9's behavior. And although the selection rule will clearly be different for S14 (S14, for example, selects *two* problems), the protocol does not contain any evidence for a radically different mechanism.

Conclusion

What does an analysis and comparison of two protocols tell us? It does not tell us how *the* student and *the* expert think, or how they approach the task of financial analysis. Nor does it *prove* the exact nature of the differences in behavior between this particular student and this particular expert. It does, however, demonstrate what may be learned through this particular protocol analysis approach: namely, the wealth of information captured by the protocols, and the rigorous analysis and interpretation possible within the current state of the art. The analysis presented here is clearly not definitive. For one thing, although the analysis of the student's protocol has been backed up by an actual, operational computer program, which proves that the structures and processes specified are indeed able to generate the observed behavior, this is not the case for the professional. More research is needed to fill this gap, and to substantiate and further operationalize the elements of expert behavior.

This paper has tried to highlight some critical differences in diagnostic analysis behavior. It explored differences in the phases of information examination and the formulation of relations. It also demonstrated a surprising lack of diagnostic reasoning processes in student behavior, which was in sharp contrast to the expert's processes of formulating summaries, searching for common problems, and formulating problem–hypotheses. Admittedly, this comparison of two protocols is only a beginning but I hope one that will stimulate further research and development in this area of decision making.

APPENDIX A: A Set of Financial Statements
Case 1

ACCOUNTING INFORMATION

Case 1

Balance sheet/December 31 1970, 1971, 1972, 1973 (in guilders)

	12-31-1970		12-31-1971		12-31-1972		12-31-1973	
Equipment	300000		475000		475000		1250000	
Acc. depreciation	112000 –		144500 –		142000 –		242000 –	
Total value		188000		330500		333000		1008000
Inventories								
Raw materials	36836		62216		90640		67972	
In process	3600		36000		36000		36000	
Finished goods	238800+		240000+		61200+		198600+	
Total		311636		338216		187840		302572
Accounts receivable		47253		21042		85916		23387
Cash		30057		30330		130998		30931
Total Assets		576946		720088		737754		1364890
Capital stock								
f 10 par value	30000		60000		60000		150000	
Premium on capital stock	70000		125850		125850		313400	
Retained earnings	160696+		164396+		172474+		126826+	
Total owners equity		260696		350246		358324		590226
Long-term debt	200000		300000		300000		550000	
Accounts payable	40250		68842		79430		147664	
Notes payable	76000+		1000+		– +		77000+	
Total liabilities		316250		369842		379430		774664
Total equities		576946		720088		737754		1364890

ACCOUNTING INFORMATION

Income statement over 1971, 1972, 1973 (in guilders)

	1971		1972		1973	
Revenues	197400		438400		263550	
Cost of goods sold	110400		326400		146400	
Manufacturing losses (due to a lower efficiency)	4660		2936		4828	
Operating expenses	5520		16320		7320	
Depreciation expenses	47500		47500		125000	
Interest expenses	17120+		19980+		25650+	
Total costs	185200 –		413136 –		309198 –	
Income before taxes	12200		25264		–45648	
Taxes	4800 –		9150 –		–	
Net income	7400		16159		–45648	
Financial ratios						
Net earnings per share = net income after taxes / number of shares	f 2.47	(4.30)*	f 2.69	(7.10)	f –3.04	(7.10)
Return on common equity = net earnings per share / book value of share	0.02	(0.07)*	0.045	(0.12)	–0.08	(0.12)
After-tax return on assets = (income before taxes and interest charges) × (1-tax rate) / total assets	0.035	(0.04)*	0.05	(0.06)	–0.15	(0.06)

*The figures between parentheses are averages of the industry as a whole.

FINANCIAL INFORMATION

Case 1

	12-31-1970		12-31-1971		12-31-1972		12-31-1973	
Short-term debt	f 76000		f 1000		f –		f 77000	
Long-term debt	f 200000		f 300000		f 300000		f 550000	
Equity	f 100000		f 185850		f 185850		f 463400	
Retained earnings	f 160696		f 164396		f 172474		f 126826	
Debt/equity ratio = $\dfrac{\text{long-term debt}}{\text{owners equity} + \text{long-term debt}}$	0.55	(0.50)*	0.51	(0.50)	0.51	(0.50)	0.57	(0.50)
Quick ratio = $\dfrac{\text{cash} + \text{accounts receivable}}{\text{accounts payable} + \text{notes payable}}$	0.67	(1.00)*	0.74	(1.00)	2.74	(1.00)	0.24	(1.00)
Current ratio = $\dfrac{\text{cash} + \text{acc. rec.} + \text{inventories}}{\text{accounts payable} + \text{notes payable}}$	3.35	(2.00)*	5.58	(2.00)	5.10	(2.00)	1.59	(2.00)
Stock market price	f 33.00	(f46.00)*	f 37.00	(f46.00)	f 40.00	(f46.00)	f 27.00	(f46.00)
Interest rate of additional debt	0.05	(0.05)*	0.05	(0.05)	0.05	(0.05)	0.05	(0.05)
Capital cost of additional equity	0.06	(0.06)*	0.05	(0.06)	0.06	(0.06)	0.12	(0.06)
Pay-out ratio = $\dfrac{\text{dividends paid}}{\text{net income after taxes}}$	0.50	(0.50)*	0.50	(0.50)	0.50	(0.50)	0.00	(0.50)

*The figures between parentheses are averages of the industry as a whole.

SALES INFORMATION

Case 1

	1971		1972		1973	
	Units	Guilders	Units	Guilders	Units	Guilders
Demand*	188	f 197400	548	f 438400	251	f 263550
Estimated demand	410	f 430500	682	f 545600	640	f 672000
Units sold	188	f 197400	548	f 438400	251	f 263550
Demand lost**	—	f —	—	f —	—	f —
Market share		0.15		0.30		0.15
Sales price		f 1050		f 800		f 1050
Average sales price (of industry)		f 800		f 1050		f 800
Profit margin = $\dfrac{\text{net income after taxes}}{\text{sales revenue}}$		0.04		0.04		−0.17
Average profit margin (of industry)		(0.10)		(0.10)		(0.10)
Inventory turnover ratio = $\dfrac{\text{sales revenue}}{\text{total inventory}}$		0.63		1.65		1.08
Average inventory turnover ratio (of industry)		(1.50)		(1.50)		(1.50)

*All figures are year totals.
**There is no demand backlog.

Case 1

PRODUCTION INFORMATION

Average capacity*

	1971	1972	1973
Machine A	215	270	505
Machine B	215	270	510
Machine C	215	315	530

*The capacities are expressed in units/year.

Utilization

	1971	1972	1973
Machine A	1.00	0.94	1.00
Machine B	0.93	0.93	1.00
Machine C	1.00	1.00	1.00

	1971	1972	1973
Production planned	195	270	495
Amount produced	190	250	480

Production efficiencies:

	1971	1972	1973
Material efficiency of			
Component A	0.86	0.92	0.86
Component B	0.86	0.86	0.84
Labor efficiency of			
Component A	0.86	0.92	0.86
Component B	0.95	0.99	0.94
Assembly	0.87	0.94	0.84

Inventory levels

	12-31-1970		12-31-1971		12-31-1972		12-31-1973	
Raw materials	f 36836	30**	f 62216	50**	f 90640	25**	f 67972	42**
In process A	f –	–	f –	–	f –	–	f –	–
In process B	f –	–	f –	–	f –	–	f –	–
Finished components A	f 17600	16	f 17600	16	f 17600	6	f 17600	13
Finished components B	f 16000	28	f 16000	28	f 16000	7	f 16000	15
In process/assembly	f 2400	1	f 2400	1	f 2400	1	f 2400	1
Finished goods	f238800	10	f240000	110	f 61200	11	f198600	75

**This figure gives the number of days the firm could operate on this size of inventory (as a constant rate of production).

APPENDIX B: *Two Protocols*

Protocol of subject S9/Case 1*   Time 7:45

E1   CHECK
1.   If we look at case 1, at the balance sheet of 70–71 and further,
     + ...
2.   we then see a large increase + in the capital equipment during the
     more recent years . . . + .
3.   And it appears to be an expansion in the area of buildings or
     machines + ...
4.   The raw materials inventory has, compared + to last year, declined
     somewhat . .
5.   The in-process inventory has remained on the (0.30) same level . . .
6.   And the finished goods inventory . . . + has about tripled . . relative
     to last year, . + . .
7.   but last year that inventory was very small, relative to the years
     + previous to that . .
8.   The total inventory value is at about the same level as during the
     years + 70–71 . . .
9.   Accounts receivable and + cash . . . . have . . declined (1.00), . .
     also again relative to 72 . . . +
10. The total owners equity . . has grown to + 59 thousand . .
11. The total liabilities have + . . . eh . . increased very strongly . .
     to 1 million + 300 thousand . . .
12. So that means a debt/equity ratio of + about . . 2½ to 1 . . . (1.30) . .
13. The sales revenues show a decline + over 1973 relative to 1972 . . . + .
14. The manufacturing losses, the + efficiency losses have . . somewhat
     increased . . . +
15. Operating expenses have decreased.
16. The depreciation expenses have increased very much . . +

E2   EXPLAIN
17. Which, of course, is related to the new acquisitions of last year . . .

E3   CHECK
18. The (2.00) interest expenses have also increased.
19. Total costs . . . + they have added up to a total of 309000 . . .
20. This means + . . that there are no net profits left in this year either
     . . + . .
21. The net earnings per share . . was 2.69 guilders last + year, . . which
     was far below the average of the industry.
22. Has now been turned + into a loss of 3 guilders . . .
23. The return on common equity, . . (2.30)
24. as well as the after-tax return on assets, have also turned negative
     . . + ... +
25. The short-term debt . . . now amounts to 77000 + guilders, . . .
26. and the long-term debt has increased + by 250000 guilders to a
     . . eh . . 550000 + guilders . .
27. The total equity . . . (3.00) . . has also increased enormously . .
28. The retained + earnings have decreased somewhat . . .
29. The debt/equity + ratio . . . is 0.57, + which is also about the
     industry average . . .
30. And as far as this ratio + is concerned the company . . has remained
     at approximately the same level through the years + . . .
31. The quick ratio . . shows a (3.30) figure of 0.24, . . which is very
     low with respect to . . the other companies

32. and especially since it still was 2.74 + last year . . .
33. The current ratio . . has + also fallen back from 5.1 to 1.59, . . + as the company average is 2 . . . + .
34. We see that the stock market price has declined from 40 guilders in 72 (4.00) to 27 guilders in 73 . . . + .
35. The interest rate . . of additional, + of additional debt has remained on 0.05, . .
36. as + the capital cost of additional equity has increased . . . + .
37. There has been no dividend paid out during the last year . + ... (4.30).
38. We see that in 1973 the demand . . shows a large decline + relative to 1972 . . .

E4 EXPLAIN
39. The estimated demand + . . therefore appears to be way too high . . + .

E5 CHECK
40. The amount sold is equal . . to the amount made, +
41. and they have no lost demand . . .
42. The market share + is back again to the level of 1971, . .

E6 PROBLEM FORMULATION
43. Which makes one suspect (5.00) that 1972 has been a one-time thing, . . .
44. which may + very well have led to . . unwarranted expansions . . +

E7 CHECK
45. The sales price of the product . . is also back again to the level + of 1971, . . .
46. which is + above the average sales price of the industry . . + .
47. The company has always had a profit margin of 0.04 . . (5.30) and has now fallen back to minus 0.17 . .
48. And the inventory + turnover ratio is still only a little above 1 . . + ... + . .
49. The average . .the utilization during the periods + 71 72 73 . . . shows + that we have been fully occupied during 1973 (6.00) . .
50. It was less in 1972, while the utilization was high too in 1971 + . . .
51. And that while the capacity was a lot higher in 1973 + . . than in 1972 . . . + .
52. The production planned . . + during 1973 . . was a little bit above the + actual production, . . .
53. was about 200 units above the production of 1972 (6.30) . . . . +
54. With respect to the inventory levels we can now also see that . . the company + got stuck with a large finished goods inventory, . . .
55. and a somewhat + . . and in comparison with last year . . a somewhat smaller raw materials + inventory . . .
56. But no more in process inventory,
57. and a + decent amount of finished components . . . (7.00) . . . . .
58. The raw material + efficiencies are roughly at the 0.85 level . . . +
59. And so are the labor efficiencies.
60. Only . . . for machine B, + the efficiency . . is higher, . . . + . .
61. although it did decrease with respect to 1972 . . + . .

E8 FINAL EVALUATION
62. The impression is that . . (7.30) an incidental demand increase has taken place in 1972, . .

63. that on + the basis of that they have decided to increase
    capacities, . .
64. which has led to + larger expenses for the company,
65. because in 1973 the demand has declined again to the level of
    71 + . . .

Recall of significant facts, subject S9/Case 1

The main thing which I am able to remember is that . . eh . . the
depreciation expenses had increased enormously . . as a consequence of
an expansion . . while however in that same year the demand . . did
decrease . . so they had . . apparently counted on an increase of the
demand . . which did not materialize . . therefore had to make higher
expenses . . and therefore resulted in a loss . . . and as far as these
ratios are concerned . . . eh . . . I just don't remember very much of
that anymore . . . .

*The protocols of subjects S9 and S14 have been translated from Dutch into English. The translation is as
literal as possible. However, occasionally a free translation is used when a literal translation would have
resulted in loss of meaning.

"+" marks 5-second intervals.

Protocol of subject S14/Case 1   Time 18:58

1. I am looking at the balance sheet totals, . . + .
2. and there I see, ... quite a bit + of growth . . from eh 70 to
   71, . + . 72 stable, and then a substantial jump *again* going to
   73 . . + eh.
3. Are there . . any components + which are not company-tied? . .
4. In process inventory, . . (0.30) finished goods, accounts
   receivable, *no* . .
5. The cash policy, + . . it does kind of hit me . . that at the end +
   of 72 they suddenly had a whole lot of cash . . +
6. It looks to me a bit excessive to have so much money available,
   but it could very well be . + .
7. Capital stock . . from 3000 to 6000, + so a stock issue . . eh
   60000 . .
8. And *another* issue over here (1.00) . .
9. We see the same thing in the premium on capital stock . . . + . .
10. The retained earnings + are also increasing regularly . .
11. Wait a minute, . . + it goes . . 160, 164, 172, + . . and then dives
    to 126 + . . .
12. *Well,* in that case we get hold of the income statement, (1.30)
    . . . . . + the income statement . .
13. Production, sales information, + financial information . . ah,
    here + . . .
14. Ah, they indeed really run into + losses in 73 . .
15. Yes, so that means, that then is + the decrease of the retained
    earnings . . . (2.00)
16. Nice for those shareholders who had then bought these shares . . + .
17. Long-term debt . .
18. 316, + 369, 379 . . + 774 . . so the balance ratio + ... + .
19. In 72 about fifty-fifty, . . (2.30) in 73 + . . . excess 77, 60, 77 + . .
20. Well still, isn't it, still a reasonable + solvency . .
21. The liquidity . . what's that one doing . . +
22. Accounts receivable, cash . . + ... (3.00) . . so that is 53000 . . +
    liquid debt . . 147 . + . and 77 accounts payable . . + .

23. Well, . . what the heck + did they do over here . . + . . .
24. Oh, they have made here a huge (3.30) investment . . . + .
25. With what did they cover it? . . . +
26. With . . a 90000 stock issue, . + . and a premium on capital stock . .
27. Yes, that's all + covered *very* well . .
28. Total finished goods inventories increase + . . very . . . (4.00) . .
29. I think I would like . . + . . to see the ratio sales revenues to finished goods inventory . + ... + .
30. 438, 400, . . and in 73 + it tumbles down to 263, . .
31. while the finished goods + inventory is increasing enormously .
32. Yes, . . so they virtually . . started to produce for inventory (4.30) . .
33. And as a consequence . . they are now hurting, + with respect to their financing . .
34. Accounts payable grow large . + .
35. What happens to the accounts receivable, do they still pay well . . .
36. Accounts receivable + are decreasing . .
37. Sales revenues are also decreasing . + .
38. It looks like they've put a little bit of pressure on the accounts receivable, collecting + . .
39. Cash is now a hundred thou, yes . . (5.00)
40. Well, but where are . . those losses . + . .
41. That is, in the first place, . . + . we should just have a look over here . . at the estimate . .
42. The demand + is 188, 548, 251 + . .
43. Yes, here they have completely missed with their estimate .
44. Have made a fail-investment on that basis + . .
45. Estimated demand, 410 . . (5.30) 682 . . 640 + ... + .
46. So they have absolutely not anticipated this decline + of the market . .
47. Market share . . + ... let's have + a look . . . . . (6.00)
48. They increase it from 71 to 72, . . and in 73 they fall back again to their + own old market share . . . .
49. So did + they have any incidental sales possibilities?
50. What is the industry + doing over here . . .
51. There are no . + . . oh, yes, you do have them, of course, you have the industry figures through + the market share.
52. The industry sales hold their own . .(6.30)
53. Let's see . . yes, it does hold its own . . +
54. But *they* have been intoxicated by . . a small market success + ... +
55. Average sales price . . 1050 + 800 . .
56. What is again the difference between sales price + in guilders and average sales price?
57. Oh, *industry* average, yes . . yes (7.00) . . .
58. *Here* they were below the industry + with their price, . . . and *here* they raise above it . + .
59. Yes, this could point at a wrong market policy . + . .
60. Yes, because it is *one* homogeneous product . . +
61. So they are not using the product mix,
62. they are not playing with the + product specifications.
63. They are playing with the price, and that goes wrong . .
64. That's about it, (7.30) isn't it . . . . eh
65. Sales price, . . + do I see it right, . . here they are below the market,
66. adjust themselves to the + market, . . . but alas . . + . .
67. A pretty good chance that they have been operating exactly against the market trend,

68. that their competitors . + . have started to reduce prices on the basis of the prices that *they* were asking . . here . .
69. And now they + are stuck . . . .
70. The profit margin is (8.00) small, . . also relative to the industry, the industry is at 0.10, and they are only + at 0.04, so that . .
71. Inventory turnover 0.63, + 1.65, 1.08, . . . the industry is + at 1.5 . . . + . .
72. Now let's have a look again at this return . + ... (8.30) . . . . + .
73. After-tax return on assets . . + 0.035, 0.04, . . 0.05, + 0.06, . . so they again are a little bit below the industry . . + .
74. But a rather meager return on assets . + .
75. What do they have to pay for borrowed money . . (9.00)
76. There is something given about that over here, I believe . .
77. Rate of . + .*additional* debt, oh, that is 0.05 . .
78. So + . . here we've got the situation . . + that the leverage is *indifferent* to . . the marginal + debt . . . + .
79. And what is the return on the common equity? . . . eh (9.30)
80. Do I have that one too, return on common equity, . . 0.02, + . . that is just terrible . . + 0.045 . . .
81. And on that basis + there is a stock issue! . . . + . .
82. And, and the tax rate, + how much is that one, ... 0.05 . . (10.00) . . . . . +
83. (other side of tape)
84. 40 percent, I would say, a bit below that, 35 percent . .
85. Yes, + . . in that case a return on assets of 0.05 is, of course, too low + . .
86. Particularly, given that this interest rate of debt, of additional debt is 0.05 + . . .
87. I don't understand . . . that they succeeded with this + stock issue, . . . given these figures . . (10.30)
88. For they did do . . . + ...
89. Stock market + price, of a 10 guilders share I assume, . . yes, + 27, 40 to 27 . .
90. The balance sheet book + value . . . + . .
91. Ah, wait a minute, yes, . . the balance sheet book value, that's of course what they are being fooled by (11.00) . . . . . + . .
92. There are . . 6000 shares with a quotation + of . . of way over 30 . . + . . .
93. Are they still paying any dividend?
94. Yes, I'll + bet they do, because of this stock issue . . . + .
95. Dividends, . . eh . . (11.30) half of the profits . .
96. And + how much is that in absolute, eh per share, dividends per share . . +
97. (E: Here you have given the profits per share . . .)
98. Oh, yes, . . + . profits per share . . is, so + eh, so dividends per share is 100, . . is f 1.20 + per 10, so 12 percent, . . (12.00) . . . 12, let's see, eh.
99. So dividend is + . . 120 and 130, . . + f 1.20, f 1.30 . .
100. And owners equity per share, + . . do we have that as well, somewhere over here, or do I have to compute that myself + ... + ... (12.30) . . . . +
101. Financial information + ... + ... + ... + ... (13.00) . . .
102. I just see, in passing, that the quick ratio + is getting abominable in 12-31-73 . .
103. Even though it still was fine in + the year before that.
104. Is of course also a bit understandable . . . +

105. And the current ratio, of course, goes down in a similar manner . .
106. Yes, + . . eh owners equity, . . this is the + market value per share, that was f 40.00 over here (13.30) . .
107. And they get . . f 1.30 + . . .
108. So that means, + . . eh . . a . + . coupon eh, a dividend yield of . . 3 + to 4 percent . . .
109. Well, in that case, + . . a quotation . . in the order of magnitude of 40 guilders is (14.00)
110. This issue, it . . has, considering the growth in the premium on capital stock, . . it has also been sizeable . +
111. That can only be motivated if there have been considerable growth expectations . .
112. Which haven't come through . + . .
113. Well, is that caused by the production or is it caused by the sales . + .
114. I must see whether we can find out some more over here . .
115. Estimated demand + . . yes, that market estimate has been way off over here . +
116. The pricing policy, we have seen that already, . . should have a question mark placed behind it.
117. So that may (14.30) explain a lot . . . .
118. Do we have + any data about sales expenses . . . + .
119. Income statement . .
120. Cost of goods + sold . .
121. Due to a lower efficiency . . + .
122. Operating expenses.
123. Depreciation expenses . .
124. (E: The sales expenses are part of the operating + expenses.)
125. Yes, so the, . . yes, you see, (15.00) typical operating expenses . .
126. From 71 to 72, . . + tripled, just to decline again to less than half + . .
127. That really would also require more detailed information about what has happened here, and about what + has been booked on operating expenses, respectively.
128. Did they also hide there . + . these issue costs . .
129. Yes, but then this should also have happened in the following year + . .
130. And that again does not appear to . . (15.30) . . . . + ... +
131. Finished goods inventory, 110, 110, . . 11, so then + they *really* started to sell . . .
132. And now this finished goods inventory has pretty much come back up again + ...
133. Planned + .
134. The capacities, . . . machine A, B, C, (16.00) . . 500 . . +
135. The production efficiencies . . from 0.92 + to 0.86, . . they are not terribly . + ... + . .
136. The utilization, + where is that one . .
137. (E: It's at the top of this page) (16.30) . .
138. Oh, yes . . . 1, + 0.93, 1 . . . 0.94, 0.93, 1, + 1, 1, 1, 1, . . + . . so the rate of utilization is . . . 100 + percent . .
139. Capacity of 505, 530 + . . .
140. And their production is only (17.00) 480 . . . . +
141. Yes, but if I compare 480 + with this 530, . . . then I don't have a utilization + of 1, isn't it, . . . then I stay below, . . . below 1 +
142. (E: That is due to the production efficiency . .)
143. Oh, + that's where this efficiency mess comes back again, . . yes . . (17.30) . . .

144. Only I can't see, + what this lower efficiency actually *costs* . .
145. I see, . + . . *wait* a minute, here of course, there is still something to look at . . + .
146. Amount produced 190, . . and those + , those are good products that are being finished . . .
147. Capacity big enough . + .
148. 250 here . . (18.00) .
149. Yes, taking into account the efficiency losses, they may + have run into capacity problems over here.
150. And here 1 . + .
151. Yes, what plays a role here as well is how you define the whole business, isn't it?
152. Whether you only look at the accepted production + when you're calculating the utilization.
153. Or whether you also include the rejected production, or disposed of production, + or whatever you call it, . . waste production, . . whether you take that into account as well . + .
154. (E: Yes, there is a lot of information one would need (18.30) in order to develop a complete picture. That information is not given. The objective of this analysis, however, only is to develop a general impression, + and to indicate, for instance, the areas where you suspect certain problems, + the areas where you would want more information. That would be a conclusion.)
155. Well, the marketing + is . . . .
156. Their expectations have been completely wrong over here, that really would be a final conclusion + . .
157. Yes, . . because they have the insolence to increase prices,
158. and then, + the competition goes down.
159. Consequence: . . sales gone.

An Information-Processing Model of Intrafirm Dynamics and Their Effects upon Organizational Perceptions, Strategies, and Choices

Francis D. Tuggle, *Rice University*
Donald Gerwin, *University of Wisconsin-Milwaukee*

A synthesis of the two areas of corporate strategy and organization theory provides a broader conception of the organization useful in organizational design, theory development, and policymaking. One attempt to synthesize the two is to be found in Tuggle and Gerwin (1980). By itself, the corporate strategy literature views the policymaker as a focal point while placing less emphasis on the context in which he or she operates. It has also tended to be atheoretical and lacking in empirical orientation (Mintzberg 1975c). Organization theory focuses on the context within which the enterprise's decisions are made at the expense of the study of strategic choice. It has been characterized by theoretical developments and offers considerable empirical results. Tuggle and Gerwin (1980) demonstrated via an information-processing simulation model of organizational perception, policymaking, and choice that precise theories of the strategic decision-making process are, at once, a way of synthesizing these two views and, at the same time, a way of ascertaining some of their limitations.

In this paper, we report on an extension of that earlier computer-simulation model, an extension which explicitly considers the effects of organizational coalitions upon the simulated firm's perceptions, strategies, choices, and eventual performance. This extension, and the implications drawn from its effects, illustrate the range of powerful conclusions which may be derived from an information-processing synthesis of corporate strategy and organization theory ideas, precepts, and principles.

By adopting an information-processing approach, the axes of organizational design issues revolve around the symbol-processing, problem-solving, and decision-making systems of the firm. The three central issues of organizational design therefore are (1) what data from their environments, both external and internal, should firms be sensitive to, (2) what processing mechanisms should the firm apply to that set of extracted signals, and (3) what actions should the firm take based upon the results of applying those processing mechanisms to the extracted data? As opposed to many other research designs, information-processing simulation models provide the experimenter with the flexibility and power to try a wide variety of organizational designs in a multitude of environments in order to inductively develop assertions of comparative advantage. The level of detail present in the information-processing simulation models either ties the results to a specific industry (or firm, in the case of a great deal of specificity in the model) or captures broad characteristics of many organizations. We adopt the latter course for the present study.

The Information-Processing Approach

The information-processing (IP) approach (for example, Cohen, March, and Olsen 1972; Cyert and March 1963; March and Simon 1958; Miles and Snow 1978) provides a way of developing a testable theory of contextual effects on organizational choice and of organizational impacts on the environment in which corporate strategy plays a fundamental role. The questions addressed by the IP approach include: Where do problems originate? When problems occur simultaneously, which one is attended to first? How are problems dealt with? What are the factors that affect choice? And how are choices made? The IP approach deals with all of these issues by focusing attention both on the amount and type of information available to problem solvers and decision makers and on the step-by-step processes of information usage.

The IP approach views the organization as an interrelated set of symbol-processing, problem-solving, and decision-making systems. Each subsystem inputs information which defines the problem it must solve, assembles a program of action using general decision-making methods, and outputs an answer which serves as part of the input for other systems. Many of these problems are well structured, in that there exist fairly complete definitions of the situation and reasonably precise general methods for devising programs. They typically involve middle- and lower-level managerial decisions made within the context of overall corporate strategy. Virtually all existing applications of the IP framework have studied well-structured, routine operating problems such as pricing and output determination (Cyert and March 1963), trust investment (Clarkson 1962), advertising (Rados 1972), and budgeting (Weber 1965). Unstructured problems are characterized by hazy input information and vague general methods from which policies rather than programs must be fashioned. Corporate strategy formulation is an example. Unfortunately, the IP approach has virtually never been applied to this issue, an exception being Carter's (1971) qualitative account of investments and acquisitions in a computing services company.

In order to rigorously apply the IP framework, it is necessary to develop a systematic characterization of the strategic decision-making process. Arguing by analogy with the process of scientific discovery (Kuhn 1969), one can posit that the process consists of at least seven phases: (1) existence of an organizational crisis; (2) pattern-finding activity; (3) a new environmental theory to explain regularities in events; (4) a new corporate strategy based on the theory; (5) elaboration of theory and strategy; (6) observation of a critical anomaly; and (7) wait for Phase 1 to recur.

Every organization possesses some theory of its environment or model of the world (Beer 1973). An environmental theory may indicate the pertinent organization, the ways in which the external institutions are related to each other (the casual texture of the environment according to Emery and Trist 1965), and how these relationships change over time. An environmental theory is needed for the development of organizational strategy because it allows predictions of the consequences of administrative actions. When a theory and its associated policy are generally accepted they are likely to serve as a set of decision premises for the organization. They provide a basic framework, by specifying problem statements, criteria, and methods, within which further elaboration of both theory and policy is carried out. Thus, while a particular set is in force, much organizational decision making can be of the well-structured variety.

How can we account for the successive transitions from one set of premises to another which result in fundamental reorientations in theory and policy? Since no environmental theory is perfect, because it is continually being extended, and because the environment is changing, there will always be events it cannot explain. Eventually, a set of events may occur that question the very basis of the decision premises. The events can neither be disregarded nor the theory adjusted to explain them. The resulting anomaly is likely to be associated with an organizational crisis and therefore, may provide the motivation for attempting to find new ways of explaining environmental data. This will involve a search for patterns or regularities in the anomalous data from which to construct a new theory. Even if some individuals in the organization are able to articulate a new set of premises, they will probably find it difficult to convince others of their new view. Because holders of competing sets interpret facts in different ways, rational arguments are not very useful. The result may be a temporary immobilization of the firm with change likely to come only from an outside force. A case study by Emery and Trist (1965) illustrates this view.

The EPASP2 Model

Overview

In order to explicate and investigate these relationships between environmental theories, corporate strategy, and procedures of decision making, a computer-simulation model has been developed. It is called EPASP, for Environmental Perceiver and Strategy Planner (see Tuggle and Gerwin 1980). (A complete listing of the model is available from the authors.) EPASP has been designed for a hypothetical profitmaking firm since it is straightforward to evaluate the performance of such organizations by quantitative metrics such as dollar profits, unit price, dollar costs, unit inventory, and unit production.

EPASP2 is an extension of EPASP. EPASP2 presumes a business firm with a functional form of organizational structure, one having three major departments: marketing, production, and finance. EPASP2 explicitly considers the effects of each department having its own unique set of organizational preferences and deriving its own perceptions of the state of the world by filtering data according to its own needs and desires. Naturally, the departments repeatedly form and dissolve temporary coalitions, either to freeze out the third department or to try to combat corporate headquarters. A complete program listing of EPASP2 is to be found in the appendix (pp. 186–194).

A variety of model forms are available to express this model of organizational perceptions, strategies, and choices: verbal, analytic, and simulation, among others. Verbal models have the virtue of being able to capture subtle nuances in behavior, yet do so at the expense of parsimony. Analytic models are quite explicit about assumptions and predictions yet occasionally sacrifice reality for tractability. Simulation models represent a midpoint of all those features, both desirable and undesirable. We rejected the verbal form of model, as we desired a model which would utter reasonably specific predictions from different settings of input parameters. We rejected the analytic model form, as neither closed-form results nor tractability was particularly relevant for our study. The simulation-model form seemed to represent an agreeable compromise for EPASP and EPASP2. Svenson (1979, p. 94) agrees with this choice, arguing that the simulation approach ". . . is much needed at the present stage of our knowledge about individual decision making."

Basically, EPASP and EPASP2 are structured around the flow of information and intelligence activities as stated by Child (1972). Figure 1 provides a depiction of this structure. The firm perceives its environment and posits a theory of the world in which it must function. From those data, the wishes of the dominant coalition, the perceived strengths and weaknesses of the firm, and the history of the firm's products, markets, and performance, a strategy is developed. The strategy, which determines how the firm will deploy its resources, is then translated into day-to-day operating decisions. For example, personnel are hired, products are produced, research and development are performed, and warehouses are stocked. Finally, the effects of the operating decisions may eventually feed back to influence management's desires and the firm's environment. In this paper, we shall concentrate on examining the differences between EPASP2 and EPASP; that is, we shall consider most carefully the role of the wishes of the dominant coalition.

EPASP2 fits within the tradition of IP models. It addresses the symbol-processing, problem-solving, and decision-making systems of the firm via information creation, transmission, and use. It contains aspects of routine choice procedures (how many goods to produce during a time period), well-structured choice procedures (how many goods to produce when product quality has been changed), and unstructured choice procedures (when to change product quality and by how much). EPASP2 addresses the process of strategic choice; it has several perceptual components. It links perception with strategy formulation, strategy formulation with well-structured choice procedures, well-structured choice procedures with routine ones, and routine choice procedures with the state of the firm's environment, which in turn links back to the firm's perceptions.

Organization

EPASP2 is organized as a main program and seven subprograms. The main program reads in the values of thirteen parameters determined by the user and

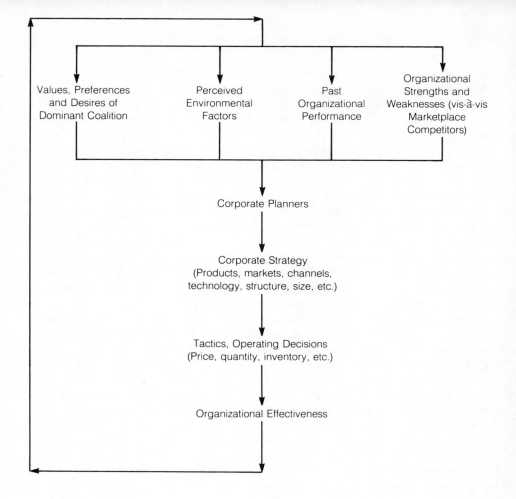

FIGURE 1   The Perception-Strategy-Operating Processes

sets initial values for several variables such as cost coefficients. It also sets up a loop which tests the number of time periods, as specified by the user, to call on the subprograms.

The function RANDO1, used only by DEMAND, produces a pseudorandomly distributed variate according to the normal distribution with a mean of zero and a standard deviation of one.

The subroutine DEMAND calculates current market demand and current market price. The level of demand is found by adjusting a base level for trend, the current stage of the business cycle, and a random fluctuation whose mean and variance are specified by the user. A similar process generates the market price. The user is free to establish *any* desired relationship between demand

and price. Our firm is a price taker in the sense that it cannot affect the quantity demanded or the price offered. It can change the *apparent* quantity and price by altering the product quality or type in the subroutine STRTGY. However, this is a shift in demand curves or markets rather than the firm's proactive intervention within a market. Furthermore, demand is treated as an aggregated mass. A more elaborate model than EPASP2 could segment consumers into clusters and depict the firm's distinctive interaction with each segment. Then it would be possible to investigate the effects on the firm of different brand loyalties, and the ways the firm can change brand loyalty through advertising and product characteristics.

The subroutine PERCEV chooses a theory of the firm's marketplace. Five different theories are possible: (1) STAB, the market is mostly stable; (2) UP, there is some mild growth in the market which means either the firm's market share is increasing, or its share is constant and underlying demand as a whole is growing; (3) OPOR, there is explosive growth in the market leading to an opportunity for the firm; (4) DOWN, there is a mild decline in the market; or (5) CRIS, there is a precipitous decline in the market leading to a crisis for the firm. Which environmental theory is adopted by the firm depends upon corporate headquarter's perception of and sensitivity to changes in profits, unit demand, and price over time and upon the perceptions of the functional subgroups. If perceptions don't change for three consecutive periods, the firm *adopts* the current level of operations as the new status quo position. In other words, the firm *adapts* its baseline perception.

Strictly speaking, EPASP2 is only capable of making parametric changes within a given market theory rather than being able to intuit a revolutionary new theory equally descriptive of market conditions. Miles and Snow (1978) also describe four adaptive organizational forms (defender, prospector, analyzer, and reactor) without describing how one organizational form could be switched to another. However, EPASP2's modest theory switching is sufficient to exhibit nontrivial phenomena. The modeling of true theory inducement and shift will prove to be quite challenging (for example, see Gerwin and Newsted 1977).

The subroutine DOMCOL calculates the current perceptions of the marketing, production, and finance departments and then aggregates their preferences into those of the coalition. The marketing department has an unvarying preference for (in decreasing order) first, unit demand increasing, second, falling prices, and third, increasing inventories. If all three of these conditions hold, the marketing department feels that the whole firm needs a more optimistic theory. If only the first two conditions are met, the marketing department feels that continuation of the current theory is in order. Otherwise, they opt for a more pessimistic view of the world.

The ordered preferences of the production department are for first, manufacturing costs falling, second, inventory levels falling (note the conflict with the marketing department), and third, number of units produced rising. Like the marketing department, the production department feels that a more optimistic theory is needed only if all three conditions are realized. If only the first two conditions are met, the production department favors continuation of the current theory. Otherwise, the production department prefers a more pessimistic theory.

The ordered preferences of the finance department are for first, costs falling, second, number of units produced falling (note the conflict with the production department), and third, inventory levels falling (note the conflict with the marketing department). In line with the other two departments, the finance department feels that a more optimistic theory is called for only if all three conditions are met. The finance department favors continuation of the current theory only if the first two conditions alone are satisfied. Otherwise, the finance department prefers a less optimistic theory.

Finally, the perceptions of the three departments are aggregated. If the perceptions of any two departments agree, that coalition's preference is taken as the aggregation, unless the third department prefers the polar opposite theory, in which case the compromise choice is for the status quo. See Figure 2 for a representation of these relationships.

In subroutine PERCEV, corporate headquarters makes use of the aggregate preferences emanating from the three operating departments. That advice is ignored if corporate profits are falling or if corporate profits are rising at a rate exceeding the corporation's sensitivity. Also, if the departmental advice is to continue the status quo theory, corporate headquarters will examine changes in demand and price to see whether a more optimistic or pessimistic theory is called for from their perspective. Otherwise, corporate headquarters adopts the advice from its three operating departments.

The subroutine STRTGY formulates a strategy based upon the firm's past environmental theory, current environmental theory, and current environmental conditions. Given different "contexts," the *same* environmental theory can result in *different* corporate strategies being formulated. For example, consider a firm which perceives a mild growth market. A choice to track that growth will depend upon contextual factors such as whether or not there are sufficient resources and how accurate past perceptions have been. The base strategy is to maintain the status quo, which means to continue the current mode of operation.

Four types of modifications may be made to the base strategy. The first is to improve the quality of its products, which results in a rise in prices, an increase in demand, an increase in costs, and additional plant capacity. Usually, after the firm improves the quality of its products, it goes back to a status quo strategy but at a different base level. The second strategy is to enter new markets, possibly with new products. This causes a large increase in costs and necessitates a huge addition in plant capacity. It also results in higher prices for any new products now offered and higher total demand. The third strategy is to use cheaper input materials and less skilled labor and to close down some of the productive machinery. This lessens costs, but demand falls due to the inferior nature of the products offered, and the market can only support a lower price for the firm's goods. The fourth strategy is for the firm to significantly consolidate its market position by reducing the size of its product line, closing some plants and warehouse sites, laying off personnel, and withdrawing from some markets. This produces major cost savings but also significantly

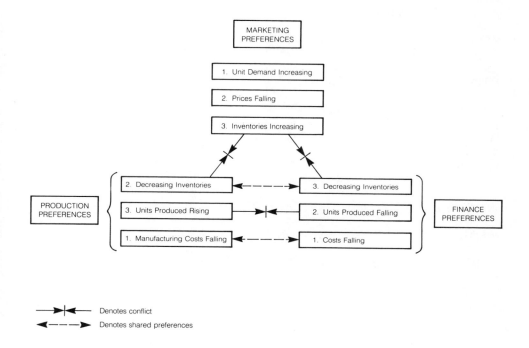

FIGURE 2   Interactions Between Departmental Preferences (for EPASP2's Subroutine DOMCOL)

reduces demand for its remaining products and the prices they command.

The DECIDE subroutine makes standard operating decisions for the firm such as how much to produce, whether overtime should be scheduled, how much to sell, and how much to put in inventory.

The PRINTO subroutine prints out each time period's results including demand, price, perception, strategy, inventory, unit sales, dollar sales, costs, profits, and cumulative profits.

Input Data

Figure 3 indicates a sample dialog between program and user. The user must enter thirteen data values for the dialog to proceed. Table 1 shows the range of parameter settings used for the computer runs performed to date.

The first four parameters are self-explanatory. The fifth, the business cycle, is sinusoidal with period equal to the number typed in. By setting the sixth

```
RUN
WHAT IS THE BASE DEMAND, IN UNITS?
2000
WHAT IS THE BASE PRICE, IN DOLLARS AND CENTS?
10.00
HOW MANY PERIODS DO YOU WANT TO SIMULATE?
18
WHAT IS THE (PLUS OR MINUS) GROWTH TREND?
        (IN THE FORM  . XXX . . . . .)
−.05
WHAT IS THE LENGTH OF THE BUSINESS CYCLE?
        (IT MUST BE A POSITIVE, NONZERO NUMBER.)
6
WHAT IS THE MAX AMPLITUDE OF THE CYCLE?
400
WHAT IS THE MEAN OF THE ERROR DEFLECTION?
0
WHAT IS THE STANDARD DEVIATION OF THE ERROR?
100
WHAT IS THE TREND IN MARKET PRICE?
        (IN THE FORM . XXX . . . . .)
.1
WHAT IS THE MEAN OF THE ERROR IN PRICE?
0
WHAT IS THE STANDARD DEVIATION IN PRICE ERROR?
1.0
WHAT IS THE FIRM'S ENVIRONMENTAL THEORY?
        (IT SHOULD BE ONE OF THE FOLLOWING)
            'OPOR'
            'UP'
            'STAB'
            'DOWN'
            'CRIS'
STAB
WHAT IS THE TEST CRITERION FOR THEORY CHANGE?
.5
```

FIGURE 3   Sample Input to EPASP2

parameter to zero, the business cycle is suppressed. All computer runs used a value of six for the length of the business cycle.

The seventh and eighth parameters are the mean and standard deviation, respectively, of the error in generating the units demanded. Setting both to zero makes the process error-free; setting only the mean to zero produces an unbiased random fluctuation. The tenth and eleventh parameters are the mean and standard deviation for the error in price, and they are analogous to the seventh and eighth parameters.

The twelfth parameter is the firm's initial theory of its marketplace. As mentioned earlier, there are five possibilities: OPOR, for an opportunity situa-

TABLE 1   Parameters and Range of Parameters

PARAMETER NUMBER	PARAMETER NAME	RANGE OF VALUES USED
1	Base demand	2,000 units
2	Base price	$10.00
3	Length of simulation run	18 periods
4	Growth trend in units demanded (percent of base)	−20%, −10%, −5%, 0%, +5%, +10%, +20%
5	Length of business cycle	6 periods
6	Maximum cycle amplitude (percent of base demand)	40%, 20%, 5%, 0%
7	Error in demand (mean)	0
8	Error in demand (standard deviation)	25%, 10%, 5%, 0%
9	Growth trend in price (percent of base)	−20%, −10%, −5%, 0%, +5%, +10%, +20%
10	Error in price (mean)	0
11	Error in price (standard deviation)	25%, 10%, 5%, 0%
12	Environmental theory	OPOR, UP, STAB, DOWN, CRIS
13	Environmental sensitivity	1.0, .5, .1

tion; UP, for mild growth; STAB, for stability; DOWN, for mild decline; and CRIS, for a crisis situation. The thirteenth parameter indicates the firm's willingness to change its perception of the environment, that is, its sensitivity to environmental change. A value of 1.0 implies that key variables such as profit, demand, and price have to change in value by 100% before the firm changes its theory. Using the value of 0.5, the key variables only have to change by 50%, and so forth.

Output from EPASP2

In order to illustrate the types of phenomena generated by the model, consider Figure 4, which indicates what is printed out when the input data are as in Figure 3. Figure 4 traces the history of the firm for periods 3, 4, and 5, when the firm is faced by a cyclical market with unbiased error in both demand and price, a modest long-term downward decline in demand, and a somewhat larger growth trend in price.

In period 3, all three departments are in favor of a more pessimistic theory — marketing because demand has dropped from 2435 to 1978 units, production because costs have risen from $22,707.25 to $24,634.57, and finance for the

THE SALES DEPT. IS IN FAVOR OF
  A MORE PESSIMISTIC THEORY
THE MANUFACTURING DEPT. IS IN FAVOR OF
  A MORE PESSIMISTIC THEORY
THE FINANCE DEPT. IS IN FAVOR OF
  A MORE PESSIMISTIC THEORY
THE CHOICE OF THE COALITION IS FOR
  A MORE PESSIMISTIC THEORY
THE CURRENT DEMAND IN PERIOD 3 IS 1978. UNITS,
  WHILE THE CURRENT PRICE IS $13.18
THE FIRM'S CURRENT ENVIRONMENTAL THEORY IS STAB
THE FIRM'S CURRENT STRATEGY IS TO
  KEEP THE STATUS QUO FOR THE NEXT PERIOD
THE INVENTORY IS NOW 2549. UNITS
    ON SALES OF 1978. UNITS, WHICH PRODUCES
    REVENUES OF $26077.85 WHILE EXPERIENCING
    COSTS OF $22903.40   THERE WERE
    CURRENT PROFITS TO THE FIRM OF $3174.45
     YIELDING CUMULATIVE PROFITS OF $1958.58

THE SALES DEPT. IS IN FAVOR OF
  A MORE PESSIMISTIC THEORY
THE MANUFACTURING DEPT. IS IN FAVOR OF
  THE STATUS QUO THEORY
THE FINANCE DEPT. IS IN FAVOR OF
  A MORE OPTIMISTIC THEORY
THE CHOICE OF THE COALITION IS FOR
  THE STATUS QUO THEORY
THE CURRENT DEMAND IN PERIOD 4 IS 1522. UNITS,
  WHILE THE CURRENT PRICE IS $14.28
THE FIRM'S CURRENT ENVIRONMENTAL THEORY IS STAB
THE FIRM'S CURRENT STRATEGY IS TO
  KEEP THE STATUS QUO FOR THE NEXT PERIOD
THE INVENTORY IS NOW 2585. UNITS
    ON SALES OF 1522. UNITS, WHICH PRODUCES
    REVENUES OF $21735.30 WHILE EXPERIENCING
    COSTS OF $20507.89   THERE WERE
    CURRENT PROFITS TO THE FIRM OF $1227.41
     YIELDING CUMULATIVE PROFITS OF $3185.99

THE SALES DEPT. IS IN FAVOR OF
  A MORE PESSIMISTIC THEORY
THE MANUFACTURING DEPT. IS IN FAVOR OF
  A MORE PESSIMISTIC THEORY
THE FINANCE DEPT. IS IN FAVOR OF
  THE STATUS QUO THEORY
THE CHOICE OF THE COALITION IS FOR
  A MORE PESSIMISTIC THEORY
THE CURRENT DEMAND IN PERIOD 5 IS 1271. UNITS,
  WHILE THE CURRENT PRICE IS $13.84

THE FIRM'S CURRENT ENVIRONMENTAL THEORY IS DOWN
THE FIRM'S CURRENT STRATEGY IS TO
   USE CHEAPER LABOR AND INPUT FACTORS
THE INVENTORY IS NOW 2561. UNITS
         ON SALES OF 1271. UNITS, WHICH PRODUCES
         REVENUES OF $17590.97 WHILE EXPERIENCING
         COSTS OF $16536.59   THERE WERE
         CURRENT PROFITS TO THE FIRM OF $1054.38
            YIELDING CUMULATIVE PROFITS OF $4240.37

FIGURE 4   Sample Output from EPASP2

same cost reason. Corporate headquarters chooses to ignore this advice as profits have increased dramatically — from a loss of $469.83 to a profit of $3,174.45. The reasons for the turnaround are that prices have increased about 10% while volume has remained roughly constant, and production fell in the period by 52 units.

In period 4, the three departments disagree with one another so only a status quo recommendation evolves, which agrees with the perceptions of corporate headquarters and so it is readily assimilated. The marketing department sees demand falling from 1978 units to 1522 units and so is pessimistic. The production department experienced a drop in costs (from $24,634.57 to $22,903.40) but the number of units produced dropped by 420 units. Thus, they favor the status quo. Meanwhile, the finance department pushes for an optimistic theory as costs dropped, the number of units produced fell, and the level of inventory slackened (from 2579 to 2549 units). The firm plunges forward with an unchanged strategy, and, thanks to reduced production and another 10% hike in prices, again enjoys a sizeable profit ($1,227.41).

Finally, in period 5 (the last one reported here although this run continues on through period 18), two departments (marketing and production) temporarily coalesce to advocate a more pessimistic theory; theirs becomes the collective judgment of the three operating departments, and it is accepted by corporate headquarters. Note that the firm's environmental theory is now "DOWN" and that its strategy has changed to include the use of cheaper labor and input factors. The marketing department is again pessimistic as demand continues to drop, to 1271 units. The manufacturing department is pessimistic, as it found an increase in inventory from 2549 units to 2585 units (due to unsold items) coupled with a decrease in the number of units produced. As a result of the firm using cheaper labor and input factors, it is still able to exhibit a comfortable profit ($1,054.38).

Simulation Results from EPASP

Before we go on to discuss the performance of EPASP2, it should be helpful to know the results of the EPASP simulation first, as a basis for comparison. About fifty computer runs were made with EPASP to study three intuitively obvious hypotheses about strategy formulation. The model showed them to be valid only if they are narrowly qualified. Furthermore, it allowed one to deduce why those propositions needed to be refined. Although a variety of performance metrics were available to study these hypotheses, the status of the cumulative profits was chosen since it captures, albeit crudely, the stock-holders' valuation of a firm. The three simplistic hypotheses shown to be in need of more narrow qualification were (with the qualifications added):

Hypothesis 1: A firm will do better, in terms of larger cumulative profits, in a more munificent environment than in a less munificent one. Qualification: This is true only to the extent it has slack resources to exploit the munificence.

Hypothesis 2: A firm more sensitive to random changes in its environment will outperform a less sensitive firm. Qualification: This is true if the market environment contains business cycles.

Hypothesis 3: The less predictable is a firm's environment, the worse that firm will perform. Qualification: This is true to the extent that the firm lacks slack resources and is relatively sensitive to environmental changes.

These three hypotheses and EPASP were "validated" by illustrating their consistency with a variety of business policy cases: the *Saturday Evening Post*, the J. I. Case Company, and the watch industries in Switzerland, Japan, and the United States, especially the Timex Corporation. Flushed with the apparent success of EPASP, the authors developed EPASP2 and now will report on the salient performance differences of EPASP2 as compared with EPASP.

Performance of EPASP2

Many of the computer runs of EPASP were compared against a "baseline" run. In the baseline condition, demand was a *constant* 2000 units, price was a *constant* $10 per unit, the business cycle was suppressed, and there were no errors or fluctuations in prices or quantities. In EPASP, the simulated baseline firm earned a constant $3,000 profit per period, for a total of $54,000 profit over the total 18 simulated periods.

Experiments with EPASP then consisted of varying one or more of the input parameters and comparing the resultant computer output to the baseline computer output. For example, one of the experiments involved changing only one input parameter: It was established that price would increase 5% each period. This results in total profits to the firm (that is, at the end of 18 periods) of $76,950, while the profit in the last period alone is $5,550. The difference in profitability between the two computer runs ($22,950 total profit and $2,550 18th period profit) can be attributed *solely* to the parametric changes, that is, in this case, the effects of a constant 5% growth in price.

For reasons discussed next, there is no natural "baseline" condition with EPASP2. Even when EPASP2 is run on the "baseline" parameter settings of EPASP, which represents as much external environmental constancy as we could build into the system, the *internal* environment of the simulated firm contains its own dynamics, which in turn prevents constancy from occurring. For example, when running EPASP2 on the "baseline" parameter settings for EPASP, in the very first period the marketing and production departments collude to force the entire organization to change its perceptions of the environment from STAB to UP, with a resulting change in strategy. Further internal dynamics ensue. Over the 18 periods, EPASP2 on the "baseline" conditions exhibits 9 changes in perceptions and strategy. Instead of earning a constant $3,000 per period, EPASP2's earnings vary from a low of $1,557.61 (period 2) to a high of $4,951.14 (periods 15 and 16). Instead of total earnings over the 18 periods of $54,000, EPASP2 earned $51,257.12. One can only attribute the difference (negative $2,472.88) to the presence of coalitional dynamics, as that is the *only* difference between EPASP and EPASP2. Let us state the issue more clearly and forcefully: there is a significant cost to the firm emanating from intrafirm disagreements.

However, perhaps there is an advantage to the firm from having different perspectives on its external environmental situation. Perhaps by being sensitive to a wider range of environmental phenomena, the firm in EPASP2 will prove to be more adaptable to more complex environments. Table 2 contains the data which allow one to resolve these open questions.

Table 2 contains a list of a variety of external environmental conditions, their specification in terms of variation from the "baseline" conditions, the total 18-period profitability of EPASP, and the total 18-period profitability of EPASP2. In teasing out the effects of having shifting coalitions in EPASP2, one can compare that performance to three other items: (1) the same condition in EPASP; (2) the "baseline" in EPASP; and (3) the "baseline" performance of EPASP2. These comparisons are reported in the form of percentage ratios in

TABLE 2   Environmental Conditions, Variations, and Profitability

| | TOTAL PROFITABILITY OF | |
CONDITION	EPASP	EPASP2
BASELINE	$ 54,000.00	$ 51,257.12
MUNIFICENCE		
+20% growth in units demanded	47,723.01	46,528.35
+ 5% growth in units demanded	57,400.00	53,432.10
+20% growth in price	145,800.00	22,559.18
+ 5% growth in price	76,950.00	13,118.36
ADVERSITY		
−20% drop in units demanded	−20,098.84	−25,071.72
− 5% drop in units demanded	37,268.81	14,747.44
−20% drop in price	7,475.25	4,694.22
− 5% drop in price	31,050.00	28,350.27
BUSINESS CYCLE		
Maximum cycle amplitude is 40% of base	−20,759.57	−3,027.64
Maximum cycle amplitude is 20% of base	28,137.42	9,540.98
Maximum cycle amplitude is 5% of base	32,672.46	14,968.05
ERRORS		
5% fluctuation in both price and demand	34,151.06	12,435.49
10% fluctuation in both price and demand	29,998.64	12,435.82

TABLE 3   Environmental Conditions, Variations, and Profitability

| | COMPARISON OF EPASP2 WITH | | |
	COMPARABLE CONDITIONS OF EPASP	"BASELINE" CONDITION OF EPASP	"BASELINE" CONDITION OF EPASP2
MUNIFICENCE			
+20% growth in units	97%	86%	91%
+ 5% growth in units	93	99	104
+20% growth in price	15	42	44
+ 5% growth in price	17	24	26
ADVERSITY			
−20% drop in units	80%	−46%	−49%
− 5% drop in units	40	27	29
−20% drop in price	63	9	9
− 5% drop in price	91	53	55
BUSINESS CYCLE			
40% maximum amplitude	686%	−6%	−6%
20% maximum amplitude	34	18	19
5% maximum amplitude	46	28	29
ERRORS			
5% fluctuations	36%	23%	24%
10% fluctuations	41	23	24

Table 3. To interpret the table, consider the figure of 86% (the middle entry in the top row). This means that under the condition of 20% growth in the number of units demanded, EPASP2's total profitability over the 18 time periods was only 86% of the total profitability of EPASP run under the "baseline" condition. Negative percentages indicate that the performance was in the opposite direction from that desired.

In scanning this table, one looks for (positive) percentages which exceed 100%, for they signify a comparative advantage for EPASP2. There are only two: (1) 104% when comparing EPASP2 under the condition of 5% growth in the number of units demanded to the "baseline" condition of EPASP2; and (2) 686% when comparing EPASP2 under the condition of a business cycle whose maximum amplitude is 40% of base demand (that is, since 2000 units is the base, the cycle runs from a trough of 1200 units to a peak of 2800 units) to the performance of EPASP under the same condition. The first case is discardable, because, relatively speaking, EPASP outperforms EPASP2. That is, if both EPASP and EPASP2 exhibit the same "baseline" performance, and then if both are run under the same condition (of a 5% growth in the number of units demanded), EPASP2's performance is only 104% of its baseline performance while EPASP's performance is 106% of its baseline (99% ÷ 93%, or consult Table 2). To put it differently, if a firm's Chief Executive Officer (CEO) knew that the firm was about to go from "stability" conditions to a 5% growth in units demanded, the CEO would prefer to run the firm along the lines of EPASP rather than EPASP2.

But the situation is just reversed with the second case (686%) — the firm's CEO would strongly prefer an EPASP2-like firm under the conditions of a business cycle with large swings. Since EPASP2 shows a compelling comparative advantage, the business cycle conditions merit more thorough investigation. The results of that experimentation are reported in Table 4, and the results are interpreted through the percentage-ratio format in Table 5.

From those tables, one can see that EPASP2 clearly outperformed EPASP in two conditions: 40%-amplitude cycle for a 1.0 insensitive firm reduced a $20,000 loss to a $3000 loss, and 20%-amplitude cycle for a 0.5 insensitive firm converted a $9,500 loss into a $9,500 gain. In two other cases, the performances of EPASP and EPASP2 were identical (except for computer rounding error): 40%-amplitude cycle for a 0.1 insensitive firm, and 20%-amplitude cycle for a 0.1 insensitive firm. In the other cases, EPASP convincingly outperforms EPASP2.

TABLE 4   Environmental Conditions, Variations, and Profitability

| BUSINESS CYCLE CONDITION | | TOTAL PROFITABILITY | |
AMPLITUDE	INSENSITIVITY	EPASP	EPASP2
40%	1.0	−$20,759.57	−$ 3,027.64
40	0.5	− 710.74	− 5,416.48
40	0.1	− 37,268.60	− 37,268.31
20%	1.0	28,137.42	9,540.98
20	0.5	− 9,441.47	9,540.98
20	0.1	2,850.74	2,850.91
5%	1.0	32,672.46	14,968.05
5	0.5	32,672.46	4,531.33
5	0.1	31,190.11	4,531.33

TABLE 5   Environmental Conditions, Variations, and Profitability: Comparison of EPASP2 with Comparable Business Cycle Condition of EPASP

| CONDITION | | |
AMPLITUDE	INSENSITIVITY	RATIO
40%	1.0	686%
40	0.5	13
40	0.1	100
20%	1.0	34%
20	0.5	—*
20	0.1	100
5%	1.0	46%
5	0.5	14
5	0.1	15

*EPASP showed a $9,000 loss in this condition, while EPASP2 exhibited a $9,000 gain.

TABLE 6   Aggregated Performance of Each Computer Program on Each Condition

| | AGGREGATED PROFITABILITY | |
CONDITION	EPASP	EPASP2
40% Cycle	−$58,738.91	−$45,712.43
20% Cycle	21,546.69	21,932.87
5% Cycle	96,535.03	24,030.71
1.0 Insensitive	$40,050.31	$21,481.39
0.5 Insensitive	22,520.25	8,655.83
0.1 Insensitive	− 3,227.75	− 29,886.07

In determining the relative merits of EPASP and EPASP2 from these data, it is helpful to turn to Table 6, which provides the aggregated performance of each computer program on each condition. Consider the leftmost figure in the top row (−$58,738.91); this is obtained by adding together the total profitability of EPASP for the 40% amplitude condition over all of the three insensitivity conditions (see Table 4).

Four conclusions may be drawn from the data in Table 6. First, in general, one's intuition is corroborated about the relation between performance and the volatility of business cycles. As the maximum amplitude decreases from 40% to 20% to 5%, performance monotonically improves — in EPASP, from −$58,000 to $21,000 to $96,000; in EPASP2, from −$45,000 to $22,000 to $24,000.

Second, as the firm becomes less insensitive and more sensitive to external environmental change, its performance worsens monotonically. The explanation for this is that by being more sensitive, the firm overreacts to fluctuations and fails to distinguish between persistent, structural environmental changes and mere epiphenomena. Note that as insensitivity lessens from 1.0 to 0.5 to 0.1, performance declines in both EPASP (from $40,000 to $22,000 to −$3,000) and EPASP2 (from $21,000 to $8,000 to −$30,000).

Third, EPASP, as with all the other conditions of Table 5, outperforms EPASP2 for all three insensitivity conditions ($40,000 versus $21,000, $22,000 versus $8,000, and −$3,000 versus −$30,000).

Fourth, the results are mixed for the business cycle conditions, but the explanation is strongly suggested by the detailed data of Tables 5 and 6. As the comparative merits of EPASP and EPASP2 cross over near the 20% maximum amplitude point, it is apparent that EPASP2's relative superiority exists with progressively more volatile business cycles. Given the stronger performance by EPASP in *all* other conditions, apparently this is EPASP2's *only* advantage.

Conclusions

While the principles of corporate strategy and the results of organization theory have a great deal to offer the policymaker, they are subject to some important limitations. The former underestimates the impact of contextual forces and is atheoretical in nature. The latter deemphasizes the role of strategic choice. The IP framework, on the other hand, permits the development of precise, testable theory concerning the interplay of organizational decisions, strategy formulation, and environmental factors.

In order to apply the IP framework, strategy formulation is conceptualized as a seven-phase process. It starts with an organizational crisis brought on by new events which cannot be handled by the current environmental theory and corporate policy. An attempt is then made to understand the events by finding patterns which can be used as the foundation for a new theory. The theory, in turn, facilitates development of a revised strategy, which subsequently becomes the basis for the firm's decision making until a critical anomaly once more appears and the process is repeated.

Using this framework, we have constructed computer simulation models of a synthetic firm in its own artificial environment. Validating EPASP was very challenging, albeit mostly successful (see Tuggle and Gerwin 1980). Trying to corroborate the procedural premises of EPASP2 (the shifting coalitions and their preferences) and the simulation results of EPASP2 (always inferior to those of EPASP, except in the case of large business cycles) will prove nearly impossible, since few firms would readily reveal that they are plagued by internal discord and "politics."

However, if EPASP2 begins to properly depict some of the realities in coalition formation and dissolution, then the range of experimentation with EPASP2 suggests some rather sharp conclusions. Specifically, if the CEO of a firm finds coalitions in the firm, he or she should either ignore their advice or try to redesign the organizational structure which permitted or encouraged the formation of the coalitions (for example, frequent job rotations, or adoption of a matrix structure) to try to minimize their occurrence.

There are three important caveats to those recommendations. First, EPASP and EPASP2 clearly show that advice to be exactly backwards in the case of business cycles with large swings. Second, there may be unexplored combinations of cases where EPASP2 outperforms EPASP, for example, a condition of 30% growth in units demanded, −10% drop in price, 10%-amplitude business cycles, and 20% error fluctuations, all happening at the same time. Third, the individual units in the firm may, with a different set of preferences and perceptions, upon banding together, outperform EPASP by being sensitive to a broader spectrum of environmental signals. Ultimately, given that firms are information-processing systems and therefore need to "read," "interpret," "understand," and "plan for" their environments, the three central design issues facing firms are (a) what data firms should extract from their environments; (b) what internal processing of that data should occur; and (c) what response should be made to that data.

While resolution of the second and third caveat awaits further research, our research with EPASP2 to date strongly suggests that coalitions in firms usually detract from their performance. That is, we have a partial, although negative, statement about the second central design issue (b). Further extension to and experimentation with EPASP and EPASP2 may allow more definitive and more constructive statements to be made about all three organizational design issues (a–c).

Regardless of the specific action recommendations, EPASP and EPASP2 could also be used to assist the training of top managers and strategic planners. The trainers would specify the input parameters concerned with market characteristics, how long the simulation session is to last, and so forth. The trainee would specify the initial environmental theory, the degree of environmental sensitivity, and so forth. The trainee and computer programmer would have to work together to specify the appropriate components in the environmental sensitivity function, parameter settings in the standard operating procedures, coalition members and their specific preferences, and so forth.

The development and elaboration of models such as EPASP and EPASP2 will require field research in a number of different areas. Detailed case studies involving verbal thinking-aloud protocols, questionnaires, and analysis of documents should help reveal the contents of environmental theories as well as other aspects of the process. Cognitive maps (Axelrod 1976) and the assertions of policymakers concerning the causal structure of their belief systems provide a tool for operationalizing different individuals' environmental theories. Mapping techniques can be used to ask whether theories are rich in detail or restricted to narrow aspects of the immediate marketplace.

The full richness of EPASP and EPASP2 are only beginning to be explored and exploited. The results suggest that it would be beneficial to continue extending our synthesis of corporate strategy and organization theory. Our results imply that the major unstructured decision processes in organizations merit more rigorous study, and indicate that environmental theories and perceptual processes are significant explanatory concepts which can no longer be ignored in the formation of theories of organizational decision and intelligence. Information-processing models appear to have great benefit for theory construction, policy recommendations, training of key personnel, and resolution of certain issues in organizational design.

ACKNOWLEDGMENT

This paper is an extension of an earlier paper, "An information processing model of organizational perception, strategy, and choice," published in *Management Science*, 1980, *26* (6), pp. 575–592. The portions of this paper that are taken from that article are reprinted with permission from the publishers of *Management Science*.

APPENDIX: Computer Program Listing for EPASP2

```
0010 C    EPASP-II, A SIMULATION OF ORGANIZATIONAL GOAL AGREEMENT,
0020 C                        PERCEPTION,
0030 C    STRATEGY FORMULATION, AND DECISION MAKING.
0040 C
```

```
0050 C    THE MAIN PROGRAM READS IN THE NUMBER OF PERIODS IN THE
0060 C    SIMULATION AND THE PARAMETERS ASSOCIATED WITH THE MARKET
0070 C
0080 C    THE SUBROUTINE 'DEMAND' COMPUTES THE CURRENT DEMAND
0090 C    AND MARKET PRICE
0100 C
0110 C    THE SUBROUTINE 'PERCEV' PRODUCES THE CURRENT
0120 C    ENVIRONMENTAL THEORY FOR THE FIRM
0130 C
0140 C    THE SUBROUTINE 'DOMCOL' AGGREGATES
0150 C    THE PREFERENCES OF THE DOMINANT COALITION
0160 C
0170 C
0180 C    THE SUBROUTINE 'STRTGY' PRODUCES THE STRATEGY FOR THE FIRM
0190 C
0200 C    THE SUBROUTINE 'DECIDE' MAKES STANDARD OPERATING
0210 C    DECISIONS FOR THE FIRM
0220 C
0230 C    THE SUBROUTINE 'PRINTO' PRINTS OUT THE RESULTS OF THE
0240 C    SIMULATION FOR ONE PERIOD
0250 C
0260 C    THE FUNCTION 'RANDO1(.)' PRODUCES 0,1 NORMALLY
0270 C    DISTRIBUTED RANDOM VARIABLES
0280 C
0290      DOUBLE PRECISION D SEED,IST,TWOPI
0300      INTEGER OPOR,UP,STAB,DOWN,CRIS,ETHERY
0310      INTEGER O1THRY,O2THRY,O3THRY,O4THRY
0320      INTEGER AGTHRY
0330      DATA OPOR,UP,STAB/4HOPOR,2HUP,4HSTAB/
0340      DATA DOWN,CRIS/4HDOWN, 4HCRIS/
0350      DSEED=123457.DO
0360      PRINT,'WHAT IS THE BASE DEMAND, IN UNITS?'
0370      READ,BASEDM
0380      PRINT,'WHAT IS THE BASE PRICE,IN DOLLARS AND CENTS?'
0390      READ,BASEPR
0400      PRINT,'HOW MANY PERIODS DO YOU WANT TO SIMULATE?'
0410      READ,NPEROD
0420      PRINT,'WHAT IS THE (PLUS OR MINUS) GROWTH TREND?'
0430      PRINT, '(IN THE FORM .XXX.....)'
0440      READ,TREND
0450      PRINT,'WHAT IS THE LENGTH OF THE BUSINESS CYCLE?'
0460      PRINT,'(IT MUST BE A POSITIVE, NONZERO NUMBER.)'
0470      READ,CYCLEL
0480      PRINT,'WHAT IS THE MAX AMPLITUDE OF THE CYCLE?'
0490      READ,CYCLEA
0500      PRINT,'WHAT IS THE MEAN OF THE ERROR DEFLECTION?'
0510      READ,AMU
0520      PRINT,'WHAT IS THE STANDARD DEVIATION OF THE ERROR?'
0530      READ,SIGMA
0540      PRINT,'WHAT IS THE TREND IN MARKET PRICE?'
0550      PRINT,'(IN THE FORM .XXX.....)'
0560      READ,TRENDP
0570      PRINT,'WHAT IS THE MEAN OF THE ERROR IN PRICE?'
0580      READ,AMUPR
0590      PRINT,'WHAT IS THE STANDARD DEVIATION IN PRICE ERROR?'
0600      READ,SIGMAP
```

```
0610        PRINT,'WHAT IS THE FIRM'S ENVIRONMENTAL THEORY?'
0620        PRINT,'(IT SHOULD BE ONE OF THE FOLLOWING)'
0630        PRINT,'  "OPOR"'
0640        PRINT,'  "UP"'
0650        PRINT,'  "STAB"'
0660        PRINT,'  "DOWN"'
0670        PRINT,'  "CRIS"'
0680        READ (5,11)ITHERY
0690 C      FROM THIS POINT ON HAVE STD FO'TRAN FO'
0700     11 FORMAT(A4)
0710        PRINT,'WHAT IS THE TEST CRITERION FOR THEORY CHANGE?'
0720        READ,CRITER
0730        PLTCAP = 1.4 * BASEDM
0740        IF(ITHERY.EQ.OPOR)ISTRAT=5
0750        IF(ITHERY.EQ.UP)ISTRAT=4
0760        IF(ITHERY.EQ.STAB)ISTRAT=3
0770        IF(ITHERY.EQ.DOWN)ISTRAT=2
0780        IF(ITHERY.EQ.CRIS)ISTRAT=1
0790        CSTNVT = .1
0800        CSTPRD = .6
0810        CSTSLS = .15
0820        CURDMD = BASEDM
0830        CURPRC = BASEPR
0840        VENTRY = BASEDM
0850        PRODCE = BASEDM
0860        OLDDM = CURDMD
0870        OLDPR = CURPRC
0880        OLDINV = VENTRY
0890        OLDPRD = PRODCE
0900        SALES = 0.
0910        REVNUE = 0.
0920        COSTS = 0.
0930        OLDCST = COSTS
0940        OLDPRF = 999999.
0950        PROFIT = 999999.
0960        CUMPRF = 0.
0970        TEMPRF = PROFIT
0980        CALL PRINTO(0,BASEDM,BASEPR,ITHERY,PROFIT, ISTRAT,SALES,
0990       & REVNUE,COSTS,CUMPRF,VENTRY)
1000        IF(ITHERY.EQ.OPOR)ETHERY = 5
1010        IF(ITHERY.EQ.UP)ETHERY = 4
1020        IF(ITHERY.EQ.STAB)ETHERY = 3
1030        IF(ITHERY.EQ.DOWN)ETHERY = 2
1040        IF(ITHERY.EQ.CRIS)ETHERY = 1
1050        O4THRY = 3
1060        O3THRY = 3
1070        O2THRY = 3
1080        O1THRY = 3
1090        DO 1 II=1,NPEROD
1100        I = II
1110        OLDDM = CURDMD
1120        OLDPR = CURPRC
1130        CALL DEMAND(BASEDM,TREND,CYCLEL,CYCLEA,AMU,
            SIGMA,I,
1140       & BASEPR,TRENDP,AMUPR,SIGMAP,CURDMD,CURPRC)
1150        CALL DOMCOL(OLDDM,CURDMD,
1160       &OLDPR,CURPRC,OLDINV,VENTRY,
1170       &OLDCST,COSTS,OLDPRD,PRODCE,AGTHRY)
```

```
1180        CALL PERCEV(ETHERY,OLDPRF,PROFIT,OLDPR,CURPRC,
1190      & OLDDM,CURDMD,CRITER,AGTHRY)
1200        IF(ETHERY.EQ.5)ITHERY = OPOR
1210        IF(ETHERY.EQ.4)ITHERY = UP
1220        IF(ETHERY.EQ.3)ITHERY = STAB
1230        IF(ETHERY.EQ.2)ITHERY = DOWN
1240        IF(ETHERY.EQ.1)ITHERY = CRIS
1250        O4THRY = O3THRY
1260        O3THRY = O2THRY
1270        O2THRY = O1THRY
1280        O1THRY = ETHERY
1290        CALL STRTGY(ISTRAT,ETHERY,O1THRY,O2THRY,O3THRY,PLTCAP,
1300      & BASEDM,BASEPR,CSTNVT,CSTPRD,CSTSLS,CURDMD,CURPRC,
1310        O4THRY, & ITHERY)
1320        OLDINV = VENTRY
1330        OLDPRD = PRODCE
1340        OLDCST = COSTS
1350        CALL DECIDE(CURDMD,CURPRC,PLTCAP,CSTNVT,CSTPRD,CSTSLS,
1360      & PROFIT,SALES,REVNUE,COSTS,VENTRY,PRODCE,CRITER)
1370        CUMPRF = CUMPRF + PROFIT
1380        CALL PRINTO(I,CURDMD,CURPRC,ITHERY,PROFIT,ISTRAT,SALES,
1390      & REVNUE,COSTS,CUMPRF,VENTRY)
1400        OLDPRF = TEMPRF
1410        TEMPRF = PROFIT
1420   1    CONTINUE
1430        STOP
1440        END
1450 C
1460 C      THE 'DEMAND' COMPUTING SUBROUTINE
1470 C
1480        SUBROUTINE DEMAND(BASEDM,TREND,CYCLEL,CYCLEA,AMU,SIGMA,
1490      & I,BASEPR,TRENDP,AMUPR,SIGMAP,CURDMD,CURPRC)
1500        DOUBLE PRECISION TWOPI
1510        DATA TWOPI/6.2831853/
1520        PERNUM = I
1530        GROWTH = BASEDM + TREND * (PERNUM - 1.0) * BASEDM
1540        CYCLE = CYCLEA * DSIN((PERNUM/CYCLEL) * TWOPI)
1550        ERR = AMU + SIGMA * RAND01(I)
1560        CURDMD = GROWTH + CYCLE + ERR
1570        PGROTH = BASEPR + TRENDP * (PERNUM - 1.0) * BASEPR
1580        PERR + AMUPR + SIGMAP * RAND01(I)
1590        CURPRC = PGROTH + PERR
1600        IF(CURDMD.LT.0.)CURDMD = 0.0
1610        IF(CURPRC.LT.0.)CURPRC = 0.0
1620        RETURN
1630        END
1640 C
1650 C      THE 'PRINTOUT' SUBROUTINE
1660 C
1670        SUBROUTINE PRINTO(I,CURDMD,CURPRC,ITHERY,PROFIT,ISTRAT,
1680      & SALES,REVNUE,COSTS,CUMPRF,VENTRY)
1690        WRITE(6,1)I,CURDMD
1700   1    FORMAT(1X,'THE CURRENT DEMAND IN PERIOD',I3,' IS', F8.0,
1710      & ' UNITS,')
1720        WRITE(6,2)CURPRC
1730   2    FORMAT(2X,'WHILE THE CURRENT PRICE IS $',F8.2)
1740        WRITE(6,3)ITHERY
1750   3    FORMAT(3X,'THE FIRM'S CURRENT ENVIRONMENTAL THEORY IS ',A4)
```

```
1760        WRITE(6,300)
1770    300 FORMAT(3X,'THE FIRM'S CURRENT STRATEGY IS TO')
1780        IF(ISTRAT.EQ.1)GO TO 31
1790        IF(ISTRAT.EQ.2)GO TO 32
1800        IF(ISTRAT.EQ.3)GO TO 33
1810        IF(ISTRAT.EQ.4)GO TO 34
1820        IF(ISTRAT.EQ.5)GO TO 35
1830    31  WRITE(6,311)
1840    311 FORMAT(6X,'CONSOLIDATE ITS MARKET POSITION')
1850        GO TO 36
1860    32  WRITE(6,321)
1870    321 FORMAT(6X,'USE CHEAPER LABOR AND INPUT FACTORS')
1880        GO TO 36
1890    33  WRITE(6,331)
1900    331 FORMAT(6X,'KEEP THE STATUS QUO FOR THE NEXT PERIOD')
1910        GO TO 36
1920    34  WRITE(6,341)
1930    341 FORMAT(6X,'IMPROVE PRODUCT QUALITY')
1940        GO TO 36
1950    351 FORMAT(6X,'ENTER NEW MARKETS WITH NEW PRODUCTS')
1960    35  WRITE(6,351)
1970    36  CONTINUE
1980        WRITE(6,301)VENTRY
1990    301 FORMAT(5X,'THE INVENTORY IS NOW ',F6.0,' UNITS')
2000        WRITE(6,4)SALES
2010    4   FORMAT(4X,'ON SALES OF ',F6.0,' UNITS, WHICH PRODUCES')
2020        WRITE(6,5)REVNUE
2030    5   FORMAT(4X,'REVENUES OF $',F10.2,' WHILE EXPERIENCING')
2040        WRITE(6,6)COSTS
2050    6   FORMAT(4X,'COSTS OF $',F10.2,' THERE WERE')
2060        WRITE(6,7)PROFIT
2070    7   FORMAT(4X,'CURRENT PROFITS TO THE FIRM OF $',F10.2)
2080        WRITE(6,8)CUMPRF
2090    8   FORMAT(5X,'YIELDING CUMULATIVE PROFITS OF $',F10.2)
2100        WRITE(6,100)
2110    100 FORMAT(1H0)
2120        RETURN
2130        END
2140 C
2150 C      THE '0,1 NORMALLY DISTRIBUTED RANDOM VARIABLE' FUNCTION
2160 C
2170        FUNCTION RAND01(I)
2180        DOUBLE PRECISION TWOPI,DSEED
2190        DSEED=123457.D0
2200        DATA TWOPI/6.2831853/
2210        R1 = GGUBFS(DSEED)
2220        R2 = GGUBF(DSEED)
2230        RAND01 = SQRT(-2.*ALOG(R1))*DCOS(TWOPI*R2)
2240        RETURN
2250        END
2260 C
2270 C      THE SUBROUTINE TO CALCULATE THE AGGREGATE PREFERENCES
2280 C      OF THE DOMINANT COALITION
2290 C
2300        SUBROUTINE DOMCOL(OLDDM,CURDMD,OLDPR,
2310      & CURPRC,OLDINV,VENTRY,OLDCST,COSTS,
2320      & OLDPRD,PRODCE,AGTHRY)
2330        INTEGER AGTHRY,SLTHRY,MFTHRY,FNTHRY
```

```
2340 C
2350 C      SALES DEPT. PREFERS (IN ORDER)
2360 C      DEMAND RISING, PRICE FALLING, AND INVENTORY RISING
2370 C
2380        IF (CURDMD.GE.OLDDM) GO TO 1
2390        SLTHRY = −1
2400        GO TO 50
2410    1   IF (CURPRC.LE.OLDPR) GO TO 2
2420        SLTHRY = −1
2430        GO TO 50
2440    2   IF(VENTRY.GE.OLDINV) GO TO 3
2450        SLTHRY = 0
2460        GO TO 50
2470    3   SLTHRY = 1
2480   50   PRINT,'THE SALES DEPT. IS IN FAVOR OF'
2490        IF (SLTHRY) 5,6,7
2500    5   PRINT,' A MORE PESSIMISTIC THEORY'
2510        GO TO 55
2520    6   PRINT,' THE STATUS QUO THEORY'
2530        GO TO 55
2540    7   PRINT,' A MORE OPTIMISTIC THEORY'
2550 C
2560 C      MANUFACTURING DEPT. PREFERS (IN ORDER)
2570 C      COSTS FALLING, INVENTORY FALLING, AND PRODUCTION RISING
2580 C
2590   55   IF (COSTS.LE.OLDCST) GO TO 101
2600        MFTHRY = −1
2610        GO TO 150
2620  101 IF (VENTRY.LE.OLDINV) GO TO 102
2630        MFTHRY = −1
2640        GO TO 150
2650  102 IF (PRODCE.GE.OLDPRD) GO TO 103
2660        MFTHRY = 0
2670        GO TO 150
2680  103 MFTHRY = 1
2690  150 PRINT,'THE MANUFACTURING DEPT. IS IN FAVOR OF'
2700        IF (MFTHRY) 105,106,107
2710  105 PRINT,' A MORE PESSIMISTIC THEORY'
2720        GO TO 155
2730  106 PRINT,' THE STATUS QUO THEORY'
2740        GO TO 155
2750  107 PRINT,' A MORE OPTIMISTIC THEORY'
2760 C
2770 C      FINANCE DEPT. PREFERS (IN ORDER)
2780 C      COSTS FALLING, PRODUCTION FALLING, AND INVENTORY FALLING
2790 C
2800  155 IF (COSTS.LE.OLDCST) GO TO 201
2810        FNTHRY = −1
2820        GO TO 250
2830  201 IF (PRODCE.LE.OLDPRD) GO TO 202
2840        FNTHRY = −1
2850        GO TO 250
2860  202 IF (VENTRY.LT.OLDINV) GO TO 203
2870        FNTHRY = 0
2880        GO TO 250
2890  203 FNTHRY = 1
2900  250 PRINT ,'THE FINANCE DEPT. IS IN FAVOR OF'
2910        IF (FNTHRY) 205,206,207
```

```
2920  205 PRINT,' A MORE PESSIMISTIC THEORY'
2930      GO TO 255
2940  206 PRINT,' THE STATUS QUO THEORY'
2950      GO TO 255
2960  207 PRINT,' A MORE OPTIMISTIC THEORY'
2970 C
2980 C      NOW AGGREGATE THE DEPARTMENTAL PREFERENCES
2990 C
3000  255 NT = SLTHRY + MFTHRY + FNTHRY
3010      AGTHRY = 0
3020      IF (NT.EQ.(-2) .OR. NT.EQ.(-3)) AGTHRY = -1
3030      IF (NT.EQ.(+2) .OR. NT.EQ.(+3)) AGTHRY = +1
3040      PRINT,'THE CHOICE OF THE COALITION IS FOR'
3050      IF (AGTHRY) 301,302,303
3060  301 PRINT,' A MORE PESSIMISTIC THEORY'
3070      GO TO 400
3080  302 PRINT,' THE STATUS QUO THEORY'
3090      GO TO 400
3100  303 PRINT,' A MORE OPTIMISTIC THEORY'
3110  400 RETURN
3120      END
3130 C
3140 C      THE 'PERCEIVING' SUBROUTINE
3150 C
3160      SUBROUTINE PERCEV(ETHERY,OLDPRF,PROFIT,OLDPR,CURPRC,
3170      & OLDDM,CURDMD,CRITER,AGTHRY)
3180      INTEGER ETHERY,AGTHRY
3190 C
3200 C      STATEMENT LABEL '101' IS FOR A MORE OPTIMISTIC THEORY
3210 C      STATEMENT LABEL '102' IS FOR A MORE PESSIMISTIC THEORY
3220 C
3230      IF(PROFIT.LT.0.)GO TO 5
3240 C
3250 C      IF PROFITS ARE MUCH BETTER, EXHIBIT OPTIMISM
3260 C
3270      IF(((PROFIT-OLDPRF)/OLDPRF).GT.CRITER)GO TO 101
3280 C
3290 C      IF THE PROFITS ARE ABOUT THE SAME, ,
3300 C      GET THE DOMINANT COALITION'S ADVICE
3310      IF (AGTHRY) 102,8,101
3320 C
3330 C      IF THE DOMINANT COALITION RECOMMENDS CONTINUING
3340 C      THE STATUS QUO, TEST UNIT SALES
3350 C
3360    8 IF(((CURDMD-OLDDM)/OLDDM).GT.CRITER)GO TO 101
3370      IF(((OLDDM-CURDMD)/CURDMD).GT.CRITER)GO TO 102
3380 C
3390 C      IF UNIT SALES ARE ABOUT THE SAME, TEST PRICE
3400 C
3410      IF(((CURPRC-OLDPR)/OLDPR).GT.CRITER)GO TO 101
3420      IF(((OLDPR-CURPRC)/CURPRC).GT.CRITER)GO TO 102
3430 C
3440 C      OTHERWISE, DON'T CHANGE THE CURRENT THEORY
3450 C
3460      GO TO 100
3470 C
3480 C      TEST TO SEE IF NEGATIVE PROFITS ARE GETTING BETTER
3490 C
```

```
3500   5    IF(PROFIT.GT.OLDPRF)GO TO 100
3510        GO TO 102
3520   101 IF(ETHERY.EQ.5)GO TO 100
3530        ETHERY = ETHERY + 1
3540        GO TO 100
3550   102 IF(ETHERY.EQ.1)GO TO 100
3560        ETHERY = ETHERY − 1
3570   100 RETURN
3580        END
3590 C
3600 C     THE 'STRATEGY' FORMULATING SUBROUTINE
3610 C
3620        SUBROUTINE STRTGY(ISTRAT,ETHERY,O1THRY,O2THRY,O3THRY,
3630        & PLTCAP,BASEDM,BASEPR,CSTNVT,CSTPRD,CSTSLS,CURDMD,
3640        CURPRC, & O4THRY,ITHERY)
3650        INTEGER ETHERY, O1THRY,O2THRY,O3THRY,O4THRY,STAB
3660        DATA STAB/4HSTAB/
3670        ISTRAT = 3
3680 C
3690 C     IF THE FIRM'S PERCEPTIONS HAVE NOT CHANGED FOR THE LAST THREE
3700 C     PERIODS, ASSUME A NEW ERA OF 'STABILITY' HAS BEEN ENTERED
3710 C
3720        IF(O2THRY.NE.O3THRY.OR.O3THRY.NE.O4THRY)GO TO 20
3730        IF(O2THRY.EQ.3)GO TO 20
3740        ITHERY = STAB
3750        ETHERY = 3
3760        O1THRY = 3
3770        O2THRY = 3
3780        O3THRY = 3
3790        O4THRY = 3
3800        WRITE(6,10)
3810   10   FORMAT(/1X,'THE FIRM ASSUMES A NEW PERIOD OF STABILITY.'//)
3820        GO TO 100
3830   20   CONTINUE
3840 C
3850 C     IF THE FIRM'S PERCEPTIONS HAVE NOT CHANGED, OR HAVE GONE BACK
3860 C     TO WHERE THEY WERE TWO PERIODS AGO, KEEP THE STATUS QUO
3870 C
3880        IF(O2THRY.EQ.ETHERY .OR. O3THRY.EQ.ETHERY) GO TO 100
3890 C
3900 C     OTHERWISE, CHANGE THE FIRM'S STRATEGY (AND ITS OPERATING
3910 C     CONDITIONS)
3920 C
3930        IF(O3THRY.EQ.O2THRY)GO TO 1
3940 C
3950 C     MAKE A DRAMATIC CHANGE IN THE FIRM'S STRATEGY
3960 C
3970        ICHNGE = (ETHERY − O3THRY)/2
3980        ISTRAT = ISTRAT + (2 * ICHNGE)
3990        CHANGE = ICHNGE
4000        CREMNT = .25 * CHANGE
4010   50   CONTINUE
4020        PLTCAP = PLTCAP + PLTCAP * CREMNT
4030        BASEDM = BASEDM + BASEDM * CREMNT
4040        BASEPR = BASEPR + BASEPR * CREMNT
4050        CURDMD = CURDMD + CURDMD * CREMNT
4060        CURPRC = CURPRC + CURPRC * CREMNT
4070        CSTNVT = CSTNVT + CSTNVT * (CREMNT / 10.)
```

```
4080        CSTPRD = CSTPRD + CSTPRD * (CREMNT / 10.)
4090        CSTSLS = CSTSLS + CSTSLS * (CREMNT / 10.)
4100        GO TO 100
4110 C
4120 C      MAKE A MODEST CHANGE IN THE FIRM'S STRATEGY
4130 C
4140   1    ICHNGE = ETHERY − O2THRY
4150        ISTRAT = ISTRAT + ICHNGE
4160        CHANGE = ICHNGE
4170        CREMNT = .1 * CHANGE
4180        GO TO 50
4190   100 RETURN
4200        END
4210 C
4220 C      THE 'PRICE AND OUTPUT DECIDING' SUBROUTINE
4230 C
4240        SUBROUTINE DECIDE(CURDMD,CURPRC,PLTCAP,CSTNVT,CSTPRD,
4250        CSTSLS, & PROFIT,SALES,REVNUE,COSTS,VENTRY,PRODCE,CRITER)
4260 C
4270 C      DECIDE HOW MUCH TO SELL AND HOW MUCH TO ADD TO INVENTORY
4280 C
4290        IF((CURDMD + .01) .GT.VENTRY)GO TO 1
4300        SALES = CURDMD
4310        PRODCE = .8 * PRODCE
4320        IF(CURDMD.LT.0.001)PRODCE = 0.0
4330        VENTRY = VENTRY − SALES + PRODCE
4340        GO TO 4
4350   1    SALES = VENTRY
4360        VENTRY = PRODCE
4370        IF(CURDMD.GT.PLTCAP)GO TO 3
4380        PRODCE = CURDMD
4390        GO TO 4
4400   3    PRODCE = PLTCAP
4410   4    CONTINUE
4420        IF(((CURDMD−PLTCAP)/PLTCAP).LT.CRITER)GO TO 5
4430        PLTCAP = PLTCAP + .05 * PLTCAP
4440   5    CONTINUE
4450 C
4460 C      CALCULATE REVENUES, COSTS, AND PROFITS
4470 C
4480        REVNUE = SALES * CURPRC
4490        COSTS = 0.
4500        COSTS = COSTS + VENTRY * CURPRC * CSTNVT
4510        IF(CURPRC.LT.0.001)COSTS = VENTRY * CSTNVT
4520        COSTS = COSTS + PRODCE * CURPRC * CSTPRD
4530        COSTS = COSTS + SALES * CURPRC * CSTSLS
4540        PROFIT = REVNUE − COSTS
4550        RETURN
4560        END
```

The Economics of Protection Against Low Probability Events

Howard Kunreuther, *University of Pennsylvania*

There has been a growing literature emerging in the social sciences on the failure of consumers to protect themselves against events which they perceive as having a relatively low probability of occurrence even though it may produce substantial damage to their property, cause them personal injury, or perhaps even loss of life. In some cases, firms have also been reluctant to offer protective options to individuals or they devote little effort to promoting these products.

The following two examples illustrate these points.

1. Many drivers did not voluntarily purchase automobile insurance until they were required to do so (Bernstein 1972). Today, most states in the United States regulate rates and there have been charges of discrimination in the pricing and distribution of automobile insurance (MacAvoy 1977).

2. Flood insurance was not offered to U.S. residents in hazard-prone areas on a large scale until 1968, when a subsidized joint federal–private program was initiated.[1] Even though the federal government highly subsidizes the premium, few residents purchase policies today unless they are required to do so as a condition for a new mortgage. Most insurance agents have also not encouraged their policyholders to purchase this coverage nor provided them with information on the availability of this insurance (Kunreuther et al. 1978a).

Both of these examples indicate the inability of the private market to provide protection against low probability events. A principal reason for such market failures is that consumers and/or firms have limited information on both the nature of the hazards they face as well as the available protective options.[2] These empirical findings were anticipated by Adam Smith in his

---

1. The early history of flood insurance sheds some light on the reasons why companies have been reluctant to market policies. In 1897, an insurance company in Illinois offered flood coverage to property owners residing along the Mississippi and Missouri rivers. Two severe floods in 1899 created catastrophic losses for the company, even washing away the home office. In the mid-1920s some insurance companies again attempted to market flood policies, but severe flooding in 1927 and 1928 discouraged all responsible companies from continuing this coverage (Manes 1938).

2. The theme of imperfect information and its effects on individual and market behavior has played an important role in recent literature in economics (Arrow 1963, Akerlof 1970, Williamson 1975, and Thaler 1980), as well as in psychology (Tversky and Kahneman 1974; Slovic, Fischhoff, and Lichtenstein 1977; Slovic 1978; Kahneman and Tversky 1979b; Einhorn and Hogarth 1981a).

Wealth of Nations when he noted:

> Taking the whole kingdom at an average, nineteen houses in twenty, or rather perhaps ninety-nine in a hundred, are not insured from fire. Sea risk is more alarming to the greater part of people, and the proportion of ships insured to those not insured is much greater. Many fail, however, at all seasons, and even in time of war, without any insurance. This may sometimes perhaps be done without any imprudence. When a great company, or even a great merchant, has twenty or thirty ships at sea, they may, as it were, insure one another. The premium saved upon them all may more than compensate such losses as they are likely to meet with in the common course of chances. The neglect of insurance upon shipping, however, in the same manner as upon houses, is, in most cases, the effect of no such nice calculation, but of mere thoughtless rashness and presumptuous contempt of the risk.   (Page 97, Volume I.)

This paper systematically explores how different types of imperfect or partial information affect consumer and firm interactions in the context of the above two examples. It also examines the effect of alternative prescriptive measures, such as incentive systems or government regulations on performance. Specifically, the following questions will be addressed.

1. How do the decision processes of consumers affect the performance of the market? What effect do systematic biases and simplified decision rules have on equilibrium price-quantity values?

2. How do firms and consumers update their information through learning? What role does statistical data and personal experience play in the dynamics of the decision process?

The next section of the paper details a framework of analysis and the relevant assumptions. Subsequent sections illustrate the framework by considering the preceding two examples. The concluding section summarizes the findings and suggests directions for future research.

Framework for Analysis

Relevant Assumptions

The framework which guides the analysis is presented in Figure 1, where the adjustment process and flow of information are depicted between the two relevant parties — consumers and firms. To simplify the analysis, assume that there are at most two groups of consumers at risk, each of whom faces a single loss (X) which is correctly estimated. Consumers in group H have a relatively high probability of a loss, while those in group L have a relatively low chance of a loss. At the end of period t, each group i has their own perception of the probability of loss (ψ_{it}) which may differ from the true probability (Φ_{it}) $i=L,H$. Consumers base their estimate of Φ_{it} on some weighted average of their previous estimate. Consumers may revise their estimate ψ_{it} as t changes by incorporating new data such as a recent experience with the hazard. This updating process may occur even if the true probability Φ_{it}, remains stable over time. Unless specifically stated, Φ_{it} is independent of human action so there are no problems of moral hazard.[3]

---

3. For a more detailed discussion of the problems of moral hazard and its impact on insurance purchase decisions see Shavell (1979).

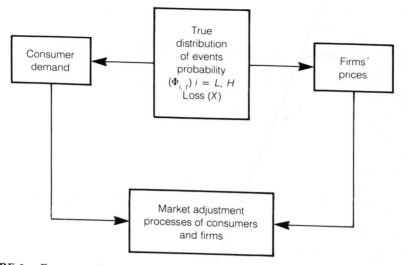

FIGURE 1   Framework for Analysis

Firms also correctly estimate the loss, but may perceive the probability of its occurrence to group i in period t to be different from ψ_{it}. The firm markets a protective measure (for example, insurance, safety devices) and may discriminate between consumers by charging them different prices based on the risk classification scheme which they utilize. As we shall see in the next section, firms may have a menu of more than two prices even though there are only two risk groups, because they have imperfect information on individuals. As data are accumulated over time, the set of prices will also change. Let P be the price charged during period t to consumers in classification j. At the end of period t, demand for the protective activity by a consumer in group i who is in classification j is denoted by Q_{jt}^i where

$$Q_{jt}^i = f\left(\psi_{it}, P_{jt}, X\right)$$

with

$$0 \le Q_{jt}^i \le X.$$

Firms set their prices P_{jt} as a function of their ability to classify consumers and their perceptions of consumer demand ($\bar{Q}_{jt}^i$) at different prices. If firms had perfect information on each individual's demand curve and its risk group, then there would be only two prices — one for the high- and one for the low-risk groups. Since $i=j$, we specify demand and premiums in this situation as simply Q_{it} and P_{it} $i=L,H$. The other extreme would be the case where the firm had no information on any consumer, and sets one price for both groups possibly based on misinformation regarding the true risk, Φ_{it}, and the consumer's decision rule. If the firm charges only one price in period t to both risk groups, this will be denoted as Pt.

In the three examples which follow, I am interested in exploring the nature of the equilibrium between supply and demand at the end of any period t. Specifically, what prices are charged for the protective measures? How are these prices affected by the type of information which firms and consumers have on the probability of a loss, the types of decision rules which consumers utilize, and firms' perceptions of this behavior? What are the welfare implications of these prices to high- and low-risk consumers and how might government policy help rectify any imbalances?

The resulting equilibrium will also depend upon the number of firms marketing the product and the degree of competition between them. We will consider two extreme cases: (1) the firm is a monopolist; and (2) the firm is in a competitive market where it is costless for new firms to enter or exit from the industry, and consumers have *no* search costs in obtaining data on premiums. These polar cases enable us to determine the sensitivity of information imperfections to market structure so as to understand more clearly when alternative policy prescriptions such as incentives and regulations may be desirable.

An Illustrative Example

To illustrate the above framework more concretely, let us consider the case where both the consumer and firm have perfect information. The resulting equilibriums in this ideal world can then be contrasted with the more realistic cases to be explored in the next two sections when the informational assumptions for the firm and consumer are relaxed. For this example and later ones, graphical analysis and numerical examples will depict the resulting equilibriums.

Figure 2 depicts a situation where consumers have the option of purchasing insurance to cover a portion or all of their loss of X dollars should a disaster occur. Firms offer coverage to consumers in each risk group i at a price per unit coverage of P_{it} $i=L,H$. If the probability of a loss for each group remains stable over time, then so will the price of insurance. Consumers are assumed to be averse to risk, estimate the probability of a loss to be Φ_{it}, and choose the optimal amount of insurance by maximizing expected utility. Then the demand curves for consumers in each risk group is given by D_{it} $i=L,H$, and full coverage will be purchased if $P_{it}=\Phi_{it}$. Firms are assumed to know Q_{it} as well as Φ_{it}. If losses are not correlated between individuals, then it is realistic to postulate that in this ideal case firms will set their premiums so as to maximize expected profits for each risk group which we denote as $E(\Pi_{it})$.

The equilibriums for the two polar cases are also illustrated in Figure 2. When the firm is monopolist it will set the premiums at P'_{it} so that each consumer purchases less than full coverage. In a purely competitive environment with costless entry or exit by firms, and no costs of search by consumers, the equilibrium price will be at $P_{it}=\Phi_{it}$ and $E(\Pi_{it})=0$ $i=L,H$ for each firm in the industry. If a firm sets $P_{it} < \Phi_{it}$ it will lose money; if $P_{it} > \Phi_{it}$ then other firms can charge a price between P_{it} and Φ_{it}, make positive profits, and attract all consumers in risk group i.

A numerical example depicted in Figure 3 illustrates the premium structure for both the monopolist and purely competitive industry for the case where $X=40$ $\Phi_{Lt}=.1$ and $\Phi_{Ht}=.3$. Consumers all have the same utility function $U_i(Y)=-e^{-cY}$ with the risk aversion coefficient $c=.04$. If the firm is a monopolist it will set P_{it} so as to maximize

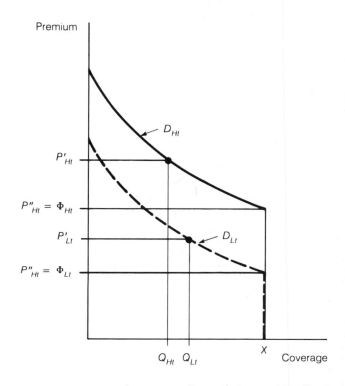

FIGURE 2   Premium Structure for Monopolist and Competitive Firms with Perfect Information

$$E(\Pi_u) = (P_{it} - \Phi_{it})Q_{it} \qquad (i = L,H)$$

knowing that Q_{it} is determined by each consumer maximizing his or her expected utility. As shown in Figure 15.3, the optimal premium structure in this case is $P'_{Lt} = .22$ and $P'_{Ht} = .49$ which results in $Q_{Lt} = 17.7$ and $Q_{Ht} = 19.3$ and yields expected profits of $E(\Pi_{Lt}) = 2$ and $E(\Pi_{Ht}) = 3.77$ for the two respective risk groups. In a purely competitive industry, the respective prices charged for the high- and low-risk groups will be the actuarial fair rates of $P''_{Lt} = .1$ and $P''_{Ht} = .3$ and full insurance will be demanded since consumers are risk averse. By definition, expected profits for all firms in the industry will be zero.

Let us now briefly turn to the impact of market structure on consumer welfare. It is clear from the above example, and true in general, that competition improves the welfare of each of the risk groups from what it would have been in a monopoly situation. The threat of new firms entering the market forces each firm to set the lowest premium consistent with their information on the risk and the consumer's demand curve. In contrast, the monopolist can exploit his or her uniqueness by charging higher rates. The question as to when regulation is appropriate for improving welfare thus hinges on the type of market situation which consumers face. As we shall see in the next section, it also depends on information imperfections by firms.

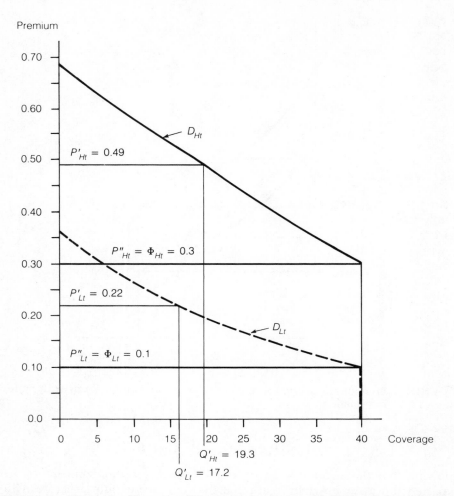

FIGURE 3 Illustrative Example of Premium Structure with Perfect Information

Imperfect Information by Firms: The Case of Automobile Insurance[4]

Relevant Assumptions

Suppose that firms have imperfect information on the risk characteristics of consumers. A typical example would be firms marketing automobile insurance to drivers, some of whom may be considered to be high-risk and others low-risk. In the context of the above framework, these two categories reflect different probabilities of having an accident.

In this section, we will consider the case where firms know what the probabilities are of an accident by a good or bad driver as well as the proportion

4. The material in this section summarizes recent research by Mark Pauly and myself. A more detailed discussion appears in Kunreuther and Pauly (1980).

of each type driver in the population. To focus on the impact of imperfect information by firms, we assume that consumers know whether they are good or bad drivers, but a firm cannot classify any new applicant, and hence, is initially forced to charge a single premium.[5] Over time, the firm learns about the characteristics of its old customers through their loss experience. This information enables them to classify consumers through a Bayesian updating procedure and charge differential prices. The real-world counterpart of this behavior is the common practice followed by insurance firms of "experience rating" whereby those with good driving records are charged lower premiums than those who have had accidents.[6]

The other institutional consideration which forms a part of this analysis is the differential information that firms have on the characteristics of consumers desiring insurance. Insurance companies who obtain specific knowledge of their customers' characteristics through experience have no incentive to share this information with other firms. Hence, these uninformed firms have no way of confirming whether a new applicant is telling the truth about his past experience.

Given the above assumptions, we can examine the characteristics of the market and contrast the resulting equilibrium with the ideal case discussed in the previous section. Let us start the analysis by first considering how premiums are set when firms have no information on the risk characteristics of the specific applicant. For concreteness, we will assume that firms are maximizing expected profits and that consumers maximize expected utility. Similarly, firms are assumed to utilize Bayesian updating procedures for incorporating loss experience into their classification scheme.

Figure 4 graphically depicts the resulting prices in the initial period 0 for the monopolist (P'_0) and for a firm in a purely competitive industry (P''_0) using the parameters from the previous example and assuming there are an equal percentage of good and bad risks in the population.[7] Turning first to the monopolist, the contrast with the case of perfect information is striking. Since the firm cannot distinguish between the high and low risks, it finds that the optimal price to charge is $P'_0 = .49$, a value so high that low-risk consumers will not demand any insurance. It is thus no coincidence that the initial price is the same as the premium charged to high-risk customers when the monopoly firm had perfect information.

5. The above problem has been examined by Rothschild and Stiglitz (1976), Spence (1978), and others in the context of static market equilibrium. These analyses assume that firms market price-quantity pairs of insurance contracts as a way of differentiating between high and low risks in contrast to the assumption here, similar to Pauly (1974), that firms set a price per unit of coverage without restricting the amount which any group can purchase.

6. A more detailed description of the practice of experience rating followed by firms in the United States appears in a detailed report of current practices by the insurance industry undertaken by the Stanford Research Institute (1976).

7. This assumption is equivalent to assigning an equal weight to the high- and low-risk groups in computing expected profit so that a meaningful comparison can be made with Figure 3. If the high-risk group has a larger relative weight, then the resulting premium will also be higher.

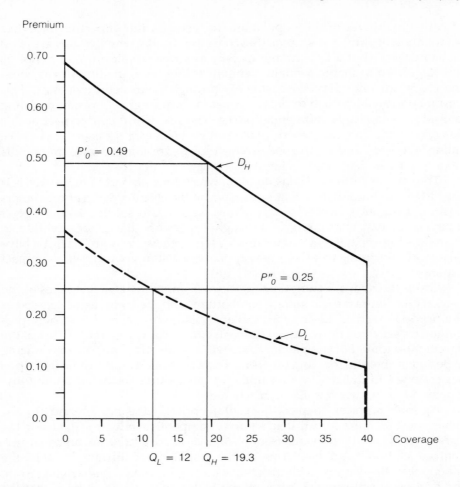

FIGURE 4   Illustrative Example of Initial Premium Structure by Firm with Imperfect
Information

This particular example illustrates the phenomenon of adverse selection
which has been discussed in the economics literature as a cause of market
failure (see Arrow 1963 and Akerlof 1970). In this case *adverse selection* refers to
the ability of the individuals at greater risk to take advantage of the supplier's
imperfect knowledge. Because a firm has imperfect information on the risk
characteristics of potential customers, it charges a premium which is so high
that only the highest-risk individuals demand coverage.

Where there is costless exit and entry, then each firm in the competitive
industry sets a premium which yields zero expected profits as shown by
$P''_0 = .25$ in Figure 4. In this case the high-risk individuals naturally buy full
coverage (that is, $Q_H = 40$). Low-risk individuals subsidize the high-risk group,
and hence, purchase only partial coverage ($Q_L = 12$). Compared to the case of
perfect information illustrated in Figure 3, the high-risk individuals clearly gain
at the expense of low-risk applicants. This phenomenon is a fairly general

one in markets with imperfect information. Those who are the worst risks get lumped together with better risks, and therefore benefit by not being identifiable as long as the equilibrium premium induces both groups to buy coverage.[8]

Let us now turn to the case where firms learn about the characteristics of their customers through loss data. During each time period, an individual can suffer at most one loss, which if it occurs will cause X dollars damage. That information is recorded on the insurer's record, and a new premium is set for the next period which reflects his overall loss experience. Informed firms do not disclose their records to other firms. Individuals who are dissatisfied with their new premium can seek insurance elsewhere. Other firms will not have access to the insured's record and hence cannot verify whether an applicant has had few or many losses under previous insurance contracts. Hence, the uninformed firms just treat the individual as a new customer.

The premium structure for the informed firm is determined in the following way. Let period t be defined as the length of time a group of customers has remained with the same firm. Then there will be $t + 1$ different classifications reflecting the number of losses j ($j=0,1...,t$) during this interval of time. Let P_{jt} represent the price charged to those consumers who have suffered exactly j losses in a t period interval. The premiums $P_{jt}, j=0...t$, have to be sufficiently low so that the uninformed firms cannot undercut these prices to attract customers from the informed firms and still make a profit.

A little reflection suggests the nature of the solution. As j increases then P_{jt} will also increase, since the proportion of high-risk consumers increases with j. Hence, if an uninformed firm charges a premium less than P_{jt} it will attract all those customers with j or more losses. Hence, each premium P_{jt} must be sufficiently low so that the uninformed firms cannot make a profit by attracting customers with j through t losses.[9] Let these values be designated as $\bar{P}_{jt}$. In essence $\bar{P}_{jt}$ represents an upper bound on the set of prices offered on the market. If the informed firm finds that it maximizes profits for any given classification j by setting $P_{jt} < \bar{P}_{jt}$ then, of course, it is in the firm's best economic interest to do so. Due to imperfect information by firms on the true risk, some of the high- and low-risk consumers will be misclassified on the basis of their losses. Over time, these statistical errors will decrease as the population sorts itself into appropriate groups.

An Illustrative Example

Figure 5 illustrates the nature of the solution by considering a simple one-period example (that is, $t=1$) with two classifications based on $j=0$ or 1. Using the same parameters as in the previous problem (see Figure 3) we find that the

8. The low-risk group could have had such a small probability of an accident that its demand for insurance could have shifted sufficiently downward that the only premium yielding zero expected profits would have been at $P''_0 = .30$. In this case, the high-risk group would pay the actuarially fair premium and the low-risk group would not have demanded any coverage, a case of adverse selection.

9. Consumers are assumed not to have any search costs. If they had, then informed firms could capitalize on this transaction cost by charging even higher premiums than the ones specified above.

optimal premiums P''_{jt} in the competitive industry are $P''_{11}=.29$ and $P''_{01}=.25$, yielding expected profits of $E(\Pi''_{11})=0$ and $E(\Pi''_{01})=.23$ respectively. In the case of $j=1$, the resulting price yields zero profits, because any $P_{11} > .29$ would have led an uninformed firm to set a lower price, inducing all of those consumers with one loss to purchase from them while still making a profit. For $j=0$, the informed firm can exploit its information on losses and make a profit by charging the same premium that a new firm would charge if it could not distinguish between risk classes, $P''_{01}=P''_0=.25$. The informed firm estimates that the proportion of low-risk customers with zero losses is .56 rather than their initial estimate of .5. This enables them to make a profit for customers with zero losses.

The case of monopoly behavior over time is uninteresting for this example, since the firm has set its initial premium so high that only the high risks will purchase insurance. Thus, the premium remains stable over time unless there is a change in the estimated probability of a loss. Had the monopolist set a price

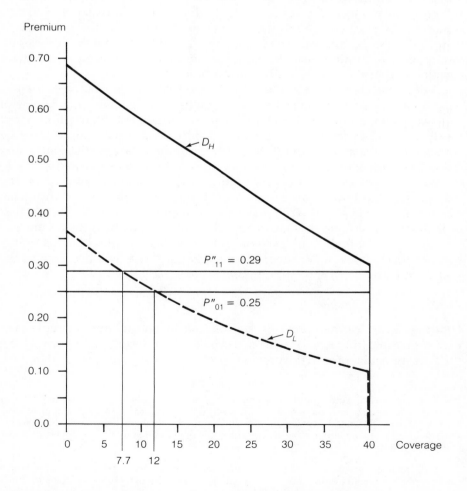

FIGURE 5   Premium Structure for Informed Firms at End of Period 1

where both high- and low-risk consumers purchased a policy, then the updating procedure would have been identical to the one described above, except that $P'_{jt}\,j=0...t$ would be determined by maximizing $E(\Pi'_{jt})$ for each classification j, since there would be no uninformed firms with which to concern oneself. Prices would thus be the same or higher than in the competitive case.

Welfare and Policy Implications

What are the welfare implications of the above analysis of firm imperfections? Two principal points emerge. First, adverse selection may create a situation where low-risk individuals will *not* demand insurance because the premium is too high. Secondly, when both groups have coverage, low-risk individuals will *always* subsidize high-risk consumers whether or not they have an accident. Those who suffer a loss will be misclassified into a higher rate category as indicated by P_{11}. Those who do not suffer a loss will pay a lower premium than P_{11} but it will be above the actuarial rate because some high-risk individuals will also be in this category.

The results of this dynamic model of learning have an interesting interpretation in the context of Cyert and March's 1963 study on the behavioral theory of the firm and Williamson's 1975 work on impacted information. Suppose we view policyholders as an integral part of the firm, as in a mutual insurance company where every insured individual is a member of the company. Any time there is a subsidy, we can refer to this situation as one of organizational slack. As defined by Cyert and March, "slack consists in payments to members of the coalition in excess of what is required to maintain the organization" (p. 36). In the context of this example, those in the highest risk class have no economic incentive to leave their insurance firm because their premiums are either actuarially fair or being subsidized.

The low-risk group has the reverse reaction — all the members are being charged more than the actuarial rate, but other firms cannot distinguish their special status because of impacted information. They are thus forced to remain with their current firm because others in the industry are not privy to the information on their relative risk. This suggests that if firms do not have perfect information on their clients, insured individuals who are worse than the average will remain because of organizational slack while those who are better than average will not switch because of problems of impacted information.

What are the implications of this behavior for prescriptive analysis? Obviously public disclosure of the information that firms use to set their rates would benefit the low-risk consumers at the expense of the higher risk group. Suppose drivers could present a certified copy of their accident record from Company A to a competitor. To the extent that this option was pursued by consumers, impacted information would be reduced and monopoly profits curtailed.

Monopoly profits by firms also provides some justification for regulating insurance premiums. Many states currently have a prior approval regulatory system where justifications for rate increases must be filed with state insurance commissioners along with supporting documents. According to these laws, rates are not to be excessive, inadequate, or unfairly discriminatory. As in all questions involving regulation, one has to balance the potential benefits of forcing firms to reveal information with the paperwork and transaction costs involved in having the company justify each rate increase. More empirical data is needed to provide a better data base on which to judge these impacts. The material reported in MacAvoy (1977) is an excellent start in this direction.

Future Research Questions

Future research on firm behavior can investigate the following sets of questions in the context of the above framework.

1. What are the implications for market behavior if firms utilize updating procedures which differ from a Bayesian analysis? For example, suppose firms develop a rate-classification scheme which only changes the premium if a driver incurs two or more accidents in a given time period. Alternatively, suppose firms have only three or four classifications no matter how many periods the individual is insured with the firm. If consumers have no losses for a certain number of consecutive years, they are automatically placed in the lowest risk classification. How will these systems affect price and quantity equilibriums for the high- and low-risk groups?

2. Suppose one introduces search costs into the analysis so that consumers are reluctant to seek out new companies unless their premiums increase from period t to $t + 1$ by more than s dollars or z percent. What are the implications of this action on firm behavior as well as on market equilibrium values?

3. How does one incorporate equity considerations, such as income level, as well as societal concerns regarding discrimination by age or sex into this analysis? There is considerable controversy now on this topic stimulated by the Massachusetts hearings on automobile insurance rates in 1977.

4. What are the likely differences to emerge between insurance premiums and the level of protection in states which are highly regulated (for example, New Jersey), moderately regulated (for example, Texas), or which rely on market forces (for example, California)?[10] An understanding of the decision processes utilized by firms and the degree of imperfect information on characteristics of consumers are important factors to incorporate in the analysis of this comparative problem.

5. Finally, we have assumed throughout this analysis that consumers have perfect information on their own risk classification. What is the impact of different types of market or regulatory systems if consumers have misperceptions of their risk and behave in ways which differ from maximizing expected utility? This very broad topic requires considerable research. The next section introduces some of the impacts of consumer imperfections on prices and market structure.

---

10. See MacAvoy (1977) for a description of the different types of regulatory systems and comparisons of the performance of the insurance industry in a highly regulated state (for example, New Jersey) and one in which open competition prevails (for example, California).

Imperfect Information by Consumers: The Case of Flood Insurance

Let us now reverse the coin from the previous section by considering the case where firms have perfect information on the risk characteristics facing the consumer, but individuals threatened with a loss of X dollars are imperfectly informed of the risk which they face. An example of this situation is the provision of flood insurance to residents of hazard-prone areas. Hydrologic data have been analyzed by groups such as the Corps of Engineers to determine the actuarial risk faced by different structures in the flood plain, but residents of the area may perceive the risk incorrectly.

Misestimation of Probability

To begin the analysis, suppose that consumers misestimate the probability of a loss. There is considerable empirical evidence from recent laboratory experiments supporting this assumption. Tversky and Kahneman (1974) describe the biases and heuristics which cause systematic misestimates of probability even by mathematically sophisticated individuals such as statisticians and engineers. They characterize one of these heuristics as availability whereby one judges the probability of an event by the ease with which one is able to imagine it. In the case of the flood hazard, two individuals with the same objective risk may estimate the probability of a future flood differently depending upon whether they have recently experienced a disaster. Fischhoff, Slovic, and Lichtenstein (1980b, in press) have categorized a set of biases in perceptions that individuals exhibit with respect to low-probability events. These findings are based on a series of laboratory experiments and field survey data which they and others have undertaken.

An Illustrative Example

What is the impact of such misestimation on equilibrium prices and demand for insurance protection? The simplest way to illustrate this effect in the context of the previous example is to assume that all individuals in the hazard-prone area have the same objective risk — Φ_{Ht}. Some individuals in the group correctly perceive the probability of a disaster while others underestimate its value, perceiving it to be Φ_{Lt}. To isolate the effect of misperception of probability on market adjustment processes, consumers are assumed to choose the amount of protection which maximizes their expected utility. The demand curve for consumers who correctly estimate $\varphi_{Ht}=\Phi_{Ht}$ is designated by D_{Ht}. Those who incorrectly estimated the risk to be $\varphi_{Ht}=\Phi_{Lt}$ have their demand curve given by D_{Lt}. Firms know the true probability and the decision rule on which the consumer bases his or her decision. However, they cannot differentiate between consumers who correctly perceive the risk and those who do not. Hence, they set just one premium, P''_t, for the competitive situation and P'_t for the monopoly case.

Figure 6 illustrates the resulting equilibria for the case where $\Phi_{Ht}=.3$ and some consumers correctly estimate its value while others assume $\varphi_{Ht}=.1$. In a competitive market, the premium will always remain at $P''_t=\Phi_{Ht}=.3$ because any higher premium would induce firms to enter the industry, charge a slightly

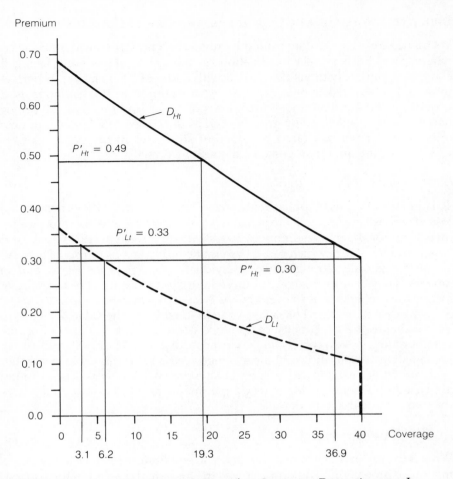

FIGURE 6   Premium Structure with Imperfect Consumer Perceptions on Φ_H

lower price, but one above .3, and still make a positive expected profit. Any lower premium would create losses. If consumers underestimate the probability of a disaster, they will find this premium to be relatively unattractive to them and purchase little insurance protection, in this example $Q_{Lt}=6.2$. In fact, it should be clear from this analysis that if the consumer sufficiently underestimates the chances of a flood, he may desire no insurance simply because the premium is too high relative to the perceived utility of protecting himself.[11]

Monopolists want to set their premium so they maximize expected profit. If the monopolist assumes that individuals correctly estimate the chances of a disaster, then he or she sets the price at $P'_{Ht}=.49$, the same value as the one given in Figure 3 when both parties were assumed to have perfect information. In this case, those individuals who misperceive the probability to be

11. Consumers who overestimate Φ_{Ht} will purchase full coverage since they perceive the premium to be subsidized.

$\varphi_{Ht}=.1$ will purchase no coverage while consumers with accurate information will buy $Q'_{Ht}=19.3$. At the other end of the spectrum, the monopolist may assume that all individuals estimate $\varphi_{Ht}=.1$. In this case, the monopolist sets the premium to maximize profit given the demand curve D_{Lt} and chooses a value of $P'_{Lt}=.33$, thus eliciting a demand of $Q'_{Lt}=3.1$. Those who correctly estimate Φ_{Ht} will purchase 36.9 units of insurance. If the monopolist assumes that there is a fraction w who correctly estimate the probability, and another fraction $(1-w)$ who misestimate it, then the premium which maximizes expected profits will be somewhere between .33 and .49.

This simple example illustrates a somewhat obvious conclusion. Even if the market is competitive with free entry and exit, individuals will purchase limited protection if they underestimate the risk. Firms will not set the premium below the actuarial rate unless they also underestimate the risk. Hence, the equilibrium price makes the purchase of a large amount of insurance relatively unattractive to those who perceive the risk to be smaller than it actually is.

Impact of Behavioral Decision Rules

The above model still assumes that individuals are behaving as if they maximized some objective function such as expected utility. There is considerable empirical evidence which suggests that actual behavior of individuals regarding low-probability events is based on a different decision process than the one described above. Building on the work of Herbert Simon, one can hypothesize that individuals' actions are constrained by their limited ability to collect and process information. Hence, they attempt to satisfy some objective through the use of simplifying heuristics rather than optimizing behavior. One such heuristic which appears to explain protective behavior regarding low-probability events is a threshold model of choice, whereby individuals do not concern themselves with the consequences of an event unless they perceive the probability of its occurrence to be above a specified level φ_i^* (Slovic et al. 1977).

Field survey data of 3000 individuals in flood- and earthquake-prone areas, half of whom were insured and the other half not, suggest that individuals utilize a sequential model of choice in determining whether to purchase coverage or not, where a threshold probability is an important part of the choice process (Kunreuther et al. 1978a). Unless individuals perceive the hazard to be a serious problem and have engaged in discussions with friends and neighbors about insurance, they are unlikely to buy coverage. The most important variable determining the perceived severity of the problem is past experience with the hazard, thus suggesting that the probability of the disaster occurring has been raised above some critical threshold φ_i^*. Once the individual has decided that he is interested in protection, there is a tendency to utilize simplified decision rules which reflect human limitations in formulating and solving complex problems.

There has been considerable work in recent years to determine the process of choice once the individual has reached the stage where he or she wants to balance costs and benefits. For the single-attribute problem discussed here, where the trade-offs are in monetary terms, [12] Kahneman and Tversky (1979b) have formulated prospect theory as an alternative to utility theory. Thaler (1980) has also provided a number of examples illustrating the tendency of consumers to incorporate regret into their decisions and their failure to ignore sunk costs as part of the analysis of a problem.

The importance of accurately describing the factors influencing the consumer's demand curve for protection cannot be overemphasized. Unless one understands the process by which choices are made, it will be difficult to evaluate how well the market is likely to work and the prescriptive alternatives which may be appropriate.

To be more concrete on this point, suppose that the consumer has reached the state in the sequential decision process whereby he or she is seriously interested in some protective mechanism, such as insurance. There are several heuristics which appear to play a role in the final purchase decision. Rather than viewing the situation probabilistically, individuals may consider the cost of a policy in relation to the amount they are likely to collect should a disaster occur. This *price/loss ratio* may explain the popularity of flight insurance, where for a very small premium, one can receive thousands of dollars worth of coverage. A comment from a homeowner in a flood-prone area illustrates how the perceptions of the premium in relation to the loss may be important, particularly after a past experience with the event.

> I've talked to the different ones that have been bombed out. This was their feeling: the $60 (in premiums) they could use for something else. But now they don't care if the figure was $600. They're going to take insurance because they have been through it twice and they've learned a lesson from it. (Kunreuther et al. 1978a, p. 112.)

A second factor which influences the decision on taking protective action is the *price* itself. If the premium is above some critical level, then this will discourage the purchase of coverage even if the risk is perceived to be high. In trying to understand the impact of an income or budget constraint on coverage, one uninsured homeowner in a flood-prone area noted:

> A blue-collar worker doesn't just run up there with $200 (the insurance premium) and buy a policy. The world knows that 90 percent of us live from payday to payday. . . . He can't come up with that much cash all of a sudden and turn around and meet all his other obligations. (Kunreuther et al. 1978a, p. 113.)

A final factor, which may determine how much protection an individual is likely to purchase, is the tendency to view this expenditure as an *investment* rather than a contingent claim. In other words, the person wants to purchase insurance if he or she feels that there is a good chance of obtaining some return on the investment. This may explain the great popularity of first dollar cover-

---

12. It is interesting to speculate whether protective decisions are viewed by individuals as having multiple attributes such as reducing anxiety, social norms, in addition to monetary trade-offs. The sequential model of choice suggests one way of dealing with this problem. An alternative approach would be the method of preference trees proposed by Tversky and Sattath (1979) for describing the purchase of consumption goods such as automobiles or choosing a meal in a restaurant.

age and the preference for low deductibles on the part of individuals.[13] It also is related to the concept of regret, utilized by Thaler (1980) as an explanation for this behavior. Once an uninsured individual has experienced a disaster, he or she may regret not having purchased a policy. The natural response of such a person is self-protection against such future events by purchasing a large amount of coverage. The same phenomenon also explains why individuals cancel their insurance policy after not collecting on it after a few years; they regret having made an investment which has not paid off.

A simple schematic model illustrating how the above heuristics could be incorporated into a demand curve for insurance is depicted in Figure 7 for persons whose threshold probability is above φ_t^*. As in the previous example, we assume there is only one risk, Φ_{Ht}, but that there are two groups of

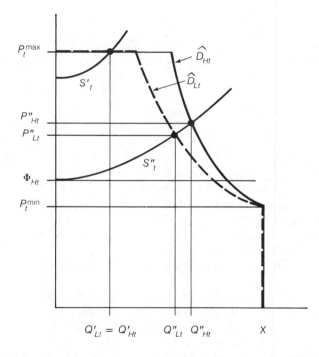

FIGURE 7   Example of Premium Structure with Behavioral Consumer Decision Rules

13. This *ex ante* behavior on the part of consumers is particularly interesting in light of the reluctance by victims to collect on a policy if the loss is relatively small. For example, an individual with a $50 deductible who suffers a $75 loss from an automobile accident may be reluctant to collect the $25 because of the processing costs as well as the fear that his insurance rates will be raised the next year. It would be interesting to confront him with this action and inquire why he did not initially take out a $100 deductible or whether he plans to do this on renewing his policy.

consumers: those who correctly perceive the risk with demand curve $\hat{D}_{Ht}$, and those who incorrectly perceive it to be Φ_{Lt} with demand curve $\hat{D}_{Lt}$. Once the premium is above some critical upper limit (P_t^{max}), it is assumed there will be no interest in insurance by either group of consumers because of a budget constraint. If $P_t=P_t^{max}$, an individual is likely to buy a relatively large amount of coverage because of concerns of regret and the view of insurance as a good investment. As the premium decreases, the individual will increase coverage until the premium/loss ratio is sufficiently low that he or she wants to purchase full protection. We have denoted this lower bound as P_t^{min}. Both P_t^{max} and P_t^{min} are assumed to be independent of the probability of a disaster since they are influenced by factors such as budget constraints or premium/loss ratios. According to the above discussion, the following factors appear to influence the shape of the demand curve for each risk group i.

A. $\varphi_{it} \leqslant \varphi_{it}^*$ $\quad\quad\quad\quad\quad$ φ_{it} $\quad\quad\quad\quad$ *(threshold concept)*

B. $\varphi_{it} > \varphi_{it}^*$

$\quad$ $P_{it} \geqslant P_t^{max}$ $\quad\quad\quad\quad$ $Q_{it}=0$ $\quad\quad\quad$ *(budget constraints)*

$\quad$ $P_t^{min} < P_{it} < P_t^{max}$ $\quad\quad$ $0 < Q_{it} < X$ *(premium/loss ratio considerations)*

$\quad$ $P_{it} \leqslant P_t^{min}$ $\quad\quad\quad\quad$ $Q_{it}=X$ $\quad\quad\quad$ *(sufficiently low premium/loss ratio)*

Let us now turn to the supply side. Firms have an additional problem in marketing coverage against a disaster such as a flood where damages between individuals are highly correlated. They must concern themselves with the possibility of a catastrophic loss which may have adverse consequences on their financial stability and short-run operations. There are two principal ways in which they can protect themselves against this possibility: (1) they can only offer coverage to a maximum number of consumers at a fixed premium per dollar of protection; or (2) they can purchase reinsurance to cover the loss above a certain amount and can charge a premium per dollar coverage which increases as the amount of coverage increases. This type of premium schedule reflects risk aversion on the part of the firm and the need to reinsure a portion of the loss.

We have depicted the latter situation in Figure 7 for both the competitive and monopoly firms. The upward sloping supply curves, S_t' and S_t'', reflect the case where firms are risk averse and concerned with possible catastrophic losses. Consumers who underestimate the probability of a disaster will thus pay a lower premium than those who correctly estimate the risk because they will be demanding less coverage. In the case of a competitive industry, the optimal premiums and quantity pairs will be (P_{Lt}'', Q_{Lt}''), and (P_{Ht}'', Q_{Ht}'') for the individuals who underestimate and correctly estimate their losses, respectively. We have drawn the monopolist's supply schedule S_t' to illustrate a case where both those who underestimate the risk and those who correctly estimate Φ_{Ht} will purchase the same amount Q_t' at the premium P_H^{max}. The upward sloping supply curve discourages consumers from buying more than that quantity of insurance.

Welfare and Policy Implementation

The simple analysis here has only suggested at the dynamics of the problem by suggesting how people's perceptions of the probability of an event may change over time due to past experience. From the welfare point of view, it is clear that consumers will purchase limited, if any, protection when they underestimate the chances of an event occurring. After a disaster, they may regret not having purchased insurance and may revise their *ex post* estimate of the probability upwards. This type of reaction raises an important philosophical problem regarding the role of the private and public sectors in dealing with situations where there is wide diversity between *ex ante* and *ex post* estimates of the probability of an event occurring.

The history of disaster relief illustrates the point rather clearly. Most individuals in flood- and earthquake-prone areas have not protected themselves against these hazards with insurance because they perceived that the chances of an event were so small that they did not have to worry about the consequences. Little attention was given prior to the disaster by uninsured individuals to the possibility of receiving federal relief to aid them in their recovery. After the event, victims pressured their representatives in Congress for special relief, and new legislation was frequently passed providing people with generous aid. For example, Tropical Storm Agnes in June 1972 caused over $750 million in damage to private housing, but only 1583 claims totaling approximately $5 million were paid under the National Flood Insurance Program. As a result, the federal government offered victims $5,000 forgiveness grants and percent loans for the remaining portion of their loss (Kunreuther 1973). After the event, victims may increase their subjective probability of the recurrence of this type of disaster. Yet liberal relief also may have had the effect of discouraging some victims from voluntarily purchasing flood insurance in the future.

There are a set of policy-related questions stimulated by this *ex ante/ex post* question. Specifically, can one make individuals more aware of the risks associated with a particular hazard so that they will want to voluntarily protect themselves by focusing on the factors which influence their demand for protection? One way to encourage individuals to purchase insurance is to present information so that they perceive the probability of an event occurring to be above their critical *threshold level*. For example, in describing the chances of a 100-year flood, the insurance firm or agent could note that for someone living in a house for twenty-five years, the chances of suffering a loss at least once will be .22. Consumers may then be willing to view the situation as serious, where they would not if data were presented in terms of the annual probability of a flood. By presenting the same information in different forms or contexts, people may behave differently.[14] If the principal reason for not purchasing coverage is the unusually high price in relation to an income or budget constraint, then a reduction in the premium may be deemed desirable.

14. Empirical evidence on this point with respect to insurance decisions and other choices under risk has been presented in a number of recent studies including Payne (1976); Fischhoff, Slovic, and Lichtenstein (1978); Grether and Plott (1979); Schoemaker and Kunreuther (1979); Hershey and Schoemaker (1980a); Schoemaker (1980a); and Tversky and Kahneman (1981).

The appropriate prescriptive measures depend on the market situation. If firms have some degree of monopoly power, premium regulation may induce more consumers to purchase coverage. In the case of flood insurance, where the industry had not offered coverage because of previous catastrophic losses, some form of government reinsurance may induce them to market policies at premiums reflecting risk. In addition, some type of federal subsidy on premiums may encourage residents to buy coverage, although the experience of the National Flood Insurance Program is not encouraging in this regard.

If none of these incentives are successful, and the public sector wants to reduce its financial commitments after a disaster, then some form of required coverage may be necessary. The simplest policy would be for banks and financial institutions to require insurance as a condition for a mortgage as a way of protecting their own investments. An alternative to the above recommendations is for the federal government to provide relief to disaster victims, using taxpayers' money to finance this effort. The latter action explicitly assumes that disasters are a public rather than a private responsibility.

Future Research Questions

From the point of view of future research, the following questions need to be investigated to gain a better understanding of the interaction between firms and consumers.

1. How can learning be more explicitly incorporated into an analysis of consumer demand over time? A protective mechanism can be viewed as an innovation which takes time to be adopted by large segments of the population. The diffusion process may be very important because of the impact that social norms may have on individual behavior. Schelling (1978) has treated this phenomenon in some detail and provides a number of interesting examples illustrating stable and unstable equilibriums.

2. How is firm behavior affected by changes in the demand curve of consumers over time because of past experience and personal influence? Both these factors appear to play an important role on the decision process over time.

3. What impact do concepts such as regret, threshold behavior, and consumer misperceptions have on market behavior and equilibrium price and quantities?

4. What are the *ex ante/ex post* implications of alternative market and public sector solutions? What are the appropriate roles of the public and private sectors with respect to protective activities and recovery measures after a disaster?

Summary and Conclusion

This paper began by citing two examples where empirical data revealed that the market did not provide consumers with adequate or equitable protection against low-probability events. The analysis which followed revealed that markets do not perform well in these cases because of information imperfections by consumers and/or firms.

In the case of automobile insurance, firms frequently use experience rating to differentiate between drivers with different loss records. This process enables them to make monopoly profits because other firms do not have access to this information. The inability of firms to classify drivers with perfect accuracy also means that low-risk individuals subsidize those in the high-risk group.

In the case of flood insurance, consumers have not voluntarily purchased highly subsidized rates because they either underestimate the probability of a loss and/or they utilize decision processes which rely on factors other than trade-offs between costs and benefits. As a result, the public sector has provided uninsured victims with liberal relief following a catastrophic disaster.

Proposed prescriptive measures for coping with the problems of protection against low-probability events should address these descriptive findings. What is the role of presenting information to consumers so they better appreciate why one may want to take preventive measures before a disaster occurs, rather than regretting not having done so after it is too late? Are there economic incentives which can aid in this process? What is the appropriate place of regulation in coping with problems of market failure?

There are no easy answers to these questions. What has become clear is that people do not do a good job in collecting and processing information regarding low-probability/high-consequence events. We must accept this empirical observation and incorporate it into our theory. This paper represents a small step in this direction. Considerably more work is needed.

ACKNOWLEDGMENT

The research report in this paper is supported by the *Bundeministerium fuer Forschung und Technologie*, F.R.G., Contract No. 321/7591/RGB 8001. While support for this work is gratefully acknowledged, the views expressed are the author's and not necessarily shared by the sponsor. This paper reflects discussions with a number of individuals in the course of my work on decision processes for low-probability events. In particular, my thinking on many points has been clarified through interchanges with Baruch Fischhoff, Jack Hershey, Paul Kleindorfer, Sarah Lichtenstein, Mark Pauly, Paul Schoemaker, Paul Slovic, and Amos Tversky, as well as with my IIASA colleagues John Lathrop, Joanne Linnerooth, Nino Majone, Michael Thompson, and Peyton Young.

On Improving Applied Decision Making: Comments on the Bouwman, Tuggle and Gerwin, and Kunreuther Papers

Ronald N. Taylor, *University of British Columbia*

The three papers included in this section represent applications of information-processing and decision-making theory and research in the fields of accounting (Bouwman), business policy and strategy (Tuggle and Gerwin), and public policy (Kunreuther). Such studies reflect the current concern for improving applied decision making through understanding the behavioral aspects of decisions made in these real-world contexts, as well as in other professional areas (for example, trust investment, graduate student admission, and design of management information systems). In commenting on these papers, I shall attempt to highlight issues which appear to me to be important for improving applications of decision-making theory and research. My focus for this critique is the implications of cognitive phenomena of human judgment and choice for applied decision making in organizational contexts — particularly with regard to how humans cope with excessive informational demands and seek information in the face of uncertainty. Suggestions pertaining to potentially profitable directions for future advances in applied decision making are made regarding: (1) advances in theory development; (2) reevaluation of research methods; and (3) strategies for applied decision making. These issues are discussed below, drawing upon the research reported in the papers included in this session.

Theory Development and Applied Decision Making

Theories to account for behavioral aspects of information processing and decision making typically have been drawn from the literature of the behavioral sciences, or they have emerged from biases and inefficiencies observed in human decision-making research. Few well-developed theories exist to explain the behavioral aspects of information processing and decision making. Typically, limited theories have been proposed to explain rather specific biases or heuristics that have been observed in empirical research (for example, representativeness or conservatism). The papers by Kunreuther and by Bouwman report some limitations in human information processing and judgment which have been observed and explore their implications for applied decision making. This approach to theory development has several limitations.

Since theory follows empirical research in an effort to explain empirical research findings, important aspects of information processing and decision making may be omitted. The papers by Bouwman and by Kunreuther consider a topic that has received relatively little attention in the literature on decision making — the manner in which problems are "found" or recognized in applied settings, priorities for solution attempts are set, and problems are formulated or reformulated prior to solution.

Some attention has been directed toward this topic, for example, problems frequently have been perceived as "gaps" between existing state and desired state (Newell et al. 1958, Reitman 1964), and Ansoff (1965) has described ways in which existing and desired states can change to produce decision problems. In addition, some research has suggested that the informational base used to identify problems can contain biases which may mislead decision makers when information is communicated upward in organizations (Woods 1966, Cohen 1958) and when the communicators perceive information as negative (Rosen and Tesser 1969). Decision makers also have demonstrated that perception of uncertain events may be consciously or unconsciously distorted by ignoring aspects of a decision problem that may cause anxiety (see, for example, Rokeach 1960) or be potentially hazardous. The latter point is demonstrated in the Kunreuther paper, since low-probability/high-consequence events may be disregarded, for example, flood threats (White 1964). Similarly, one may disregard fluctuations in interest rates or antitrust policies (Cyert and DeGroot 1970). These developments hold promise for augmenting prior attention to problem perception, for example, selective perception (Dearborn and Simon 1958), and level of aspiration (Hansburger 1969), and may lead to more coherent theories of problem recognition and formulation. Aspiration level is appropriately incorporated into problem perception by Kunreuther as a threshold that must be surpassed before individuals will be motivated to take protective actions in the face of low-probability threats.

The utility of limited theories explaining specific biases and heuristics in information processing and decision making can be increased if they are grounded in more general behavioral science theories of individual and collective choice. For example, the "gambler's fallacy" or "representativeness heuristic" could be understood more fully if these research findings were integrated into a more general theory of probabilistic judgment. Finding isolated situations in which judgments deviate from "standards" is a useful way to empirically generate hypotheses regarding judgmental processes; but understanding these processes can be furthered by mapping them within the domain of related theories of cognition, motivation, and/or perception. Some efforts have been made to develop more general theories to explain biases and heuristics in information processing and judgment, for example, integration theory (Anderson 1973), prospect theory (Kahneman and Tversky 1979b), alpha utility theory (Chew and MacCrimmon 1979), my own "contingent process" model (1976), and Kunreuther's information-processing model of risky choice (1976). An abundant literature on cognitive processes is developing (for example, see Bourne et al. 1979) and advances have been made in placing human judgment more firmly within the literature on social interaction (for example, Rappoport and Summers 1973). Attempts to integrate literature from the various fields related to decision making, such as the discussion of findings from judgment and attribute theory research (Fischhoff 1976), are promising avenues for developing more complete theories to explain information processing and judgment behaviors. In addition to deriving theories to *account for* research findings, it would be useful to propose general theories to *guide* the search for biases and heuristics in information processing and judgment.

Drawing upon psychological research on cognitive processes, models of human information-processing mechanisms can be used to develop decision aids (for example, Goodman et al. 1978). For example, the concept of "expert" judgment examined in the Bouwman paper may involve a trade-off between information processing and memory. In human information processing, the more material learned (that is, stored in memory), the fewer the computations to perform (that is, information-processing operations) and the easier the task becomes. A trade-off between processing and memory can be seen in the nature of "expertise" in many areas of competence — in learning to play soccer, to become a competent lawyer, or to become a chess master. Useful reviews of cognitive processes are provided by Neimark and Santa (1975) and Falmagne (1975). An intriguing observation reported in the Bouwman paper was greater variability in diagnostic processes for "experts" compared to "novices." While the differences in diagnostic processes between expert and novice subjects would be expected, one might anticipate that CPAs would tend to exhibit greater similarity in their diagnostic processes during the course of their professional training. It seems appropriate to interpret these findings — reported for one novice and one expert — with caution, despite the report that, while not representative of novices and experts, these two subjects were "typical" of their respective populations. The nature of "expertise" in professional judgments is a topic with considerable import for applied decisions, and a topic which requires much more attention in the literature of information processing and decision making.

Despite the view expressed in the Bouwman paper that subjects tend to exhibit little variability in the problem space they perceive, a growing body of research evidence on the psychological characteristics of decision makers has shown that, for example, they differ markedly in their susceptibility to cognitive strain (see MacCrimmon and Taylor 1976). Although human information-processing ability is sharply limited, some decision makers have much greater capacity to process information than do others. Susceptibility to cognitive strain has also been shown to be influenced by a decision maker's cognitive styles, and a good deal of research has dealt with the impact of two cognitive styles — "field independence" and "field dependence" on information systems acceptance and use (for example, Bariff and Lusk 1977).

Finally, papers included in this section represent the different levels of analysis that are highlighted by the papers in this book. The Bouwman paper focuses on individual diagnosticians, the Kunreuther paper deals with consumers who may be either individuals or collectives, and the Tuggle and Gerwin paper examines intraorganizational processes. Expanding the analysis of information-processing and decision-making behavior to encompass a policymaker's decision processes, organizational processes (that is, coalition formation), and the influence of the organization's environment is an important advance if we are to improve decision making in organizational contexts. This thrust represents a merging of individual decision making, organizational behavior, and policy analysis that appears to be gaining momentum in the literature of these fields.

Research Methodology and Applied Decision Making

The three papers included in this section use a variety of research methods: analysis of verbal protocol elicited by think-aloud instructions, computer simulation of organizational processes, and an economic analysis of courses of action. As such, these papers reflect the increasing use of a range of research methods in investigating information processing and decision making. Research on judgment and choice has tended to take advantage of appealing research paradigms (for example, in investigations of opinion revision) — appealing in that quantitative measures of behaviors can be used, objective norms can be specified in judging the quality of these behaviors (for example, Bayes's theorem), and the research can be performed in the laboratory using rigorous experimental designs. Yet, Cartwright (1973) has pointed out, in the context of the risky-shift paradigm, the dangers of limiting research to a single paradigm — values shared by researchers working within the paradigm may tend to inhibit critical testing of the theories advanced by this same group.

Also, relatively little concern has been expressed concerning experimental artifacts which may result from reactions of subjects to the experimental setting, the tasks, or the experimenter; yet these issues have received considerable attention in experiments done by social psychologists. The research evidence demonstrates that serious distortions in research findings can be produced by these reactive effects. The question of the reliability and validity of measures used in studies of judgment and choice have seldom been raised. An exception to this was an attempt to determine the convergent validity of a group of measures presumed to measure risk-taking propensity (Slovic 1972). Yet, the reliability of measures places limits on conclusiveness of research findings, and invalid measures can be misleading with regard to what construct has been measured. Research on the behavioral aspects of information systems design and use also suffers from lack of attention to the psychometric aspects of measurement (for example, Taylor and Benbasat 1980).

Important research questions may be neglected because they cannot be researched by the traditionally used research methods. Problem identification, for example, is generally regarded as crucial to the decision-making activities that follow (see, for example, Connolly 1977), yet, as noted above, it has received little research. This may be partly due to difficulties in finding an appealing research methodology for the less objectively observed and quantifiable aspects of decision making. The need for research on problem identification has been raised in reviews of the literature (Slovic et al. 1977), and it appears likely that an increasing amount of research will be addressed to this topic in the future. Also, as reflected in the Bouwman paper, there is a need for other research methods — perhaps longitudinal studies — to investigate learning effects or other developmental processes involved in information processing and decision making.

Finally, the frequent use of laboratory experiments has limited the extent to which findings can be generalized to the world outside the laboratory. When the findings are taken from the laboratory to an organization, there remains the question of whether important, real-world decisions are biased in the manner found in the laboratory. Increasingly, however, research on decision making is being conducted in field settings on topics such as technological hazards (Kates 1977). In these situations, it is particularly advisable to use multiple research methods to overcome the limitations of any single method for deriving research findings to guide applied decision making.

Strategies for Applied Decision Making

Much of the attention directed to improving applied decision making has taken the form of assisting decision makers to compensate for their limited information-processing and judgmental ability. For example, the "bounds" placed on effective decision making by cognitive strain can be expanded by operating upon the decision maker, the decision environment, or both, to achieve a correspondence between the amount of information required for making an effective decision and the processing capacity of a decision maker. Such a correspondence can be produced in three ways: (1) decision makers with high information-processing capacities can be selected; (2) decision makers can be trained to overcome the informational limitations and biases that lead to cognitive strain; or (3) the informational demands of a decision problem can be reduced by applying appropriate decision aids (for example, information formats or levels of aggregation) or by restructuring the decision problem (for example, decomposing, segmenting). The discussion by Kunreuther suggests a number of methods to aid decision makers in overcoming biased perceptions of low-probability events, as when he suggests that they acquire information regarding the rules firms use to set insurance rates.

Other theorists have approached the difficulty of explaining how choices are reached in organizational contexts by proposing alternate models of choice. Some have suggested that the central role of goals in many views of choice, that is, the use of goals to direct decision-making activity and to evaluate outcomes, can be changed either by replacing them with either broadly defined directions as in Braybrooke and Lindblom's disjointed incrementalism (1965), or by models which do not include goals, for example, the "garbage can" model (Cohen, March, and Olsen 1972), or the so-called "enacted" environments (Weick 1977). The search for alternate ways to represent how choices are made in organizational contexts seems to hold some potential for suggesting ways to more accurately reflect the psychological, social, and organizational influences on choices. It would, in my opinion, be useful to approach the task of improving applied decision making from the perspective of multiple models of decisions and multiple research methodologies. The three papers reviewed here reflect these features of research on applied decision making.

Applications of Information-Processing and Decision Theories: A Discussion

John W. Payne, *Duke University*

The information-processing approach to behavioral science, in general, and research on decision behavior, in particular, have always had a strong applied orientation. Simon (1979a), for example, explicitly notes the close relationship maintained between information-processing psychology and research on artificial intelligence. Similarly, Einhorn and Hogarth (1981a) comment on the strong engineering emphasis of decision research. It seems perfectly appropriate, therefore, that a large part of our dialogue here be devoted to presentations concerned with applications of information processing and decision making.

The papers by Bouwman, Tuggle and Gerwin, and Kunreuther, which I have been asked to discuss, present a wide sampling of current efforts to apply information processing and decision theories. In fact, the differences between these three papers are far greater than their common elements. Consequently, I will not try to fit all three papers into a single framework. What I plan to do is just highlight a couple of general methodological and theoretical trends that one or more of these papers illustrate.

Recently, there has been emphasis in information processing and problem-solving research on the study of expertness in ill-structured, complex, and semantically rich task domains (Simon 1979a). The potential benefits of shifting the focus of problem-solving research from tasks that can easily be represented in the laboratory (for example, Tower of Hanoi puzzles) to tasks that are closer to the kinds of complex tasks facing individuals in business, government, and medicine are clear. On the basic research side, we are able to test the power of our theoretical ideas against the complexity of real-world behavior. The work by Bouwman, Tuggle and Gerwin, and Kunreuther certainly deserves praise for attempting to deal with more complex problem-solving and decision environments.

It should be recognized, however, that our understanding of the behavior of individuals when faced with the apparently simple decision tasks that have been studied in the laboratory is far from complete. For example, one of the most studied decision tasks involves the choice between two or three outcome gambles. From our research, we now know that expected utility theory does not, at least in standard forms, provide an adequate explanation of risky choice behavior. On the other hand, the development of an alternative general theory is just beginning. Prospect theory by Kahneman and Tversky (1979b) is a major step toward such an understanding of decision behavior under risk. It appears to account for a number of the violations of the standard expected utility model. Nonetheless, as acknowledged by Tversky and Kahneman (1981, p. 454), prospect theory should only be viewed as "an approximate, incomplete, and simplified description of the evaluation of risky prospects." Much more research is still required to test and extend or revise prospect theory.

It should also be pointed out that the applied value of understanding responses to laboratory decision tasks such as simple gambles does exist. In part, this is because of the large increase in the last ten years of efforts to use decision analysis (see Keeney and Raiffa 1976) to solve real-world decision problems. A basic input into decision analysis are the responses resulting from a decision about simple hypothetical gambles. The nature of such responses needs to be well understood. In a related area, computer based decision support systems are also likely to include judgmental responses to simple trade-off problems. Again, we need to understand how such judgments may be affected by such things as the response made and other task variables.

In addition to illustrating a shift in the kinds of problems being studied, the papers by Bouwman and Tuggle and Gerwin illustrate two methodologies for the study of problem solving and decision making. The first methodology is the use of verbal protocols to collect detailed data of the time-course of decision behavior. Since the general advantages and disadvantages of verbal protocols in decision research are discussed elsewhere (Hayes, this volume, pp. 61–77; Payne, Braunstein, and Carroll 1978), let me just touch on two issues of verbal protocol analysis that are illustrated by the Bouwman paper. On the positive side, the Bouwman paper clearly indicates how verbal protocol techniques may be used in exploratory studies of decision making in ill-structured task environments. I believe that this use of verbal protocols to do such exploratory research is one of the major advantages of the technique.

Unfortunately, the Bouwman paper also demonstrates one of the weaknesses of many recent verbal protocol studies of decision making. That weakness is the relative lack of summary measures of behavior that will allow the reader to make some inferences regarding the generalizability of the results obtained. Now, I recognize that the information-processing approach to problem solving is famous for its concern with examining the behavior of individual subjects in great detail. There are merits to such efforts at the level of basic research (see Newell and Simon 1972). However, I wonder about the value of such an approach in more applied research. Bouwman states that the objective of his paper is to explore the differences in expert versus novice behavior in order to better teach novices how to become experts. Later in presenting a comparison of verbal protocols he states that we will not learn how *the* expert approaches the task but will learn what typical differences may be observed between the experts as a group and the students. However, the analysis presented by Bouwman is based on one novice subject and one expert subject. We are told that the two subjects are "typical" of their respective populations. No evidence on the degree to which these two subjects are typical is given. I believe that such evidence is essential if we wish to take what we learn from the individual protocol analyses and apply that knowledge in the form of prescriptions for the training of better decision makers.

The other methodology highlighted by the Bouwman and Tuggle and Gerwin papers is the use of computer simulation techniques. Computer simulation has long been a characteristic of the information-processing approach. In part, this is because information-processing theorists have dealt with forms of problem-solving behavior that are clearly going to be a function of numerous variables interacting in a complex fashion. Computer models seem to be the best, and perhaps the only, way to handle such complex interactions. While both the Bouwman research and the Tuggle and Gerwin research utilize computer models, there are interesting differences between the ways computer models are being used. Bouwman's work appears to place the emphasis on the computer model as a formalism that forces him to be more precise in his description of observed behavior. That is, the development of an operational computer program is said to back up the analysis of the novice's verbal protocol. It is clear that in the Bouwman work, the approach is one of first collecting a dense amount of empirical data and then to validate, in some sense, the analysis of that data by building a computer model that appears to simulate the observed behavior.

In contrast, consider how Tuggle and Gerwin utilize computer simulation. There are no empirical data presented at all. Instead, they appear to adopt what has been called a "program-first" approach to research. A computer model of a decision-making unit, in this case a hypothetical profit-making firm, is developed. The model is then exercised in order to generate hypotheses about how the system being simulated might behave. While I am sure the researchers see a contact between their simulation and empirical data, at this stage in the research the correspondence is not made explicit.

This computer-simulation approach has also been used recently by several other researchers concerned with decision processes. Cohen (1980a, b), for example, uses a very similar approach to that of Tuggle and Gerwin to explore the issue of how an organization consisting of individuals, each with conflicting values and limited information-processing abilities, is able to successfully adapt to complex environments. Thorngate (1980) has explored the efficiencies of various decision heuristics in leading to an optimal choice. Together with the Tuggle and Gerwin work, these studies support the position by Simon (1969) that the program-first method can be a powerful method for generating insights into the behavior of complex, poorly understood systems.

But the Tuggle and Gerwin paper also illustrates some of the problems of complex simulation models. Let me just mention two. First, the complexity of models such as those developed by Tuggle and Gerwin makes the interpretation of their results very difficult. For example, Tuggle and Gerwin identify a situation in which a firm with conflicting subunit goal structures will outperform an organization that does not have such goal conflicts, a result that is very interesting. It is also supported by the recent simulation work by Cohen (1980a). The problem comes in trying to understand why subunit goal conflict might be valuable to the firm. In particular, why is such conflict useful in situations of volatile business cycles? Is the reason that organizations with subunit conflict are less likely to be sensitive to external environmental change? I suspect so. However, the interpretation of the result is certainly not clear.

Second, I am concerned about the method used to later validate the simulation model. The approach seemingly suggested by the authors in the present paper, and the approach followed in a closely related paper by Tuggle and Gerwin (1980), is to validate the model by pointing out the consistency of the simulation results with a variety of business policy cases. Such an approach to model validation, while interesting, is not sufficient in my opinion. There is a clear need to collect other forms of data on how organizations perform in setting strategies. One suggestion for such data would be the collection of verbal protocols from managers while engaged in either the actual or simulated policy-setting process. Acquiring such a collection would be a very difficult task, but I believe it is needed.

So far, I have focused my remarks on the Bouwman and Tuggle and Gerwin papers. Let me conclude my remarks with a few comments on the paper by Kunreuther.

The paper by Kunreuther addresses an important applied issue. Apparently, there is a market failure in providing consumers with protection against events which have a low probability of occurrence, but also very serious consequences if these events do occur. Kunreuther addresses the question of why such a market failure exists. He also discusses how the government might deal with such a market failure.

The first half of the paper presents a fairly standard economic analysis of these issues. Standard behavioral assumptions, such as expected utility maximization on the part of consumers, are used. The most interesting results concern the impact of under- or overestimates of the probabilities of loss on the behavior of consumers and firms.

The second half of the paper extends the economic analysis by considering alternative models of consumer decision making. In particular, a two-stage model is suggested. The first stage involves a probability-of-loss threshold used by consumers to determine whether to concern themselves with a potential hazard and possible protective behaviors. The idea is that consumers will only consider cost/benefit types of trade-offs if the perceived probability of loss is above some threshold value. Note that the trade-offs considered may not be the ones suggested by normative theories at the second stage; for example, a price/loss rule is suggested for flight insurance, and perhaps for air bags. Kunreuther also suggests that prospect theory may describe the trade-off processes at this second stage.

Other factors that Kunreuther suggests are the protection an individual is likely to purchase, including the concept of regret and the view of insurance as an investment rather than a contingent claim. The last idea supports the importance that problem framing has recently received in the decision literature (Tversky and Kahneman 1981). The notion of regret is related and also interesting because it introduces the possibility of consumers viewing the insurance problem as having a regret attribute as well as a monetary loss attribute. A similar notion recently has been advanced by Keeney (1980) to account for the risk-seeking behavior that has been documented by Kahneman and Tversky (1979b) and Payne, Laughhunn, and Crum (1980).

Overall, the Kunreuther paper illustrates the value of bringing together in the analysis of an applied problem concept data drawn from psychology experiments, field surveys, and economic market analyses.

ACKNOWLEDGMENT

Preparation of this paper was supported by a contract from the Engineering Psychology Program, Office of Naval Research.

6 Applications of Information-Processing and Decision-Making Research, II

Behavioral Process Research: Concept and Application in Consumer Decision Making

Robert W. Chestnut, Columbia University
Jacob Jacoby, New York University

Decision Support Systems: Their Present Nature and Future Applications

George Huber, University of Wisconsin—Madison

Decision Analysis for Complex Systems: Integrating Descriptive and Prescriptive Components

Howard Kunreuther, University of Pennsylvania
Paul J. H. Schoemaker, University of Chicago

Commentaries:

Comments on the Huber, Kunreuther and Schoemaker, and the Chestnut and Jacoby Papers

Henry Mintzberg, McGill University

Decision Making: An Interdisciplinary Focus

John Slocum, Southern Methodist University

While the first group of application papers is strongly committed to a general theoretical point of view, with distinctive methodologies, the second group is more eclectic in nature. The paper by Chestnut and Jacoby examines research on individual information processing in the context of consumer purchase decisions; Huber discusses the potential application and impact of decision support systems; and Kunreuther and Schoemaker integrate elements affecting the demand for protection against the threat of financial ruin in the event of disaster.

Chestnut and Jacoby elaborate on their notion of "behavior process research," developed as a methodology to study the variety of ways in which the individual makes purchase decisions. These studies have, in general, much that is similar to the process-tracing approach (Newell and Simon 1972). The prototypical method would be to present subjects with increasingly complex and large amounts of product information via specially designed display boards, and to examine what information is used and not used. From this general procedure, the researchers have been able to make inferences regarding the nature of the information used, how information is used, and, to a limited extent, why certain types of information are selected. One example cited is the consumer's tendency to "chunk" information under a brand name, and use the chunks of information associated with the brand as a substitute for obtaining new product information. Other techniques used by researchers in this area include verbal protocols, eye-fixation analysis, and field experiments.

In the next paper of this series, Huber discusses the potential of the "decision support system" (DSS). DSS can be distinguished from decision aids in that DSS is enhanced: "computer enhanced . . . contain[ing] computer-retrievable and manipulable models or algorithms" (p. 249). Moreover, a DSS contains procedures for examining the desirability of various decision alternatives, and therefore is often associated with, or designed as a part of, a management information system. A DSS can also incorporate a descriptive model of the firm's cash flow, for example, which would then allow managers to assess the impact of controllable variables in the model on the firm's performance.

Huber suggests that DSSs can be used, by both "hands-on managers" as well as supporting staff. Although he concedes his data on their use are impressionistic at this time, his interviews with three large corporations indicate overwhelming optimism regarding DSS use. However, Huber states that the design of DSSs should take into consideration specific links with the organizational environments in which they function. Citing four models of organizational decision environments, he suggests how DSSs might be designed into each situation.

The last paper in this series, by Kunreuther and Schoemaker, examines the role of descriptive and prescriptive analysis in organizational decision making. The authors argue that traditional decision analysis has failed to realize its full potential because of its limited concern for the descriptive aspects of problem solving.

Descriptive aspects that need to be taken into account include the organizational structures and the cognitive limitations of the decision makers. A framework is then employed to illustrate the integration of descriptive and prescriptive analyses. Specifically, the role of insurance agents in the marketing of socially desirable flood insurance is discussed using a bounded rationality model that takes into account the nature of the inevitably sequential acquisition of information by the consumer.

In their commentaries on these three papers, Mintzberg and Slocum present issues regarding the informational environment in which decision support systems (Huber), consumers (Chestnut and Jacoby), and purchasers of flood insurance (Kunreuther and Schoemaker) operate. Citing problems created by a manager's need for current information, Mintzberg addresses the need to integrate formal decision aids, which are designed into DSSs, with a manager's own intuitive diagnostic processes. Specifically, DSS may displace or drive out intuition by forcing the rationalization and programming of some decisional processes. Thus, DSS designers should be aware of what they are doing, in order to obtain a better appreciation of which aspects of decision making are best supported by their systems.

This theme is pursued in his critique of the Kunreuther and Schoemaker paper. Mintzberg lauds these authors for their attempt at integrating descriptive and prescriptive decision making, but then raises questions on the price we might pay for favoring technique and formalization, since these may encourage attention to choice at the expense of diagnosis and intuition.

Mintzberg's concern for understanding the messier aspects of the decision process provides a basis for his critique of the Chestnut and Jacoby paper. Mintzberg suggests that laboratories may be valuable for cognitive psychologists who study natural behavior in the lab, but not useful for social psychologists and consumer behaviorists who are purportedly interested in real-world decisions. He argues that social simulations in the lab are relatively naive, and that social reality is difficult to replicate. Mintzberg concludes by raising some issues related to labeling, typologies, and the need for a better description of the term *decisions*.

Slocum's commentary starts with references to the work of Simon. We are reminded that, according to Simon, the ultimate challenge for theorists is not to focus on information *per se* but rather on attention. Therefore, Slocum is happy to report that all of these papers focus on attentional aspects of the use of information in the decision process. He points out that the values, goals, or preferences of the decision maker play an important role in the manner in which information is conceptualized in these studies. The use of information results from two major factors: access and weight. Citing various empirical studies, Slocum shows that "gatekeepers," and "boundary-spanners" both have considerable impact on who gets to use information, when it is transmitted, and what form it takes. A related issue is that information access is often determined by the influence of group dynamics on the decision situation. This may be an especially acute problem for the designers of decision-support systems. Once information is transmitted, the problem of subjective weighting by the decision maker becomes very relevant to its use. Again, various empirical studies are cited to demonstrate the variety of ways in which decision makers subjectively weight information, even often restructuring weights at different points in time. Lastly, Slocum reminds us that organizational power and politics are significant determinants of information usage, and should therefore be included in one's analysis.

Behavioral Process Research: Concept and Application in Consumer Decision Making

Robert W. Chestnut, *Columbia University*
Jacob Jacoby, *New York University*

Decision making is increasingly a multidisciplinary topic. Relevant findings are to be found in a variety of literatures and appear to reflect entirely different styles or approaches to research. So diverse are the contributions that one recent monograph (Hammond, McClelland, and Mumpower 1980) refuses even to try to integrate the material; instead, it reviews each approach separately in what is termed a loose "kinship" system. The assumption is that, at least in our present stage of theoretical development, we are better off appreciating the variety of what is available. Each approach or discipline offers its own unique potential for understanding the problem. We can utilize this potential only if we are tolerant of more, rather than fewer, concepts of the decision-making process.

With this in mind, the present account focuses on a new concept and an approach labeled *behavioral process research* (BPR). BPR is a fairly recent addition to the decision-making area and is limited for the most part to applications in consumer behavior. In the course of its few short years of existence, however, it has evolved quite rapidly. The greatest change has come with regard to the complexity and scope of its activities. It has gone from a simple testing procedure, only one of several process measurement techniques introduced into applied research in the early 1970s (Wright 1974, Van Raaij 1976), to a complex array or "technology" of methods, measures, and analyses (Jacoby 1977a). More than just a procedure or operationalism *in* research, it has emerged as a general paradigm *for* research.

The impact of this paradigm promises to be substantial. Although it is not our intent to review fully all its contributions at this time (the reader is instead referred to a series of articles: Jacoby 1974a, 1975b, 1977a; Chestnut and Jacoby 1978, 1979; see also Jacoby and Chestnut 1980), certain trends in its development are worth noting. First, acceptance and actual use of the approach is growing. Whereas initial studies were confined to one specific program of research at Purdue University, subsequent developments have diffused to a number of different institutions and working groups. Research papers, dissertations, and articles are beginning to appear throughout the United States and in Europe. Second, with this widening circle of results we are fast approaching what seems to be a kind of critical mass or weight of evidence. Replications firming up the conclusions of earlier work and patterns of convergence across independently conducted studies can be seen. Finally, those involved in this research are beginning to realize that the approach has barely scratched the surface of its application. Expanding out from the concerns of marketing and public policy, it faces numerous and interesting issues in organizational behavior, strategy formulation, financial decision making, and so on.

There is but one major problem. The underlying concept of BPR is not yet clear. What exactly do we mean by the words: behavioral process research? What do they imply for an understanding of the behavior of decision making? Unfortunately, these questions find not one but several distinct answers. Bettman (1979, pp. 196-197), for example, equates BPR to the study of internal processing conditions and discusses it in conjunction with verbal protocol techniques and correlational analysis. Wilkie (1979, pp. 250-251) questions this interpretation and, although he cites the approach for its creativity, leaves it undefined, saying only that it gives some insight into the preliminary importance of information. We ourselves have spoken at different times of information importance (Jacoby et al. 1976), strategies of choice (Bettman and Jacoby 1976), conscious decision making (Chestnut and Jacoby 1978), and information acquisition (Jacoby, Chestnut, and Silberman 1977).

To cut through all these interpretations and give substance to the existing research, we turn in this paper to the development and presentation of a concept that we feel is central to the approach. Explaining this concept and, in so doing, providing answers to the above questions is not an easy task. We will attempt it in three stages. The first stage is a brief review of BPR, highlighting the development of its applied science perspective on decision making. The second stage builds on this account by elaborating the key basic science concept implied and discussing the manner in which BPR has modified or advanced this concept. Finally, a third section presents selected applications and their results in an attempt to better understand the role of BPR on research in decision making.

The Development of Behavioral Process Research

It is important to note at the outset that, although BPR developed in an applied rather than a basic science context, it has not been without a strong connection to theory. Attempts were made quite early in its development to ground the approach in a general information-processing analysis of decision making. With the benefit now of hindsight, however, we can detect and describe certain changes in BPR's perspective on theory. A review of these changes will be useful in setting the stage for a more precise definition of the approach.

Initially, BPR was not an attempt to investigate the processes of decision making. Primarily through a methodological issue, it was only related to research which did seek such an investigation. A sequence of three studies in the early 1970s (Jacoby, Speller, and Kohn 1974; Jacoby, Speller, and Berning 1974; Jacoby, Kohn, and Speller 1973; for an extended discussion and critique see Russo 1974; Wilkie 1979; Summers 1974; Jacoby, Speller, and Berning 1975; Jacoby 1977b) had generalized a well-known information-processing phenomenon to the consumer literature. While marketing academicians were arguing for an upgrading of the informational contents of advertising, and public policy officials were regulating under the assumption that more information was better (Jacoby 1974a), empirical research on consumer performance was showing quite strongly the opposite. Given larger and larger quantities of information, consumers rapidly lost their ability to select an ideal brand and began to exhibit all the symptoms of information overload.

> The most significant of the many findings of these investigations can be summarized thusly: As quantity of information increased, subjects felt more satisfied, more certain, less confused, and desired less additional information regarding both the available brands and a hypothetical new brand. In contrast to these linear relationships, a curvilinear "information overload" relationship was obtained between quantity of information and both amount of time spent attending to the information and "correctness" of the purchasing decision. Subjects devoted less time to attending to and reading the information they were given and, more importantly, made demonstratively poorer purchase decisions, at both low *and* high levels of information load, in contrast to intermediate levels of information load. Thus, "more" was definitely not "better." Despite the fact that people felt better when provided with more information, high levels of information load led to reduced attention to the information and poorer purchase decisions. (Jacoby 1974b, p. 3)

Graphically, the axes of *performance* versus *information load* depicted what might well be a severe problem in real-world purchasing. The loads of information used in this research were not atypical of those to be found in retail outlets, and the subject's motivation to perform was, if anything, greater than the normal motivation in purchasing nondurables. Given the increasing availability of advertising or package information, both through competitive marketing activities and federal regulation, consumers might be expected to acquire more and more information with the consequence of having less and less of an effective ability to make decisions (see the solid arrows in Figure 1). Or would they? The linear relationship with satisfaction suggested that this would be the case, but one important methodological issue needed to be considered.

Overload had been obtained under experimental conditions. One condition was that of forced exposure; subjects in this research had no option but to consider the information load presented to them. That is, they were brought into a test environment and given an organized table or array of information. The table was in the format of a $p \times q$ matrix (brands by attributes) and was of a size fixed by the experimenter to represent a specific load of information. Subjects were required by their instructions to evaluate all information within the matrix in arriving at their purchase decision. Performance in this situation declined as the matrix took on larger dimensions and overload began to occur.

But if the interests of this research were to re-create the natural conditions under which overload might occur, then certainly forced exposure was inappropriate. Consumers, not experimenters, fixed the size or amount of information to be employed in their own purchase decisions. Would consumers in fact select the full amount of information present in the matrix? Exactly how much would they select or acquire? Given a large enough matrix to represent the actual environment, might some consumers acquire an optimal amount of

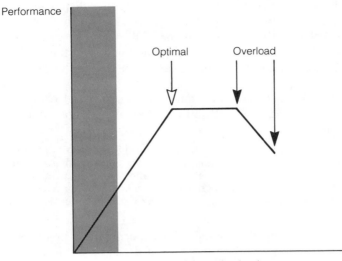

FIGURE 1   Information Overload Phenomenon

information (see hollow arrow, Figure 1) and, if so, what would that information contain?

Fortunately, these were all empirical questions. Their answers were a matter for further research, research predicated on a method or methods which would allow for a subject-generated process of information-acquisition behavior.

> On a conceptual level, the most basic form of the methodology involves presenting the subject with an array of product information. . . . The format adopted consists of presenting information via a specially designed information display board (IDB) which presents information arranged in the form of a $p \times q$ matrix. (Entries in this matrix represent specific "information values." It should be noted that these values are not openly displayed but rather require some overt action or behavior to acquire. Typically, brand-name values are treated as a given, visually present as headings for each of the p columns of q attributes.). . . Subjects are placed into a simulated shopping situation and instructed to purchase one brand from among the set of brands provided in the information display. They are informed that, using the IDB, they are to "shop" for the product as they usually do, taking as much or as little time and acquiring as much or as little information from the matrix as they desire. . . . When information values are selected (that is, the behavior necessary to acquire a specific value is observed) a process record is formed . . . which can then be analyzed in terms of the depth (how many values?), sequence (acquired in what order?), and content (what type?) of the information acquired. (Jacoby et al. 1976, p. 307)

These were the general outlines of BPR as it first emerged. The results in terms of the overload phenomenon were quite dramatic. Actual information-acquisition behavior directed at package labeling in a nondurable purchase was practically nonexistent. To simulate the full range of consumer action, subjects were allowed to acquire what was in effect zero values of information. That is, they simply looked at the brand-name labels openly displayed on the IDB, named their choice of brand, and avoided all costs and effort of search (if, indeed, they believed this to be their usual response in purchasing). With brand names available, immediate brand-name choice was the modal observed behavior. External search, other than brand name, was the exception rather than the rule.

Many of the initial findings pertained to the product class of breakfast cereal where a 16 brand by 35 attribute matrix of package label information could be specified.

> Of the 560 values available, half the sample found it necessary to acquire less than 2%. . . . Given that the methodology employed, if anything, should have increased search (that is, through potential demand characteristics and minimization of acquisition costs relative to such costs in an actual supermarket setting), this degree of selectivity is striking (Jacoby et al. 1976, p. 328; see also Jacoby, Chestnut, and Fisher 1978).

For those that did engage in some search or acquisition behavior, the depth of their decision varied greatly. One way of describing this variance was to separate out response into categories of light, moderate, and heavy acquisition, and then to examine the salient characteristics of each category separately (Table 1). Even at its heaviest, though, the consumer's acquisition involved an average of only 28 percent of the brands, 21 percent of the attributes or dimensions, and little more than three to four minutes of deliberation (data from Jacoby and Chestnut 1977, p. 85).

The reason for this selectivity was obvious. Consumers relied on their memory, their internal resources of knowledge and experience, rather than on their environment. An investigation of the consumer's tendency to "chunk" information via brand name (Jacoby, Szybillo, and Busato-Schach 1977) supported this conclusion. Yet, even with brand names removed (consumers were told that the matrix had been collected on new brands, unavailable in the market and identified only through the numbers 1 to 16), acquisition behavior was limited. For the product classes of margarine and headache remedies, the percent of matrix acquired was 7 percent and 12 percent respectively. Although most brands were considered at least once, 69 percent and 75 percent, still relatively few attributes were acquired, 30 percent and 54 percent (Jacoby and Chestnut 1977, pp. 83–94). Consumers were simply excluding information, now quite arbitrarily.

The problem in purchase was that of "underload." Far too little information was entering into the decision (shaded zone, Figure 1). Of course, it could be argued that the actual observed acquisition had been augmented by internal stores of knowledge up to a point more closely resembling optimal, or even overloaded, processing. But then the response would be that these recollections at time of purchase, especially given the relatively small amount of time spent in deliberation, could hardly resemble the facts as they really existed. They might reflect gross judgments or recodings of the facts, but it is doubtful whether precise information would be stored or, once stored, accurately retrieved and placed into the decision. Ask a consumer to play back the nutritional characteristics of his or her favorite brand of breakfast cereal. Would the result really be that of a specific nutrient listing as present in the U.S. Recommended Daily Allowance?

TABLE 1 Descriptive Statistics on Depth of Search for Breakfast Cereal Brand-Name Present

	NUMBER OF VALUES ACQUIRED	NUMBER OF SUBJECTS	MEDIAN NO. OF VALUES ACQUIRED	MEAN NO. OF BRANDS CONSIDERED	MEAN NO. OF DI-MENSIONS CONSIDERED	MEAN DECISION TIME (SECONDS)
I. BRAND-NAME CHOICE	0	71	0	0	0	0
II. INFORMATION SEARCH						
Overall	1–47	127	6	3.16	4.55	140.16
Light	1– 4	39	3	1.82	1.90	57.05
Moderate	5– 8	42	6	2.95	4.95	119.02
Heavy	9–47	46	12	4.48	6.43	229.91

More than just a commentary on performance, however, BPR now provided a technique for the internal analysis of decisions. Acquisition behavior could be taken apart and examined in detail. With this examination, a basic change in research interest and perspective had occurred. The search was on for the "strategies" by which consumers selected their brands. Developments came rapidly through a variety of new measures and analyses particularly adapted to the process data base. The implication was clear. ". . .Once effective decision making strategy is identified in a given sphere, the approach has considerable potential to be employed as a training device" (Jacoby 1977c, p. 19).

The underlying theory was relatively straightforward. BPR measured information coming in from the external environment and being placed into a conscious decision-making process (Chestnut and Jacoby 1978). By definition, it measured elements of what went on in the ultimate choice of a brand. To describe acquisition behavior was in effect to describe a decision. Instead of elaborating this perspective, emphasis was placed on the methodological advantages of BPR. Information acquisition was not by itself a particularly new area of study. Prior to the advent of BPR, and, in fact, continuing today in a majority of the marketing research available, data had been collected using verbal reports of past purchasing behavior. Consumers were simply asked if they had ever paid attention to specific attributes.

BPR offered several major improvements on this traditional approach. First, it was *behavioral*. Although it simulated behavior, it did measure what was really of interest, not what consumers said they used, but what they actually did use in purchasing. A number of different problems could be pointed out in the rather weak link between verbal reports and acquisition behavior (Jacoby and Chestnut 1980). These problems were borne out in consistently low correlations (+.3 to +.4) between the reported and simulated referencing of attributes (see Jacoby et al. 1978).

Further, to be able to report on acquisition implied that consumers actively went around thinking about what they acquired. There was the interesting possibility, however, that acquiring information in decision might be more a matter of acting than thinking (or, at least, verbally thinking). Given that nondurable purchasing is likely to be a routine, low-involvement task, much of its processing may center on quick, automatic response or habit (Kassarjian 1978).

> When one considers the advantages of habit and realizes that thought does not necessarily (and probably does not often) generate a significantly better response than habit, there is scarce reason to invoke thought when faced with a familiar encounter (Thorngate 1976a, p. 32).

BPR easily picked up these habitual patterns of behavior, patterns which were likely to disappear in a process made overly deliberate or verbal through measurement.

A second advantage was that data were collected in an ongoing sequence or *process* of events. This altered the very nature of measurement, making possible measures and analyses of the sequence in which values were acquired, and introduced a new level of complexity. The data comprised more than a series of isolated events. Each event was linked up over time to suggest the

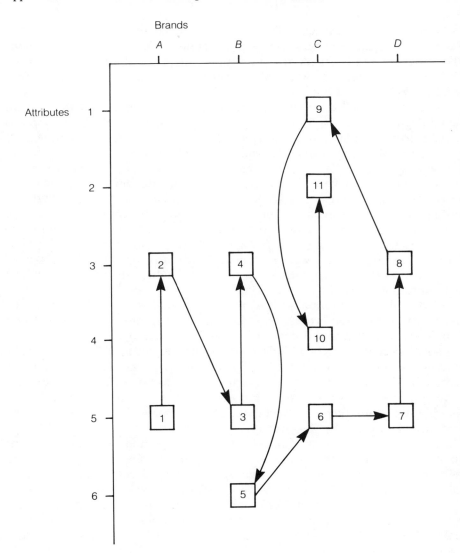

FIGURE 2   Example Pattern of Matrix Acquisition

Note: Numbers in boxes represent the order in which values were acquired.

mechanisms by which the environment was being used (Figure 2). The language that had grown up around the study of information processing could now be applied to acquisition behavior. Investigators could talk of phased decision strategies, paired comparisons between brands, transition analysis, spectator versus participant information testing, and so on. In short, although choice was in no way directly observed, a reflection of choice was present, step-by-step for all to see.

Other advantages related to the evolving character of BPR as an "experimental simulation" (see Fromkin and Streufert 1976). BPR was increasingly a *descriptive, realistic,* and *flexible* approach to decision making (Jacoby et al. 1976).

It did not attempt to prescribe the consumer's behavior. Instead, it sought to guarantee the maximal amount of freedom. When a procedural element inevitably intruded on this freedom (for example, the physical arrangement of the IDB), this aspect was either counterbalanced or studied to assess its impact (Jacoby, Szybillo, and Busato-Schach 1977).

Realism was maintained throughout, even though at times it was a realism more imagined (that is, in the mind of the subject) than actual. Simulations do not have to present the same characteristics as that of the real world; they have only to present those analogous to the real world, ones with which the subject can behave in a similar or same manner. In simulating in-store purchase information, for example, a number of individual attributes were identified (price, net weight, and so on). Dividing these attributes and physically representing them down the columns of a large display did not represent a package. However, one could behave toward that display in very much the same manner as actually picking up a package and reading specific values. Further, what differences did exist were not particularly worrisome. They represented boundary variables or conditions on the design which in themselves posed new topics for research.

This ability to systematically explore a simulated environment and its impact on the decision process was perhaps BPR's greatest advantage. It was completely flexible and did not need to be tied down to any one operational form. Although there arose a tendency in the literature to label this approach by the name of its earliest technique ("IDB research," Bettman 1977), such labeling became hard to accept in light of the variety of methods which soon developed. By the mid-1970s physical display boards had given way to electronic display boards and the unique potential of the computer to provide information via the CRT (see, for example, Chestnut 1977).

Unfortunately, all this emphasis on method seemed to lead in only one direction. Investigators became involved with a comparison of different methods and found themselves arguing the relative pros and cons of measurement. Which method was best: eye-fixation analysis, behavioral process research, or verbal protocols? The naive assumption was made that all the available methods measured roughly the same concept — that is, decision making — and, therefore, one could pick the least biased, most productive method for further research.

It was soon apparent that this was not the case (Russo 1978b, Chestnut and Jacoby 1979). Considering the study of consumer decision making only on the merits of method was indeed putting the cart before the horse. The meaning of research was in the concept assessed and, clearly, different approaches or methods had different concepts. But what were these concepts?

This question brings us to the present time and to the objective set out in the introduction. Hopefully, we have imparted some idea of how BPR has developed and, at least, one concept of what is involved: namely, a measurement and analysis of self-selected exposure to information — what goes into a decision at time of purchase.

Over the course of our experience with this approach, however, we have become interested with a second, somewhat different, albeit implied, concept. BPR is also a measurement and analysis of what is left out of decision at time of purchase. Given its emphasis on experimental simulation, it has concentrated more than other research on an understanding of the external task or environment. This is a domain of knowledge which we have often sacrificed in our pursuit of studying the internal or processing environment.

> A concept which has not been applied to any great extent in consumer research . . . is the idea of task analysis. Newell and Simon (1972) argue quite forcefully that the structure of the task being undertaken by a subject greatly influences what processes will be used. That is, the task itself imposes certain constraints . . . (Bettman 1977, p. 344).

We argue that one of the strongest elements in any task structure is the simple overabundance of information. Not to use this information is to place a constraint on the nature and processes of the decision which then ensues. The implications of this constraint are only seen when we attend to the environment and to the information not acquired. It is the information left out of a decision that forms the background against which the figure of search takes on meaning.

At the outset, we rather boldly contended that this was a "new" concept. That is not entirely the case. The concept is new, but just in terms of application and collection of data. The idea behind the concept has long been recognized and is an integral part of a theory first expressed in economics.

Bounded Rationality and a Concept of Limited Acquisition

> We cannot afford to attend to information simply because it is there. I am not aware that there has been any systematic development of a theory of information and communication that treats attention rather than information as a scarce resource (Simon 1978a, p. 13).

Information is present in abundance for most decisions, it is our attention which is the scarce resource. Simon's observation is the exact opposite of that predicted by classical economics. It is not, however, particularly shocking or revolutionary to most economists. The reason is perhaps that Simon first introduced his observation twenty-five years ago. The above quote merely bemoans the fact that, despite our acceptance of what he has to say, we still have relatively little understanding of attention scarcity and its implications for decision making.

In the mid-1950s two papers appeared almost simultaneously, one in economics and the other in psychology. The papers (Simon 1955, 1956) advanced what has come to be known as "bounded rationality." Decision making was seen to operate within certain boundaries or constraints. As noted by March (1978, p. 590), "it started from the proposition that all intendedly rational behavior is behavior within constraints." One constraint was that of information acquisition behavior.

Until Simon's writings, economists had assumed that people's appraisal of their decision environment was "if not absolutely complete . . . at least impressively clear and abundant" (Simon 1955, p. 99). The only recognized constraint was that of the environment. If an alternative were completely absent from the environment, then certainly it could not be included in a

modeling of choice behavior. Simon pointed out that this was just the beginning of the constraint. Decision makers acted on their environment, taking it
"within the skin of the biological organism." The true constraint was not the
environment: it was the decision maker's "approximation" thereof. Given
people's general abilities and level of motivation, this was likely to contain
considerably less information. A concept of limited acquisition was proposed.

Over the years, this concept has changed in fundamental ways. Several of
these ways are worth noting. One concerns the magnitude by which we tend to
approximate. In making decisions we do not just compose smaller, more
simplified models of the available information; instead, we radically depart
from the informational contents of our environment.

> The decision maker's information about his environment is much less than an
> approximation to the real environment. The term "approximation" implies that the
> subjective world of the decision maker resembles the external environment
> closely. . . . In actual fact, the perceived world is fantastically different from the
> "real" world (Simon 1959, p. 272).

So little information enters into a decision in fact, that a completely different perspective on acquisition behavior is called for. It is a perspective which
recognizes the absence rather than the presence of information. "The sins of
omission in perception are more important than the sins of commission"
(Simon 1959, p. 272).

The omission of information is an active process. It is a process of deciding
what information to exclude and how to exclude it. "The filtering is not merely
a passive selection of some part of the whole, but an active process involving
attention to a very small part of the whole and exclusion, from the outset, of
almost all that is not within the scope of attention" (Simon 1959, p. 273).

Two interpretations are possible here. The first stresses our inadequacy as
decision makers. Quite simply, environments are too complicated and our
abilities are too limited. We are $7 + 2$ organisms in a world better made, given its
large quantities of information, for computers. Our only defense is to cut the
problem down to size, often hacking it beyond recognition.

A second interpretation stresses precisely the opposite view. We are more
than adequate in decisions. In comparing our abilities to those of the computer,
one stands out above the rest. It is the ability to "recognize" rather than "search
out" solutions. Computers waste their vastly superior talents on information
that the human decision maker would never even approach. "Clearly the use of
selective heuristics (to avoid information), a characteristic of many artificial
intelligence programs, is even more highly developed in human thinking"
(Simon 1978b, p. 503). We succeed in making our decisions by what we manage
not to acquire.

In actuality, both interpretations are probably correct. It would all depend
on both the decision maker and the environment. We really have little, if any,
theory (as Simon points out) to help us decide. One reason is our lack of data,
descriptive data, on the extent and parameters of limited acquisition.

BPR provides this data. It does so with two crucial modifications in
decision-making research. The first is with regard to the definition of information itself. Information is defined to exist outside or external to the decision
maker. Many theorists would have otherwise. If defined at all, information is

thought to exist only in the mind of the decision maker (see Jacoby and Chestnut 1980). We feel that this confuses the existence of information with the impact of information. Information must be at least described externally if we are ever to measure the exclusion of information.

BPR has developed a nomenclature for this description. It is, in a way, a means of task analysis (Chestnut 1977, Jacoby and Chestnut 1980). Briefly, it involves a matrix listing of all "units" or values of information present in a given environment. The dimensions of this matrix, although others may be specified, are those of source (the origin of information), option (the alternative to which information is related), and property (the attribute or type of information). These are all reasonable means of categorizing values, in that they are also the means by which the decision maker is likely to approach the environment and to direct or code acquisition behavior.

The second modification has already been mentioned. BPR exhibits the properties of an experimental simulation (Fromkin and Streufert 1976). Among these properties is a tendency to seek realism in the design of environments. As Fromkin and Streufert point out, realism is a matter of "judgment" and, depending on one's judgment, the simulation can be designed differently. By systematically testing the different designs, the investigator can gradually build a working model of the major parameters involved. This appears to be quite close to what Simon (1974) has recently argued for in his switch from "hypothesis-testing" to "parameter-estimating" research.

Before proceeding on to the data produced by this approach, one final point should be made. We have tried to emphasize the importance of an environmental perspective on the information which decision makers purposively leave out of decision. We have labeled this concept *limited acquisition* and have contended that BPR offers a unique potential for its investigation. From a measurement standpoint, however, it must be admitted that the inclusion and exclusion of information are really two sides of the same coin. We can and do describe limited acquisition by the specific values acquired. But note that the importance of the description resides in its implications vis-à-vis the environment which is thereby excluded.

Selected Applications

Evoked Sets

Since the theoretical work of Howard and Sheth (1969, and see also Howard 1977), a major interest in marketing has been that of determining the consumer's evoked set at time of purchase. Marketers, as one might expect, are most interested in selectivity when it affects the consideration of their brand. Evoked set is a recognition of the fact that consumers usually focus their deliberations on some finite number of brands. "An evoked set is the set of alternatives that the buyer would actually consider. . . . Marketers have a strong interest in the size and content of the evoked set at each decision point" (Kotler 1980, p. 152).

BPR alters the notion of a finite set to that of an extremely restricted set of brand considerations. It presents the opportunity to study these sets in their development and to explore the parameters which tend to influence their size and content. By contrast, the traditional method of verbal report is static in assessment and, in all likelihood, a composite recollection across multiple purchase occasions.

One way to measure an evoked set is simply to total all those brands considered. This is closest to the concept defined in theory. For most of the nondurables already tested by BPR, the effort required is not great. Table 2 presents data on the mean size of evoked set for three different product classes (Jacoby and Chestnut 1977). The total number of brands available in each case is sixteen. The percent of the environmental set considered is thus between 20 percent to 30 percent, or a quarter of the brands available. If we look back to the data under brand-name absent conditions, the influence of information chunking can be seen. Without memory, evoked sets increase dramatically in size.

Correlations of set size with consumer characteristics provide a description of the extended versus the limited shopper (Jacoby and Chestnut 1977). The descriptions vary with product class, but then that is a traditional problem in consumer research and consistent with the differences which must exist across products. For breakfast cereal, extended shoppers (that is, with larger sets) are more educated, rate themselves higher on product knowledge, and engage in paired-comparison between brands. Limited shoppers are older, attach less significance to the product, are less likely to try a new brand, and concentrate their search on finding out more about the alternatives favored. Interestingly, brand loyalty, which does appear in significant correlations for other products, has no relationship to evoked set in the sample tested, a representative sample of 200 housewives.

Simply totalling the brands considered, however, does not do justice to the richness of the descriptive data. An alternative approach is to define evoked sets in terms of the depth of search per brand, that is, the number of values or even properties. A factor analysis is used to correlate the consumer's brand interests and to form a competitive map in which clusters of brands represent sets. Depending on the solution chosen, sets will range in size from 1 to n

TABLE 2   Mean Evoked Set Size

PRODUCT CLASS	MEAN EVOKED SET	PERCENT ENVIRONMEN-TAL SET
BREAKFAST CEREAL	3.16	20%
MARGARINE	4.59	29%
HEADACHE REMEDIES	3.39	21%

brands. An eight-factor solution for the data on breakfast cereal explaining 71 percent of the variance, for example, produces a clear picture of each brand's nearest competitor. Further internal analysis of the search between these empirically defined competitors can shed still more light on the nature of the evoked set.

Multiple Decision Making

Russo (1974) suggests an interesting parameter in nondurable purchasing. Consumers rarely go into a store to buy just one product, as is often assumed in the simulations. They go into a store to engage in a "shopping trip" in which several different products are purchased in succession. Multiple decisions raise new costs in terms of time and effort. As these costs increase in terms of the number of products shopped for, will the consumer begin to alter his or her decision-making behavior?

Chestnut (1975, 1979a) addresses this question in a between-subject design with either one, four, eight, or twelve products shopped for. The expectation is that, as the number of decisions increase, the depth of acquisition for any one decision decreases. The results confirm this (Figure 3). Acquisition behavior is literally cut in half by the increasing costs of multiple decisions.

Several additional findings are worth noting. First, associated with this decrease in total values, there is an increase in the tendency to avoid search altogether. With a long shopping trip ahead of them, many consumers fall back on a rapid identification and choice of brand. Second, for those that do continue to search, there is a hierarchy of the ways by which values are reduced. Time in decision, then properties, and then, as a last resort, brands are sacrificed from search. Finally, since the study controlled for order effects, the position of the product in the shopping trip as a potential influence on search could be examined. A significant positive correlation, $+.4$ to $+.5$, depending upon the search variable correlated, is found between position and depth of search. Consumers tend to overestimate the impact of multiple decisions, cutting search sharply in initial purchasing and then gradually lengthening search as the trip wears on.

Product Comprehension

Leaving nondurables for the moment, we turn to an entirely different order of decision making. It involves perhaps the most complex of all consumer purchases: life insurance. A study by Chestnut and Jacoby (1980) looks at the role of high versus low comprehension in a consumer's selection of policy. Without going into any great detail, subjects in this study are asked to evaluate two different strategies — permanent and term/invest. Information selectivity (an average of 17 percent of the matrix is acquired) is approximately the same for both high- and low-comprehension groups. A ratio reflecting the relative emphasis between strategies, however, proves significant and interesting. Consumers low in product comprehension, the ones least likely to appreciate the implications of a term/invest strategy, are the ones most likely to search in this direction. The reasons for this are relatively clear and touch on a variety of public policy implications.

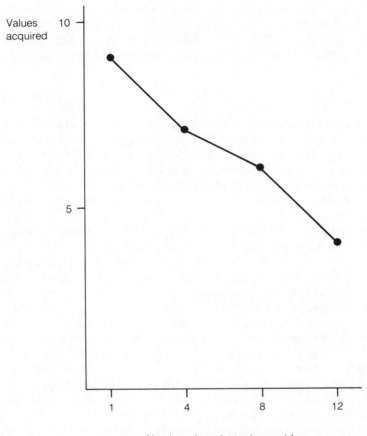

FIGURE 3   Impact of Multiple Decisions

Product Learning

Lehmann and Moore (1980) provide data on a consumer's information acquisition over time. A longitudinal design of six-purchase trials is used. Consumers are asked to select from among several brands of a common food product — bread. They receive the brand that they select and are told to return at weekly intervals to repeat the process. A variety of parameters are modeled during the course of the six-week simulation, including the important addition of product usage — the actual consumption of the brand purchased.

As expected, there is a significant decline in the use of externally provided information. Consumers start by acquiring an average of around 40 percent of the matrix in what is, in essence, a brand-name absent condition, the higher-than-usual percentage being perhaps best explained by the smaller-than-usual matrix of 45 values. By the end of the simulation, they have reduced this amount to around 10 percent.

One way of looking at this decline in information acquisition is to describe the general case of any two purchase trials. What happens to the consumer's acquired set of information from t_1 to t_2? Figure 4 depicts the three probabilities. First, there is a 23 percent chance that a value is simply excluded at t_2; that is, the mean percentage by which acquisition is reduced on each of the trials. Second, there is a 37 percent chance that a value changes in content; that is, a new value is acquired in its place. Finally, there is a 40 percent chance that the exact same value is reacquired. This last probability of reacquisition indicates a substantial amount of consistency from one trial to the next, of concentrating search or going back to the same information over and over again.

The implications for consumer memory are interesting. It appears that we engage in a rehearsal process by which we might learn more about information remaining in, rather than being excluded from, the acquired set of values. Some have argued that consumers can well afford to be selective and limit their acquisition. After all, they are engaged in a process of learning by which the environment is systematically sampled and stored away in memory.

Suppose you are a consumer in the above simulation. It is trial 4 and you have become tired of your most preferred brand (MPB). In the midst of reacquiring MPB information you suddenly acquire a value from one of its competitors and decide to switch your brand allegiance. The assumption is that you have considered this competitor in the past and that your switch of brands is not ill considered. You are an experienced shopper, you know your environment, and the values not acquired externally are retrieved internally. A corollary assumption is that BPR's record of your relatively trivial acquisition is only a partial assessment of the values entering into processing.

Neither of these assumptions receives support. Tests at the end of the simulation indicate that the best predictor of value storage is repeated acquisition of the value over time. We are likely to know much about where we concentrate our acquisition and little about where we merely sample or compare. Internal resources do not so much complement the values acquired as duplicate them.

Comparative Advertising

Sheluga and Jacoby (1978) tested for an interaction between advertising and decision-making behavior. The focus here was on comparative claims and their

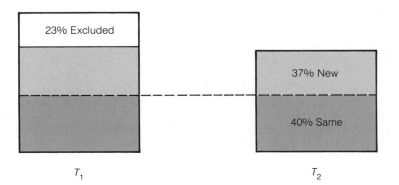

FIGURE 4   Probabilities of Value Existence Between Purchase Trials

ability to promote an actual comparison of brands at time of purchase. The procedure used in the experiment is direct. An experimental group is exposed to a message regarding two brands of cameras. The message states that Brand X "out-performs" Brand Y. A control group receives no message. Both groups are then placed into a simulated purchase with an assortment of eight different brands (including X and Y). The expectation is that of an increase in comparative activities specific to X and Y. Although the results indicate that the message is retained in memory, the claim of superiority does not translate into an evaluation of superiority. No significant differences are found between experimental and control groups. Advertising and product information appear to be treated quite separately.

We could continue here in this review for some time. Our purpose, however, is not to present findings. It is only to spur an interest in these findings and their application. Other studies which might have been mentioned include data on: source effects (Chestnut 1979b), demographic influences (Schaninger and Sciglimpaglia 1980), cross-cultural variation (Raffee et al. 1979), the estimation of brand preference (Sheluga, Jaccard, and Jacoby 1979), brand loyalty (Lehmann and Moore 1980), health and safety information (Jacoby and Jaccard 1981), nutrition information (Jacoby, Chestnut, and Silberman 1977), contraceptive decision making (Hoyer 1979), and socioeconomic status (Capon and Burke 1980).

Summary

Our summary is brief. The problem identified in this paper, and we hope to some extent resolved, is that of the concept of BPR. Our position on this concept has changed over the years but, we believe, always in the direction of a better understanding of decision making in general. This is indeed the purpose of science, and one of the particular advantages of paradigmatic research.

BPR is an attempt to measure and explore one state of the process of decision making: the input of information from the external environment. And by considering this stage, a second and potentially more interesting concept is addressed. Limited acquisition is a process by which we all set external boundaries on our ability for decision making. These boundaries exist whether we talk of consumer decision, management decision, or any other area. Through its emphasis on an analysis of task and a simulation of environmental parameters, BPR provides a unique opportunity to systematically investigate these boundaries and their influence.

Decision Support Systems: Their Present Nature and Future Applications

George P. Huber, *University of Wisconsin—Madison*

And I told Orville and Wilbur, I said, "It won't happen today, it won't happen tomorrow, and it will never happen." That's what I told Orville and Wilbur. (Graffiti observed near Kitty Hawk, North Carolina, c. 1903.)

The purposes of my presentation are to describe a relatively new decision-aiding technology, Decision Support Systems, and to speculate on the nature of the information and decision aids that these systems may employ in the future as they are applied in environments of decision making.

Many people are familiar with the general nature of Decision Support Systems but are not quite certain what they are and how they differ from Management Information Systems. Let me make clear the difference between these two technologies and, at the same time, put them in perspective. It might be useful for us to begin by reminding ourselves of a fact we all know but sometimes forget: every manager has and uses a management information system (*mis*), a combination of information sources and channels, and procedures for drawing on these sources and channels. Such systems typically consist of the trade magazines, file cabinets, vendor representatives, recollections, telephones, organization charts, and the other resources and programs the manager uses when seeking to answer a "What is . . .?" question. With this perspective in mind, we see that a Management Information System (MIS) is the portion of a management information system (*mis*) that deals with computer-stored, and perhaps processed, data.

Second, we might remind ourselves that every manager also has and uses a decision support system (*dss*), a set of procedures and mechanisms for examining the desirability of possible choices. Such a system might include decision rules, policy manuals, recollections, and advisors among the programs and resources that the manager uses when seeking to answer a "What if. . . ?" question. With this fact also in mind, we see that a Decision Support System (DSS) is the portion of the decision support system (*dss*) that is computer enhanced, that is, contains computer-retrievable and manipulable models or algorithms. Conventional use of the term also implies that the relationship between the computer and the decision maker is highly interactive; that is, that the DSS includes a personal terminal that accesses an on-line processor, and that the DSS is designed to fit the needs and style of the particular decision maker.

Some DSSs contain descriptive models. For example, I recently visited one corporation where a cash flow "model of the business" has been developed for each of the corporation's several hundred profit centers and for each hierarchical aggregation of these profit centers, including, at the top of the stack, a "model of the corporation." These models allow the corporation's managers to determine the effects on any dependent performance variable of changes in the level of any of the exogenous or controllable variables. All that is required for such an analysis is the following instruction, "Change X. . .X [a single-word English-language designation of the chosen exogenous or controllable variable] in time period YY to Z. . .Z to [any number]." The relationships among variables in the model can be either deterministic or probabilistic. This DSS was regarded as a real breakthrough at the strategic decision-making level, as it allowed top management to examine many possible courses of action in two or three hours, instead of the two to three weeks that is used to take to rework all of the subordinate unit budgets using the new assumptions (where *new assumptions* meant the new levels of exogenous or controllable variables).

Some DSSs contain as components optimization models and algorithms, such as linear programming models and decision trees. For example, I visited a company recently that used a linear programming model to examine the transportation-cost aspects of a plant-location–production-allocation problem, as part of the overall process of using a descriptive model of long-term cash flow to determine whether to expand in a region where raw materials were expected to increase in cost.

Finally, some DSSs contain no models at all. Instead, they contain the language, software, and sometimes instructions necessary for creating whatever model seems appropriate for aiding the decision maker. These latter systems have been referred to as "DSS generators," as contrasted with "specific DSS" (Sprague 1981).

It is interesting to note that while in practice many DSS access computer-stored data bases (that is, they are linked to an MIS), this is not a necessary condition for their existence. There are DSSs that draw solely upon data entered via the user's terminal at the time of use.

At this point it may be useful to address a few questions. For example, "Have DSSs progressed, in number, beyond a few prototypes?" Yes, they have. The MIS-related literature is actually becoming cluttered with descriptions of Decision Support Systems, in contrast with the fact that hardly any such systems existed until the mid- to late-1970s. National meetings of ORSA/TIMS and AIDS invariably contain sessions devoted to descriptions of existing Decision Support Systems. I know of one company in this field that has over 150 installations of the system it designed and marketed, and some of these installations have scores of users.

The more important question is, "Once in place, are they used?" The answer is, again, yes. I recently had hour-long interviews with each of sixteen Decision Support System users in three large corporations. The corporations were not randomly selected, nor were the users: both the corporations and users were converts to the DSS movement. Nevertheless, what I heard was convincing. First, almost all of those interviewed volunteered the opinion that the systems greatly reduced the time to conduct individual decision-related analyses. No one suggested anything to the contrary. Second, everyone with whom I spoke mentioned that decision-related analyses were more thorough with the Decision Support System than they had been without it. The frequently voiced explanation was that more alternatives were examined because the system made a timely examination possible. A less frequently voiced explanation was that there were fewer computational errors made, and that this fact encouraged the use of more complex analyses. Several of the managers volunteered the conclusion that the increased exploration of alternatives led to better decisions.

Let me add an important aside. Many DSSs are advertised as being "operable by the decision maker him- or herself." While this may be true, I found that managers who had strong staff support were generally not hands-on users of the Decision Support System. Although there were exceptions, most managers with strong staff support relied on staff to carry out the appropriate analysis. On the other hand, without exception, these same managers, several of whom were top-level managers, knew very well what the system capabilities were, and they often asked for analyses that, given the time constraints, could be conducted only with the aid of the Decision Support System. In this sense, then, these decision makers were users, but not hands-on users.

In contrast to managers with strong support staffs are those without such staffs. These latter were the managers who were hands-on users. They tended to be at lower levels in the organization, in manufacturing, or in positions of responsibility without authority or resources, such as might be the leader of a product management team. I do not know if these observations, that managers at all levels were users but that only middle- and lower-level managers were hands-on users, would be replicated with a more sophisticated study.

Most of us approach the study of decision making from a behavioral perspective. With this as a rationale, let us turn to the possible penetration of the DSS technology into various decision-making environments and to the information and decision aids that it might employ if it does penetrate into these environments.

Extensiveness of Future Decision Support System Applications

The first Decision Support Systems were implemented in the mid-1970s. The first book with the words *Decision Support Systems* in its title was published in 1978 (Keen and Scott Morton 1978). Today the number of DSS users is in the thousands, but probably less than 10,000. What is the future of Decision Support Systems? Will their use become extensive and then fade, as did that of decision-aiding technologies such as group brainstorming and queuing theory; or will their use become extensive and persist for some time, as has been the case for the nominal group technique and Monte Carlo simulation?

I expect that the use of DSS will become extensive and that it will persist for some time. Of course, there are natural forces that will retard its penetration into certain managerial environments, and there may appear decision technologies that will supersede it, but there are nevertheless reasons to believe that the range of future DSS application will be considerable. Let me highlight two of these reasons.

The first concerns the nature of the "postindustrial world," as this is described by Simon (1973), Bell (1973, 1979), Toffler (1980), Phillips (in press), and others.

> In the postindustrial state, first there is a shift from the production of goods to the selling of services. Services exist in all societies but, in preindustrial societies, there are primarily domestic services. In industrial societies, these services are ancillary to the production of goods, such as transportation, utilities, and financial services. In postindustrial societies, the emphasis is on human services (education, health, social services) and on professional services (computing, systems analysis, and scientific research and development) (Bell 1979, p. 22).

The importance of this fact for new directions in decision making is that:

> Organizational decision making in the organizations of the postindustrial world shows every sign of becoming a great deal more complex than the decision making of the past. As a consequence of this fact, the decision-making process, rather than the processes contributing immediately and directly to the production of the organization's final output, will bulk larger and larger as *the* central activity in which the organization is engaged. In the postindustrial society, the central problem is not how to organize to produce efficiently (although this will always remain an important consideration), but how to organize to make decisions — that is, to process information (Simon 1973, pp. 269–270).

If the nature of the postindustrial world causes organizations to focus on and be designed around decision making and information processing, it is reasonable to believe that technologies that aid in these tasks will become more widely used. The fact that DSSs are specifically designed to aid in decision making and information processing suggests that these systems may play a prominent role in the management of postindustrial organizations.

The second reason to believe that the range of DSS application will be considerable follows from the fact that modern communications technology and modern computer storage and retrieval technology allow decision makers access to immense quantities of information. However, as Ackoff (1967), Simon (1973), and others remind us, in a great many decision settings the problem is not that there is insufficient information but rather that the decision maker does not possess the cognitive ability to appropriately process the available information.

> The information-processing systems of our contemporary world swim in an exceedingly rich soup of information, of symbols. In a world of this kind, the scarce resource is not information, it is processing capacity to attend to information (Simon 1973, p. 270).

Here, though, is where DSS can help, as these systems are specifically designed to carry out some of the decision maker's information-processing load. From what I've seen, even at this early stage of their development, they do this very well. So the second reason why the use of DSSs may become widespread is that these allow decision makers to make use of the data that other technologies are making more and more available.

When we consider this idea, that DSSs allow the decision maker to use available data in a way not heretofore possible, we must keep in mind the work of Henry Mintzberg (1975). He and others tell us that much of the information used by high-echelon decision makers is not stored in the organization's archives, for example, in its computers. This is true in part because really timely information tends not to be available from the computer, as it has not yet arrived there. It is also true because high-echelon decision makers are among the organization's principal gatherers and users of information about the organization's environment, and environmental information is not, in general, available from the organization's computers. Thus, the question arises, are DSSs going to be used at the higher organizational levels?

I think they will be. There are two supporting arguments for this view. One is that tomorrow's high-echelon managers are today's middle managers, and today's middle managers are or will be DSS users. And although it may be true that the nature of managerial work at higher echelons is such that DSSs are less appropriate than at lower levels, managers, as other learning organisms, tend to rely on proven methods even when these methods become less appropriate. Of course, if the use of DSS at higher echelons is inappropriate, *and* if decision makers see this, they will unlearn their reliance on DSS technology. These are big ifs, however, and I expect that the tendency will be for some managers at least to continue to use a tool that has previously served them well.

The second argument supporting the view that higher echelons will be users of DSS is that two of top management's important tasks are organizational design and resource acquisition. For example, top-level managers are frequently involved in mergers, acquisitions, and the addition or deletion of product lines or services. In today's world, such matters involve the examination of fairly complex alternatives that are largely described in quantitative terms. Further, the data relating to these matters are usually available and easily fed into the computerized data bases and models that characterize Decision Support Systems. The "What if . . .?" question-answering capability of DSS is ideally suited for examining matters such as these, and I found that top managers in two out of three corporations examined were using their DSS to study mergers, acquisitions, and other forms of reorganization, as well as alternative forms of financing for capital acquisitions.

It is important to note that in spite of the enthusiasm associated with this new technology, today's DSSs assist managers in understanding only a small portion of their total decision environments. Increases in the scope of their data bases, and in the variety of the decision aids they offer, will enable tomorrow's DSSs to assist managers in understanding a much larger portion of these environments. In particular, we can expect that tomorrow's DSSs will assist managers to more fully understand and account for the organizational environments in which their decisions are made.

This development of an explicit linkage between DSS and the organizational environments in which they function seems inevitable. Consider two facts. First, managerial decision processes are affected by the environment in which they are conducted. For example, formalization, organizational slack, goal ambiguity, and several other components of the organizational decision environment have been found to affect managerial decision making. Second, "a main argument of the DSS approach is that effective design depends on the technician's detailed understanding of management decision processes" (Keen and Scott Morton 1978, p. 1). Together these facts suggest that those who design user-specific, decision-aiding technologies such as DSS will not long allow consideration of organizational decision environments to go unattended.

Let us turn now to examining what the nature of future applications of DSS might look like if, in fact, the DSSs are designed to aid the manager in understanding and accounting for the organizational decision environment.

Decision Support System Application in Various Organizational Decision-Making Environments

A number of authors have considered the use of different conceptual models for viewing organizational decision environments (Allison 1969, Hah and Lindquist 1975, Pfeffer 1981b). The four most commonly discussed of these models are the Rational Model, the Political/Competitive Model, the Garbage Can Model, and the Program Model. In examining the forms that DSS might take in various organizational environments, we will draw on this categorization of conceptual models. Let us begin by briefly reviewing the nature of the models themselves. Later we will examine the information requirements of each model, and we will discuss how computers might assist decision makers in the retrieval or processing of this particular information. We begin with the Rational Model, since the other three models are invariably portrayed as relating to it in some way, for example, as an alternative or as a complementary elaboration.

The Rational Model

The Rational Model suggests that *organizational decisions are consequences of organizational units using information in an intendedly rational manner to make choices on behalf of the organization.* The qualifier "intendedly" acknowledges the fact that although decision makers may attempt to use normatively correct decision procedures, they are generally unsuccessful, due to either intellectual or resource constraints.

A number of bodies of literature are related to this model. One of these bodies of literature consists of reports on the use of normative procedures such as operations research or program evaluation in organizational decision making (Howard, Matheson, and Miller 1976; Kaplan and Schwartz 1977). Another consists of reports on the apparently rational use of information by individuals in simulated organizational environments (Huber 1974; Mobley and Meglino 1977). Most of these latter studies are attempts to test the applicability of behavioral decision theory (Slovic, Fischhoff, and Lichtenstein 1977) in organizational settings. The third body of literature consists of authoritative descriptions of the nature of managerial decision making (Simon 1947; March and Simon 1958; Downs 1966; Mintzberg, Raisinghani, and Theoret 1976). Although the rational model is extremely important, both because it is publicly ascribed to, and because it is often the target of those who espouse alternative models, it is easy for some of us to forget that it is simply a model, an abstraction of reality, a fragmentary representation of what actually occurs, and therefore an inadequate basis for the design of the relatively encompassing Decision

Support Systems that I believe will become more commonplace as this decision-aiding technology matures.

The Political/Competitive Model

The Political/Competitive Model emphasizes that *organizational decisions are consequences of the application of strategies and tactics by units seeking to influence decision processes in directions that will result in choices favorable to themselves.*

Each of us has no doubt encountered organizational decision environments that were readily describable with the political/competitive model. The model highlights the fact that different participants in the decision process often have different goals. There is a good deal of literature related to the issue of organizational politics, although a composite model or theory is not yet available. Some of this literature concerns organizational power, particularly how such power is acquired (Mechanic 1962; Pettigrew 1972; Pfeffer 1981b). Another part of the literature consists of field studies where the decision processes and outcomes are interpreted as having political bases (Pfeffer, Salancik, and Leblebici 1976; Hills and Mahoney 1978). Expositions on the role of politics in complex organizations are provided by March (1962), Pettigrew (1973), and Lerner (1976).

The literature on conflict and bargaining is also related to the literature on organization politics, but with a few exceptions (Walton, Dutton, and Cafferty 1969; Schmidt and Kochan 1972) it is not based on studies undertaken in the complex and hierarchical organizations where DSSs are most commonly found.

The relationships between the rational model and the political/competitive model are not well understood, either by organizational scientists or by managers. It is fair to say that not everyone agrees about the nature of the relationships. At the one extreme are those who believe that appeals to the public interest (or the stockholders' interests), and the rational/analytic studies that seek to find means for fulfilling these interests, are merely weapons used by parties seeking to achieve their own interests and operating according to the political/competitive model. At another extreme are those who believe that political behavior is a rational approach for determining the relative weight to be given to subgoals in the development of the organizational goal, and that such behavior fits within an enlarged definition of the rational model. Still another point of view is that organizations can design their reward systems such that their members will make choices in keeping with organizational objectives rather than personal objectives, and in this way they can eliminate the competitive behavior highlighted in the political/competitive model.

The Garbage Can Model

This is a relatively new model. Although the basic concept was alluded to in 1963 (Cyert and March 1963), the model itself was not fully explicated until 1972 (Cohen, March, and Olsen 1972). The essence of the Garbage Can Model is that *organizational decisions are consequences of intersections of problems looking for solutions, solutions looking for problems, and opportunities for making decisions.* These three variables, problems, solutions, and choice opportunities, along with a fourth, participants, are portrayed by Cohen, March, and Olsen (1972) and later by March and Olsen (1976) as being tossed into and churning about in a garbage can.

The garbage can model highlights the roles of chance and timing in determining organizational choices. In spite of the appearance of superficiality imparted by its name, this is an important model if for no other reason than that, on the one hand, it is apparently very useful in interpreting choices in certain organizational settings and yet, on the other hand, it relies so little on available behavioral or normative theories of decision making. The model is thought-provoking to say the least (Moch and Pondy 1977), or as Perrow (1979, p. 153) chooses to say, "aggravating."

The Program Model

In 1888, James Bryce observed that "to the vast majority of mankind nothing is more agreeable than to escape the need for mental exertion . . . to most people nothing is more troublesome than the effort of thinking." Sixty years later Chester Barnard made a similar observation in his book, *The Functions of the Executive.*

> The making of decisions, as everyone knows from personal experience, is a burdensome task. . . . Accordingly, it will be observed that men generally try to avoid making decisions, beyond a limited degree when they are rather uncritical responses to conditions (1938, p. 189).

In 1978, Herbert Simon won the Nobel prize for, among other professional contributions, his writings suggesting that organizational decision making was significantly and adversely affected by the cognitive limitations of the human decision maker (Simon 1947; March and Simon 1958). In 1966, Anthony Downs suggested that the nature of a manager's task environment was not conducive to making high-quality decisions, a point of view that seems supported by Mintzberg's studies (1975).

This evidence and authoritative testimony lead one to ask, "When rationality and analysis do not guide organizational decision making, what does? The Program Model identifies two factors that seem to determine many organizational decisions. One is "programs." Our everyday observations and a good many empirical studies remind us that decision-making behavior in organizations is affected by standard procedures, group norms, budget limitations, and other forms of action-directing or action-constraining organizational "programs." The other factor that seems to guide decision making is "programming." Again we have our own observations and an abundance of empirical evidence attesting to the fact that the behavior of decision making is influenced by prior professional training, planned and accidental reinforcements of past decision-related behavior, on-the-job training, and other forms of cognitive or motivational "programming."

The Program Model emphasizes the effect of these programs and programmings on organizational decisions. In its most rudimentary form, the model is captured with the following statement: *Organizational decisions are consequences of the programs and programming of the units involved.* Since an organization's programs are slow to change, and since the effects of programming are hard to erase, decision-making behavior at time T is largely predictable from decision making behavior at $T-1$, irrespective of whether this is appropriate.

Let us be clear at this juncture on two points. One is that these four are not the only models of organizational decision environments that appear in the organizational science literature. Other models have been developed that focus on particular types of situations, such as crises (Snyder and Paige 1958; Smart and Vertinsky 1977) and capital allocation (Cyert, DeGroot, and Holt 1979), or that demonstrate the goodness-of-fit of process or phase models (Weber 1965; Smith 1968; Mintzberg, Raisinghani, and Theoret 1976; Gerwin and Tuggle 1978). These four are, however, the only conceptual models that have an empirical base, and in sum they do seem to capture the relevant features of organizational decision environments.

The second point to be clarified is that, while these four models are alternative ways of interpreting organizational decisions, in almost all important decision situations all four have validity. Part of what goes on is interpretable with one model and part with another. The great majority of significant organizational decisions have their rational aspects, their political aspects, their predictable process aspects, and their chance or garbage-can aspects.

This review of alternative models of organizational decision environments reminds us that most managers are faced with multifaceted decision situations, and it suggests that in many instances the most useful information elements and decision aids might be other than those commonly associated with the rational model. It would seem useful, then, for the designers of Decision Support Systems to consider the possibility of aiding decision makers operating in each of the environments just reviewed. To further this end, in the next few pages we will examine the nature of the information and decision aids that might be employed in the DSSs of managers operating in each of these environments.

Information Requirements and Decision Aids

Today's DSSs are almost all designed to serve in organizational settings that can be portrayed most appropriately with the rational model. The encompassing list of data requirements for this model is the following. Of course, not every decision requires all the data types listed.

Basic Data

1. What are the alternatives? (For example, Who are the possible suppliers?)
2. What are the future conditions that might be encountered? (For example, What are the possible interest rates?)
3. What are the criteria to be used in evaluating alternatives? (For example, Is overhead a required component of the cost analysis? Is community reaction to be considered?)

Elaborating Data

4. What are the probabilities of the future conditions?
5. What is the relative importance of the various criteria?

Performance Data

6. What are the payoffs (or costs) associated with various outcomes?
7. What are the constraints on the payoffs or costs? (For example, Is there a minimum rate of return? Is there a budget limit?)

Analytic aids for the rational model settings include those familiar to us all, such as break-even and rate-of-return models, linear programming algorithms, and simulation languages and models.

In some cases the numerical data for DSS in the rational model setting are directly retrievable from computer-accessed data bases, and the proportion of DSSs for which this is the case will increase dramatically in the next several years, as data-base management systems and interfacing software make their impact. Of some interest will be the inclusion within tomorrow's DSS of existing computer-aided judgment-eliciting technologies, such as computer-automated Delphi studies (Turoff 1972) or computer-enhanced social judgment analysis (Hammond et al. 1977), for obtaining information such as the identity of alternatives or estimates of the probabilities of future conditions. Of similar interest will be the increased computer storage and accessing of nonnumerical data. With regard to the first question in the list above, "What are the alternatives?," for example, it is inevitable that a great deal of information about the identity of vendors and suppliers, and their most up-to-date offerings and prices, will be computer accessible using the desired product or service as a key word retrieval cue, just as nonnumerical information about job candidates and job openings is available on today's computer-aided employment systems.

With respect to the political/competitive model, the organization science literature and my own experience as a professional lobbyist together suggest that decision makers with the responsibility just described frequently deal with the following questions:

1. Who are the parties involved in the decision process?
2. What is the potential influence of each of these parties?
3. Which alternatives does, or should, each of these parties, or my competitors, favor?
4. How can I influence these parties or my competitors?
5. Which strategies might my competitors choose and how likely are they to be chosen?

It is interesting to note that DSSs are currently being used in environments characterized by the political/competitive model. For example, during labor–management negotiations and utility–municipality negotiations (over utility rates), on-line DSSs are being used to assess, during the negotiations, the impact of proposals and counterproposals. Similarly, DSSs are being used in negotiations between contractors and subcontractors, and in mergers and acquisitions, for determining the benefits to both parties that will be derived from various financial arrangements.

It seems likely that future DSSs will be of particular assistance in answering the first of the above questions, especially in situations such as those described by Shumway et al. (1975), where there are many parties involved in the process of decision making. We can expect they will contain, for example, the identities of all executives with authority for approving funding or enactment of the decision, all members of committees involved in the organizational decision processes, the staff advisors of each of the committee members or executives, and the phone numbers and addresses of all these parties.

Other DSSs will be useful in answering the second, third, and fourth questions. For example, solicitors of government contracts, marketers of industrial goods, lobbyists, heads of government agencies, and perhaps even corporate division managers must, as a primary responsibility, choose among strategies for influencing other decision makers, and they do this in settings readily portrayed by the political/competitive model. In order to assist such decision makers, it seems likely that tomorrow's DSSs will be even more capable than today's in providing information about the nature of previously approved contracts and the success rate of competitors for soliciting contracts; the nature of previously made purchases and the success rate of competitors for marketing industrial goods; political affiliation, voting record, and primary supporters for lobbying; the missions, mandates, and budgets of superordinate units for obtaining authorizations; and new corporate policy or strategy proclamations for packaging divisional budget requests.

Finally, with respect to the fifth question concerning the competitor's strategies, we should note that there are DSSs today that support the decision making of managers operating in formally competitive environments. For example, the computer-accessible data bases of professional sports managers contain information about the probabilities of certain strategies being adopted by the opposing teams, information that is developed from historical data bases.

Besides convenience, having these several types of information available in an on-line DSS will allow for easy updating, and datedness is an important problem in the hard-copy maintenance of information of this kind.

With respect to decision aids, we might suppose that game theory would be useful to decision makers operating in a political/competitive environment. This supposition seems not to have been fulfilled in practice, however, perhaps because of the restrictive assumptions necessary for most game-theory models to apply. It does seem, though, that in the future decision aids might be devised that will aid in employing information such as that described above. For example, today's industry lobbyists use information concerning how individual legislators feel about each of a bill's key features as they make the trade-offs and compromises necessary to ensure passage. Especially when the number of key features and/or the number of legislators is large, computer-actualized optimization algorithms would be of immense benefit and could be easily designed. It may be that mathematical studies of coalition formation are already addressing this question. (See for example Tuggle and Gerwin's article on pp. 168–194.)

Let us turn now to the garbage can model. Recall that this model emphasizes environments where decisions are largely intersections in time of problems looking for solutions, solutions looking for problems, and opportunities for decision making. A further thrust of this model is that in many settings the nature and occurrence of problems, solutions, and opportunities for decision making are not fully predictable. What, then, are the questions that a decision maker operating in such a setting might wish to have assistance in answering? They would include the following:

Problems and Opportunities

1. What are the problems and opportunities that might be forthcoming?
2. How likely is it that these problems and opportunities will occur?
3. When might they occur?

Solutions

4. What are the potential solutions that might be forthcoming?
5. How likely is it that these solutions will occur?
6. When might they occur?

Opportunities for Decision Making

7. What are the potential opportunities for decision making that might be forthcoming?
8. How likely is it that these opportunities will occur?
9. When might they occur?

Could DSSs, like those now in existence, be of assistance in answering such questions? Yes, in situations where the occurrence of an event is a consequence of other predictable events. For example, current DSSs can provide probabilistic estimates of income streams and capital availability, and also probabilistic forecasts of certain events leading to cash outlays, such as equipment failures. Thus, they can forecast the intersection of anticipated solutions and problems, and in this rudimentary manner they can be useful in organizational decision environments describable with the garbage can model.

In some respects, however, the preceding example misses the point; the unique thrust of the garbage can model is its focus on events that are not readily predictable. This simultaneous consideration of (1) the dynamic, probabilistic nature of the environment characterized with the garbage can model and (2) the fact that much of the information a manager seeks is used to build a mental model of his or her environment (Mintzberg 1975) suggests that for a manager operating in a garbage-can environment, a primary need would be for a DSS that would help in efficient environmental scanning. Such decision aids are, of course, within easy reach of today's technology. For example, we can expect tomorrow's DSSs to store trade journals, newspapers, and segments of television broadcasts, and to access these and other media through key-word searches. In other words, they will be timesaving, effectiveness-enhancing aids to "the manager [who] perpetually scans his environment for information" (Mintzberg 1975, p. 56). Similarly, especially considering the fact that "a good part of the information the manager collects in his monitor role arrives in verbal form" (Mintzberg 1975, p. 56), we can expect tomorrow's DSS to contain the names, attributes, and locations of people, both inside and outside the organization, who are experts on certain aspects of the environment, and for it to conduct searches of this file on the basis of key words.

Somewhere between a DSS's use for forecasting events in modelable stochastic environments and its use for aiding the manager in obtaining information with which to build models of his or her environment, is the potential use of the DSS for monitoring the environment in order to seek preselected opportunities or problems. For example, routine monitoring of stock market transactions, patent applications, and financial reports could identify potential investment opportunities or possible candidates for acquisition.

With respect to the inclusion of decision aids for DSSs designed for garbage-can environments, it may be that some forms of search theory would be useful. For example, it is likely that decision trees will be incorporated in future DSSs for determining the merits of dealing with an available problem or solution versus waiting to see if the problem goes away of its own accord or if the solution is replaced by another of greater utility.

The program model is the last to be discussed. Recall that this model emphasizes that in many environments organizational decision-making behaviors are largely the consequences of programs and programming and, further, that because these are slow to change, organizational decision processes and outcomes are largely predictable from historical data.

Managers whose organizational environments conform to this model have both a special challenge and a special opportunity. The special challenge is to make sure that the decision processes they manage do not become dysfunctionally routine and inflexible. While programs often increase the user's efficiency, they also tend to "stay in place," and to be employed long after the circumstances that initiated their use have changed. Thus, "when an organization discovers a solution to a problem by searching in a particular way, it will be more likely to search in that way in future problems of the same type" (Cyert and March 1963, p. 124). Similarly, an organization's structural characteristics and reward systems create routine routings of information (Huber, forthcoming), and in this way lead to routinization of decision-making behavior.

Although there seems to be no scientific studies that directly test the hypothesis that decision-aiding technologies themselves lead to routinization of decision-making behavior, it seems reasonable to believe that, to the extent that the technologies are found helpful, their helpfulness will reinforce their use. Thus, while all managers should avoid the calcification of decision-making processes in their units, their caution is especially important when their overall organizational decision environment can be validly described by the program model, and may be even more important with the implementation of a DSS.

A special opportunity for managers operating in program model environments comes from the routineness that leads to predictability, which, in turn, increases the availability and reliability of information that can be used in managing decision-making efforts. Examples of such information include:

1. The frequency distributions of the time necessary for subordinate or adjacent units to produce decision-related information or recommendations.
2. The expected accuracy and precision of this information, including data concerning the nature and expected magnitude of the biases that may be involved.
3. The frequency distributions of the time and cost for decision-implementing units to carry out their assignments.

Data of this nature are relevant to the decision support system (*dss*) of any manager. They could also be an important component of a Decision Support

System (DSS). Certainly, today's MISs already contain "standard times" for organizational activities, varying in scope from operator hand movements to construction of subassemblies, and DSSs already monitor the relationship between forecasts and outcomes using the findings to update the DSS's exponential smoothing forecasts and models. We can expect that data of this nature will be commonly accessible in tomorrow's DSSs, especially for those designed for use in program model environments. Further, tomorrow's DSSs will more frequently contain decision aids that will assist managers in capitalizing on the availability of these data. For example, we can expect them, more often than not, to contain Gantt charts, and critical path and PERT-cost algorithms and displays.

Concluding Comments

Today's Decision Support Systems have shown themselves to be useful in the organizational environment characterized by the rational model of organizational decision making. It seems likely that future DSSs will also be designed for use in organizational decision environments other than those characterized by the rational model. Whether this is true or not, I hope that by examining that possibility I have provoked thought on the nature and impact of decision-aiding technologies, and on the nature of the information that might be useful in various organizational decision settings. These matters are important both to students of decision making and to those interested in organizational behavior. Such matters, finally, might be best studied with a perspective, or by research team, that reflects both of these interests.

ACKNOWLEDGMENT

This research was supported in part by the Army Research Institute for the Behavioral and Social Sciences, and in part by the National Science Foundation.

Decision Analysis for Complex Systems: Integrating Descriptive and Prescriptive Components

Howard C. Kunreuther, *University of Pennsylvania*
Paul J. H. Schoemaker, *University of Chicago*

Decision theory, in both its prescriptive and descriptive form, has much to say about organizational behavior. The descriptive models aid in understanding what actually happens or what might happen; the prescriptive ones point out directions for improvements. Nevertheless, decision theory has not had the impact on organization theory and managerial behavior many had hoped for or expected (Behn and Vaupel 1976, Grayson 1973, Brown 1970). In light of this disappointment, the present article develops a framework for decision analysis in complex social systems. The focus will be on the following three components:

1. Descriptive analyses of organizational environments and decision models.
2. Prescriptive analyses, including decision methodology and decision technology, to aid decision makers.
3. The relationship between descriptive and prescriptive analyses: on the one hand, prescriptive tools must reflect the complexity of organizations and the needs of managers; on the other hand, descriptive theory is needed to identify the cognitive limitations of managers in collecting and processing information.

To illustrate these ideas, we shall first present a theoretical framework which is then applied to a policy example — the marketing of flood insurance by agents. In developing the framework, a class of complex problems was envisioned in which (1) conflicting goals would be present within and among stakeholder groups; (2) varying degrees of stakeholder interaction would exist; (3) limited information would be available on which to base decisions; and (4) uncertainty would prevail.

The discussion is particularly aimed at showing the importance of descriptive analyses, as these will both precede and run parallel to prescriptive analyses.

A General Framework

Let us assume that some problem area has been identified for analysis. This problem may have originated from historical, planning, imposed, or extraor-

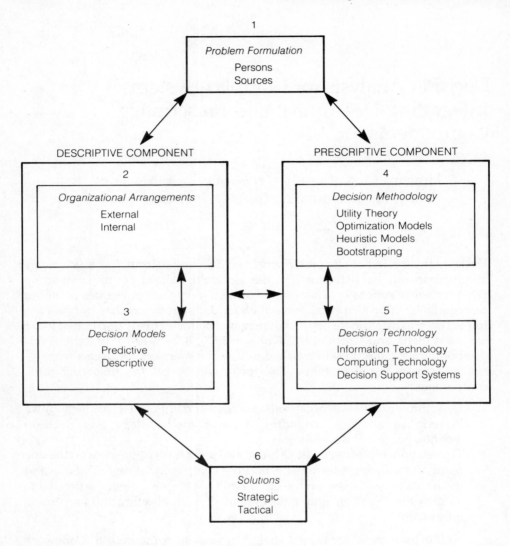

FIGURE 1   A Framework for Decision Analysis

ganizational sources (Pounds 1969). As a first step, it is important to understand the sources and reasons underlying the current problem perception, as this may lead to changes in problem definition. Figure 1 shows this first step (Box 1), and suggests that from it follow both descriptive and prescriptive analyses, both of which may provide feedback regarding the problem formulation.

The descriptive component involves the two interrelated elements of *organizational arrangements* (Box 2) and *decision models* (Box 3). The former concerns the structure of the system or organization in relation to the problem area, and the flow of information among the affected parties (that is, stakeholders). The latter concerns the manner in which information is collected and used to arrive at decisions.

The prescriptive component in Figure 1 involves the body of theory on how to represent preferences, constraints, and choice procedures, as well as the technology that exists for solving models derived from this theory. These two aspects will be referred to as *decision methodology* (Box 4) and *decision technology* (Box 5) respectively. Examples of decision methodology are multi-attribute utility theory (Keeney and Raiffa 1976), mathematical optimization, and heuristic programming. Decision technology refers to decision support systems that assist managers in their choice processes, and which improve the effectiveness of their actions (Keen and Scott Morton 1978).

The basic premise in this article is that the descriptive component is a vital ingredient to the prescriptive one. Specifically, understanding organizational arrangements and decision processes defines a set of constraints which should be explicitly considered in designing prescriptive models. The solutions (Box 6) which emerge should represent an integration of these two strands.

A Policy Example[1]

To illustrate the framework in the context of a concrete example, consider the problem of protecting residents in hazard-prone areas via flood insurance. Homeowners who live in such areas have had an opportunity in recent years to purchase coverage at rates highly subsidized by the federal government. Relatively few of such homeowners, however, have availed themselves of this subsidized insurance so that they have turned to the government for disaster relief after their property was damaged from flooding. The large postdisaster debts incurred by these uninsured homeowners, as well as the cost of federal relief borne by the general taxpayers, make this a social problem of some importance and concern. The specific problem we will be discussing here is the role of insurance agents in marketing flood insurance to potential victims. In general, agents do not inform their policyholders of the availability of this attractive coverage, so that the majority of inquiries regarding flood insurance have been personally initiated by the consumer himself. The three key questions to be addressed are the following: What factors have led agents to behave as they do (the descriptive component)? What decision tools and technology might be useful to the agent in improving their behavior (the prescriptive component)? And what are the policy implications of integrating these two strands (that is, what solutions should be proposed)?

Descriptive Component

Given a specific problem, the descriptive component provides insight into the historical context, as well as the organizational arrangements which define informational and authority relationships among the parties. A perspective on historical events may indicate that existing arrangements are not working well. For example, in their study of the flood insurance program on ten New York communities in the Susquehanna River basin affected by Tropical Storm Agnes in 1972, Preston, Moore, and Cornick (1975) found that many insurance agents

1. This section builds on a program of research on the role of the insurance agent initially developed by Cummins, Kunreuther, and Schoemaker (1977).

expressed little interest in the flood program. The agents felt there would be little money in marketing coverage because the volume of business would be low, and because they did not expect to pick up much other business as a result of developing new contacts.

Organizational Arrangements

To gain a better perspective on where the agent fits into the flood insurance program, it is useful to know who the relevant stakeholders are, how they interact, how they obtain information, and what their perceived and stated responsibilities are. In the case of flood insurance, the relevant stakeholders are the residents of flood-prone communities, the insurance agents, insurance companies, and the federal government as represented by the Federal Insurance Administration.

The National Flood Insurance Program was enacted in 1968 as a means of offering federally subsidized flood insurance on a nationwide basis through the cooperation of the Federal Insurance Administration and the commercial insurance industry. Up until the end of 1977 the writing of flood insurance was overseen by the National Flood Insurers Association (NFIA), an organization that represented a pool of 130 of America's major property and casualty insurance companies. Beginning in 1978, the FIA ended its partnership with the NFIA. Private insurance agents still market flood policies but the underwriting of risks for the insurance is now completely assumed by the federal government. Hence, the agents have to deal directly with the federal government in marketing policies, rather than dealing with their own companies. Hence, they serve as the intermediary between the consumer and the federal government. A natural question which thus arises is what role insurance companies play in influencing agents to promote or not promote this type of coverage. Understanding the types of incentive systems that currently exist in different companies with respect to the marketing of coverage might be a first step in understanding the agent's behavior.

More generally, the interaction of the agent and his or her company can be viewed in the context of the organization's design as shown in Figure 2. As can be seen from the diagram, the following five interacting subsystems will impact on the behavior of the organization: its structure, processes, reward systems, people, and task and technology.

As Galbraith (1977) points out, changes in any of these subsystems may require reinforcing changes in others. For example, adopting new technologies (as in designing and marketing new products) may require structural changes in the direction of product or matrix designs to accommodate the increased uncertainty and associated need for information processing. The interdependence among the five subsystems suggests a notion of fit; changes in organizational arrangements should be assessed within that context.[2]

---

2. A comprehensive framework for organization assessment has recently been developed by Van de Ven (1976), building extensively on the work of March and Simon (1958), Thompson (1967), Perrow (1967), Child (1975a,b), and Galbraith (1977). This framework, developed more fully in Van de Ven and Ferry (1980), provides an operational theory and methodology for constructing a network of relationships among persons and offices involved with a certain problem area.

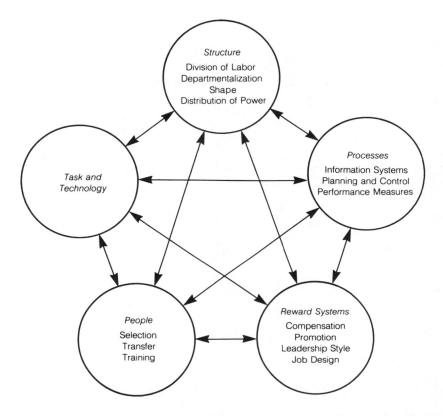

FIGURE 2   Schematic Representation of the Design Variables (From Galbraith, J. and Schoemaker, P., "Technology and organizational design: A managerial assessment." In *Studies in operations management*, ed. A. C. Hax. Adam, Holland: North Holland Publishing Co., 1978. Reprinted with the permission of the publisher.)

Decision Processes

Perhaps the most important aspect of descriptive analysis, and often the most neglected, is understanding the decision processes of each of the different actors involved. We define *decision processes* as the collection, processing, and dissemination of specific types of information in determining a specific course of action. For the problem at hand, our interest is in the factors influencing the agent's propensity to promote flood insurance. Two alternative models of choice lend themselves for comparison: an economic model based on the concepts of expected utility (EU) theory and a behavioral model based on bounded rationality (BR) notions (Simon 1957). Figure 3 depicts which variables would play a role in each of these two models.

The two models differ considerably in their underlying assumptions and in their implications for possible interventions and solutions. We shall first outline how the models differ in content and what procedures might be used to ascertain which best describes reality. Later we will discuss how the models differ in solutions and policy implications.

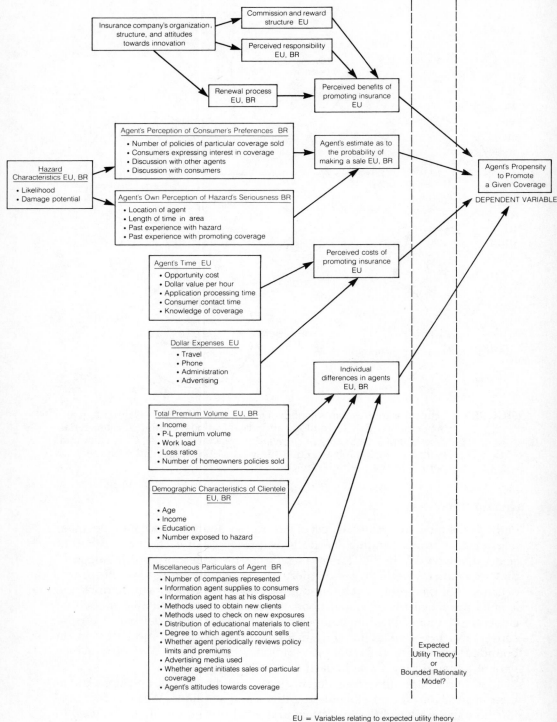

EU = Variables relating to expected utility theory
BR = Variables relating to bounded rationality model

FIGURE 3   Factors Influencing the Agent's Propensity to Promote Flood Insurance

An expected utility model assumes that the agent determines the expected costs and benefits associated with promoting or not promoting flood insurance and makes his or her choice by such a rational calculation. The utility of promoting will be determined by the costs and benefits associated with contacting the client and transacting a sale. Typical costs are time, consisting primarily of the opportunity cost of spending time that could have been channeled into other revenue-generating activities, and actual dollar expenses such as travel, telephone, and administration. The primary benefits are the commission plus the prospect of future commissions should the homeowner decide to renew his or her policy or recommend the agent to other homeowners.

If the agent promotes coverage but does not complete a sale to a particular homeowner, the primary expenses are time and dollar costs, whereas the tangible benefits are zero. However, if one includes such factors as changes in consumers' attitudes as a result of a contact and changes in the company's attitude (particularly for exclusive agents) as a function of how the agent allocates time, then intangible benefits may accrue from an unsuccessful sales attempt. Thus, an agent may still decide to market a certain type of coverage even if the profit resulting from a transaction, weighted by the probability of a successful completion, is less than the costs incurred. This is especially likely if the agent considers it a professional responsibility to inform his or her clients of the availability of coverage, even when this is a costly process. The appendix to this paper contains a simplified mathematical summary of an agent's decision process as suggested by the expected utility framework.

A model based on bounded rationality generally assumes that the agent utilizes simpler decision rules than those suggested by expected utility theory. It implies that the agent will not initiate promotion of a new coverage until some external event induces him or her to do so. Examples of external events are a recent disaster, disaster warnings, consumers expressing interest in the coverage, and discussions with other agents. Figure 4 offers a plausible bounded rationality model of the agent's decision whether or not to actively promote flood insurance.[3]

The agent's perception of the hazard (Stage 1) will be influenced by personal hazard experiences in the past, as well as information supplied to him or her by the insurance company, friends, professional colleagues, or community and government officials. The agent's knowledge of the coverage (Stage 2) will also be directly related to the type of information provided by the insurance company or trade associations, as well as by friends and colleagues.

The agent's perceived likelihood of completing a transaction (Stage 3) will depend on the agent's perception of consumers' insurance preferences, his or her past experience selling coverage, the nature and frequency of the hazard, and the type and quality of information presented to the agent by the insurer, trade associations, other agents, and community officials. A bounded rationality model might predict that the agent will not promote coverage unless the likelihood of a sale exceeds some probability threshold. This minimum probability level may partially reflect the costs of marketing a policy in relation to the benefits associated with a sale. However, the bounded rationality model

3. The bounded rationality model described here was primarily developed by Brad Borkan as part of the Cummins, Kunreuther, and Schoemaker (1977) research program.

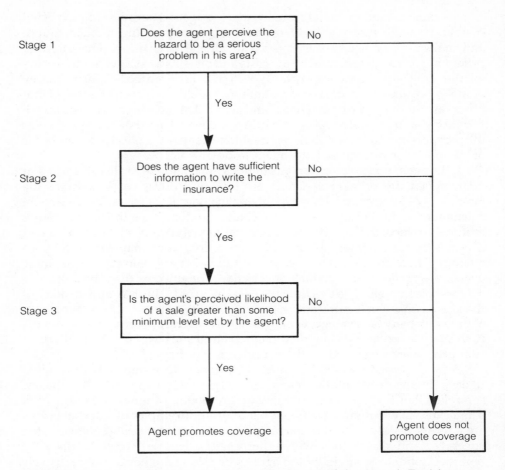

FIGURE 4   Hypothetical Bounded Rationality Model of the Agent's Decision to
Actively Promote Coverage

suggests that the agent will not consider this trade-off explicitly in setting the
probability level.

Empirical Evidence

Recent empirical studies in field and laboratory settings have shed light on the
behavioral processes associated with collecting and utilizing information and
the impact these phenomena may have on the prescriptive component. In
particular, Tversky and Kahneman (1974) have shown that individuals exhibit
systematic biases in their processing of information. One common heuristic is
availability, according to which individuals judge the probability of an event by
the ease with which relevant instances are retrieved from memory. Such a
heuristic implies that past experience will be a critical variable in an agent's
decision to market flood coverage. If the agent resides in an area that has been
severely flooded, he or she is likely to be deluged with requests for coverage
and, hence, will want to promote the insurance.

There is also extensive literature which suggests that individuals do not understand the concept of probability well, and that they process information on it poorly (Hogarth 1975; Tversky and Kahneman 1974). Empirical studies in a field setting (Kunreuther et al. 1978a) and in controlled laboratory experiments (Slovic et al. 1977) provide evidence that consumers have little interest in insurance against events such as floods when they perceive the probability of occurrence to be small, even if the potential losses are very high. Also, people's risk-taking attitudes are greatly affected by contextual influences (for example, problem presentation), as was recently shown by Schoemaker and Kunreuther (1979), Hershey and Schoemaker (1980a), and Schoemaker (1980b). These findings have relevance to agents' decision processes. They may not promote coverage because they feel consumer interest will not be high due to a low perceived probability of occurrence; however, if they do decide to market policies, the way they present information on the consequences of the event to prospective buyers may have a significant effect on their sales success.

Regarding the process associated with collecting information, Cyert and March (1963) suggest that the search for new alternatives (for example, promoting new coverage) is normally generated by a situational response such as a personal experience with misfortune or a crisis within the organization. Personal sources such as friends or close business acquaintances are likely to be critically important in determining where actual data will come from as indicated by the extensive literature on the diffusion of innovations (Rogers and Schoemaker 1971). Another feature of the decision process is the limited amount of data that individuals are likely to collect before taking action. Thus, rather than obtaining information on the various costs and benefits of a large number of alternatives, agents are likely to focus on relatively few variables and consider only a limited set of options (March and Simon 1958).

The aforementioned research suggests various biases and influences that might exist in the agent's decision processes. If not uncovered, prescriptive recommendations may fail because of fallacious behavioral assumptions. Hence, modeling and understanding the descriptive aspects is crucial. Indeed, part of the modeling process may have to involve experimentation, as we shall discuss next.

Critical Experiments

After having concluded interviews with agents regarding their decision process, some critical experiments may have to be conducted to discriminate better between the two choice models. For the problem under discussion, the experimental approach has three important comparative advantages over more traditional survey or interview methods.

1. It has the advantage of not relying on the agent's own insights into his or her decision process, but requiring only that the agent is able to make realistic decisions in hypothetical choice situations. For example, one may not want to ask an agent whether there exists a critical probability threshold associated with the sale of a policy that determines whether or not he or she promotes insurance coverage. Rather, one can infer whether or not such a threshold exists by analyzing the agent's decisions for hypothetical situa-

tions in which the probability is systematically varied. This comparative advantage is important since research on cue utilization (for example, Slovic, Fleissner, and Bauman 1972) indicates that decision makers often do not know the relative importance of cues (that is, decision parameters) or the ways in which they combine into a judgment (Nisbett and Wilson 1977). Hence, some of the limitations of protocol and survey methods (for example, people not knowing how they make decisions) can be overcome through the experimental approach.

2. A second advantage of the experimental method is that decision or insurance parameters can be varied systematically and over a *wider range* than in the real world. For example, suppose that survey data show that commissions for flood insurance vary only slightly across insurance companies. In that case, it may be difficult to say anything about the role of commissions on the basis of field data. Experimental data, however, may determine at what commission levels agents will become interested in promoting the coverage. The greater variance in the experiments enhances cue-identification and decision-rule modeling.

3. A third advantage is that the agent's decision process can be analyzed at different stages in which the experimenter controls all cues. For example, by means of hypothetical questions, one can study the effect of changes in loss magnitudes on the agent's willingness to promote insurance, while keeping all other variables constant. This procedure allows for testing the sequential model of choice in a way more systematic than that allowed by attitude data collected in a field survey.

Figure 5 contains a more detailed diagram of the factors presumed to influence directly an agent's propensity to promote flood insurance. As an illustration, the figure suggests that experiments could be designed which address (1) the influence of hazard characteristics on the agent's own perception of the seriousness of a hazard; (2) the agent's perceptions as to how seriously his or her clients will consider protecting themselves against the consequences of a certain hazard; and (3) how costs, benefits, and the probability of a sale are combined in the agent's decision process. Such experiments could determine whether expected utility or bounded rationality models better describe agent behavior. Since these two models lead to very different policy recommendations, as discussed later, developing a realistic model of the agent's decision process becomes particularly important.

Prescriptive Component

If the descriptive analyses show that agents do not maximize expected utility, neither objectively nor subjectively, normative decision methodology might be invoked to improve agent decision making. However, the extent of normative analysis is constrained through its cost by the degree to which current decision making by agents is suboptimal. Recognizing the trade-offs between model realism and solution complexity, as well as other cost/benefit trade-offs, it may not be easy to determine what strategy to follow.

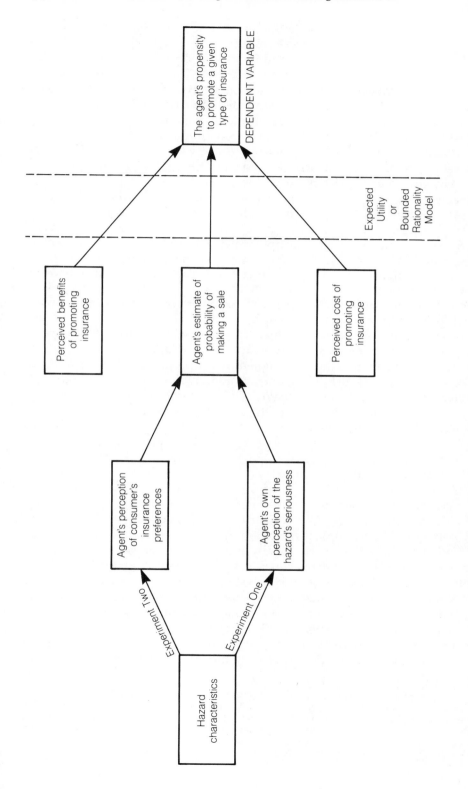

FIGURE 5   Variables and Relationships to Be Examined Experimentally

Several mathematical programming models for sales effort allocation decisions have been formulated: for example, Davis and Farley (1971); Lodish (1975a,b, 1976); Shanker, Turner, and Zoltners (1975); Zoltners (1976); Lodish and Fudge (1977); and Beswick and Cravens (1977). These models, together with their solution algorithms or heuristics, are part of current decision methodology and would have to be studied and adapted to the insurance agent's task, recognizing the latter's cognitive limitations.

At an organizational level, the available methodology for modeling preference structures (for example, multiattribute utility theory) could be employed to assess more precisely the organizational priority to be given to flood insurance.[4] Incentives and decision procedures could then be designed, on the basis of the best descriptive decision model, to evoke behavior on the part of the agent that is compatible with the priority level assigned to flood insurance. The art of applying multiattribute utility theory is well covered in Keeney and Raiffa (1976). Their book shows how to approach attribute specification, goal hierarchies, and preference elicitation. It contains case descriptions of several successful applications of the theory, ranging from corporate planning to choosing an airport location. Hence, joining the multiattribute utility approach with traditional optimization techniques of management science may lead to more powerful decision analyses.

Of course, the problem's complexity, together with the time and computational constraints, may not allow for such a thorough approach. As an alternative, heuristic methods may be designed that explicitly consider the costs of collecting and processing information (for example, Kleindorfer and Kunreuther 1978). Hence, when optimality (defined narrowly) is too expensive, it may be advisable to develop rules of thumb or to incorporate existing managerial decision rules into the model itself. This latter approach has been successfully used in bootstrapping studies of organizational planning decisions.

The general idea is to retain that which is good in existing managerial decision behavior and to eliminate noise and inconsistencies associated with the execution phase. The essence of this technique is to build a model of a manager, based, for example, on past decisions, and have the model outperform the manager subsequently. Numerous studies in psychology (for a review see Dawes 1973) have shown that simple linear regression models based on the past judgments of some expert typically outperform the person him- or herself. The regression weights of the linear model usually provide a sufficient approximation to the human decision model, be this linear or not, so that the former's prediction error will on average be less than that of the human, whose future judgments will typically contain considerable execution error.

In this vein, Bowman (1963) and Kunreuther (1969) show in the context of business decisions that substituting an "average" rule for human decision making may lead to better decisions, even though the average rule is nothing

---

4. For a given multiattribute preference structure or a subset thereof several so-called independence conditions may hold which would allow for relatively simple mathematical representations. Keeney (1973) provides a brief overview of these independence conditions and how they limit the functional form of the associated multiattribute utility function. Exploiting independence conditions in this manner may lead to more realistic objective functions than those typically used in management science applications.

more than a good statistical model of past human decisions. Hence, bootstrapping models are a form of decision support. In the context of the flood insurance problem, agents can examine the suggested decisions resulting from the model and then decide whether they would like to follow the prescribed advice or modify it because of special factors not considered in the model.

Decision Technology

Recent developments in computer technology have allowed for nonoptimizing approaches in which human and machine interact. Such techniques are called *nonoptimizing* because no explicit problem formulation occurs, and, hence, no clear optimization criterion exists. However, the outcome of such a human–machine interaction is not necessarily less of a contribution than mathematically optimal solutions to more narrowly defined problems.

Indeed, the interaction between a person who possesses intimate knowledge of real organizational problems and a computerized system that instantly provides key information may represent a vast improvement over traditional management science methods. Advantages may accrue because of a reduced danger of solving elegantly and optimally the wrong problem, or the right one too late. Keen and Scott Morton (1978) provide a thorough discussion of the philosophical and substantive aspects of such interactive decision support systems. Examples of this approach are described in Hurst (1977) for technical decision problems, in Katz and Miller (1977), and in Kunreuther et al. (1978b) regarding policy analysis for natural hazards.

In the context of our insurance problem, several types of decision support could be considered. At the organizational level, policy formulation and priority setting could be aided by so-called symmetrical linkage systems. Pioneered by Hammond et al. (1977), this approach links interactive computer models of the environment with interactive models of human judgment. By presenting policymakers with hypothetical decision situations, the system provides feedback on the consequence of the decisions (for example, via simulation), as well as on the implicit weighting of various criteria, and the shapes of imputed value functions for that particular policymaker. It represents a new form of vicarious learning, in which policy formulation occurs as an iterative process of simulated judgment with feedback on consequences and implied priority levels.

At the agent level, it may be advisable to develop a decision support system to aid the agent in servicing his or her clients. The information to be provided (for example, information on exposure, current coverage, deductibles, and tax implications) would depend on the decision model the agent currently uses or will be encouraged to use.

Without an in-depth knowledge of the descriptive component, prescriptive analyses remain limited to ad hoc applications of existing tools. The real challenge lies in developing prescriptive analyses that do justice to the existing cognitive limitations of organizations and individuals, and the varying perceptions as to organizational goals and problems.

Proposing a Solution

Returning to Figure 3, we can identify several variables that play a role in either a bounded rationality model, an expected utility model, or both. For example, as shown in Figure 3, an agent's own perception of a hazard's seriousness would be considered a key variable in a bounded rationality model but not in an expected utility model. In general, the bounded rationality model is primarily concerned with information processing and subjective variables concerning past experience, whereas expected utility deals with more precise cost/benefit analyses. Hence, the perceived costs of promoting a policy will be an important factor in the expected utility model but relatively unimportant in a bounded rationality approach. As shown in Figure 3, the perceived probability of completing a sale plays an important role in either model.

The solutions implied by the two preceding choice models are distinctly different. The expected utility model suggests that raising the commission to a level where the benefits of promoting coverage outweigh the costs will be sufficient inducement for the agent to promote coverage. The sequential model implies that the agents must first be aware of the hazard and the need for promoting the coverage before becoming sensitive to commission or bonus inducements. Even if the agent has reached this state, the probability of completing a sale may be the primary determinant of his or her future action rather than an explicit benefit/cost trade-off.

Let us now turn to policy questions. After having analyzed the agent's decision processes, it will become clearer whether private markets are appropriate mechanisms for administering federally subsidized flood insurance. If the agent's current decision model is far removed from the prescriptive one, there will be a serious question as to whether the agent's rationality can be enhanced just through changes in organizational arrangements and the use of decision methodology and technology, or whether institutional changes are called for.

The Issue of Integration

The preceding policy example has illustrated the types of descriptive and prescriptive analyses that would have to be conducted for the particular societal problem of flood insurance, particularly regarding the role of insurance agents. A meaningful set of policies will only emerge if the descriptive and prescriptive components become well integrated. We turn now to this important integration issue, taking a more theoretical perspective.

Put very simply, the descriptive analyses will tell us where we are and what we are capable of, and the prescriptive ones where we would like to be or should be. Since the actual state and the desired state usually do not coincide, there is a question as to how much either state is to be modified. For example, the descriptive component may reveal that existing organizational arrangements and decision processes make it impossible to attain the desired state as identified by prescriptive analysis. This tells us that the prescriptive analysis was unrealistic and has to be scaled down in recognition of the existing constraints (cognitive or otherwise).

Descriptive and prescriptive analyses should be conducted in the realization that organizational problems are faced by people who (1) have limited time and attention capacity, (2) limited training and cognitive abilities, (3) varying needs, (4) different cognitive styles, and (5) varying problem perceptions.

For example, consider cognitive style as a potentially important decision variable. McKenney and Keen (1974), Kilmann and Mitroff (1976), and others have shown that people prefer different modes in which to utilize their perceptual and judgmental faculties.[5] Some prefer making decisions at an emotional level, others at a more cerebral one; some value information for its specific content and others for how it supports or disconfirms prior beliefs and cognitive models of the world. A manager's personality may influence his or her problem perception (Schoemaker 1980b), the preferred organizational arrangements (Kilmann and Mitroff 1976), the preferred type of organizational activity (Mitroff, Barabba, and Kilmann 1977), and the type of information desired.

To illustrate the importance of psychological type, let us just consider the design of a decision support system. Using Mason and Mitroff's (1973) framework this involves matching the user's psychological type with (1) a class of relevant problems, (2) methods of evidence generation, (3) an appropriate organizational context, and (4) a mode of presentation. Each of these involves choices. With respect to the methods of evidence generation, the decision analyst must choose from competing philosophical bases in designing his or her inquiring system (Churchman 1971). For example, a Leibnitzian inquiring system would primarily be based on more traditional operation research models and, hence, would be most appropriate for well-structured problem environments. Alternatively, a Hegelian system would have to be conflictual in nature, providing data from different points of view, models, or premises. It would therefore best work in ill-structured problem situations.

In summary, prescriptive theories are based on philosophical premises which may have varying appeals to different organizational decision makers and varying degrees of appropriateness in a given situation. The reductionist philosophy underlying much of recent management science might well be rejected by politically motivated decision makers who think holistically about their problems, and to whom gestalt is more important than a machine representation of a system or organization. Accordingly, the basic values and needs of the users will determine in important ways the desirability, acceptability, and usefulness of traditional prescriptive decision science. Inadequate appreciation of this constraint may have been an important factor in limiting the role of normative decision theory in complex social systems.

---

5. With respect to corporate cognitive style, there may, for example, be a real question as to whether an insurance company would desire and accept a formal multiattribute utility representation of its goals and objectives. Even though Keeney (1975) successfully applied such a methodology in a highly professional consulting organization, it is not clear that the same would work in a conservative, large, and probably more complex insurance company. Indeed, techniques requiring less detail as to the definition and measurement of attributes (for example, Saaty 1978), may initially be preferred.

Summary

In this article we have examined the role of descriptive and prescriptive analysis in organizational decision making. Recognizing the separate cultures underlying these two components (McKenney and Keen 1974), we argued that much more integration is needed before analysis will assume its rightful role in complex decision making.

Recent reviews of the cognitive limitations of man (for example, Connolly 1977; Simon 1979a) clearly suggest that humans are poor and unsystematic decision makers. On the other hand, however, available prescriptive decision tools are seldom used, possibly because they belong to a culture vastly different from the managerial one. The present article has presented a general framework which may be useful in bridging this cultural gap. In particular, we feel that prescriptive theorists have not fully appreciated the importance of understanding organizational arrangements and decision processes.

To illustrate the challenges and difficulties of doing justice to the descriptive component, a policy example was discussed concerning the role of insurance agents in the marketing of flood insurance. The example focused on the importance of developing realistic decision models of agent behavior, and pointed out avenues for doing so. Particular emphasis was given to the role of experimentation in developing realistic decision models, as inputs to prescriptive analysis.

In conclusion, the theoretical part of the article and the example both suggest that the organizational context of the decision maker and the nature of his or her decision rule critically influence the type of prescriptive analyses that should be conducted as well as the type of solutions to be proposed. The practical challenges for decision analysis may be more in this latter area than in further development of normative methodology.

ACKNOWLEDGMENTS

Reprinted from *Knowledge* Volume 3, Number 2, (1981), pages 389–412, by permission of the publisher, Sage Publications, Beverly Hills, CA. Acknowledgment is made to Brad Borkan for helpful comments. The research for this article was in part supported by the Office of Naval Research project "Incentives in Systems Acquisitions," under contract #N00014-77-C-0171.

Appendix

A Simplified Expected Utility Model of the Agent's Decision Process

Input Parameters

P = probability of the hazard occurring (per year)

L = loss incurred by client if hazard occurs (per year)

c = premium client must pay for coverage (per year)

R = commission (or revenue) to the agent for one policy sold

T = time value of agent (per hour)

K = cost of making a client contact (includes T plus administrative and transportation costs)

t = time it takes agent to process an application (after having made a sale)

Estimates

p_s = perceived probability of sale = $f(p, L, c)$

$U(S)^*$ = utility of sale = $U(R - Tt - K)$

$U(\bar{S})$ = utility of no sale = $U(-K) < 0$

Decision

Promote insurance if: $p_s U(S) + (1 - p_s) U(\bar{S}) > 0$

or
$$\frac{U(S)}{|U(\bar{S})|} > \frac{1 - p_s}{p_s}$$

*The utility function represents changes in wealth. We assumed $U(0) = 0$.

Comments on the Huber, Kunreuther and Schoemaker, and Chestnut and Jacoby Papers

Henry Mintzberg, *McGill University*

I should like to make some comments on each of these papers, in the order in which I read them, and then use these comments as a lead into more general conclusions on the study of decision making in organizations. Those conclusions deal with the use of labels, the development of typologies, and our application of the concept of decision itself.

Huber

I am tempted to open my comments on the Huber paper with a citation of some graffiti that someone surely must have seen on a bathroom wall in the Pentagon, around 1961: "And I told Bob, I said, 'PPBS won't happen today, PPBS won't happen tomorrow, and it will never happen.' That's what I told Bob." Well the Program Planning Budgeting System happened, but only for a short time, before it crashed. Had PPBS been accompanied with more critique instead of being treated — as we tend to treat all new management techniques — as the "one best way," it might have gotten off the ground. I do not wish to imply that Decision Support Systems (DSSs) will not fly, but rather that we cannot just assume that a new idea will fly because the plane at Kittyhawk did. To launch DSSs safely, we must be prepared to look carefully and realistically at their failures as well as their successes.

In this regard, I welcome Huber's survey of applications. Unfortunately, his paper says little of the results, but I look forward to their eventual publication. I would urge him, however, to avoid using the survey to demonstrate that DSS is working, a tendency I see in his early comments. Rather, I hope he will study what is not working, as well as what is, and why. To use an example from his paper, it is not the existence of a cash flow model that is important, not even the fact that it allows "top management to examine many possible courses of action in two or three hours. . ." (p. 250). Rather, we need to know if there were specific applications of that model made, and how they affected the decisions managers made.

Decision Support Systems and Managerial Intuition

What appeals to me about the orientation of the DSS literature in general (for example, Keen and Scott Morton 1978) is its sympathy with the needs of the manager and its sensitivity to the findings of descriptive research. It is refreshing to see these computer systems recognized as "support," and to encounter a part of the management science literature that puts down neither the manager nor his or her intuition. This provides a healthy basis on which to develop and introduce these systems into organizational decision making.

The Huber paper follows in this tradition. In fact, it goes one better than previous writings by seeking to tie these systems into four models of decision making, essentially Allison's (1971) three models coupled with March and Olsen's (1976) garbage can. After I read what Huber was trying to do I thought, "How is he going to be able to find applications in some of those situations?" In fact, his lists of possible applications are plausible in terms of the information needs of different situations of decision making. However, I would fault him for not discussing the monumental problems involved in developing such applications.

While I understand Huber's wish to see applications in all four models, I believe that Decision Support Systems are really oriented to two of them: rational and program models. The applicability to the garbage can and political models is more forced. Specifically, I see the DSS as an attempt to force rationality on the organization (even the garbage can) by programming at least in part its decision processes. In other words, the DSS functions in the spirit of two of the models more than in that of the other two.

Furthermore, I believe a fifth and very important model is missing — that of intuition. Organizational decision making appears to be largely intuitive, and it is this characteristic above all — more than politics or the confusion of the garbage can — with which Decision Support Systems must learn to live. My main comments on the Huber paper, which follow, relate to this fifth model.

As I implied in my opening, many a new technique in management generated a great deal of enthusiasm while revving up, but, rather than taking off like Orville and Wilbur's airplane, crashed at the end of the runway. Few have been able to fly in the atmosphere of intuition. One can talk of PPBS and the strategic planning of the 1960s, financial models of the firm in the early 1970s, and so on. I think DSS may have planned a better flight path, but it may not fly as high as some people hope.

Huber raises what I see as one of the major problems — the manager's need for very current information. Often managers need information before it gets documented — for example, as rumor that an important customer was seen golfing with a competitor, rather than as fact, that a contract was lost. But Huber drops the point. I think DSS people need to think more about this. Likewise, as I have argued elsewhere (Mintzberg 1975a and 1979), the use of formal systems is impeded by the manager's reliance on soft information, information inaccessible to the computer, yet very rich in nature — mood in the factory, sense of product quality, personal reactions of customers. Again, DSS people should give a good deal of attention to what their systems miss, so they can decide where and how these systems best fit in with managerial decision making — and don't.

I suspect that overselling of DSS may prove a more serious problem than underselling. Underselling means lost opportunity to clarify intuition by analysis. Overselling means driving out appropriate intuition. Earlier systems sought to displace intuition and the managers who use it. Support systems, while not displacing the manager, may displace his or her intuition. My concern is that the convenience of the terminal will discourage managers from using their senses to collect data. In other words, it may keep managers in their offices, rather than out on a tour of the factories, or out meeting customers. My image is of the terminal installed at the door to the manager's office, blocking the exit. If that image is even partially accurate, we may pay a high price for these systems.

A major problem in today's large organizations, in my opinion, is that the senior managers are too removed, too detached. Intuition is driven by the senses — by hearing, touching, seeing (and not just print), smelling, tasting, and picking up some kind of vibration through that elusive sixth sense. All kinds of factors currently block senior managers from using these senses to their fullest — hierarchies, distances, procedures, and so on. I fear that Decision Support Systems may aggravate this problem, and, in the process, render organizations even more detached, insensitive, and essentially bureaucratic than they currently are.

I wish not to be misunderstood. I do believe that intuition needs to be fortified with systematic analysis. And the DSS strikes me as a sensible form of systematic analysis. But I worry about the consequences of the enthusiastic promotion of such systems. Up to some point, they must improve decision making. Beyond it, they may prove a serious liability if our organizations are to be sensitive to our needs as clients, workers, and citizens — our very human needs.

One last point: I like Huber's contrast of *dss* and DSS. It reminds me of Shapero's (1977) biting comparison of MANAGEMENT with management — of what techniques propose versus what managers actually do. In the light of my comments I wonder if we shouldn't be thinking of *ds*S. By this I mean decoupling the system from the computer — in simple terms, building managerial support systems around clever analysts instead of fancy hardware. This, of course, is how operations research began. Maybe the DSS people, with their managerial orientation, can rediscover what operations research seems to have lost.

Kunreuther and Schoemaker

The Kunreuther and Schoemaker paper is obviously compatible with the Huber one. In particular, I am very sympathetic with their premise that the "descriptive component (of decision making) is a vital ingredient to the prescriptive one." What these authors do is show us how to "load in" decision making relevant descriptive theory that is interesting and, in many cases, relevant, in order to comprehend problems as well as to analyze them.

Of course, there is no shortage of literature pursuing either of these themes. On the descriptive end, while we have been somewhat remiss in the field of management, the literature of public policy sciences treats at length the role of the expert and the use of knowledge — of descriptive theory — in policymaking. And, of course, our own management literature deals at length — at times ad nauseam — with the use of prescriptive theory.

What makes this paper unique is its attempt to pull these two perspectives together — to integrate them. I welcome that effort, but wish that it had been further developed. In particular, the paper does not tell me a great deal about the intersection of these two perspectives. I can only hope the authors will pursue their theme in the future.

This paper also draws me back to some of the points I made about the Huber paper, especially regarding intuition. We need not only make a plea for the use of theory and technique, but also address the issue, at what price theory, at what price technique? What do we lose by explicating, articulating, analyzing? We sometimes seem intent on driving out intuition — approaches to decision making that are inexplicit, unarticulated, essentially inaccessible. Should we? What would be the effect of loading decision-making processes to the hilt with formal knowledge and technology? Our techniques, for example, are almost all focused on the selection of alternatives, at the back end of the process of decision making. Yet our own study of decision making (Mintzberg, Raisinghani, and Theoret 1976) suggests that what really matters is diagnosis, at the front end, which remains largely outside the realm of analysis, and within that of intuition. Favoring technique — and formalization — in my view will encourage more attention to choice at the expense of diagnosis, resulting in poorer decisions. Of course, I welcome theories and techniques that will help in diagnosis. But I have so far seen little effort in this regard.

Kunreuther and Schoemaker claim that "recent reviews of the cognitive limitations of man . . . clearly suggest that humans are poor and unsystematic decision makers" (p. 277). Compared to what (or whom)? Who wrote their paper? Humans, I assume. What could have written it instead? Rather than disparaging managers and intuition, we would do better to recognize their amazing abilities, and design our technologies to complement them. It is we theorists who are the poor decision makers. So intent are we on promoting our own perspective that we blind ourselves to reality.[1]

Chestnut and Jacoby

I have more difficulty with the Chestnut and Jacoby paper. Perhaps that is because I know nothing about consumer behavior (aside from my own). But

---

1. The authors claim that "numerous studies in psychology . . . have shown that simple linear regression models based on the past judgments of some expert typically outperform the person him- or herself" (p. 274). As I recall this literature (for example, Bowman 1961), the cost curve proved to be disk-shaped, so that the experienced human, who typically did not vary too greatly from the norm, proved to be almost as effective as the formal model (and a lot more flexible, and often much cheaper). In fact, Peters, Hammond, and Summers (1974) show us that while the intuitive approach is less often precisely correct than the analytic one, it tends to have a far lower variance. In other words, when the analytic approach is wrong, it can really be quite wrong. On a disk-shaped cost curve, that would render analysis far more costly, on the average.

since they are presenting it in a book on decision making, I have to consider their paper in the light of this field.

Their paper seems to be written to clarify what they call *Behavioral Process Research* (BPR), but for me, it serves to confuse. While the authors claim to be describing a methodology, I end up with the impression that what distinguishes BPR is not methodology but a focus of attention — namely on the acquisition of information. As a result, the methodology part of their paper works less well for me, although the results of their studies — reviewed briefly at the end — seem more interesting.

I am also bothered by what in Herzberg's terms might be called a hygiene factor (Herzberg et al. 1959) — pushing one's work a little too aggressively. The tone of this paper is a bit annoying. I believe the researcher must promote his or her ideas, but this should be done in the publication of his or her research. Once this is done — and the mousetrap is published, so to speak — then it is up to others to beat a path to its door. Let others decide if the approach is valid and useful. The research is public; it should speak for itself.

The Pursuit of Realism in Research

More importantly, I have trouble with the claim of realism. Again we are back to frame of reference. Picking data off a chart concerning product may be more realistic than filling out a consumer behavior questionnaire, but that sure isn't how I buy my canned kumquat!

Chestnut and Jacoby's frame of reference is the psychologist's laboratory, with all its neat control. Mine is the manager's office, with all its messiness. How do we know what's in a simulation? How can we determine what is lost in a simulation? The comment about Russo's discovery that consumers buy more than one product on a shopping trip — which will come as no surprise to my ten-year-old daughter — suggests how removed from reality laboratory researchers can be. The authors claim that, "simulations do not have to present the same characteristics as those of the real world; they have only to present those analogous to the real world, ones within which the subject can behave in a similar or same manner" (p. 240). But how do you know? How can you ever know? The authors talk of "realism more imagined . . . than actual" (p. 240). What does this mean? They claim that "what differences did exist were not particularly worrisome" (p. 240). To whom?

I have a different image of their subject: not of a consumer ignoring information in a purchase, but of a student anxious to collect his money and get back to his homework. So he sits on the edge of his chair, scans the data as fast as he can, collects his money and his chocolate bar or whatever, and runs. Then the researchers build a theory about the limited acquisition of information. But the subject's real choice was not about the product, but about engaging in the experiment in the first place. And for that he had all the information he needed. Maybe we should draw conclusions about the *complete* use of the *relevant* information.

In his comments in Section 7, Louis Pondy lists a number of points about how to make laboratory experimentation more realistic. I have three reactions. First, he only knows about these points because he has done field research and read about other field studies of real decisions. Had he never gone into the field, he would never know what was missing in the laboratory. Second, I doubt that many of his suggestions for approximating reality can be effectively simulated in the laboratory. Recalling Ken MacCrimmon's comments in Section 2, how do you simulate Mr. Iacocca's problems at Chrysler? And third, how can we ever know that there is not yet another factor, that renders the simulation naive? In the field, that factor is present, even if we are blind to it. In the laboratory, we never know. Claims of "realism" and of differences not being "particularly worrisome" have no meaning. Perhaps there is always just one more unconsidered factor, like the city planners who are always sure that *next* time they plan a city, it will be just right.

I must add one qualification. Why, I ask myself, do I find laboratory work of this nature, and most of what is done in social psychology in general, of so little use in management, and yet often find the results of laboratory work done in cognitive psychology of great interest? I guess it must be a matter of simulation. Former researchers typically try to simulate some real-world phenomenon — leadership, consumer behavior, groups with a purpose. But these simulations always seem artificial to me. Naturally occurring groups, for example, have some real purpose; their members and leaders come together through complex social processes; the groups typically last; and so on. Those conditions are difficult to replicate in the laboratory. The cognitive psychologist, on the other hand, seems to capture a reality, perhaps because the focus is on mental, rather than on social, processes. This can be made to occur in the laboratory much as it does outside. In a sense, the cognitive psychologist seems not to be simulating but just bringing natural behavior into the laboratory. And so I conclude that while we should learn from the laboratories of the cognitive psychologists, we should get our social psychologists, and consumer behaviorists, out of their laboratories. Let them study the real world of social behavior, the messy one. Let them face a little uncertainty for a change. Maybe then they will discover startling things.

Reflections

I have three related comments to make in conclusion, on labeling, on typologies, and on the concept that we call *decision*.

Labeling

I was struck by the labeling in two of the papers. As a compulsive labeler, I see an example of good and bad labeling here.

Decision Support Systems is a wonderful label, and shows the full value of labeling. A good label creates a community. It focuses attention on a theme, pulling people together in their pursuit of that theme. Conferences can be held, and the relevant people will know to attend. The label works for Decision Support Systems because the words were chosen carefully, and indeed, Keen and Scott Morton (1978) devote a good deal of attention to the reasons behind the selection of each of the three words. The key word for me is *support* because, as I already noted, it sets this attempt at the use of analysis in organizations off from a long stream of unsuccessful predecessors. The role of managers, and by implication, of intuition, is recognized and accepted. Those interested in decision systems are cordially invited to attend so long as they see their systems as a support.

Just as a good label can clarify and create a community, so can a poor one confuse and mislead, creating either no community or an artificial one, reifying a concept. Behavioral Process Research is a poor label. While Jacoby and Chestnut may do BPR, all of us do *bpr*. My own research — tracing strategies as patterns in streams of decisions — is certainly behavioral, and it is concerned with process. Call a conference on Behavioral Process Research, and unless you attract everybody, you risk getting nobody. So labels are important. (In this regard, I cannot help but reveal my suspicion that the only thing that some of the different communities represented in this book seem to have in common is the word *decision*. Just because we happen to use the same word does not mean that we are capable of communicating with each other. Again, we need to be more careful about our labels.)

The Need for a Typology of Decisions

Labeling brings me to a second point, one I have been wanting to make in print for some years now. In organization theory, we are badly in need of a set of labels for the decisions organizations make. In other words, we need a decent typology. We have had one for decades, going back to Parsons (1960): coordinative, allocative, and policy decisions (or, more popularly, operating, administrative, and strategic decisions), but it is not of much help. In my opinion, the greatest block to progress in organization theory is the lack of a decent typology of organizational decisions. How can we realistically discuss decentralization or participation or virtually any other organization concept without such a typology?

In principle, the creation of such a typology need not be difficult. Someone has to go into an organization (a small one will do) and write down everything that seems to be a decision, and then describe various characteristics of each seeming decision. From this, with a dose of imagination, can come one or a number of useful typologies.

Decisions

One difficulty will be encountered in the creation of a typology. To delineate the decisions of an organization, we shall have to be clear on what we mean by *decision*. I have no problem with defining the term as "a specific commitment to action, (usually a commitment of resources)" (Mintzberg, Raisinghani, and Théoret 1976, p. 246). But I do have a problem with operationalizing it. To my great surprise, no one has raised the issue in this volume. *Decision* is a given, as if it exists in organizations — like doorknobs and desks. It certainly exists in the laboratory — the researchers make sure of that. But are we so sure about it in organizations? Consider the European automobile firm whose senior management was reputed to have hired a management consulting firm in order to find out who "decided" to introduce a major new model.

What makes us so sure that *decision* is so clear-cut a word? Maybe we have been fooled by the artificial certainty of the laboratory. Some decisions are clear enough — the selection of a new Chief Executive Officer, for example. But a decision can just emerge too, as a kind of implicit consensus or a gradual reorientation of one's world view. People just change their ways. There is action, but no formal commitment. *Formal* is the key word, because I think it underlies what we mean by *decision*. We don't just reorient our product lines over time, we "decide" to, on Tuesday, the 13th, at 3:51 P.M. We don't just have children, we "decide" to. We don't just live our lives, we make decisions. We pronounce, and we commit formally before we act.

In a world that believes this, the onus is on the actor to decide. If by chance he or she has decided implicitly, or perhaps subconsciously, or maybe even not at all, then it becomes necessary to decide retroactively. In other words, we must rationalize, or explain, as if we really did decide. And next time we shall know better. We *shall* decide. Behavior must be *formal*, conscious, articulated, and pronounced upon. In fact, probably no society has ever been more hung up on articulation than ours of North America, thanks in good part to Mr. Freud. From protocols in the laboratory to encounter groups in the mountains, we drive ourselves crazy articulating.

The important word is *formal*, because it means bureaucratic. It allies the label *decision* with the label *bureaucracy.* Who but the bureaucracies are so obsessed with "deciding" everything? And we as researchers fit right in. By pretending that all action must be preceded by "decision," and by implicitly accepting an unambiguous use of the word, we evoke and even encourage bureaucracy and only bureaucracy — without even realizing it. That is how we look at the world. That *is* our world. Of course, by that token — and a number of others[2] — the laboratories of many of our social psychologists seem to qualify as bureaucracies. We know that intuition can deny decision, as we use the word, not to mention articulation. So it should come as no surprise that we would deny intuition, or put it down when it rears its informal head.

2. An example is the obsession with reducing uncertainty and standardizing behavior.

Decision Making: An Interdisciplinary Focus

John W. Slocum, Jr., *Southern Methodist University*

Interdisciplinary research is like the weather; people are always talking about it, but most never do anything about it. In reading the three papers in this section, I felt like a person looking out of a hotel window, not able to see across the street because of a dense fog. In the background, the television weather forecaster is predicting clear skies. The disparate scope of these papers has made a theoretical synthesis difficult and the fog dense. Only time will tell if the fog has actually cleared.

An organization's very existence is the outcome of a process of decision making. An individual or group of individuals must have made a decision to organize in order to carry out some activity. In order for organizations to be effective and efficient, they are dependent upon the decisions of individual members to actually engage in the activities required for effective performance of their tasks.

Microeconomic theory generally contains two basic postulates regarding the behavior of decision making: first, that people's goals are given and, second, that people are rational. The parsimoniousness and pervasiveness of these assumptions is readily understandable. Empirical research, however, has concluded that these assumptions are untenable (Simon 1979b).

The notions of bounded rationality and satisficing have been introduced by Simon in an attempt to develop a more realistic and valid description of decision making. In 1979, Simon extended his examination of limited rationality. A distinction was made between "substantive" and "procedural" rationality. According to Simon, behavior is substantively rational when it is appropriate to the achievement of stated goals within the limits imposed by given conditions and constraints. On the other hand, behavior is procedurally rational when it is the outcome of appropriate deliberation; its procedural rationality depends on the process that generated it. Simon (1979, p. 504) argues for economic theory focused primarily on substantive rationality. As problems have arisen with this approach, economists have attempted to deal with them by broadening the criteria for substantive rationality. Recognizing these problems, Simon maintains that ultimately an adequate theory of rational behavior must account for both procedural and substantive rationality. However, more research needs to be focused toward the development of a theory of procedural rationality. This calls for: (1) the analysis of the processes of decision making as they actually occur in organizations, and (2) an examination of the mechanisms designed to facilitate the work of decision making in organizations.

Simon indicates that the ultimate challenge for theorists is not to focus on information *per se* but rather on attention. He argues that for many decisions, information may be an expensive luxury since it may distract the decision maker's attention from truly important aspects of the problem. The attention process is analogous to the "enactment" process proposed by Weick (1979). By studying how organizations distribute the scarce resource of managerial attention, how they develop and implement heuristics for problem solving, how they use past experience to generate feasible solutions, the process of decision making can be advanced.

All three of these papers focus on the attentional basis of decision making. The paper by Chestnut and Jacoby in this section focuses on the external informational cues provided to consumers in making choice decisions. Using Simon's construct of attention, their literature review indicates that if consumers are overloaded with information, they begin to lose their ability to make a choice. They have developed a methodology, Behavioral Process Research (BPR), to measure what Simon labeled procedural rationality. BPR addresses the facets in the decision maker's cognitive schemas that have an impact on this choice process. George Huber's paper examines the impact of Decision Support Systems (DSSs) on the manager's ability to make decisions. DSSs are designed to help the manager process information. The types of information to be processed are a function of the manager's decision environment. The final paper by Kunreuther and Schoemaker focuses on a descriptive model of decision making. Recognizing the cognitive limits of decision makers, they present a general paradigm integrating prescriptive and descriptive models. The decision-making processes of life insurance agents were studied using these two models. Factors considered salient in the prescriptive model were thought not to be salient in the descriptive model. A proposed integration of these different models was attempted.

Informational Basis of Decision Making: Goals

In all three papers, two important facets were considered: (1) the values, goals, or preferences of the decision maker, and (2) the information available to the decision maker about the environment and alternative choices. Let us consider how the goals of the decision maker can affect the information used and sought, and, conversely, how the information available to the decision maker may affect his or her goals.

Classical economists postulated that consensual goals exist throughout an organization. Given the internal conflict within most organizations, the perspective seems naive. A number of theorists (Hrebiniak 1978 and Pfeffer 1981b) have developed the position that agreement on overall goals is tenuous. Limited goal consensus is achieved as a result of temporary agreements between members or stakeholders who hold goals of differing compatibility (Arnold, Evans, and House 1980). The actual content of these goals reflects the political structure of the organization, the stakeholders' personal and departmental goals, and the task(s) facing this loose coalition of organizational members. Using this perspective, the minimal aspiration levels of each stakeholder become constraints that the organization must satisfy to maintain its viability. Kunreuther and Schoemaker explore this perspective with their model of decision making.

The cognitive style of the decision maker is a potentially important decision variable affecting goal congruence. McKenney and Keen (1974), Mitroff and Kilmann (1975), Hellriegel and Slocum (1980), and Steckroth, Slocum, and Sims (1980) have shown that managers differ in their preference modes of perception and judgment. Based on the model of C. G. Jung, judging is represented by a continuum of feeling to thinking. Some managers are aware of others' feelings and emphasize affective and personal goals in reaching a decision; others try to fit problems into standardized formulas and use a rational process to make a choice. The perception continuum is anchored by the functions of sensing and intuition. Sensing managers gather highly specific information about their environment, are good at working on details, and like to solve structured problems. Intuitive managers tend to view their environment from a gestalt perspective and like to solve "ill-structured" problems. These researchers have found that people with differing cognitive styles prefer different kinds and amounts of information, organizational tasks, and different goals to attempt to satisfy through the organization.

The Jungian system has implications for Huber's Decision Support System research. Huber proposes that DSSs will be used by managers who are confronted with "ill-structured" decisions. It would seem that intuitive thinkers or intuitive feelers who use a Hegelian inquiry system would work best on these types of problems. Sensation thinkers or sensation feelers, who approach problems with a Leibnitzian inquiry system, would not work well in these environments.

Use of Information

There are two major factors that affect whether or not a particular piece of data will be used by the decision maker. First, whether or not the individual has access to the information and, second, the weight of the information.

Accessibility

Mintzberg (1973), and Aldrich and Herker (1977), among others, have found that information sources for *boundary spanners* are usually their subordinates and business associates. These researchers have also found that the acquisition of information is dependent upon the individual decision maker's position in a network, and the extent to which the individual reciprocates information needed by others in the network. These "gatekeepers" carefully control the flow of information between sets of independent decision makers. An interesting study by Hirsch (1975) of the record and pharmaceutical industries highlights the importance of organizations managing their environments through the cooptation of "gatekeepers."

A major role of the boundary spanner is to absorb uncertainty. This process occurs when the person coalesces the raw information and edits it prior to transmission. The process is influenced by the boundary spanner's interpretation of his or her power in the organization, his or her personality, and the company's strategy toward managing its environment. How personality factors affect the ability of a boundary spanner to process uncertainty has been addressed by several researchers. Driver (1979) and Hunsaker (1975) have found that individuals who have a highly tolerant General Incongruity Adaptation Level (GIAL) use more information before aggregating and transmitting it than individuals with a lower tolerance. If the environment is too "rich" or munificent for the individual, the person will attempt to downgrade this by limiting the search process to capture only a few variables. Unfortunately, this downgrading process does not always result in high performance (Downey and Slocum 1981). When the environment provides too little uncertainty, high GIAL individuals will seek new inputs or engage in other informational processing activities to enrich their environment. Jacoby and Chestnut's and Huber's research relies on the person processing information. Given the previous research by Jacoby and his associates, larger quantities of information may overload cognitively simple individuals, rendering it impossible for them to make a purchase decision. Similarly, if an organization establishes a Decision Support System, it may overload individuals, or individuals may choose to ignore much of the information's attributes. In either case, a performance decrement might occur.

An issue that DSS will have to address is the impact of group dynamics on information processing. By including more decision makers and persons who occupy diverse interests, integrating techniques (such as liaison roles or task forces) tend to open up decision situations. The consideration of more alternatives, more potential outcomes, and more evaluation criteria may create uncertainty for decision makers in integrative structures (Gifford, Bobbit, and Slocum 1979). For example, O'Connell, Cummings, and Huber (1976) found that in loosely structured groups there was no relationship between uncertainty and information specificity. In tightly structured groups, low information specificity was associated with high uncertainty.

Weight of the Information

Once the information has been communicated to the decision maker, its use is still problematic (Chestnut and Jacoby, pp. 232–248), Kunreuther and Schoemaker, pp. 263–279). Two factors may influence its use: (1) individual bias and (2) organizational bias.

Tversky and Kahneman (1973), Einhorn and Hogarth (1981a), among others, indicate that there are several factors affecting the weight an individual assigns to a piece of information in making a decision. Some of these factors are:

1. Individuals have differential access to information from their environment.
2. Information must be stored in the individual's memory and reaccessed when needed for decision making.
3. Information that is stored is affected by its: (a) emotional relevance, (b) specificity, and (c) temporal ordering.
4. After storage, information is further enhanced by the ability of the decision maker to generate associative networks and rehearse or muse over it.

These factors are highly relevant to the research of Chestnut and Jacoby and others studying choice. According to Chestnut and Jacoby, consumers rely on evoked sets to make purchase decisions. If consumers arbitrarily exclude external information from their evoked decision-making sets, the antecedents of this exclusion process may be rooted in individual biases. In a study of job choices, Sheridan, Slocum, and Richards (1975) found that nurses used different evoked sets during a six-month job search process. Various attributes of the job alternatives changed as the individual acquired additional data over time. According to Janis and Mann (1977), people are reluctant decision makers because making decisions evokes stress reactions. As one would expect, the intensity of the stress varies with the importance of the decision, that is, the magnitude of anticipated gains and losses, and the individual's ability to cope. For minor decisions, this stress is often manifested in hesitation, vacillation, and feelings of uncertainty. For more difficult decisions, stress is manifested by a desire to escape the distressing choice dilemma, reliance on credible others for advice, and self-blame for putting oneself into the predicament of having to choose. This paradigm might explain an agent's reluctance to sell flood insurance or the buyer's decision process in the purchase of nondurable goods.

Even if the individual decision maker has the information available and it is accessible and representative of the real situation, the power/politics bias in the organization may affect its usage. Work by Crozier (1964), Perrow (1972), and Hickson et al. (1971) illustrate that to the extent subunits or individuals can cope with the uncertainty facing the organization, the power of the subunit increases relative to those subunits that cannot cope with this uncertainty. Furthermore, these researchers posit that other subunits in the organization place greater weight on this unit's preferences and the factual information it supplies. Following this line of inquiry, users of Decision Support Systems might posit a series of "what if" questions that could help an organization muddle through uncertainties by helping it understand its own internal power relationships. Unfortunately, even if the subunit has the formal power to cope with uncertainty, the politics of the organization may impede its effectiveness (Pfeffer 1981b). In Sapolsky's case analysis of the Polaris submarine and missile system, he concludes:

> If . . . the Polaris experience has any lesson it is that programs cannot be distinguished on the basis of their need. . . . The success of the Polaris program depended upon the ability of its proponents to promote and protect the Polaris. Competitors had to be eliminated; reviewing agencies had to be outmaneuvered; congressmen, admirals, newspapermen, and academicians had to be coopted (1972, p. 244).

We come to similar conclusions. On a more abstract level, the implications of this paper are that the information a decision maker attends to is a function of: (1) the decision maker's own selection biases; (2) the biases of others scanning the environment and communicating with that person; and (3) the power and political exigencies of the organization.

7 Meta-Commentaries

The meta-commentaries in this section provide further dialogue, closure, integrative judgments, personal assessments, and presentations of future developments. The papers by Larry Cummings, Arie Lewin, Louis Pondy, Ward Edwards, Amos Tversky, and Karl Weick exhibit this diversity. Overall, their themes encompass a comprehensive range of issues that define and represent the evolving nature of research on decision making.

Cummings

Larry Cummings compares, contrasts, and integrates the three state-of-the-art papers — Einhorn and Hogarth's, Hayes's, and March and Shapira's — by positioning each paper in terms of its level of analysis (individual, group, organization, and environment) and its states of analysis in examining a decision process (inputs, processes, and outcomes). Against this framework, Cummings discusses each paper, carefully pointing out its contributions and weaknesses. He concludes that the Einhorn and Hogarth paper provides a clear research agenda for further understanding individual decision making, but that it fails to elaborate on the processes thereof, that is, social modeling and learning, the emotional-affective components of decisions, and the conscious versus unconscious processes that underlie decision making. He finds that the Hayes's paper provides a well-reasoned approach for the use of protocols, but that it does not consider the impact of group or organizational contexts on the subjects' protocols. Finally, Cummings writes that the March and Shapira paper points out the similarities between individual and organizational paradigms, but that it does not sufficiently elaborate on the organizational context in which decisions are made.

In closing, Cummings suggests three unresolved issues: (1) the inadequacy of simply comparing and contrasting behavioral decision theory and organizational decision theory, (2) the unresolved role of dysfunctional behavior in evolving organizations, and (3) the degree to which decision making is thought of as being managed by information as opposed to being managed by ideology.

Pondy

Louis Pondy starts off with arguments that behavioral decision making, human problem solving, and organizational decision making engage in the study of different phenomena, use different methods, and have different agenda. Thus, it is by no means clear that the three fields should be integrated. Accordingly, he suggests six characteristics of real decisions: (1) a shifting cast of characters, (2) a history of dependence on real decisions, (3) interdependence between decision problems, (4) the difficulty of the justification as opposed to the choice, (5) the changing frame, and (6) the presence of conflict. Following a discussion of each characteristic, he presents an argument for developing both internal tools (for example, new habits of thought) as well as external tools (for example, ancillary hardware) to aid in decision making.

Lewin

Arie Lewin critiques each state-of-the-art paper by building on particular viewpoints that may represent future points of integration. He suggests that while Einhorn and Hogarth's review of behavioral decision theory is over-whelming, it is still too narrowly focused on psychological processes, and underemphasizes group and organizational influences. Lewin agrees with the general intent of the March and Shapira paper, but finds the implications of behavioral decision theory on organizational decision making underdeveloped and unclear. He argues that decision engineering is the most important area where a strong potential link between the two fields may exist. Finally, he presents his own arguments for why protocol tracing, as discussed by Hayes, is becoming an important research methodology in the empirical study of psychology.

Edwards

In a most provocative paper, Ward Edwards presents his soul-searching thoughts on the meaning of rationality, or more specifically, bounded rational-ity in decision making. Arguing that the notion of bounded rationality only becomes meaningful and controversial when one starts to explore the locations of the bounds, Edwards discusses the work of Tversky and Kahneman, of March and Shapira, and of researchers on decision making in general. He critiques researchers who have overgeneralized Tversky and Kahneman's find-ings, that "persons in psychological experiments fail to perform simple prob-abilistic reasoning tasks well," to "when people have decisions to make, they don't do very well." He cites Connolly's paper as one example in which a person's capacity for solving problems is much greater than what some theorists would suggest.

Commenting on the March and Shapira paper, Edwards presents his perplexity at the numerous implicit or explicit paradoxes in the paper. He caps this discussion by declaring that the bounded rationality of organizations lies at "zero," and in conclusion, finds some solace in discussing decision support systems. Since these systems present a sneaky approach to developing sen-sible and sophisticated questions, they introduce some sense of orderliness which Edwards finds absent from the March and Shapira conceptions of organizational decision making.

Tversky

Amos Tversky then discusses the strengths and weaknesses of present-day research in decision making. He pays particular attention to the weaknesses, for example, that decisions are ill defined and therefore difficult to study, and that theories are approximate, with boundary conditions so unclear as to prevent a present integration of behavioral decision theory and organizational decision theory. Tversky argues that the two research groups would be better off exploiting their methodological strengths rather than trying to emulate each other. In his view, it is premature to make claims on the relative superiority of one research method over another and, if anything, many different research methods need further exploration.

Finally, like Edwards, Tversky questions our working definitions of rationality, namely, instrumental rationality (when rational behavior is consistent with and fulfills stated goals) and coherent rationality (when behavior is internally consistent). The difficulty with instrumental rationality is the lack of an independent way to assess goals of the decision maker; the difficulty with coherent rationality, that internal consistency is unattainable. Tversky concludes his paper by illustrating how persons can err by treating as erroneous decisions which are in fact justifiable.

Weick

In the final paper, Karl Weick uses a soup-sampling cartoon to synopsize various themes discussed in the volume: real decisions; intuitive processes; action-outcome-feedback; hedge cutting and microadaptive rationality; decision support systems; adaptation; elimination-by-aspects; overfrequency of success; aspiration level goals and satisficing; context-free arguments, and many others. Taken together, these themes represent different ways in which behavioral decision theory and organizational decision theory may accommodate each other, specifically through a division of labor. Weick then discusses why such integration has not taken place. The difficulties with developing choices and the peripherality of decision making among collective actors are among the reasons discussed.

Weick also suggests that our methods of inquiry have led to an amplification of slight differences into large differences. Such differences arise from the ways fine issues are handled in our process of inquiry: variety, bias, boredom, degrees of freedom, and trade-offs. The predilections of behavioral decision theorists and organizational decision theorists are discussed in terms of these differences.

In conclusion, Weick notes that our biggest oversight may be how we appear to know where decisions begin and end. As in the case of a musician who continually creates modulations, or a chef who goes through the motions of soup making and sampling, it is difficult to determine the boundaries of a problem and the act of creation.

A Framework for Decision Analysis and Critique

Larry L. Cummings, *Northwestern University*

An Integrating Framework

To compare, contrast, and integrate the papers by Einhorn and Hogarth, Hayes, and March and Shapira, we will first develop an integrating framework. This framework poses two dimensions for the description and evaluation of the three papers. The first of these dimensions focuses upon the level of analysis at which one might attempt to describe and prescribe decision processes. This dimension is reflected in Table 1 on the vertical axis and is composed of four elements: the individual, the group, the organization, and the environment. The second dimension in Table 1 focuses upon the states of analysis through which one might attempt to analyze a decision process. This dimension is reflected on the horizontal axis and is composed of three elements: (1) the determinants or inputs into a decision process, (2) the processes through which these inputs are claimed to operate, and (3) the effects or outcomes achieved by these inputs via these processes.

Levels of Analysis

Decision systems can be described and analyzed at one or more of the four levels of analysis depicted in Table 1. Some analysts focus upon individual determinants or processes and outcomes as central to understanding decision making, both at the individual level of analysis *per se* and in organizational contexts. Typically, this tradition has been associated with psychology, particularly experimental and cognitive psychology. Other analysts focus upon the centrality of groups in most organizational realities, and therefore, attempt to examine determinants, processes, and outcomes as if they were each phenomenologically group characteristics. This perspective has traditionally been the domain of social psychologists, some working from psychological perspectives and others working from sociological perspectives. A third approach to analyzing decision systems assumes that meaningful decisions can only be made and understood when conceptualized as organizational phenomena. While analysts using the organizational perspective usually do not deny the existence of individual and group variations, they do argue that a complete understanding of important real-world decisions necessitates an organizational perspective. This approach to decision analysis has typically been the province of analysts coming from sociology, economics, and management theory. More recently, scholars approaching decision making from the perspectives of information system design and decision support systems have typified this perspective. Finally, from the most macroscopic perspective, some analysts assume that to fully understand decision processes and their application, an interorganizational or environmental perspective is most appropriate. Scholars approaching decision analysis from this perspective usually have backgrounds in sociology, political science, or, in a few cases, history and anthropology. Currently, there is within organization theory a popular stream of analysis which uses the environmental perspective to understand decision systems. This perspective has been variously labeled as population ecology, exchange analysis, and network structures.

It is extremely rare to find a single analysis utilizing all of these perspectives in attempting to understand a decision system. Decision theorists usually have taken a limited point of view in order to facilitate analysis and application. One of the issues we will address in this paper is to what degree the contributions by Einhorn and Hogarth, Hayes, and March and Shapira reflect one or more these levels of analysis in their approaches to decision making.

Stages of Decision Analysis

Determinants. As indicated in Table 1, decisions can be analyzed across three stages. First, one can examine decision models, at whatever level of analysis or aggregation, in terms of the determinants that are specified for decision making. Our analysis here will focus on three dimensions of these determinants or inputs. First, what does the model being analyzed specify concerning the *complexity of stimuli* that impinge upon the decision maker, the group, the organization, or the decisional environment? This dimension can be thought of

TABLE 1   A Framework for Dissecting Decision Analyses

| | | DECISION STAGES | | |
		DETERMINANTS (INPUTS)	PROCESSES	EFFECTS (OUTCOMES)
	ENVIRONMENT			
LEVELS OF ANALYSIS	ORGANIZATION	(M&S)	(M&S)	
	GROUP			
	INDIVIDUAL	Einhorn & Hogarth (E&H)[1]	(E&H) Hayes (H)[1] March & Shapira (M&S)[1]	(H) (M&S)

[1] Complete spelling of names indicates cells of major emphasis. Use of initials denotes cells of lesser emphasis.

as ranging from a focus upon extremely simple stimuli, as in many studies of engineering psychology, to more complex stimuli which affect decision systems, as in the case of environmental turbulence or uncertainty in the analysis of complex organizational decisions.

A second dimension of determinants would focus upon a situation in which the stimuli impacting a decision maker are complex and then would proceed to ask questions concerning the *form of combination or aggregation* which is assumed to take place across stimuli. This is primarily the question of ascertaining the form through which cues or stimuli are combined in order to make information storage and retrieval possible under complex stimulus environments. Of course, many decision models make and/or criticize assumptions about the ability of humans to deal with complex stimuli through simplifying mechanisms of combination and aggregation.

A third dimension of decision analytic determinants focuses upon the assumed *threshold values* necessary in order to engage the decision-making process. This dimension focuses a model's attention upon the magnitude and configuration of stimuli, either complex or simple, that are needed in order to cause a system to engage in a conscious, explicit process of decision making. Thus, this particular dimension of determinants in decision analysis centers on the question of conscious problem recognition or decision-opportunity recognition by the decision-making unit.

Processes. The second dimension important in analyzing decision states is the process or processes through which decision determinants are thought to influence decision outcomes. Models of decision making can be analyzed on a number of characteristics which articulate this dimension. For example, one can ask whether the processes assumed to be operating to link determinants and effects are primarily cognitive, emotional, or volitional. Most decision models implicitly assume that decision making is primarily a cognitive process and is best understood through elaboration of cognitive abilities and characteristics of systems of decision making. Generally, it is the case that emotional and motivational characteristics of decision systems are given relatively less emphasis in describing and prescribing effective decision systems.

A second issue centering on decision processes deals with the degree to which a decision model assumes that processes of decision making can best be described as within the consciousness of decision units. Phrased alternatively, this is the issue of the degree to which conscious articulation of decision processes is a necessary condition for decision making to occur and for the study of such decision making. Recent evidence and theory in social psychology suggest that it may well be that individuals are severely constrained in their ability to bring to consciousness the most important factors influencing attitude formation and moderating the relationship between attitudes and behavior (Nisbett and Ross 1980). To the extent that such evidence pertains to decision-making situations, it is possible that an exclusive or even primary focus upon conscious decision-making processes causes us to overlook significant underlying processes which influence decision outcomes and which are important in a thorough analysis of a decision system. Such a posture toward the study of decision making would represent a rather radical departure from most current themes and developments in the decision literature.

Even within the domain of conscious and explicit articulation of decision processes there remains the question of the degree to which a decision model assumes that the processes operating are rational or intendedly rational in nature. In general, there are trends in the organizational behavior literature suggesting that many decision systems engage in rationalization and *post facto* justification to a far greater extent and with far greater sophistication than they do processes of rationality (Staw 1980a).

Thus, the three central issues underlying the process stage of decision analysis are: (1) the degree to which a balance of psychological processes across cognitive, emotional, and volitional characteristics are emphasized in the model; (2) the degree to which a decision model assumes consciousness or explicit awareness as a necessary condition for the operation of decisional processes; and (3) given an assumption of the conscious nature of decision making, the degree to which purpose is to be positioned as an *a priori* or as a *post facto* construct in imputing rationality into the decision-making system.

Effects. A third dimension along which decision analysis stages should be analyzed and which has received relatively little attention centers on the nature of effects produced by decision making over time. There are two relevant questions here. The first is the issue of the appropriate time lags for effects of decisions to be manifest. The second asks over what time horizon the effects of decisions are to be monitored and evaluated in a context where organizational effectiveness is of concern.

The first question, of *time lags for effects,* is a question of research design or the relevant time series within which managerial decisions should become available for legitimate evaluation. This is fundamentally a question of how long it takes for a decision system to produce manifest outcomes which then may be subject to evaluation.

The second question, of *time horizon for evaluation,* assumes the presence of a tangible effect or effects in the decision system environment. It then moves to the evaluative issue of over what time horizon these effects should be assessed and these assessments accumulated before evaluation. It is obvious that the two time effects questions are interrelated, but a sophisticated decision analysis should separate the questions into the time lag for effects to appear, and the time horizon over which such effects are to be accumulated and evaluated by relevant parties.

The paper now moves to a description and evaluation of the three contributions by Einhorn and Hogarth, Hayes, and March and Shapira, within the context of the established framework.

Einhorn and Hogarth

Einhorn and Hogarth essentially focus on two of the cells in the framework presented in Table 1. Their review centers on issues and unresolved research problems at the intersection of the individual level of analysis and the determinants and processes implicit in individual decision making. To a lesser extent, they are concerned with the group and environmental contexts of decision determinants and processes.

Einhorn and Hogarth virtually exclude the organization as a relevant level of analysis in understanding decision processes. They do not present evidence suggesting the importance of organizational structure, information flows, and political systems for the formulation of decision problems or for the formulation of processes through which decisions are either made or implemented. In addition, Einhorn and Hogarth virtually exclude an analysis of the effects produced by the design of decision systems. In particular, they do not examine the effects produced by variations in organizational and environmental designs, as these relate to outcomes such as organizational performance or individual and group productivity.

What Einhorn and Hogarth have offered us is an insightful review and the establishment of an important research agenda for further understanding the phases of individual decision making. Their focus upon the importance of the strategies and mechanisms of judgment and choice as well as the phases of decision evaluation and the roles of feedback and learning in individual decision making are central to a research agenda for the 1980s.

One of the themes implicit in the Einhorn and Hogarth paper is that we know far more about the constraints upon normative and rational decision making than we do about the issues surrounding such concerns as (1) how individuals recognize the need for choice or decision; (2) the distinction between choice as a tangible, finite, time-bound human act and the processes of human judgment as a sequential and partially intuitive representation of human intelligence; (3) the issues of problem formulation and information-seeking strategies; and (4) the roles of models of learning other than simple reinforcement paradigms in understanding human judgment. In regard to this last point, the Einhorn and Hogarth paper is rather conservative in that it does not elaborate or review the important work on social modeling and social learning, insofar as that work pertains to the processes through which individuals come to understand the need for choice, the search for alternatives, and the resolution of uncertainty in choice situations.

Einhorn and Hogarth do not interpret the literature they review in a fashion that allows us to easily extend that literature. The authors spend considerable time discussing the limitations of human beings as decision makers but they do not organize this discussion in a way that allows us to expand on their interpretation. In terms of the dimensions of determinants as depicted in Table 1, Einhorn and Hogarth do not speak to the three issues of the complexity of stimuli; the forms of combination and aggregation of stimuli; and the threshold values of stimuli necessary to engage either the decision to choose, or the decision to search for relevant alternatives, or the decision to terminate choice behavior.

Einhorn and Hogarth take explicit positions regarding the state of scholarship on individual decision making as it pertains to the processes in Table 1. They clearly state that the present literature suggests that most studies on individual decision processes have focused on cognitive components to the near exclusion of emotional and affective components. To a lesser extent, they point to research on the motivational processes that may underlie less-than-optimal decision strategies used by individuals. The remaining two issues of process — that is, conscious versus unconscious and purposive versus random

— are not explicitly discussed in the paper. In many ways, this lack of explicit discussion is indeed a likely reflection of the current state of the literature on these processes. Still, it is unfortunate that more attention was not given to the need to generate sophisticated theory and derivative research programs centering on the nature of these two important processes.

Hayes

Hayes makes an explicit prescriptive appeal for the use of protocol analysis in understanding individual decision processes. In Table 1 his contribution is positioned at the intersection of individuals and processes. He claims that to understand individual decision processes, and in particular to use protocol analysis and process-tracing techniques, it is important to understand both the outcomes the individual is attempting to achieve and the inputs the individual brings to the decision task. Hayes mentions the importance of inputs and outcomes but does not elaborate or provide a framework for the articulation of the roles of these inputs and outcomes.

The Hayes paper provides a well-reasoned appeal for the use of protocol analysis, going beyond a mere exposition of the advantages of this methodology. It does so by suggesting a number of constraints on the effective utilization of protocol analysis, and by reminding us of the importance of reliability and validity checks in using what is essentially a subjective technique for understanding process analysis.

Hayes does not discuss the impact of levels of analysis other than the individual upon the utilization and interpretation of decision protocols. This is unfortunate in that much is known about the impact of group and organizational contexts upon the sense-making capabilities of both decision makers and interpreters of decisions (Pfeffer 1981a). Since protocol analysis places the decision analyst in the role of an interpreter of the phenomenology of an individual subject, it would seem central that the users of protocol analysis should be explicitly aware of the importance of group and organizational contexts in the creation of meaning. Since a decision protocol essentially provides a description of an individual's map of a situation, and since this map is subject to multiple interpretations by not only the individual decision maker but by analysts of that decision as well, it would seem crucial for the users and promoters of protocol analysis to embed the technique within what is known about the social and organizational contexts of interpretation.

It is not clear what the primary contribution of protocol analysis will be to understanding decision processes. Hayes's description and illustrations of protocol analysis present process analysis as a technique for interpreting either the description of a decision or the behavioral and verbal cues admitted by decision makers. The positioning of protocol analysis as a technique for interpretation after the fact rather than as a technique for understanding internal cognitive processes may be a contribution in its own right. However, the use of protocol analysis as an interpretive technique as opposed to a process-discovering technique may lead one to conclude that protocol analysis tells us more about decision analysts and their processes than it tells us about decision makers. A similar conclusion has often been reached concerning the use of decision models in a related area of behavioral research. The specific reference here is to our attempts to understand the performance appraisal process. Our present understanding, after twenty-five years of research aimed at predicting performance appraisal outcomes, is that most of that research tells more about appraisers than performance, or about appraisee performance in particular (Landy and Farr 1980). Hayes's description of protocol analysis and the conditions necessary for significant research using protocols may lead us to a similar conclusion.

March and Shapira

In terms of Table 1, the March and Shapira paper, by title, fits into a number of cells across the levels of analysis axis. The paper promises to speak in terms of behavioral decision theory at the individual level and organizational decision analysis at the organizational and environmental level. However, the case will be made here that the paper is essentially a dual description, using different terminologies, of individual decision making alone.

March and Shapira present an abbreviated review of what they refer to as behavioral decision theory. Their review is not the primary purpose of their paper, so the fact that it is incomplete and unelaborated relative to the Einhorn and Hogarth paper is not of central concern. Still, the description of individual decision making, its limitations, its constraints, and the behavioral theories depicting decision making does set the stage for what ends up being an artificial comparison of behavioral decision theory and organizational analysis.

The description of organizational decision theory emphasizes the uncertain, unpredictable, sometimes random, and always confusing nature of organizational decision making. It becomes apparent in March and Shapira's description of organizational decision theory that they are actually talking about *individual* decision making within an organizational context. In fact, most of their material, under the rubric of organizational decision theory, can easily be translated into individual decision analysis merely by substituting the word *individual* for *organizational*. The similarity between the description that emerges from such a substitution and the Einhorn and Hogarth paper is striking. We discover that individuals considered as individuals, and individuals within the organizational context (as in the March and Shapira description) are, indeed, best described using similar psychological constructs. Emphasis in both treatments is given to the cognitive limitations and the resulting coping strategies used by individuals to make and implement decisions in organizations.

In summary, there is actually little discussion of *organizational* decision theory in the March and Shapira paper. It is not clear that including the organizational context in the paper would make any difference in the kinds of conclusions one comes to concerning research agendas, central problems, or the evaluation of individual decision processes. Thus, in a sense, it is heartening to know that behavioral decision theorists have tapped most of the central concerns in individual decision making that are of interest to persons viewing matters from an organizational perspective. The organizational perspective, however, in March and Shapira's analysis is no more than a context for individual decision making. The level of analysis has not substantially changed, and the complexities of organizational structure, growth, and decline, as well as the interrelationships among organizations, are not dealt with in the paper. This is the case even when these phenomena might relate to changes in the underlying description and analysis of, and research on, individual decision making.

The paper does speak to emotional and motivational processes in understanding individual decision making; thus, the analysis goes beyond the rather restrictive focus upon cognitive processing in the Einhorn and Hogarth paper. March and Shapira include the possibility of unconscious processes operating in choice phenomena at the individual level, with rationalization becoming as central as rationality in individual decision making.

As with the previous two papers, March and Shapira ignore the effects of different strategies of decision making and the productivity of the individual or organizational decision-making process. As with Einhorn and Hogarth, time and temporal dimensions in decision effects are ignored.

March and Shapira provide a useful description of what they consider two separate paradigms for studying decision making. As noted above, the distinction between the paradigms is grossly overdrawn. In the latter part of their paper, however, they draw several important implications for each of the paradigms, assuming that there is some central difference between them. The underlying theme of March and Shapira's discussion of these implications seems to be that constructs included in one paradigm should be included in the other. They illustrate that issues central to behavioral decision theory can be used in organizational decision theory to bear fruit of analysis. Likewise, the reverse flow would also appear to be fruitful. However, the underlying issue that remains is the degree to which this is merely a translation of terminology from one paradigm to the other. It is unclear that the added effect of this translation amounts to much.

March and Shapira do draw interesting implications for the design and engineering of decision systems. These implications are significant in that they concern the two paradigms considered collectively for decision engineering. The paper ends commenting on how decision sciences and the design of decision analytic systems and decision support systems would be different if we took seriously the commonalities existing between behavioral decision theory and organizational decision theory.

Important Unresolved Issues

As noted earlier, March and Shapira have strained to contrast decision models at the individual and organizational levels of analysis. The strain apparent in their argument may well signify that formulating the central issue as one of contrast and similarity between behavioral decision theory and organizational decision theory is not the most appropriate direction for future research on decision making.

March and Shapira's retranslations between behavioral decision theory and organizational decision theory, also implied in Einhorn and Hogarth's review, are sufficient to draw parallels, if not identities, between individual and organizational level phenomena. This parallelism is also a current theme in other forms of theory on individual behavior within organizations. Centrality of cognitions in understanding not only decision making but processes of motivation, learning, change, leadership, influence, and socialization is appearing as a current theme in organizational behavior (Naylor, Pritchard, and Ilgen 1980).

The translation and exchange between levels of analysis does not diminish the fact that unresolved issues in decision analysis remain whether one takes an individual, group, or organizational perspective. Three examples will suffice to make the point. First, most decision theorists, regardless of the level of analysis they use, argue that the evolution of viable explanations of decision processes in the face of complexity and uncertainty is central to advancing the decision sciences. The lack of sufficient models to capture the reality of decision processes is a frequently mentioned constraint by nearly all decision scholars. Second, regardless of level of analysis, there remains the frequently cited need to balance the study of decision opportunities and constraints with the study of the development, perhaps subsequent to action, of preferences. This notion of the missing theory of preferences in decision sciences is emphasized by March and Shapira. It is also reflected in the neglect of emotional and motivational issues in the behavioral research on decision making at the individual level of analysis. Third, there is common recognition that we do not yet understand the roles of organizations as an aid or as a hindrance to individual decision making and decision implementation.

The Role of Dysfunctional Behavior in the Evolving Organization

One needs only to express general agreement with Einhorn and Hogarth's argument that persistent dysfunctional decision behavior is not inconsistent with evolutionary concepts. That is, there is no necessary functional evolutionary outcome associated with the development of individual decision-making competence across time. However, given the existence and the possible rationality of such an apparent inconsistency, one must ask what the implications are of such inconsistency for the relationship between individual decision makers and their organizational contexts. This leads to a number of unresolved questions shared by scholars of both individual and organizational decision making, namely:

1.   Do organizations reduce or increase dysfunctionality? That is, are organizations error-generating and amplifying in their effects or are they correcting mechanisms? It is, of course, likely that organizations can and do play both roles. That perspective shifts the theory and research agenda to articulating the constraints and conditions under which organizations either facilitate or hamper individual decision making.

2.   Does the possibility of the parallel existence of dysfunctional behavior in the short run, and yet the evolution of effective decision systems over time, change the kind and degree of errors and biases that decision processes are subject to? Under the parallel existence of dysfunctional and evolutionary processes, deviations from normality or from normative models provide an important and necessary input into natural selection processes. Without

the tolerance and encouragement of such deviations, which in the short-run might be viewed as dysfunctional, evolutionary processes are impossible. Selection requires variance around normality.

These questions emphasize the similarity rather than the differences between models of decision making at varying levels of analysis.

This discussion tempts one to conclude that the similarities are so great that the study of decision making has few significant themes which can engender theoretical insight and conflicting paradigms. One might conclude that the entirety of theoretical decision research consists of variations on a small set of similar themes. But this conclusion would seem to leave unanswered, or perhaps even unasked, some central questions about the basic nature of management systems and philosophical perspectives on the nature of decision making and influence.

Management by Information Versus Management by Ideology

The most central issue confronting decision scholars and designers of decision systems in this decade may be the degree to which decision making is thought of as a component in a system managed by information versus one managed by ideology. The distinction between these two approaches centers upon the classical distinction made by Simon (1976) between premises based upon values and premises based upon facts. Management by ideology assumes that the central focuses of management, that is, the things being managed, are value premises. Within this perspective decision support systems and information systems are designed to influence, inculcate, and stabilize values. Stabilization is crucial for other organizational design and decision support system principles to operate, for example, decentralization, participation, and lower participant involvement. Within this perspective, many dysfunctions and limitations of individual decision makers become advantageous. They become opportunities to be used for the design of systems which operate primarily through values and secondarily through facts.

Management and decision systems that operate primarily upon information assume that the premise of management and influence is the development, communication, and accurate interpretation of facts. This is why so little attention has been given to preference formation and preference expression in traditional behavioral and organizational decision theories, as noted by March and Shapira and Einhorn and Hogarth. Individual biases and so-called errors in decision making become disadvantages in the predictable and stable management of organizational systems. Decision supports and aids are designed to counter these individual limitations or prevent and constrain decisions so that the limitations are least likely to exhibit their effects.

One wonders what interpretation traditionally socialized and trained Japanese managers would have of the papers included in this volume. One suspects they would not be concerned about the competitive threat posed by the practical implications of much of what we say in the decision sciences today. In fact, they might argue that much of the Western approach to understanding decision making misses the central point. Alternative formulations of management through ideology imply quite different constructs and processes for understanding and enhancing choice in organizations. The relative lack of attention to preferences around organizational and cultural norms would mystify the Japanese managers. They would say that if we want to understand decision systems, we need a more generic or robust distinction among paradigms than the distinction implied by behavioral and organizational decision theory. These paradigms are just too similar to generate the intellectual spark that comes from considering conflicting, underlying approaches to theories of choice and theories of change in organizations.

On Real Decisions

Louis Pondy, *University of Illinois at Urbana–Champaign*

My assigned task in this volume was to ask how we might integrate the three heretofore distinctive perspectives on decision making: organizational decision theory, problem-solving theory (or protocol analysis), and behavioral decision theory. It is by no means clear that the three perspectives *should* be integrated. The argument against integration is that the three perspectives deal with essentially different phenomena. Behavioral decision theory deals with optimal choice processes under risk and with human tendencies toward systematic errors in use of information. Problem-solving theory, as represented in Hayes's protocol paper deals with fairly well-defined problems in structured problem environments such as chess and logic. Organizational decision theory deals with the problem of how collections of individuals make complex choices in the face of ambiguity not only in information but even in objectives.

The three perspectives use different methods of data collection and analysis, methods which may be appropriately suited to the phenomena under investigation but which are not applicable to other phenomena. For example, the use of protocol analysis to describe the "fine structure" of information processing in a major, novel, multi-actor business decision would be next to impossible, given current technology.

The three perspectives also have different agendas. Behavioral decision theory seeks to make possible the achievement of optimal human choices under conditions of probabilistic information. Problem-solving theory seeks to understand the human mind as a rule-governed system of intelligence. Organizational decision theory seeks to understand how organizational structure and environment condition collective choice.

But most fundamental is that the three perspectives take a different position on whether the aim of research is to *understand* human decision making or to *improve* decision making, perhaps by the extension of human capabilities through tools and other aids.

Rather than attempting a merger of the three perspectives we might more profitably think of alternative ways by which each perspective can inform the others, by asking what is most sophisticated about each. Let me take them in order.

Organizational Decision Theory

Organizational decision theory can make its greatest contribution by forcing us to focus on "real decisions," meaning not necessarily decisions in the field, as opposed to the lab, but decision situations with characteristics rich enough to be worthy of analysis. Let me identify six such characteristics.

First, real decisions have a shifting cast of characters, participants who come into the decision stream temporarily, stay for a while, and then leave of their own volition or are forcibly evicted by the central power figures in the decision process.

Second, there is a history dependence to real decisions, not necessarily of the continuous sequential sort that March alluded to, but what we might call "leapfrogging dependence." That is, current decisions may be dependent on commitments, bargains, and beliefs formed long ago with no discernible linkage in the intervening time period to the present moment.

A third characteristic of real decisions is the interdependence among the various decision problems faced by any organization at a given time. What is striking to me about the way both Hayes and Einhorn and Hogarth approach decision analysis is that they each have lifted decisions out of the natural context of other ongoing decisions and analyzed them in isolation. From my own observation of decision making in field contexts, one powerful characteristic is that each decision is deeply interlocked with other decisions going on at the same time. Organizations deal not only with problems surrounding a single decision but also with a portfolio problem. That is, where shall we direct our attention? Should we direct it to this decision problem, or that decision problem? How can we decouple these two decisions so that they don't interfere with one another? How can we combine or merge them so that they provide mutual support?

A fourth characteristic of real decisions is that frequently the choice process is not the crux of the problem. The choice part of the decision may be easy, but the justification to others can be hard. Inventing rationales which are persuasive to budget officers, colleagues, and competitors is often the difficult part of real decisions, not the choice.

A fifth characteristic of real decisions is that the frame of reference is constantly changing. Part of what I have observed in real decisions is that the definition of the problem shifts over the course of the decision in ways that may be only partially in the control of the decision makers. Also, problems are often unstructured. In contrast, in behavioral decision theory there is initially a high degree of structuring whereupon the concern is with the process of choice *within the given structure,* but not with the structuring of the problem in the first place. Organizational decision theory focuses our attention on the role that language and political behavior play in establishing one frame of reference over another.

The sixth characteristic of real decisions is the presence of conflict among the various decision makers.

Studying decisions that have these six characteristics in a natural field setting can be maddeningly complex, because we have few or no controls over events taking place; we cannot isolate specific phenomena for closer study. However, we might attempt to simulate several or all of the six characteristics in laboratory settings where we can gain more control over the phenomena. Thus, organizational decision theory provides a wide-angle lens that permits us to identify broad aspects of decision making that can be studied in greater detail using the other two perspectives.

Problem-Solving Theory

Problem-solving theory can make its greatest contribution by drawing exquisite attention to process detail, something that I believe the other two points of view can benefit from. I don't have a great deal to say about that, except that what I find most appealing about protocol analysis is that it may help us to understand the process of problem structuring more than it will help us to understand problem solving.

Behavioral Decision Theory

Behavioral decision theory contributes most by providing us with guidelines for what I would like to call "local" rationality, that is, prescriptions for optimal behavior within a *given* frame. What it doesn't do is raise our consciousness about the possibility of alternative frames. Let me argue that any description or representation of a primitive, undescribed situation is a joint product of both the situation and the frame of reference. A situation can admit as many descriptions or representations as the number of frames of reference applied to it. It is useful to distinguish between two levels of prescription: prescription at the *local* level, that is, prescribed actions within a given frame of reference or a given representation of problem situations; and prescription at the *global* level, which is prescription about the choice of the frame of reference to begin with. Now, whereas behavioral decision theory can provide us with information about rational behavior within a given frame of reference, it seems to me that juxtaposing the three different perspectives can raise our consciousness about global levels of rationality or prescription, that is, about design or choice of the frames of reference themselves.

Internal and External Tools of Decision Making

At the beginning of my comments I drew a distinction between understanding human decision making without attempting to improve it, and improving decision making with tools or extensions to human capabilities. I would like to make a further distinction between *internal* tools, that is, new habits or thought (for example, March's prescriptions about foolishness), and *external* tools of decision making that range from simple memory devices such as pencil and paper to computers, administrative staffs, and filing cabinets. I have been dismayed and surprised that there has been so little discussion about how we might improve decision making by inventing new tools of an external sort. There has been some discussion about the development of internal tools for improved decision making but not of external tools.

Terry Connolly has observed that despite our incompetence at processing is that it may not be too surprising that humans facing a complex decision situation, unaided by tools of any sort, do not do well relative to the expectations derived from rational models. In my judgment, what is needed is a theory of decision tools that improve the performance of person–tool combinations, not merely a descriptive theory of how humans unaided by tool extensions perform less than optimally.

The State of the Art in Decision Making: An Integration of the Issues

Arie Y. Lewin, *Duke University*

This volume is concerned with the state of the art of a research paradigm which, in a way, is still young, but whose central concepts — decision making by rule, bounded rationality, satisficing, search, and so on — were outlined by Herbert Simon more than twenty-five years ago. These concepts endure as part of the general theory and they have influenced the direction of research in fields as diverse as microeconomics, organization theory, public administration, policy science, behavioral decision theory, and the management and information sciences.

In this context it is particularly appropriate that this volume's three papers on the state of the art were directly influenced or originated by Simon's pioneering work.

Einhorn and Hogarth

The volume of research on behavioral decision making is overwhelming. A few of its important characteristics are: (1) it has focused on human decision making in the face of uncertainty; (2) it has developed much empirical insight into the deviation of behavior from statistical decision theory; and (3) most, if not all, of the research has been a study of individual choice behavior in relatively simple, well-structured situations where the normative theory can make specific predictions as to how subjects ought to behave.

The paper by Einhorn and Hogarth is very much concerned with human decision making. Its emphasis, however, is on the need for psychologists to elucidate the basic psychological processes underlying judgment and choice by focusing on the strategies and mechanisms of judgment and choice (p. 21) as they are affected by attention, memory, cognitive representation, conflict and learning, and feedback.

To some extent, the paper misses the mark as a state-of-the-art review of behavioral decision making for this volume. This is because the authors' original target was the *Annual Review of Psychology*. For this volume, a more appropriate paper would have identified promising directions of research on decision making, pointed to the need for a greater focus on real decisions, and, concomitantly, discussed the merits or demerits of a shift from carefully controlled laboratory experiments to more realistic field research. The few instances of such research include: Clarkson 1962; Smith and Greenlaw 1967; Payne 1976; Carroll and Payne 1976; Russo 1977; Fischhoff, Slovic, and Lichtenstein 1978; and Laughhunn, Payne, and Crum 1980. As Ken MacCrimmon noted earlier in his comment on the paper (pp.48–52), there is a need for a more systematic approach to research on decision making with the objective of identifying more generalized paradigms based on generalizable principles or concepts (for example, Simon's concept of bounded rationality). Finally, the paper does not discuss the implications of the research to applied decision making or to decision making in groups or organizations.

March and Shapira

Interrelating Behavioral Decision Theory and Organizational Decision Theory

A major contribution of this paper is its focus on the implications that research in behavioral and organizational decision theory have for one another. I am in complete agreement with March and Shapira when they note the need to study individual behavior in the context of real organizations, and when they note that anomalous individual choice behavior, observed in an experimental setting, may be explained in an organizational context. To a degree, March and Shapira identify variables similar to those identified by Einhorn and Hogarth when the former suggest that behavioral decision theory research, to the extent that it focuses on mechanisms and processes of choice, needs to consider conflict, history-dependent processes (learning and feedback), and preference processing. However, within an organizational context, March and Shapira point out, these variables may take on different meaning, and the organizationally based models of decision making may be more applicable for studying individual behavior (for example, conflict models and organizational learning models).

The implications that behavioral decision theory have for organizational decision theory research are less clear-cut, as March and Shapira suggest, in three areas: aspiration level theory and decision making; attention, search, and organization memory; and decision simplification and organizational decision making. They note that satisficing behavior might be sensitive to the perceived risk of decision outcomes (consequences) and that organizational decision theory could profit from an elaboration of the original aspiration level-search model. Such contributions could enhance organizational decision theory. It is not clear, though, whether they will result in major reformulations of organizational decision theory. Upon examination, similar conclusions emerge from the link between processes of attention and search from the perspective of individual behavior research, and their implications for organizational decision making (particularly when we consider the loosely coupled structure and the parallel processing of information which is so characteristic of organizations).

Implications for Decision Engineering

Another area where a strong potential link exists between behavioral decision theory and organizational decision theory involves what March and Shapira call *decision engineering*. Decision engineering involves the transformation occurring in organizations due to developments in information technology and decision support systems (Huber, this volume pp. 249–262, and Huber, in press). It is clear that the design of organizations is increasingly being driven by innovations in information technology. The trend toward distributed data processing networks, the quantum decreases in the cost of data-base management and personal computing, and the advent of videotext technology all point to an intersection of behavioral decision theory and organizational decision theory — that relatively unexplored area that March and Shapira call decision engineering.

As we become concerned with designing decision support systems to fit the limitations of the individual in the organization, it will be necessary to consider such factors from behavioral decision theory as "framing," "concreteness," "elimination by aspect," and "prospect theory" on managerial problem solving (that is, attention, problem formulation, or decision simplification, and problemistic search, communication, and choice). Similarly, the design of decision support systems will have to fit organizations as systems of decision making by being concerned with how information is dealt within the organization. For example, organizations orchestrate decisions to achieve legitimacy and avoid uncertainty; decisions are history-dependent; organizations pursue aspiration level-type goals; processes of decision making often are more important than outcomes; information is processed in a parallel manner, simultaneously, and in different places in the organization; and so on. In short, the area of decision engineering holds the potential for close interaction between organizational decision theory and behavioral decision theory.

Hayes

Controversies in the Application of the Method

Hayes's paper directs our attention to a relatively new methodology — protocol analysis — for identifying psychological processes. The use of the protocol tracing methodology is controversial. Although both Michael Posner and Sarah Lichtenstein (pp. 78–82 and 83–84) acknowledge that protocol tracing can be valuable, I interpret the overall tenor of their remarks as raising serious concerns regarding the method.

To some extent, doubts about the validity of protocol tracing are due to the perception of the method as being nonstandard. No scientific, exact aura is associated with it, as is the case with various statistical methodologies such as least squares techniques, analysis of variance, and factor analysis. The typical criticism of the method rests on three issues: subjects cannot report, reporting affects the process, and the analysis of protocols cannot be objective.

Along these lines, Posner notes that the act of verbalizing the thought process can affect the solution process by crystallizing it. In addition, he notes that unconscious processes can influence the solution process, and that protocol tracing cannot identify such unconscious processes. Lichtenstein observes that subjects, and even experts, often cannot verbalize their thoughts because they do not know how they are doing what they are doing. She also notes that the process of segmenting a protocol is a very fine art, and that different ways of segmenting will produce different results.

In reality, there have been problems with other methodologies which have been used to determine the parametric structure underlying decision making and behavior. These problems include such techniques as self-reports or critical incidents and the analysis of information acquisition behavior. The self-verbalization technique is asking a subject to recall and describe, usually in writing, an incident representing an actual example of the situation being studied. The validity of self-reports has been criticized because the reports may only represent after-the-fact rationalizations. Nisbett and Wilson (1977) cautioned that the accuracy of self-report data is impaired by the time lag between the occurrence of the process and the self-report.

Monitoring information acquisition behavior involves arranging a decision task in such a way that the information a subject selects or views can be readily monitored. The researcher records what information the subjects seek and in what order, the quantity of information sought, and the length of time the material is examined. The approach provides insights into the structure of the used information, but it does not reveal the thought process itself.

Advantages of Protocol Tracing

Protocol tracing has the potential of becoming an important research methodology in empirical psychology. The following are its possible applications:

1. It can be valuable in supporting or explaining empirical results based on another methodology. A recent example of this approach is reported in Payne, Laughhunn, and Crum (1980).

2. It can provide insights into underlying processes. Lewin and Layman (1979) used protocol tracing to explicate the process of person perception underlying peer rating in ad hoc groups.

3. It can be used to demonstrate the existence of a phenomenon. For example, Payne (1976) demonstrated the use of a phased decision strategy consisting of an elimination-by-aspect rule followed by a compensatory rule when a subject is facing a choice among many alternatives.

4. It can be used to test hypotheses or alternative theories. For example, Lewin and Layman (forthcoming) discuss how hypothetical protocols of various leadership models can be used to determine models in actual protocols of subjects making leadership attributions.

5. It can be used in combination with another method. For example, Carroll et al. (1976) concluded that combining protocol tracing with the monitoring of information acquisition behavior can determine the structure of the entire chain of thought involved in decision making (see Russo 1978b).

It seems that confidence in the application of the protocol tracing methodology will increase with use, standardization of the technique, availability of instructional manuals and primers, and the inclusion of protocol tracing as a topic taught regularly to graduate students in methodology courses. In addition, confidence is forthcoming with the increased publication of empirical studies using protocol tracing in various ways, for example, in conjunction with other methods (Carroll et al. 1976; Payne, Laughhunn, and Crum 1980), or directly testing the predictions from models derived from protocol tracing (for example, Gregg and Simon 1967; Lewin and Layman 1979; and Einhorn, Kleinmuntz, and Kleinmuntz 1979).

Summary

The three papers focused attention on behavioral decision theory, organizational decision theory, and protocol tracing — the last relatively new and underused research methodology. Decision engineering points to a new direction where a strong potential link exists between behavioral decision theory and organizational decision theory. In essence, the research agenda is to design decision support systems to fit the limitations of the individual in the organization and to fit the organization as a system of decision making.

A View from a Barefoot Decision Analyst

Ward Edwards, *University of Southern California*

I approach this volume as a simple barefooted decision analyst. The gurus of the field, who taught me almost all I know, began by emphasizing two fundamental ideas: Decisions are made by individuals called decision makers, and the goal of any decision maker is to maximize his or her own utilities. The goal of a decision analyst is to help the decision maker to achieve that goal by offering tools designed to divide the decision task into manageable parts and then put the parts back together again.

When I set out to apply these straightforward ideas I ran into trouble. First, I could not find the decision maker. In any decision situation, someone must sign off on the decision. But then if you explore the question of whether that individual is out to maximize individual utility, you discover that no thought could be further from his or her mind. The decision maker does not think alone, does not act alone, and does not maximize personal utilities — at least for significant decisions. Most important decisions are made by some form of committee.

Who then is the decision maker? I concluded that, in spite of job titles, important decisions are made by the organization. That thought brings me here, to a volume intended to bring decision analysts and organization theorists together. I had hoped that my decision analytic naiveté would be dispelled by the organizational wisdom contained herein.

The "baggage" I bring with me is familiar enough to need little exposition. Everyone is familiar with the ideas of utility, probability, their combination into expected utility, the recognition of the complexity of values embodied in multiattribute utility measurement, and simple decision rules such as maximizing expected utility. Fewer people are familiar with structuring decision problems — a curious combination of technology and art form. Perhaps my generalization, a piece of baggage, that human beings are boundedly rational will be controversial in this volume. Still, no one could possibly argue with that generalization, since the alternatives are either that human beings are unboundedly rational or not rational at all. I did not expect to see either of those propositions seriously defended in this volume, but I was wrong.

Bounded rationality only becomes meaningful, and controversial, when one starts to explore the location of the bounds. One school of thought about where the bounds lie is embodied in the work of Kahneman and Tversky and their myriad fellow travelers. A simple version of their ideas is that subjects in psychological experiments fail to perform simple probabilistic reasoning well.

The failures are sufficiently orderly that they have been given names, such as availability bias, representativeness bias, and hindsight bias.

A sweeping generalization of these ideas, encountered too often, is "When people have decisions to make, they don't do very well." This generalization is painfully inappropriate. It is unjust to Kahneman, Tversky, and most other authors in the field. Few of these authors have committed any such broad statements to print; indeed, the seminal articles are adequately supplied with careful, needed caveats against just such conclusions. The tasks, subjects, stakes, and performance criteria are all unlike ordinary, everyday decision making, and they are more unlike the tasks, subjects, stakes, and criteria of the decisions most decision analysts encounter professionally. Most important of all, subjects of psychological experiments are not allowed to use tools. An article I am currently writing starts: if a subject says that two plus two equals four, that is arithmetic. If a subject says that two plus two equals five, that is psychology.

Having unloaded my luggage, I turn to what I have acquired from this book. An early and happy discovery has been that I am not alone in rejecting the conclusion, drawn from a misinterpretation of the literature on cognitive illusions, that people are poor decision makers. Many of the points that seem so cogent to me were clearly made by Dr. Connolly: the bounds on rationality depend on various things, notably the expertise of the person or people involved, the importance of the intellectual task, and the availability of relevant tools.

A second kind of information acquired is that, if you ask a person engaged in the kind of thinking that is antecedent to decision making what is going on in his or her head at the time, you will get an answer. I am sorry to report that the conclusion I reached about these studies, like the conclusions I have reached from reading about others and from my own informal observations, is that the reports these thinkers give you are uninformative. Research on process tracing excites those who do a lot of it, and it seems to give them insight into the nature of human thought. I wish they could transfer that excitement and those insights to me.

The most important things I have learned here are about organizational decision making, and I learned them from that truly remarkable paper by Jim March and Zur Shapira. They offered a number of clear prescriptive messages about how someone like me, eager to help organizations to make better decisions, should behave. Don't encourage an individual or an organization to maximize anything, or to exercise wisdom; it might lead them to avoid errors. Avoiding errors is disastrous, because only by making errors does one learn. An implication for organizational design is to make sure that organizations reward obvious mistakes in order to make sure they do get made. Of course, it may be difficult to recognize obvious mistakes. Organizations don't know what they want. It would be folly, however, to help them find out; it would either confuse them further or give them a set of defined and understood purposes — something we want to avoid. Given the confusion about purpose and eagerness to make errors, organizations waste information, but they should not be helped to use information properly. They need information for surveillance purposes. Surveillance has no relation to subsequent action, such as a decision.

Most information consists of lies in any case. Nevertheless, organizations should continue to seek information, though it *is* both false and useless. The reason why organizations should continue to seek information is not clear from March and Shapira's paper; perhaps the point is that if the false and useless information were not collected, the organization would have nothing other than money, perhaps, to waste.

Amazingly, organizations adapt. It is difficult to understand how they adapt, since they do not know what they want and cannot recognize the difference between a good and a bad outcome. It is even more difficult to figure out how to help an organization to adapt, since the preceding discussion of organizational behavior implies that any change one might think of as adaptive will be in fact maladaptive.

This discussion of the bounded rationality of organizations implies a far broader conception of the bounds than I had ever encountered before: They lie at zero. How can an organization so described be expected to function and survive? Perhaps it will: random action is sometimes successful. I cannot, however, bring myself to abandon my lifelong belief that directed and orderly action is better.

Even barefooted decision analysts occasionally wander into the halls of organizations as I have done. In them I have encountered individuals puzzled about what to do. When someone offers them a way of thinking about what to do, they are sometimes intrigued, stimulated, willing to try it out, and delighted with the result. That, of course, is lucky for me; I make my living from their willingness to try such ways of thinking and their pleasure at the result. Of course that pleasure doesn't prove that I am doing any good. The problem of validating decision analysis or any form of advice is fascinating, nearly untouched, and in need of study.

It must be apparent by now that I have not learned from the organization theorists what I needed to learn in order to go back and apply the simple ideas my gurus taught me to organizations as decision makers. My own view has been challenged but it persists. Organizations are composed of people with considerable communalities of knowledge and of concern. If the issues at stake are important enough, these people can be encouraged to bring to bear on decision problems the analytic tools that take advantage of these communalities — in particular those communalities arising from the desire that the organization survive and prosper. Simple tools can be used to combat the incoherence resulting from the fact that many individuals play a role in most decisions. The most obvious and often the most successful tool is simply to bring those individuals together; obtain from them an orderly statement, in the form of a multiattribute utility function, of what they want; and then examine the degree to which various available actions will help the organization to get what they want.

In this kind of endeavor, I found the things that George Huber had to say about decision support systems stimulating and helpful. I liked the conception of decision support systems he presented because it was so sneaky. That is, if you ask a decision support system a question, it will ordinarily be able to answer it. Since people occasionally have simple factual questions to ask, they will ask them, get answers, find them correct, and be encouraged. This experience, often repeated, will lead them to want to be able to ask more ambitious and sophisticated questions. The more sophisticated the question, the more sophisticated must be the techniques available within the decision support system to provide the answer. That sneaky approach to building support for a system that actually gives sensible answers to even sophisticated sensible questions is brilliant, because it will work. In working, it may mitigate the organizational paradoxes so frustratingly set forth in the March and Shapira paper. Is it too hopeful to conclude that George Huber has pointed out a path toward introducing orderliness, and adherence to a few principles of good sense? Might I go further and argue that orderliness and good sense are really what the dirty word *rationality* means?

Remarks on the Study of Decision Making

Amos Tversky, *Stanford University*

An Assessment of Decision-Making Research

Decision making is a meeting ground for psychologists, economists, sociologists, organizational theorists, statisticians, philosophers, and others. It is an exciting field, endowed with a deep formal theory, a rich technology, numerous intriguing observations of individuals and organizations, and a growing body of experimental results. It is an area that could improve the quality of individual and organizational decision making. This is the good news.

The bad news is that our conceptions of decision making are not satisfactory. First, our basic problem is ill defined. At one level of analysis, any act is a decision. We decide, for example, what to say, and when and how to say it. But this conception of decision making is far too general to be useful. Instead of that conception, we normally isolate from the activity of an organism or organization distinguishable points that we treat as decisions. The distinctions, however, among automatic or semiautomatic actions, standard operating procedures, routine action, and reflective decisions are difficult to make. Second, our methods for gathering information about decision making suffer from serious limitations. Anecdotes, casual observations, and case studies lack controls, while laboratory experiments and hypothetical questions often lack realism.

Third, our theories are approximate and their boundary conditions not clear. For example, it appears reasonable that, when faced with a large number of alternatives, people reduce the choice set by a process resembling elimination-by-aspects. When the choice set is reduced to two or three alternatives, other compensatory models might come into play. However, the conditions under which elimination-by-aspect phases into a compensatory rule, such as an additive difference model, are not well understood and are difficult to formalize. Many of our choice models should probably be regarded as subroutines that could be applied to different decisions, but we lack an adequate theory predicting which subroutine will be applied to a particular choice problem. Finally, although we have a highly developed normative theory, its application to specific problems is hindered by our difficulty in describing the decision maker's objectives and our inability to fully specify utilities and beliefs.

These critical remarks are not meant to generate despair, but rather to encourage a sober, realistic assessment of what we know and do not know about individual and organizational decision making. The remarks suggest that we are not ready for an integration of behavioral decision theory with organizational theory. There is, however, room for dialogue between the two disciplines which enables us to share insights, facts, opinions, and prejudices, as this volume demonstrates.

Dialogue Between Behavioral Decision Theorists and Organizational Theorists

An exchange of views between behavioral decision theorists or cognitive psychologists and organizational theorists or management scientists can help us to place our problems and methods in a broader perspective and to realize both the potential and the limitations of our own work. In such exchanges, naturally, we not only share information but we also complain. Experimental psychologists complain that studies of organizational behavior are not properly controlled and often do not permit strong inferences, while the organizational theorists complain that experimental studies are contrived and ungeneralizable. Although both complaints have an element of truth, they are hardly constructive. A better understanding of individual and organizational decision making would be achieved if each field would exploit its methodological and substantive strengths rather than attempt to emulate the other. The lesson is not that organizational theorists should run controlled experiments and psychologists should bring the complexities of the real world into the laboratory, but rather, that we should do our best to understand the processes we study. This may help us understand other processes as well.

Let me illustrate this point by an example which has already been mentioned in Michael Posner's article (p. 79). In an ingenious experiment, Bruner and Potter (1964) showed that it is more difficult for people to identify a picture if they see it earlier in an unfocused form, presumably because the hypotheses generated by the degraded picture interfere with a proper identification afterwards. (Incidentally, Wyatt ran a similar study in the 1940s.) Although the experiment concerns perception rather than decision making, and is far removed from an organizational setting, it has important implications for the design and management of information systems because it tells us something about the formation of hypotheses.

Our present state of knowledge about decision making does not justify strong conclusions about the superiority or inferiority of controlled experiments in comparison to case studies. We need both. We are far from discovering the fundamental laws of human decision making. Rather, we are engaged in increasing, revising, and debugging our substantial lay knowledge about individual and organizational decision making. Consequently, work in the field should be evaluated on the background of lay knowledge about individuals and organizations. Decision research should be evaluated in terms of its contribution to our general knowledge, much as consultants should be judged by what they add to what the decision maker already knows.

Much research on decision making and inference has focused on the contrast between normative models and actual behavior. This strategy provides a useful tool for studying judgment and choice, which has led to some interesting observations. Recent studies of decision making indicate that people depart from the standard rational model in a predictable manner. These studies show that people are often fallible and inconsistent but not necessarily irrational or incompetent. Anybody who infers from the presence of intransitive preferences and inconsistent beliefs that people are unable to cross the street or to operate a simple machine is making an inferential error more severe than errors observed in the studies of heuristics and biases. The argument that the study of inferential errors provides a biased view of human judgment is comparable to the claim that students of perception provide a biased view of sensory mechanisms because of their concern with perceptual illusions, or that students of memory are portraying people as having poor memories because the studies employ tasks in which a great deal of forgetting takes place. The tendency to infer the message from the medium is a common error of representativeness that we should avoid.

Rationality in Research on Decision Making

The question as to whether people are rational or not is unlikely to produce illuminating answers because we do not have an adequate definition of rationality. There are two general conceptions of rationality. The first is that of instrumental rationality: behavior is rational to the extent that it fulfills its stated goals. The difficulty with this notion is that we do not have an independent way of assessing the decision maker's goals, and in the absence of such an assessment the definition becomes circular. The second conception of rationality, which underlies modern decision theory, is the notion of rationality as coherence. Behavior is rational if it is internally consistent or coherent. Recent research suggests that this criteria is unattainable, and hence not very useful for our purposes. Denis Lindley once argued that "inside every real person, there is a rational person trying to get out." Evidence suggests that this rational person, if he or she exists, has a hard time getting out.

The philosophical question of rationality notwithstanding, we constantly evaluate individuals and organizations. In interpreting people's behavior as optimal or suboptimal, wise or foolish, we can make two types of errors. We can err by providing sophisticated and devious rationalization for foolish behavior, and we can err by treating as erroneous decisions that are in fact justifiable. Sometimes we make both types of error simultaneously, as illustrated by the following anecdote.

Several years ago, Daniel Kahneman and I participated in an interdisciplinary conference with economists, management scientists, and marketeers. Danny presented some of our empirical work demonstrating systematic inconsistencies or reversals of preferences. A small group of economists was scandalized by our results and proceeded to produce a long list of objections. They claimed that (1) the results were not true; (2) they knew them all along; (3) the results would disappear if people were given monetary incentives and/or an opportunity to learn; (4) the inconsistencies would disappear at the aggregate level, and so on and so forth. I ended up joining this group for dinner, and the argument continued. After reaching an impasse, I suggested a change of topic and asked one of the critics for his views on Carter's economic policy.

"The President's policy is completely incoherent," he replied. "It is irrational, inconsistent, and counterproductive."

"This is very interesting," I replied, and posed a different question, "How would you evaluate your wife's shopping habits from the standpoint of optimal decision making?"

"You must be kidding," he laughed. "Do you know what she did the other day?" and so on.

After a few more questions, it dawned on the participants that despite their commitment to universal rationality, they were denying the rationality of any particular individual, such as the President or the economist's wife. These opposing tendencies may have a common cause, namely an inability to put ourselves in other people's shoes. The lack of empathy contributes to the generation of unrealistic theories of human behavior and to the tendency to view many decisions as irrational. A better understanding of the constraints and complexities of decision making may encourage a more realistic and charitable evaluation of human choice.

Rethinking Research on Decision Making

Karl E. Weick, *Cornell University*

In 1964 Berelson and Steiner's *Human Behavior: An Inventory of Findings* was published, a book containing 1045 established propositions about human behavior. Berelson used to summarize this book with three propositions:

1. Some do, some don't.
2. The differences aren't very great.
3. It's more complicated than that.

Those three propositions synopsize much of what the preceding papers tell us about people making decisions.

Additional recapitulations can be done in the context of the following image: soup sampling is a real decision in the real world of restaurants. That

"Mmm. The soup du jour is not cream of mushroom. It is not tomato or celery. It is not chicken, nor is it Scotch broth. It is most definitely not won ton..."

Drawing by Ziegler; © 1980 The New Yorker Magazine, Inc.

alone coordinates it with discussions by MacCrimmon, Pondy, and Mintzberg. MacCrimmon was jolted because the papers he read on behavioral decision theory seemed to contain no behavior, no decisions, and no theory. Soup sampling has at least behavior (tasting) and a decision (What shall we call this stuff?). It also implies the theory that decision making is a retrospective rather than a prospective process.

Soup sampling fits at least five of Pondy's six criteria for real decisions:

1. A shifting cast of characters: a waiter could enter the kitchen or the maitre d' leave.
2. History dependence (current decisions depend on past commitments): a commitment to being a French restaurant rules out won ton soup as a choice.
3. Interdependence among decision problems: some definitions of the soup will drive people toward higher priced items on the menu to complement it, while other definitions could drive them toward lower-priced items.
4. That choice is sometimes easy, but the justification hard: not an obvious issue here unless a gourmet happens to taste the mixture, disputes the labeling, and does so in a newspaper column reviewing the restaurant.
5. A changing frame and definition of the problem: "Whoops, the sauce for the guinea hens just burned; can the soup stock be turned into a sauce for fowl as well as or instead of a soup?"
6. And conflict: the more attractive the soup, the more people who will order it, hence, the more time it will take to serve complete dinners, meaning that fewer people can be seated before closing time.

Mintzberg conceivably would find the soup sampling a reasonable exhibit of intuitive processes, but even if he did not, the fact that the cartoon showed anything other than the laboratory would enlist his approval.

The decision sequence portrayed is action—outcome—feedback. Having cooked something, though he's not sure what, the chef tastes what he's cooked, decides what he must have decided to cook earlier in the day, and then throws in a final handful of ingredients to make the mixture a superb example of whatever he's decided the mixture has become. The actions of assembling ingredients and simmering them until customers arrive, then generating an outcome in the form of a label for what the pot apparently contains, and finally using this label as feedback to modify the initial assemblage of ingredients, shows how decision making often concludes a sequence of action rather than begins it.

Assembling the soup of the day bears some resemblance to Connolly's hedge cutting. Both involve continuous sampling and incremental adjustments. Just as the gardener repeatedly snips and inspects to create contours he had not foreseen, the chef repeatedly tastes and flavors to create a soup he had not anticipated when the process began. More generally, acting and deciding are interwoven. Each shapes the other. Action shapes the data that determine what needs to be decided next. What is decided next, however, influences which action will now seem appropriate. Subsequent acting further modifies the data with the result that acting and deciding repeatedly inform and edit one another.

The chef is in the company of other employees as he makes his decision, which is appropriate given the emphasis on organizational decision making, where multiple actors drift toward single decisions. The three people surrounding the chef might be viewed as a decision support system providing alternative labels for the soup, reminding the chef of some decision premises pertinent to his decision (for example, scotch broth was yesterday's soup of the day), and offering potential validation for certain of his proposals. The presence of multiple actors also raises the likelihood that there will be a conflict of interest. For example, if the soup is called cream of cream rather than cream of celery, customers will order more appetizers, which have to be prepared from scarce supplies, soup bowls will go unused, and there will be more congestion in the kitchen because more courses will need to be served.

The cartoon demonstrates one way in which new goals come to light in organizations. If organizations persistently follow well-defined objectives, they suffer because they become confined to these objectives, consider no new goals, and reduce their chances of adaptation. Since change has a negative expected value, the only way they may discover something new is by a bit of silliness, a bit of behavior unconstrained by past experience. Thus, the chef might discover a new house specialty, a new goal for the restaurant. He might say, for example, "Since we apparently make terrific cream of won ton, we will become the only restaurant in New York which produces that specialty."

Pondy and Connolly's discovery that the word *decision* means to cut away, as opposed to an *in*cision, which is a cutting in, helps us to appreciate how the chef makes decisions. He decides what soup he has cooked by determining what he has not cooked — the soup is *not* cream of mushroom, *not* tomato or celery, *neither* is it chicken *nor* scotch broth. Whatever is left after the elimination must be the soup of the day, just as whatever alternative survives after less attractive alternatives are discarded must be what we have decided. Ironically, the phenomenology of decision making may miss this process. We feel and report that we have decided in favor of something, when we have actually spent most of our time pruning away inferior alternatives with only the vaguest notion of what we'll be left with.

The soup sampling suggests an answer to Connolly's question, "If we're so dumb, how did we make it to the moon?" In its more general form the question is: How can we do complicated things well? One way to make a complicated soup, with measured quantities introduced at specific points in the cooking, is to cook *something* and then give it a specific label that implies a complicated prior history of careful attention to detail. The fact that the detail is an opportunistic reconstruction by the chef behind the closed doors of the kitchen is understandable and reasonable, given the intricate context of patrons impressed by labels and searching for new tastes, leftover food the use of which cuts costs, before-dinner drinks that deaden taste buds, and unforeseen interactions among ingredients as they cook.

Soup sampling is also an appropriate setting to ask about aspiration-level goals and satisficing. Is the chef asking, "Is this good enough to pass for celery soup?" or is he striving for a more optimal outcome? Does it even matter? If the chef is making do by using trusted heuristics, does it make any sense to niggle over whether this action exhibits rationality or a departure from rationality?

There is no question that observers can suggest other sequences of soup sampling that might appear more sensible and efficient when assessed against a set of criteria that are context-free. That exercise, however, has a high potential for mischief because it distracts observers into meaningless debates about the capacities of everyman for reasoning, analysis, and information processing. Questions of capacity, addressed without specification of contexts, constraints, and purposes, are little more profound than a search for the one best way, the key trait of leaders, the one ruling dimension of personality.

The Context of Action and the Consequences of Choice

Context-free arguments about limits, bounds, and biases in thought are irrelevant when applied to actors who are never free of contexts. Hogarth was sensitive to this issue when he observed that laboratory environments are not redundant. This lack of redundancy puts people at a disadvantage when they try to process information that is not confirmed in multiple ways. Redundancy that is present in the environment of soup sampling includes taste, smell, appearance, knowledge of initial ingredients, suggestions from bystanders, and memory of the original intent. March was sensitive to the issue of context when he observed that most information in organizations contains lies. If people confront suspicious inputs, why should they apply to these inputs the same practices that they apply to trusted inputs? We act as if they should apply the same practices regardless of input and chuckle in judgment when they don't.

One potential for accommodation between behavioral decision theory and organizational decision theory lies in a division of labor. Organizational decision theory specifies dimensions and clustering of these dimensions into contexts that have differential effects on the credibility of inputs and the accountability of people who process inputs into decisions. Behavioral decision theory specifies the ways in which people incorporate inputs of variable validity into decisions that have different short- and long-term implications for their own survival in, and maintenance of, the very setting that produced those variable inputs in the first place.

But if that's all it takes, why haven't we done it? There are several answers and it is appropriate to review some of them in this context of appeals for integration. To answer the question of where we go next, we need to address the related question, *how* do we work next? People seem to have things to say to one another but they may not be speaking very clearly and they aren't being heard.

The preceding inquiries into decision making are often thin on context, action, pragmatics, and consequentiality. They seldom come to grips with the centrality of choice in individual actors as portrayed in the following excerpt (Zimbardo 1969):

"He who has a choice has trouble," according to an old Dutch proverb. Man is born free, but at every opportunity he shackles himself with compulsion, ritual, obligation, and conformity in order to live thoughtlessly, to conceal his weaknesses, and to gain respectability.

Why should choice make trouble? The ability to choose first involves psychological freedom to specify what the alternatives are, or to perceive those that are available. The act of deciding upon one alternative and rejecting others requires consideration of the attributes, implications, utility, and costs of each. The commitment to take action transforms what is originally a continuum of theoretical response alternatives into a concrete dichotomy with one degree of freedom, thereby changing abstract intellectual involvement into immediate ego involvement. Since the consequences of any act cannot be fully known at the time of the choice, there is always some risk that the decision may be the wrong one. It is fear of this possibility that keeps people from choosing. If one chooses freely, then one bears personal responsibility for the consequences of the choice. If there are outcomes which can be evaluated as right or wrong, good or bad, wise or stupid, then the individual himself can be evaluated according to the consequences of his choice. Where the alternatives are mutually exclusive, the choice irrevocable, and the consequences involve important aspects of the individual's aspirations, values, and attitudes, then his very self-definition is at stake. As long as the individual knows he could have done otherwise, or that others he respects might have made a different choice, then, unlike Pontius Pilate, he cannot wash his hands of it (pp. 12–13).

The preceding papers also seldom come to grips with the peripherality of decision making among collective actors in groups and organizations. One thing we know about real settings is that indecision and the avoidance of decision is functional. This is evident in a recent study of the National Institute of Education (Sproull, Weiner, and Wolf 1978). Furthermore, we know that most people in power try to delegate only innocuous decisions to their subordinates while reserving the important ones for their own decision making. This argument has been stated most clearly by Bachrach and Baratz (1962). We also know that in most social settings people postpone rather than make decisions. This has the effect that problems originally associated with those decisions eventually wander away and attach themselves to other more timely issues. That being the case, when the original decision is finally made, it solves nothing because there are no problems attached to it. Finally, it has been observed that in most settings, events make decisions for people. There are surprisingly few snap decisions made without a great deal of prior homework, negotiation, deliberation, and development of a climate of inevitability. Fewer snap decisions are made at higher levels of organizations than people usually realize (Peters 1978).

My criticisms are not intended as cheap shots at the slow pace of scholarship when directed at overdetermined human problems. Rather they involve a perversion of Connolly's moon question: If we're so smart, how did we make it to the Bay of Pigs?

The pieces of some answers to questions such as that seem to be evident in the preceding papers. Why then, haven't they been assembled in provocative ways?

My hunch is that subtle differences in our way of inquiring have led us to see slightly different things, and that we have magnified these slight differences by associating closely with likeminded colleagues who share our biases. As a result, the differences among us look larger than they may be.

Five Issues of Inquiry

Our differences seem to arise in the ways we handle at least five issues associated with inquiry: variety, bias, boredom, degrees of freedom, and trade-offs.

Variety

Decision making is a complicated process rich in variety. The law of requisite variety suggests that it takes variety in a sensor-observer to manage and register the variety that exists in the phenomenon being sensed. The surprising recent suggestion (Daft and Wiginton 1979) is that natural language has more variety than does contrived language. Consequently natural language registers phenomena with more accuracy and in greater detail. If that's plausible, then the crucial differences among us may lie more in the subtlety and intricacy of the images we use as metaphors for decision making and less in how we operate on the data those images lead us to.

Bias

The differences among us may also represent different ways we choose to deal with bias. Most of us try to control bias by keeping some distance from the objects we study. We often treat subjects as objects in an effort to preserve some detachment from them. We've paid dearly for that distance (Weick, in press). What we observe of those objects from afar now looks to be quite different from what we would see of them if we worked close up and interacted with them. What we don't understand right now is what it means to be objective when we're close up. As we find out what that means we're also likely to get some convergence on what it means to make decisions in organizational settings.

Boredom

Arthur Koestler (1970) argued that any explanation of any phenomenon, no matter how interesting or dramatic or novel, loses its evocative power rather quickly. Once novel explanations become familiar, people lose interest in both the idea and the objects to which it refers. Koestler argues that this is inevitable. I think that it's been true of discussion about decision making as well. Satiation rather than falsification seems to have controlled the courses of work on this topic. Koestler argues that there are two basic ways to cope with the law of diminishing returns: shouting and whispering. We've seen both among these papers.

Shouting occurs when there is a resort to hyperbole, nonobvious prediction, flamboyance, spicier fare, overexplicitness, or overemphasis. Whispering occurs when explanations become more economical, more implicit, more oblique, when they suggest rather than name, when they introduce subtleties, and when greater imagination is required for comprehension. Koestler talks about whispering in terms of the "law of infolding." He points out that greater usage of implicit suggestions to combat the law of diminishing returns is not intended to make the message obscure.

On the contrary it is to make it more luminous by compelling the recipient to act as a fluorescent screen, to work out the implications by his own effort, to re-create it. Implicit is derived from the Latin *plicare*, and means "folded in," like a role of parchment. The implicit message has to be unfolded by the reader; he must unravel it, fill the gaps, solve the riddles. . . . The writer's best friend is his pair of scissors (or his eraser). . . . The law of infolding demands that the reader should never be given something for nothing; he must be made to pay in emotional currency by exerting his imagination. Otherwise one gets the dreaded "So what?" reaction. . . . The law of infolding operates even in science. . . . Only recently did we begin to realize that the unfolding of the secrets of nature was accompanied by a parallel process of infolding, because the more precise knowledge the physicist acquired, the more ambiguous and elusive the mathematical symbols he had to use; he could no longer make an intelligible model of reality, he could only allude to it by abstract equations (pp. 44–45).

It may be that differences in these styles of managing boredom are what keep us apart rather than differences in substance or assumptions.

Degrees of Freedom

We differ in a fourth way in the number and kind of observations we need to make before we think we know something. This difference can be expressed in our preferences regarding degrees of freedom.

Decision problems are often rearranged in the interest of drawing cleaner conclusions about cause and effect. Such rearrangement is often justified in the name of increased degrees of freedom, even if the increase is achieved at a substantial cost of external validity. Campbell (1975) broke this methodological lockstep when he argued that degrees of freedom can be established for single observations. To establish them, degrees of freedom are defined in terms of ideas rather than people. Implications that follow from a single theory are treated as relationships, all of which can be disconfirmed in a single setting. Thus, a single event is examined in multiple ways suggested by the theoretical derivations, and those theories disconfirmed less often are retained as more plausible explanations of what is happening. Differential preferences for numerical versus theoretical degrees of freedom, and for observations in abundance versus ideas in abundance, lie behind some of the apparent difficulties we have in building a theory of setting-specific decision behavior.

Trade-offs

Finally, we differ in how we resolve the dilemma that none of us can propose an explanation of decision making that is simultaneously general, accurate, and simple (Thorngate 1976b). To build an explanation that incorporates any two of these qualities is to forego the third. Kunreuther's effort to represent insurance accurately was at the expense of generality and simplicity. March and Shapira's effort to blend simplicity and generality in their explanation evoked objections about accuracy. Einhorn and Hogarth's attempt to combine accuracy and simplicity in the laboratory elicited skepticism about the generality of their findings.

We're all caught in this dilemma. We're all vulnerable along at least one dimension. And we all protect ourselves against this vulnerability by discounting that dimension on which we are weak. Thus people argue that it's too early in our history to be concerned with generality, or that accuracy is an illusion because the world continually changes, or that simplicity is a virtue only for simple minds. The trouble is, in a dialogue such as this book represents, one person's virtue and strength is the very thing that another equally committed person discounts. Those who tout the accuracy of their explorations are unprepared for the yawns of people who, in justifying their search for generality and simplicity, belabor the transience of accuracy. And so it goes.

Behavioral decision theorists seem to anchor their explanations in accuracy and appear ambivalent over whether to blend the accuracy with generality or with simplicity. Organizational decision theorists are more inclined to start with general explanations and to move reluctantly toward either simplicity, where they lose much of the phenomenon of interest, or toward accuracy, where they lose much of the audience of interest, for example, practitioners who have little tolerance for complex explanations.

Conclusion

Finally, perhaps our biggest oversight is acting as if we know and agree upon where decisions begin and end. My hunch is that we differ significantly on this point. Repeatedly, each one of us seems to astonish the others by what we include and exclude as decisions. Our mutual astonishment resembles closely Raymond Smullyan's (1980) reaction when someone congratulated him on solving a problem he never knew he had.

> Once when I was playing for a musician, he complimented me on the way I played a particular passage. He told me how well I handled a certain modulation and added, "You don't realize in what a remarkable way you solved this problem!"
> I must say, I was thunderstruck! In the first place, I was not even aware that there was a modulation. (That shows how much I know about music! I just don't think about them.) In the second place, I was totally unaware of any problem let alone solving one! The whole idea of "problem solving," especially in music, strikes me as so weird! Not only weird, but most disharmonious and destructive. Is that how you think of life, as a series of problems to be solved? No wonder you don't enjoy living more than you do!
> To compliment a musician, or any other artist, on having "solved problems" is to me absolutely analogous to complimenting the waves of the ocean for solving such a complex system of partial differential equations. Of course the ocean does its "waving" in accordance with these differential equations, but it hardly solves them. I do not claim to know whether the ocean is or is not a conscious being, but if the ocean does think (which wouldn't surprise me), the one thing I'm sure the ocean does not think about is differential equations.
> Perhaps I am allergic to the word *problem*. If so, I am grateful for this allergy. Some of you will say I am only quibbling about words. This is not so. It is ideas that count, not words. And I believe that one who feels he is "solving problems" lives very differently from one who does not feel this way. I believe my objection to the notion of "problem" is due to my deep conviction that the moment one labels something as a problem, that's when the real problem starts (pp. 79–80).

The chef sampling soup might be just as astonished to learn that he was making a decision as Smullyan was surprised to learn that he had solved the problem of modulation. In both cases the situated actions of the chef and the musician can be mislabeled by well-intentioned decision theorists for whom believing is seeing. The problem is not that these theorists have preconceptions. They can't help themselves, since everyone has preconceptions. The problem is that the content of decision theory preconceptions can force people to misread what is happening. Specifically, observers equipped with too little linguistic variety, too much detachment, attention spans that are too short, theories that are too arid, and aspirations for generality, simplicity, and accuracy that are too ambitious, watch situated action and draft a parody of what it involves.

We are well reminded by the papers in this volume that context makes a difference, that contemplation without action is an illusion, and that people continue to make do whether their efforts are viewed as insipid or inspired. If we continue to take these reminders seriously we should have something to say to each other and to those people who continued to live by their decisions even as we are gathered here to enumerate the reasons why they couldn't and shouldn't.

8 Epilogue

Gerardo R. Ungson, University of Oregon
Daniel N. Braunstein, Oakland University

Gregory Bateson once observed that "An explorer can never know what he is exploring until it has been explored" (1972, p. xvi). This volume represents a first, in which researchers from behavioral decision making, human problem solving, and organizational decision making have explored similarities and differences in their approaches to the study of decision making. The multiplicity of themes and positions, many of these exploratory in nature, suggests both the difficulty of integrating the fields and a reassessment of how they may be eventually integrated. The interest exhibited by contributors and others in the field as well are strong indications that the dialogue established here will continue.

In the spirit of continuing the dialogue that has begun, we would like to offer some perspectives for integrating the different research fields.

1. A theme present throughout this book is that integration should not consist of one research discipline emulating the other. That is, it is not in the common interest for behavioral decision theorists to become organizational theorists, and vice versa. Rather, each participant should be continuously aware of the others' problems while exploiting the substantive conceptual and methodological strengths of his or her own method.

2. It is possible that research disciplines may eventually incorporate into their framework of analysis some variables traditionally belonging to other disciplines. Einhorn and Hogarth's research agenda including social learning, modeling, and conflict is a step in this direction. In addition, the March and Shapira paper leaves open numerous possibilities in which organizational decision theorists may use theoretical ideas developed by behavioral decision theorists.

3. Commitment is central to any integrative effort. Karl Weick spoke to the phenomenon that behavioral and organizational decision theorists complain a lot to each other in forums and books of this nature. It may be that complaints are a redeclaration of one's conceptual domain. Perhaps an attempt at cross-pollinating the research disciplines may have to come

from people outside these areas who are committed to doing research on decision making, regardless of their conceptual domains.

4. Integration may not be directly aligned with reconciling philosophical and methodological differences, but rather with rallying around an issue in which different ideas from each research discipline are needed. The emerging interest in decision aids, decision support systems, and human engineering may provide such an avenue for this purpose. The design of such systems needs to encompass the decisional process of the individual decision maker as well as the organizational or group context in which these decisional processes are enacted.

5. Integration may not only involve the extension in use of present problem-solving tools, but the creation of new ones. Pondy astutely observed that much of the emphasis in this volume was on internal tools of problem solving, and that little attention was directed at external tools of problem solving. To properly examine both internal and external tools, we may need to create new artifacts that encompass interests shared by behavioral and organizational decision theorists alike.

In closing, we acknowledge that the process of dialogue is, in itself, an ill-structured task in which boundaries are unclear, ambiguous, and continually evolving. Therefore, we hope that this book provides a point of departure from which present research may be recast, future research may be anchored, and dialogue may be continued. While the book is directed primarily at students and researchers in the field of decision making, we hope that, through extended applications, it may also benefit practitioners of and all others interested in the understanding and improvement of decision making. If it does, the exploration demanded by Gregory Bateson as quoted in the opening of this epilogue may be fulfilled.

Bibliography

Abelson, R. P. Script processing in attitude formation and decision making. In J. S. Carroll & J. W. Payne (Eds.), *Cognition and Social Behavior.* Hillsdale, N.J.: Erlbaum, 1976.

Ackoff, R. L. Management misinformation systems. *Management Science*, 1967, *14*(4), B147–B156.

Ajzen, I. Intuitive theories of events and the effects of base-rate information on prediction. *Journal of Personnel and Social Psychology*, 1977, *35*, 303–314.

Akerlof, G. The market for "lemons": Quality uncertainty and the market mechanisms. *Quarterly Journal of Economics*, 1970, *84*, 488–500.

Aldrich, H. & Herker, D. Boundary spanning roles and organization structure. *Academy of Management Review*, 1977, *2*, 217–230.

Allison, G. Conceptual models and the cuban missile crisis. *American Political Science Review*, 1969, LXIII, 689–718.

Allison, G. *Essence of Decision: Explaining the Cuban Missile Crisis.* Boston: Little, Brown, 1971.

Anderson, N. H. Cognitive algebra: Integration theory as applied to social attribution. In L. Berkowitz (Ed.), *Advances in Experimental Social Psychology*, (Vol. 7). New York: Academic Press, 1973.

Anderson, N. H. Algebraic rules in psychological measurement. *American Scientist*, 1979, *67*, 555–563.

Andrew, B. J. An approach to the construction of simulated exercises in clinical problem-solving. *Journal of Medical Education*, 1972, *47*, 952–958.

Ansoff, H. I. *Corporate Strategy.* New York: McGraw-Hill, 1965.

Armstrong, J. S. *Long Range Forecasting.* New York: Wiley, 1978a.

Armstrong, J. S. Forecasting with econometric methods: Folklore versus fact. *Journal of Business*, 1978b, *51*, 549–564.

Arnold, H., Evans, M., & House, R. Productivity: A psychological perspective. In S. Maital and N. Meltz (Eds.), *Lagging Productivity Growth: Causes and Remedies.* Cambridge, Mass.: Ballinger, 1980.

Arrow, K. Uncertainty and the welfare economics of medical care. *American Economic Review*, 1963, *53*, 941–973.

Aschenbrenner, K. M. Single-peaked risk preferences and their dependability on the gambles' presentation mode. *Journal of Experimental Psychology: Human Perception and Performance*, 1978, *4*, 513–520.

Axelrod, R. *Structure of Decision.* Princeton, New Jersey: Princeton University Press, 1976.

Bachrach, P. & Baratz, M. S. Two faces of power. *American Political Science Review*, 1962, *56*, 947–952.

Bar-Hillel, M. The role of sample size in sample evaluation. *Organizational Behavior and Human Performance*, 1979, *24*, 245–257.

Bar-Hillel, M. The base-rate fallacy in probability judgments. *Acta Psychologica*, 1980, *4*, 211–233.

Bar-Hillel, M. & Falk, R. Some teasers concerning conditional probabilities. Paper presented at *18th Conference on Bayesian Inference and Decision Making*, University of Southern California, 1980.

Bariff, M. L. & Lusk, E. J. Cognitive and personality tests in designing MIS. *Management Science*, 1977, *23*, 820–829.

Barnard, C. I. *The Functions of the Executive.* Cambridge, Mass.: Harvard University Press, 1938.

Bateson, G. *Steps to an Ecology of Mind.* New York: Ballantine, 1972.

Beach, L. R. & Mitchell, T. R. A contingency model for the selection of decision strategies. *Academy of Management Review*, 1978, *3*, 439–449.

Becker, G. M. & McClintock, C. G. Value: Behavioral decision theory. *Annual Review of Psychology*, 1967, *18*, 239–286.

Beer, S. The surrogate world we manage. *Behavioral Science,* 1973, *18,* 198–209.

Behn, R. D. & Vaupel, J. W. Why decision analysis is rarely used and how it can be. Working paper, Center for Policy Analysis, Institute of Policy Sciences and Public Affairs, Duke University, 1976.

Bell, D. *The Coming of Postindustrial Society.* New York: Basic Books, 1973.

Bell, D. Thinking ahead. *Harvard Business Review,* May-June 1979, 20–42.

Berelson, B. & Steiner, G. *Human Behavior: An Inventory of Scientific Findings.* New York: Harcourt, Brace, & World, 1964.

Bernstein, G. K. Testimony before the U.S. Senate Subcommittee on Housing and Urban Affairs, 92nd Congress, S.2794, a bill to amend the National Flood Insurance Act of 1968 to increase flood insurance coverage of certain properties, to authorize the acquisition of certain properties, and for other purposes. Washington, D.C.: Government Printing Office, 1972.

Beswick, C. & Cravens, D. A multistage decision model for sales force management. *Journal of Marketing Research,* 1977, *14,* 135–144.

Bettman, J. R. A graph theory approach to comparing consumer information processing models. *Management Science,* 1971, *18,* 114–128.

Bettman, J. R. Towards a statistic for consumer decision net models. *Journal of Consumer Research,* 1974, *1,* 71–80.

Bettman, J. R. Data collection and analysis approaches for studying consumer information processing. *Advances in Consumer Research,* 1977, *4,* 342–348.

Bettman, J. R. *An Information Processing Theory of Consumer Choice.* Reading, Mass.: Addison-Wesley, 1979.

Bettman, J. R. & Jacoby, J. Patterns of processing in consumer information acquisition. *Advances in Consumer Research,* 1976, *3,* 315–320.

Bettman, J. R. & Kakkar, P. Effects of information presentation format on consumer information acquisition strategy. *Journal of Consumer Research,* 1977, *3,* 233–240.

Boulding, K. E. Observations on judgment and public policy decisions. In K. R. Hammond (Ed.), *Judgment and Decision in Public Policy Formation.* Boulder, Colo.: Westview, 1978.

Bourne, L. E., Dowinowski, R. C., & Loftus, E. F. *Cognitive Processes.* Englewood Cliffs, N.J.: Prentice-Hall, 1979.

Bouwman, M. J. *An information processing model of financial diagnosis.* Unpublished manuscript, Graduate School of Industrial Administration, Carnegie-Mellon University, 1978a.

Bouwman, M. J. *Financial diagnosis: A cognitive model of the processes involved.* Unpublished doctoral dissertation, Carnegie-Mellon University, Pittsburgh, Penna., 1978b.

Bowman, E. H. Consistency and optimality in managerial decision making. *Management Science,* 1961, *9* (2), 310–321.

Braine, M. D. S. On the relation between the natural logic of reasoning and standard logic. *Psychological Review,* 1978, *85,* 1–21.

Braybrooke, D. & Lindblom, C. E. *A Strategy of Decision.* New York: The Free Press, 1963.

Brehmer, B. Note on clinical judgment and the formal characteristics of clinical tasks. *Psychological Bulletin,* 1976, *83,* 778–782.

Brehmer, B. Response consistency in probabilistic inference tasks. *Organizational Behavior and Human Performance,* 1978, *22,* 103–115.

Brehmer, B. In one word: Not from experience. *Acta Psychologica,* 1980, *45,* 223–241.

Broadbent, D. E., Cooper, P. J., & Broadbent, M. H. P. A comparison of hierarchical and matrix retrieval schemes in recall. *Journal of Experimental Psychology: Human Learning and Memory,* 1978, *4,* 486–497.

Bronowski, J. *The Origins of Knowledge and Imagination.* New Haven: Yale University Press, 1978.

Brooks, L. Nonanalytic concept formation and memory for instances. In E. R. Rosch and B. B. Lloyd (Eds.), *Cognition and Categorization.* Hillsdale, N.J.: Erlbaum, 1978.

Brown, H. I. On being rational. *American Philosophical Quarterly,* 1978, *15,* 241–248.

Brown, R. V. Do managers find decision theory useful? *Harvard Business Review,* 1970, *48* (3), 78–89.

Bruner, J. S. & Potter, M. C. Interference in visual recognition. *Science,* 1964, *144,* 424–425.

Brunswik, E. Organismic achievement and environmental probability. *Psychological Review,* 1943, *50,* 255–272.

Brunswik, E. *Conceptual Framework of Psychology.* Chicago: University of Chicago Press, 1952.

Brunswik, E. *Perception and the Representative Design of Experiments* (2nd ed.). Berkeley: University of California Press, 1956.

Bryce, J. *The American Commonwealth.* London: Macmillan, 1888.

Campbell, D. T. Systematic error on the part of human links inmmunication systems. *Information and Control,* 1959, *1,* 334–369.

Campbell, D. T. Blind variation and selective retention in creative thought as in other knowledge processes. *Psychological Review,* 1960, *67,* 380–400.

Campbell, D. T. Reforms as experiments. *American Psychologist,* 1969, *24,* 409–429.

Campbell, D. T. "Degrees of freedom" and the case study. *Comparative Political Studies,* 1975, *8,* 178–193.

Capon, N. & Burke, M. Individual, product class, and task-related factors in consumer information processing. *Journal of Consumer Research,* 1980, *7,* 314–326.

Carpenter, P. A. & Just, M. A. Reading comprehension as eyes see it. In M. Just & P. Carpenter (Eds.), *Cognitive Processes in Comprehension.* Hillsdale, N.J.: Erlbaum, 1978.

Carroll, J. S. Analyzing decision behavior: The magician's audience. In T. S. Wallsten (Ed.), *Cognitive Processes in Choice and Decision Behavior.* Hillsdale, N.J.: Erlbaum, 1980.

Carroll, J. S. & Payne, J. W. The psychology of the parole decision process: A joint application of attribution theory and information-processing psychology. In J. S. Carroll & J. W. Payne (Eds.), *Cognition and Social Behavior.* Hillsdale, N. J.: Erlbaum, 1976.

Carroll, J. S., Payne, J. W., Frieze, I. M., & Girard, D. C. Attribution theory: An information processing approach. Unpublished manuscript, Carnegie-Mellon University, 1976.

Carter, E. E. The behavioral theory of the firm and top-level corporate decisions. *Administrative Science Quarterly,* 1971, *16,* 413–428.

Cartwright, D. Determinants of scientific progress. *American Psychologist,* 1973, *28,* 222–231.

Castellan, N. J., Jr. Decision making with multiple probabilistic cues. In N. J. Castellan, D. B. Pisoni, & G. R. Potts (Eds.), *Cognitive Theory* (Vol. 2). Hillsdale, N. J.: Erlbaum, 1977.

Chestnut, R. W. The expenditure of time in the acquisition of package information. Unpublished M.S. Thesis, Purdue University, 1975.

Chestnut, R. W. Information acquisition in life insurance policy selection: Monitoring the impact of product beliefs, affect toward agent, and external memory. Unpublished doctoral dissertation, Purdue University, 1977.

Chestnut, R. W. Time "costs" and external search in the purchasing of nondurables. Research working papers, 224A, Columbia University, 1979a.

Chestnut, R. W. Source attractiveness and the purchase of life insurance. Research working papers, 233A, Columbia University, 1979b.

Chestnut, R. W. Cost disclosure and the influence of agent in life insurance purchasing. Working paper, Columbia University, 1980.

Chestnut, R. W. & Jacoby, J. Consumer information processing: Emerging theory and findings. In A. G. Woodside, J. N. Sheth, & P. D. Bennett (Eds.), *Consumer and Industrial Buyer Behavior.* New York: North-Holland, 1978.

Chestnut, R. W. & Jacoby, J. Methods and concepts in consumer information processing: Toward an integrated framework. Research working papers, 141A, Columbia University, 1979.

Chestnut, R. W. & Jacoby, J. Product comprehension: The case of permanent vs. term life insurance. *Advances in Consumer Research,* 1980, *7,* 424–428.

Chestnut, R. W., Moore, W. L., & Lehmann, D. R. Brand loyalty and the development of information acquisition behavior. Working paper, Columbia University, 1980.

Chew, S. H. & MacCrimmon, K. R. Alpha utility theory, lottery composition and the Allais paradox. Working paper 686, University of British Columbia Faculty of Commerce, 1979.

Child, J. Organizational structure, environment and performance: The role of strategic choice. *Sociology,* 1972, *6,* 1–22.

Child, J. Managerial and organizational factors associated with company performance — Part I. *Journal of Management Studies,* 1975a, *11,* 175–189.

Child, J. Managerial and organizational factors associated with company performance — Part II. *Journal of Management Studies,* 1975b, *12,* 12–27.

Christensen-Szalanski, J. J. J. Problem-solving strategies: A selection mechanism, some implications, and some data. *Organizational Behavior and Human Performance,* 1978, *22,* 307–323.

Christensen-Szalanski, J. J. J. A further examination of the selection of problem-solving strategies: The effects of deadlines and analytic aptitudes. *Organizational Behavior and Human Performance,* 1980, *25,* 107–122.

Churchman, C. W. *The Design of Inquiring Systems.* New York: Basic Books, 1971.

Clarkson, G. P. E. *Portfolio Selection: A Simulation of Trust Investment.* Englewood Cliffs, N. J.: Prentice-Hall, 1962.

Claybrook, J. Letter to Reader's Digest. In *Insurance Institute for Highway Safety Status Report,* April 15, 1980, *1,* 6–7.

Cohen, A. R. Upward communication in experimentally created hierarchies. *Human Relations,* 1958, *11,* 41–53.

Cohen, L. J. *The Probable and the Provable.* Oxford: Clarendon Press, 1977.

Cohen, L. J. On the psychology of prediction: Whose is the fallacy? *Cognition,* 1979, *7,* 385–407.

Cohen, L. J. Can human irrationality be experimentally demonstrated? *The Behavioral and Brain Sciences,* 1981, *4,* 317–370.

Cohen, M. D. Conflict and complexity: Goal diversity and organizational search effectiveness. Working paper, University of Michigan, 1980a.

Cohen, M. D. The power of parallel thinking. Working paper, University of Michigan, 1980b.

Cohen, M. D. & March, J. G. *Leadership and Ambiguity: The American College President.* New York: McGraw-Hill, 1974.

Cohen, M. D., March, J. G., & Olsen, J. P. A garbage can model of organizational choice. *Administrative Science Quarterly,* 1972, *17,* 1–25.

Collins, A. M. & Loftus, E. F. A spreading activation theory of semantic processing. *Psychological Review,* 1975, *82,* 407–428.

Connolly, T. Information processing and decision making in organizations. In B. M. Staw & G. R. Salancik (Eds.), *New Directions in Organizational Behavior.* Chicago: St. Clair Press, 1977.

Connolly, T. The decision competence paradox. In R. C. Huseman (Ed.), *Proceedings of the Academy of Management.* Detroit, 1980a.

Connolly, T. Uncertainty, action and competence: Some alternatives to omniscience in complex problem-solving. In S. Fiddle (Ed.), *Uncertainty: Behavioral and Social Dimensions.* New York: Praeger, 1980b.

Cook, P. & Graham, D. The demand for insurance and protection: The case of irreplaceable commodities. *Quarterly Journal of Economics,* 1977, *91,* 143–156.

Coombs, C. H. & Avrunin, G. S. Single-peaked functions and the theory of preference. *Psychological Review,* 1977, *84,* 216–230.

Corbin, R. M. Decisions that might not get made. In T. S. Wallsten (Ed.), *Cognitive Processes in Choice and Decision Behavior.* Hillsdale, N.J.: Erlbaum, 1980.

Crozier, M. *The Bureaucratic Phenomenon.* Chicago: University of Chicago Press, 1964.

Cummins, J. D., Kunreuther, H., & Schoemaker, P. J. H. The role of insurance agents and companies in the marketing of flood and earthquake insurance. Research proposal, The Wharton School, University of Pennsylvania, 1977.

Cyert, R. M. & DeGroot, M. H. Multiperiod decision models with alternating choice as a solution to the duopoly problem. *Quarterly Journal of Economics*, 1970, *84*, 410–429.

Cyert, R. M., DeGroot, M. H., & Holt, C. A. Capital allocation within a firm. *Journal of Behavioral Science*, 1979, *24*(5), 287–297.

Cyert, R. M. & March, J. *A Behavioral Theory of the Firm*. Englewood Cliffs, N.J.: Prentice-Hall, 1963.

Daft, R. L. & Becker, S. W. *The Innovative Organization*. New York: Elsevier, 1978.

Daft, R. L. & Wiginton, J. C. Language and organization. *Academy of Management Review*, 1979, *4*, 179–191.

Davis, O. & Farley, J. Allocating sales force effort with commissions and quotas. *Management Science*, 1971, *18*, 55–63.

Dawes, R. M. Objective optimization under multiple subjective functions. In J. L. Cochrane & M. Zeleny (Eds.), *Multiple Criteria Decision Making*. University of South Carolina Press, 1973.

Dawes, R. M. Shallow psychology. In J. S. Carroll & J. W. Payne (Eds.), *Cognition and Social Behavior*. Hillsdale, N.J.: Erlbaum, 1976.

Dawes, R. M. Case-by-case versus rule-generated procedures for the allocation of scarce resources. In M. F. Kaplan & S. Schwartz (Eds.), *Human Judgment and Decision Processes in Applied Settings*. New York: Academic Press, 1977.

Dawes, R. M. The robust beauty of improper linear models in decision making. *American Psychologist*, 1979, *34*, 571–582.

Dearborn, D. C. & Simon, H. A. Selective perception: A note on the departmental identification of executives. *Sociometry*, 1958, *21*, 140–144.

DeDombal, F. T. Computer-assisted diagnosis. In Whitby & Lutz (Eds.), *Principles and Practice of Medical Computing*. London: Churchill Livingstone, 1971.

Downey, K. & Slocum, J. Uncertainty and managerial performance. Working paper, Oklahoma State University, 1981.

Downs, A. *Inside Bureaucracy*. Boston: Little, Brown, 1966.

Driver, M. Individual decision making and creativity. In S. Kerr (Ed.), *Organizational Behavior*. Columbus, Ohio: Grid Publishing Company, 1979.

Ebbesen, E. B. & Konečni, V. J. On the external validity of decision-making research: What do we know about decisions in the real world? In T. S. Wallsten (Ed.), *Cognitive Processes in Choice and Decision Behavior*, Hillsdale, N.J.: Erlbaum, 1980.

Edwards, W. The theory of decision making. *Psychological Bulletin*, 1954, *51*, 380–417.

Edwards, W. Behavioral decision theory. *Annual Review of Psychology*, 1961, *12*, 473–498.

Edwards, W. Comment. *Journal of American Statistical Association*, 1975, *70*, 291–293.

Edwards, W. Use of multiattribute utility measurement for social decision making. In D. E. Bell, R. L. Keeney, & H. Raiffa (Eds.), *Conflicting Objectives in Decisions*. New York: Wiley, 1977.

Einhorn, H. J. Decision errors and fallible judgment: Implications for social policy. In K. R. Hammond (Ed.), *Judgment and Decision in Public Policy Formation*. Boulder, Colo.: Westview, 1978.

Einhorn, H. J. Learning from experience and suboptimal rules in decision making. In T. S. Wallsten (Ed.), *Cognitive Processes in Choice and Decision Behavior*. Hillsdale, N. J.: Erlbaum, 1980.

Einhorn, H. J. & Hogarth, R. M. Confidence in judgment: Of the illusion of validity. *Psychological Review*, 1978, *85*, 395–416.

Einhorn, H. J. & Hogarth, R. M. Rationality and the sanctity of competence. *The Behavioral and Brain Sciences*, 1980.

Einhorn, H. J. & Hogarth, R. M. Behavioral decision theory: Processes of judgment and choice. *Annual Review of Psychology*, 1981a, *32*, 53–88.

Einhorn, H. J. & Hogarth, R. M. *Uncertainty and Causality in Practical Inference*. Center for Decision Research, University of Chicago Graduate School of Business, April 1981b.

Einhorn, H. J., Kleinmuntz, D. N., & Kleinmuntz, B. Linear regression *and* process-tracing models of judgment. *Psychological Review,* 1979, *86,* 465–485.

Einhorn, H. J. & McCoach, W. P. A simple multiattribute utility procedure for evaluation. *Behavioral Science,* 1977, *22,* 270–282.

Ellis, A. The basic clinical theory of rational-emotive therapy. In A. Ellis & R. Grieger (Eds.), *Handbook of Rational-Emotive Therapy.* New York: Springer, 1977.

Elstein, A. S., Shulman, L. E., & Sprafka, S. A. *Medical Problem Solving: An Analysis of Clinical Reasoning.* Cambridge, Mass.: Harvard University Press, 1978.

Emerson, R. W. Self-reliance. In *Emerson's Essays* (First Series). Cambridge, Mass.: Riverside Press, 1883.

Emery, F. E. & Trist, E. L. The causal texture of organizational environments. *Human Relations,* 1965, *18,* 21–31.

Ericsson, K. & Simon, H. A. Retrospective verbal protocols as data. Unpublished manuscript, Department of Psychology, Carnegie-Mellon University, 1978.

Ericsson, K. A. & Simon, H. A. Thinking-aloud protocols as data: Effects of verbalization. Unpublished manuscript, Department of Psychology, Carnegie-Mellon University, 1979.

Ericsson, K. A., & Simon, H. A. Verbal reports as data. *Psychological Review,* 1980, *87*(3), 215–251.

Estes, W. K. The cognitive side of probability learning. *Psychological Review,* 1976a, *83,* 37–64.

Estes, W. K. Some functions of memory in probability learning and choice behavior. In G. H. Bower (Ed.), *The Psychology of Learning and Motivation: Advances in Research and Theory* (Vol. 10). New York: Academic Press, 1976b.

Estes, W. K. Is human memory obsolete? *American Science,* 1980, *68,* 62–69.

Falmagne, R. J. (Ed.) *Reasoning: Representation and Processes in Children and Adults.* Hillsdale, N. J.: Erlbaum, 1975.

Fantz, R. L. The origin of form perception. *Scientific American,* 1961, *204,* 66–72.

Feinstein, A. R. An analysis of diagnostic reasoning: The domains and disorders of clinical macrobiology. *Yale Journal of Biology and Medicine,* 1973a, *46,* 212–232.

Feinstein, A. R. An analysis of diagnostic reasoning: The strategy of intermediate decisions. *Yale Journal of Biology and Medicine,* 1973b, *46,* 264–283.

Feinstein, A. R. An analysis of diagnostic reasoning: The construction of clinical algorithms. *Yale Journal of Biology and Medicine,* 1974, *1,* 5–32.

Fischhoff, B. Hindsight ≠ foresight: The effect of outcome knowledge on judgment uncertainty. *Journal of Experimental Psychology: Human Perception and Performance,* 1975, *1,* 288–299.

Fischhoff, B. Attribution theory and judgment under uncertainty. In J. H. Harvey, W. J. Ickes, & R. F. Kidd (Eds.), *New Directions in Attribution Research.* Hillsdale, N. J.: Erlbaum, 1976.

Fischhoff, B. Decision analysis: Clinical art or clinical science. In L. Sjöberg, T. Tyszka, & J. A. Wise (Eds.), *Human Decision Making* (Vol. 1). Bodafors, Sweden: Doxa, 1980.

Fischhoff, B. Debiasing. In D. Kahneman, P. Slovic, & A. Tversky (Eds.), *Judgment under Uncertainty: Heuristics and Biases.* New York: Cambridge University Press, 1982.

Fischhoff, B., Slovic, P., & Lichtenstein, S. Knowing with certainty: The appropriateness of extreme confidence. *Journal of Experimental Psychology: Perception and Performance,* 1977, *3,* 552–564.

Fischhoff, B., Slovic, P., & Lichtenstein, S. Fault trees: Sensitivity of estimated failure probabilities to problem representation. *Journal of Experimental Psychology: Human Perception and Performance,* 1978, *4,* 330–344.

Fischhoff, B., Slovic, P., & Lichtenstein, S. Knowing what you want: Measuring labile values. In T. S. Wallsten (Ed.), *Cognitive Processes in Choice and Decision Behavior.* Hillsdale, N.J.: Erlbaum, 1980a.

Fischhoff, B., Slovic, P., & Lichtenstein, S. Lay foibles and expert fables in judgments about risk. In T. O'Riordan and R. K. Turner (Eds.), *Progress in Resource Management and Environmental Planning* (Vol. 3). Chichester, England: Wiley, 1980b.

Fischhoff, B., Slovic, P., Lichtenstein, S., Read, S., & Combs, B. How safe is safe enough: A psychometric study of attitudes toward technological risks and benefits. *Policy Sciences*, 1978, *8*, 127–152.

Freud, S. *The Ego and the Id.* New York: Norton, 1960 (originally published, 1923).

Fromkin, H. L. & Streufert, S. Laboratory experimentation. In M. D. Dunnette (Ed.), *The Handbook of Industrial and Organizational Psychology.* Chicago: Rand McNally, 1976.

Galbraith, J. *Organization Design.* New York: Addison-Wesley, 1977.

Galbraith, J. & Schoemaker, P. J. H. Technology and organization design: A managerial assessment. In A. C. Hax (Ed.), *Studies in Operations Management.* A'dam, Holland: North Holland, 1978.

Gardner, W. R. Good patterns have few alternatives. *American Scientist,* 1970, *58,* 34–42.

Gazzaniga, M. S. & LeDoux, J. E. *The Integrated Mind.* New York: Plenum Press, 1977.

Gerwin, D. & Newsted, P. A comparison of some inductive inference models. *Behavioral Science,* 1977, *22,* 1–11.

Gerwin, D. & Tuggle, F. D. Modeling organizational decisions using the human problem solving paradigm. *The Academy of Management Review,* 1978, *3*(4), 762–773.

Gifford, W., Bobbit, R., & Slocum, J. Message characteristics and perceptions of uncertainty by organizational decision makers. *Academy of Management Journal,* 1979, *22,* 458–481.

Goldman, A. Epistemics: The regulative theory of cognition. *Journal of Philosophy,* 1978, *75,* 509–523.

Goldsmith, R. W. Studies of a model for evaluating judicial evidence. *Acta Psychologica,* 1980, *45,* 211–221.

Goodman, B., Fischhoff, B., Lichtenstein, S., & Slovic, P. The training of decision makers. *Army Research Institute Technical Report TR–78–B3,* 1978.

Grayson, C. J. Management science and business practice. *Harvard Business Review,* 1973, *51*(4), 41–48.

Green, D. M. & Laffont, J. *Incentives in Public Decision Making.* Amsterdam: North-Holland, 1978.

Green, D. M. & Swets, J. A. *Signal Detection and Psychophysics.* New York: Wiley, 1966.

Greenwald, A. G. Within-subjects designs: To use or not to use? *Psychological Bulletin,* 1976, *83,* 314–320.

Gregg, L. W. & Simon, H. A. Process models and stachostic theories of simple concept formation. *Journal of Mathematical Psychology,* 1967, *4,* 246–276.

Grether, D. M. & Plott, C. R. Economic theory of choice and the preference reversal phenomenon. *American Economic Review,* 1979, *69,* 623–638.

Hah, C. & Lindquist, R. M. The 1952 steel seizure revisited: A systematic study in presidential decision making. *Administrative Science Quarterly,* 1975, *20*(4), 587–605.

Hammond, K. R. Toward increasing competence of thought in public policy formation. In K. R. Hammond (Ed.), *Judgment and Decision in Public Policy Formation.* Denver, Colo.: Westview, 1978a.

Hammond, K. R. Psychology's scientific revolution: Is it in danger? Center for Research on Judgment and Policy Report 211. Boulder, Colo.: Institute of Behavioral Science, 1978b.

Hammond, K. R. & Adelman, L. Science, values and human judgment. *Science,* 1976, *194,* 389–396.

Hammond, K. R., Hursh, C. J., & Todd, F. J. Analyzing the components of clinical inference. *Psychological Review,* 1964, *71,* 438–456.

Hammond, K. R., McClelland, G. H., & Mumpower, J. *Human Judgment and Decision Making.* New York: Praeger, 1980.

Hammond, K. R., Mumpower, J. L., & Smith, T. H. Linking environmental models with models of human judgment: A symmetrical decision aid. *IEEE Transaction on Systems, Man and Cybernetics,* 1977, *SMC–7* (5), 353–367.

Hammond, K. R., Rohrbaugh, J., Mumpower, J., & Adelman, L. Social judgment theory: Applications in policy formulation. In M. F. Kaplan & S. Schwartz (Eds.), *Human Judgment and*

Decision Processes in Applied Settings. New York: Academic Press, 1977.

Hammond, K. R., Stewart, T. R., Brehmer, B., & Steinman, D. O. Social judgment theory. In M. Kaplan & S. Schwartz (Eds.), *Human Judgment and Decision Processes.* New York: Academic Press, 1975.

Hammond, K. R. & Summers, D. A. Cognitive control. *Psychological Review,* 1972, *79,* 58–67.

Hannan, M. T. & Freeman, J. The population ecology of organizations. *American Journal of Sociology,* 1977, *82,* 929–966.

Hansburger, R. V. Bob Hansburger shows how to grow without becoming a conglomerate. In J. McDonald, *Fortune,* October 1969.

Harris, R. J. & Monaco, G. E. Psychology of pragmatic implication: Information processing between the lines. *Journal of Experimental Psychology: General,* 1978, *107,* 1–22.

Hayek, F. A. Rules, perception, and intelligibility. *Proceedings of the Brookings Academy,* 1962, *48,* 321–344.

Hayes, J. R., & Flower, L. S. Identifying the organization of writing processes. In L. Gregg and E. Steinberg (Eds.), *Cognitive Processes in Writing.* Hillsdale, N.J.: Erlbaum, 1980.

Hedberg, B. L., Nystrom, P. C., & Starbuck, W. H. Camping on seesaws: Prescriptions for self-designing organizations. *Administrative Science Quarterly,* 1976, *21,* 41–65.

Heidbreder, E. The attainment of concepts. *Journal of General Psychology,* 1946, *35,* 173–189.

Held, R. & Freedman, S. J. Plasticity in human sensorimotor control. *Science,* 1963, *142,* 455–462.

Hellriegel, D. & Slocum, J. Preferred organizational designs and problem solving styles: Interesting companions. *Human Systems Management,* 1980, *1,* 151–158.

Hershey, J. C. & Schoemaker, P. J. H. Risk taking and problem context in the domain of losses: An expected utility analysis. *The Journal of Risk and Insurance,* 1980a, *47,* 111–132.

Hershey, J. C. & Schoemaker, P. J. H. Prospect theory's reflection hypothesis:

A critical examination. *Organization Behavior and Human Performance,* 1980b, *3,* 395–418.

Herzberg, F., Mausner, B., & Snyalerman, B. *The Motivation to Work.* New York: Wiley, 1959.

Hickson, D., Hinnings, C., Lee, C., Schneck, R., & Pennings, H. A strategic contingencies theory of intraorganizational power. *Administrative Science Quarterly,* 1971, *16,* 216–229.

Hilgard, E. R. *Divided Consciousness.* New York: Wiley, 1977.

Hills, F. S. & Mahoney, T. A. University budgets and organizational decision making. *Administrative Science Quarterly,* 1978, *23*(3), 464–465.

Hirsch, P. Organizational effectiveness and the institutional environment. *Administrative Science Quarterly,* 1975, *20,* 327–340.

Hirschleifer, J. & Riley, J. G. The analytics of uncertainty and information — An expository survey. *Journal of Economic Literature,* 1979, *17,* 1375–1421.

Hogarth, R. M. Cognitive processes and the assessment of subjective probability distributions. *Journal of the American Statistical Association,* 1975, *70* (350), 271–294.

Hogarth, R. M. *Beyond Static Biases: Functional and Dysfunctional Aspects of Judgmental Heuristics.* Center for Decision Research, University of Chicago Graduate School of Business, 1980a.

Hogarth, R. M. *Judgment and Choice: The Psychology of Decision.* Chichester, England: Wiley, 1980b.

Hogarth, R. M. Beyond discrete biases: Functional and dysfunctional aspects of judgmental heuristics. *Psychological Bulletin,* 1980c.

Howard, J. A. *Consumer Behavior: Application and Theory.* New York: McGraw-Hill, 1977.

Howard, J. A., Matheson, J. E., & Miller, K. L. (Eds.). *Readings in Decision Analysis.* Menlo Park, Calif.: Decision Analysis Group, Stanford Research Institute, 1976.

Howard, J. A. & Sheth, J. N. *The Theory of Buyer Behavior.* New York: Wiley, 1969.

Howell, W. C. & Burnett, S. A. Uncertainty measurement: A cognitive taxonomy. *Organizational Behavior and Human Performance*, 1978, 22, 45–68.

Hoyer, W. D. Contraceptive usage decision-making: An information processing approach. Unpublished masters thesis, Purdue University, 1979.

Hrebiniak, L. *Complex Organizations*. St. Paul, Minn.: West Publishing Co., 1978.

Huber, G. P. Multi-attribute utility models: A review of field and fieldlike studies. *Management Science*, 1974, 20,(10), 1393–1402.

Huber, G. P. Organizational information systems: Determinants of their performance and behavior. *Management Science*, 1982, 28, 138–155.

Hull, F. M. Diagnostic pathways in general practice. *Journal of the Royal College of General Practitioners*, 1972, 22, 241–258.

Humphreys, P. & McFadden, W. Experience with MAUD: Aiding decision structuring through reordering versus automating the composition rule. *Acta Psychologica*, 1980, 45, 51–69.

Hunsaker, P. Incongruity adaptation capability and risk preference in turbulent decision making environments. *Organizational Behavior and Human Performance*, 1975, 14, 173–185.

Hurst, E. (Ed.). Description of the Wharton ODA system. Department of Decision Sciences, Working Paper 77-11-02, The Wharton School, University of Pennsylvania, 1977.

Insurance Institute for Highway Safety. Consumer survey finds strong support for air bags. Status Report 15, August 6, 1980.

Jacoby, J. Consumer reaction to information displays: Packaging and advertising. In S. F. Divita (Ed.), *Advertising and the Public Interest*. Chicago: American Marketing Association, 1974a.

Jacoby, J. A proposal for research on amount, type, and order of package information acquisition in purchasing decisions. Grant proposal, National Science Foundation, 1974b.

Jacoby, J. Examining consumer information acquisition behavior via an emerging process methodology. Paper presented at Tilburg University, The Netherlands, 1975a.

Jacoby, J. Perspective on a consumer information processing research program. *Communication Research*, 1975b, 2, 203–215.

Jacoby, J. The emerging behavioral process technology in consumer decision making research. *Advances in Consumer Research*, 1977a, 4, 263–265.

Jacoby, J. Information load and decision quality: Some contested issues. *Journal of Marketing Research*, 1977b, 14, 569–573.

Jacoby, J. Third interim progress report (GI-43687). National Science Foundation, 1977c.

Jacoby, J. & Chestnut, R. W. Amount, type, and order of package information acquisition in purchasing decisions (GI-43687). National Science Foundation, 1977.

Jacoby, J. & Chestnut, R. W. The boundaries of decision. Working Paper, Purdue University, 1980.

Jacoby, J., Chestnut, R. W., & Fisher, W. Simulating nondurable purchase: Individual differences and information acquisition behavior. *Journal of Marketing Research*, 1978, 15, 532–544.

Jacoby, J., Chestnut, R. W., Hoyer, W., Sheluga, D. A., & Donahue, M. J. Psychometric characteristics of behavioral process data: Preliminary findings on validity and reliability. *Advances in Consumer Research*, 1978, 5, 546–554.

Jacoby, J., Chestnut, R. W., & Silberman, W. Consumer use and comprehension of nutrition information. *Journal of Consumer Research*, 1977, 4, 119–128.

Jacoby, J., Chestnut, R. W., Weigl, K. C., & Fisher, W. Pre-purchase information acquisition: Description of a process methodology, research paradigm, and pilot investigation. *Advances in Consumer Research,* 1976, 3, 306–314.

Jacoby, J. & Jaccard, J. J. Assessing the effects of science based on information on consumer technological choices. Grant PRA-7920585, National Science Foundation, 1981.

Jacoby, J., Kohn, C. A., & Speller, D. E. Time spent acquiring product information as a function of information load and organization. *Proceedings of the 81st Annual Convention of the American*

Psychological Association, 1973, *8,* 813–814.

Jacoby, J., Sheluga, D. A., Hoyer, W. D., & Chestnut, R. W. Information accessing behavior when information load varies: Two studies. Working paper, Purdue University, 1979.

Jacoby, J., Speller, D. E., & Berning, C. A. K. Brand choice behavior as a function of information load: Replication and extension. *Journal of Consumer Research,* 1974, *1,* 33–42.

Jacoby, J., Speller, D. E., & Berning, C. A. K. Constructive criticism and programmatic research: Reply to Russo. *Journal of Consumer Research,* 1975, *2,* 154–156.

Jacoby, J., Speller, D. E., & Kohn, C. A. Brand choice behavior as a function of information load. *Journal of Marketing Research,* 1974, *11,* 63–69.

Jacoby, J., Szybillo, G. J., & Busato-Schach, J. Information acquisition behavior in brand choice situations. *Journal of Consumer Research,* 1977, *3,* 209–216.

Janis, I. L. *Victims of Groupthink.* Boston: Houghton-Mifflin, 1972.

Janis, I. L. & Mann, L. *Decision-Making: A Psychological Analysis of Conflict, Choice and Commitment.* New York: The Free Press, 1977.

Jungerman, H. "Decisionectics": The art of helping people to make personal decisions. *Acta Psychologica,* 1980, *45,* 7–34.

Just, M. & Carpenter, P. A. *Cognitive Processes in Comprehension.* Hillsdale, N.J.: Erlbaum, 1977.

Kahneman, D. & Tversky, A. On the psychology of prediction. *Psychological Review,* 1973, *80,* 251–273.

Kahneman, D. & Tversky, A. Intuitive prediction: Biases and corrective procedures. *Management Science,* 1979a, *12,* 313–327.

Kahneman, D. & Tversky, A. Prospect theory: An analysis of decision under risk. *Econometrica,* 1979b, *47,* 263–291.

Kahneman, D. & Tversky, A. On the interpretation of intuitive probability. A reply to Jonathan Cohen. *Cognition,* 1979c, *7,* 409–411.

Kaplan, M. F. & Schwartz, S. *Human Judgment and Decision Processes in Applied Settings.* New York: Academic Press, 1977.

Karmarkar, U. S. Subjectively weighted utility: A descriptive extension of the expected utility model. *Organizational Behavior and Human Performance,* 1978, *21,* 61–72.

Karmarkar, U. S. Subjectively weighted utility and the Allais paradox. *Organizational Behavior and Human Performance,* 1979, *24,* 67–72.

Kassarjian, H. H. Presidential address, 1977: Anthropomorphism and parsimony. *Advances in Consumer Research,* 1978, *5,* xiii–xiv.

Kates, R. W. (Ed.). *Managing Technological Hazard: Research Needs and Opportunities.* Boulder, Colo.: University of Colorado Press, 1977.

Katz, N. & Miller, L. An interactive modeling system. Working paper 77-09-02, Department of Decision Sciences, The Wharton School, University of Pennsylvania, 1977.

Kay, N. M. *The Innovating Firm: A Behavioral Theory of Corporate R & D.* New York: St. Martin's, 1979.

Keen, P. G. W. & McKenney, J. L. The implication of cognitive style for implementation of analytic models. Sloan working paper 694, Massachusetts Institute of Technology, 1974.

Keen, P. G. W. & Scott Morton, M. *Decision Support Systems: An Organizational Perspective.* Reading, Mass.: Addison-Wesley, 1978.

Keeney, R. L. Concepts of independence in multiattribute utility theory. In J. L. Chochrane & M. Zeleny (Eds.), *Multiple Criteria Decision Making.* Missouri, S. C.: University of South Carolina Press, 1973.

Keeney, R. L. Examining corporate policy using multiattribute utility analysis. *Sloan Management Review,* 1975, *17*(1), 62–76.

Keeney, R. L. Analysis of preference dependencies among objectives. Working paper, Woodward-Clyde Consultants, 1980.

Keeney, R. L. & Raiffa, H. *Decisions with*

Multiple Objectives: Preferences and Value Tradeoffs. New York: Wiley, 1976.

Killeen, P. R. Superstition: A matter of bias, not detectability. *Science,* 1978, *199,* 88–90.

Kilmann, R. H. & Mitroff, I. I. Qualitative versus quantitative analysis for management science: Different forms for different psychological types. *Interfaces,* 1976, *6*(2), 17–27.

Kleindorfer, P. & Kunreuther, H. Stochastic horizons for the aggregate planning problem. *Management Science,* 1978, *24,* 485–497.

Kleindorfer, P. & Kunreuther, H. Descriptive and prescriptive aspects of health and safety regulation. In A. R. Ferguson & J. Behn (Eds.), *Benefits of Health and Safety Regulation.* N.Y.: Ballinger, 1981.

Kleinmuntz, B. The processing of clinical information by man and machine. In B. Kleinmuntz (Ed.), *Formal Representation of Human Judgment.* New York: Wiley, 1968.

Kleinmuntz, B. The computer as clinician. *American Psychologist,* 1975, *30,* 379–387.

Koestler, A. Literature and the law of diminishing returns. *Encounter,* 1970, *34*(5), 39–45.

Köhler, W. *The Mentality of Apes.* London: Routledge and Kegan Paul, 1925.

Kotler, P. *Marketing Management,* (4th ed.). Englewood Cliffs, N.J.: Prentice-Hall, 1980.

Krieger, S. *Hip Capitalism.* Beverly Hills, Calif.: Sage Publications, 1979.

Kubovy, M. Response availability and the apparent spontaneity of numerical choices. *Journal of Experimental Psychology: Human Perception and Performance,* 1977, *3,* 359–364.

Kuhn, T. S. *The Structure of Scientific Revolutions,* (2nd edition). Chicago, Illinois: University of Chicago Press, 1969.

Kunreuther, H. Extensions of Bowman's theory on managerial decision-making. *Management Science,* 1969, *15*(8), B415–B439.

Kunreuther, H. *Recovery from Natural Disasters: Insurance or Federal Aid.* Washington, D.C.: American Enterprise Institute, 1973.

Kunreuther, H. Limited knowledge and insurance protection. *Public Policy,* 1976, *24,* 227–261.

Kunreuther, H., Ginsberg, R., Miller, L., Sagi, P., Slovic, P., Borkan, B., & Katz, N. *Disaster Insurance Protection: Public Policy Lessons.* New York: Wiley, 1978a.

Kunreuther, H., Lepore, J., Miller, L., Vinso, J., Wilson, J., Borkan, B., Duffy, B., & Katz, N. *An Interactive Modeling System for Disaster Policy Analysis.* Boulder, Colo.: Institute of Behavioral Science, 1978b.

Kunreuther, H. & Pauly, M. Equilibrium in insurance markets with experience rating (mimeograph), 1980.

Landy, F. J. & Farr, J. L. Performance rating. *Psychological Bulletin,* 1980, *87*(1), 72–107.

Langer, E. Rethinking the role of thought in social interaction. In J. H. Harvey, W. J. Ickes, & R. F. Kidd (Eds.), *New Directions in Attribution Research.* Hillsdale, N.J.: Erlbaum, 1976.

Langer, E. The psychology of chance. *Journal of the Theory of Social Behavior,* 1977, *7,* 185–207.

Larkin, J. H. Problem solving in physics. Working paper, Carnegie-Mellon University, 1977.

Laughhunn, D. J., Payne, J. W., & Crum, R. Managerial risk preferences for below-target returns. *Management Science,* 1980, *26,* 1238–1249.

Leaper, D. J., Gill, P. W., Staniland, J. R., Horrocks, J. C., & DeDombal, F. T. Clinical diagnostic process: An analysis. *British Medical Journal,* 1973, *3,* 569–574.

Lehmann, D. R. & Moore, W. L. Validity of information display boards: An assessment using longitudinal data. *Journal of Marketing Research,* 1980, *17,* 450–459.

Leibenstein, H. *Beyond Economic Man.* Cambridge, Mass.: Harvard University Press, 1976.

Lerner, A. W. *The Politics of Organizational Decision Making: Strategy, Cooperation, and Conflict.* Beverly Hills, Calif.: Sage Publications, 1976.

Levine, M. E. & Plott, C. R. Agenda influence and its implications. *Virginia Law Review,* 1977, *63,* 561–604.

Levinthal, D. & March, J. G. A model of adaptive organizational search. Unpublished manuscript, 1981.

Lewin, A. Y. & Layman, S. S. Information processing models of peer nominations. *Personnel Psychology,* 1979, *32,* 63–82.

Lewin, A. Y. & Layman, S. S. Information processing models of leadership attribution. *Management Science,* 1982.

Lewontin, R. C. Sociobiology as an adaptationist program. *Behavioral Science,* 1979, *24,* 5–14.

Libby, R. & Fishburn, P. C. Behavioral models of risk-taking in business decisions. *Journal of Accounting Research,* 1977, *15,* 272–292.

Lichtenstein, S. & Fischhoff, B. Do those who know more also know more about how much they know? The calibration of probability judgments. *Organizational Behavior and Human Performance,* 1977, *20,* 159–183.

Lichtenstein, S. & Fischhoff, B. Training for calibration. *Organizational Behavior and Human Performance,* 1980, *26,* 149–171.

Lichtenstein, S., Fischhoff, B., & Phillips, L. D. Calibration of probabilities: The state of the art. In H. Jungermann & G. deZeeuw (Eds.), *Decision Making and Change in Human Affairs.* Dordrecht, Holland: Reidel, 1977.

Lindblom, C. *The Intelligence of Democracy.* New York: Macmillan, 1965.

Linnerooth, J. The value of human life: A review of the models. *Economic Inquiry,* 1979, *17,* 52–74.

Lodish, L. Sales territory alignment to maximize profit. *Journal of Marketing Research,* 1975a, *12,* 30–36.

Lodish, L. CALLPLAN: An interactive salesman's call planning system. *Management Science,* 1975b, *18,* 25–40.

Lodish, L. Assigning salesmen to accounts to maximize profit. *Journal of Marketing Research,* 1976, *13,* 440–444.

Lodish, L. & Fudge, W. Evaluation of the effectiveness of a model based salesman's planning system by field experimentation. *Interfaces,* 1977, *8,* 97–106.

Lopes, L. L. Doing the impossible: A note on induction and the experience of randomness. Working paper, Department of Psychology, University of Wisconsin at Madison, 1980.

Lopes, L. L. Decision making in the short run. *Journal of Experimental Psychology: Human Learning and Memory,* 1981, *7*(5), 377–385.

Luce, R. D. The choice axiom after twenty years. *Journal of Mathematical Psychology,* 1977, *15,* 215–233.

Lyles, M. A. & Mitroff, I. I. Organizational problem formulation: An empirical study. *Administrative Science Quarterly,* 1980, *25,* 102–119.

MacAvoy, P. (Ed.) *Federal-State Regulation of the Pricing and Marketing of Insurance.* Washington, D.C.: American Enterprise Institute, 1977.

MacCrimmon, K. R. Collective decision models. Paper presented at the British Psychological Society, Birmingham, England, 1976.

MacCrimmon, K. R. & Taylor, R. N. Decision making and problem solving. In M. D. Dunnette (Ed.), *Handbook of Industrial and Organizational Psychology.* Chicago: Rand McNally, 1976.

McKenney, J. & Keen, P. How managers' minds work. *Harvard Business Review,* 1974, *52,* 79–90.

Mackie, J. L. Causes and conditions. *American Philosophical Quarterly,* 1965, *2,* 245–264.

Mackworth, N. H. & Thomas, E. L. A head-mounted eye-marker camera. *Journal of the Optical Society of America,* 1962, *52,* 713–716.

Manes, A. *Insurance: Facts and Problems.* New York: Harper, 1938.

Marcel, T. Conscious and preconscious recognition of polysemous words; locating the selective effects of prior verbal context. In R. S. Nickerson (Ed.), *Attention and Performance* (Vol. VIII). Hillsdale, N.J.: Erlbaum, 1981.

March, J. C. & March, J. G. Performance sampling in social matches. *Administrative Science Quarterly,* 1978, *23,* 434–453.

March, J. G. The business firm as a political coalition. *Journal of Politics,* 1962, *24*(4), 662–678.

March, J. G. Bounded rationality, ambiguity, and the engineering of choice. *Bell Journal of Economics,* 1978, *9,* 587–608.

March, J. G. Footnotes to organizational change. *Administrative Science Quarterly*, 1981a, *26*, 563–577.

March, J. G. Decisions in organizations and theories of choice. In A. Van de Ven and W. Joyce (Eds.), *Assessing Organizational Design and Performance.* New York: Wiley, 1981b.

March, J. G. & Feldman, M. S. Information in organizations as signal and symbol. *Administrative Science Quarterly*, 1981, *26*, 171–186.

March, J. G. & Olsen, J. P. (Eds.) *Ambiguity and choice in organizations.* Bergen, Norway: Universitetsforlaget, 1976.

March, J. G. & Romelaer, P. Position and presence in the drift of decisions. In J. G. March and J. P. Olsen (Eds.), *Ambiguity and Choice in Organizations.* Bergen, Norway: Universitetsforlaget, 1976.

March, J. G. & Simon, H. A. *Organizations.* New York: Wiley, 1958.

Mason, R. O. & Mitroff, I. I. A program for research on management information systems. *Management Science*, 1973, *19*(4), 475–487.

Mechanic, D. Sources of power of lower participants in complex organizations. *Administrative Science Quarterly*, 1962, *7*(3), 349–364.

Michotte, A. *The Perception of Causality.* London: Methuen, 1963.

Miles, R. E. and Snow, C. C. *Organizational Strategy, Structure and Process.* New York: McGraw-Hill, 1978.

Mill, J. S. *Bentham.* (1838) Reprinted in *Mill on Bentham and Coleridge.* London: Chatoo and Windus, 1950.

Miller, N. E. Liberalization of basic S-R concepts: Extensions to conflict behavior, motivation, and social learning. In S. Koch (Ed.), *Psychology: A Study of a Science* (Vol. 2). New York: McGraw-Hill, 1959.

Mintzberg, H. *The Nature of Managerial Work.* New York: Harper & Row, 1973.

Mintzberg, H. Impediments to the use of management information. Paper presented at the National Association of Accountants, 1975a.

Mintzberg, H. The manager's job: Folklore and fact. *Harvard Business Review*, 1975b, *53*, 49–61.

Mintzberg, H. Policy as a field of management theory (1975). Working Paper, Université de Droit, Institut d'Administration des Enterprises, 1975c.

Mintzberg, H. Beyond implementation: An analysis of the resistance to policy analysis. In K. B. Haley (Ed.), *OR'78.* Amsterdam: North-Holland, 1979.

Mintzberg, H., Raisinghani, D., & Theoret, A. The structure of "unstructured" decision processes. *Administrative Science Quarterly*, 1976, *21*(2), 246–275.

Mischel, W. On the interface of cognition and personality: Beyond the person-situation debate. *American Psychologist*, 1979, *34*, 740–754.

Mitroff, I. I., Barabba, V. P., & Kilman, R. H. The application of behavioral and philosophical technologies to strategic planning. *Management Science*, 1977, *24*(1), 44–58.

Mitroff, I. I. & Emshoff, J. R. On strategic assumption making: A dialectical approach to policy and planning. *Academy of Management Review*, 1979, *4*, 1–12.

Mitroff, I. & Kilmann, R. Stories managers tell: A new tool for organizational problem solving. *Management Review*, 1975, *64*, 18–28.

Mobley, W. H. & Meglino, B. M. A behavioral choice model analysis of the budget allocation behavior of academic deans. *Academy of Management Journal*, 1977, *20*(4), 564–572.

Moch, M. K. & Pondy, L. R. The structure of chaos: Organized anarchy as a response to ambiguity. *Administrative Science Quarterly*, 1977, *22*(2), 351.

Mowrey, J. D., Doherty, M. E., & Keeley, S. M. The influence of negation and task complexity on illusory correlation. *Journal of Abnormal Psychology*, 1979, *88*, 334–337.

Mynatt, C. R., Doherty, M. E., & Tweney, R. D. Confirmation bias in a simulated research environment: An experimental study of scientific inference. *Quarterly Journal of Experimental Psychology*, 1977, *29*, 85–95.

Mynatt, C. R., Doherty, M. E., & Tweney, R. D. Consequences of confirmation and disconfirmation in a simulated research environment. *Quarterly Journal of Experimental Psychology*, 1978, *30*, 395–406.

Nagel, E. & Newman, J. R. *Gödel's proof*. New York: New York University Press, 1958.

Naylor, J. C., Pritchard, R. D., & Ilgen, D. R. *A Theory of Behavior in Organizations*. New York: Academic Press, 1980.

Neches, R. Personal communication to John R. Hayes, 1978.

Neimark, E. D. & Santa, J. C. Thinking and concept attainment. *Annual Review of Psychology*, 1975, *26*, 173–205.

Neisser, U. The multiplicity of thought. *British Journal of Psychology*, 1963, *54*, 1–14.

Nelson, R. R. & Winter, S. G. An evolutionary theory of economic capabilities and behavior. Unpublished manuscript, 1981.

Newell, A., Shaw, J. C., & Simon, H. A. Elements of a theory of human problem solving. *Psychological Review*, 1958, *65*, 151–166.

Newell, A. & Simon, H. A. *Human Problem Solving*. Englewood Cliffs, N.J.: Prentice-Hall, 1972.

Nisbett, R., Borgida, E., Crandall, R., & Reed, H. Popular induction: Information is not necessarily informative. In J. S. Carroll & J. W. Payne (Eds.), *Cognition and Social Behavior*, Hillsdale, N.J.: Erlbaum, 1976.

Nisbett, R. & Ross, L. *Human Inferences: Strategies and Shortcomings of Social Judgment*. Englewood Cliffs, N.J.: Prentice-Hall, 1980.

Nisbett, R. & Wilson, T. D. Telling more than we can know: Verbal reports on mental processes. *Psychological Review*, 1977, *84*, 231–259.

O'Connell, M., Cummings, L., & Huber, G. The effects of environmental information and decision unit structure on felt tension. *Journal of Applied Psychology*, 1976, *61*, 493–500.

Olson, C. L. Some apparent violations of the representativeness heuristic in human judgment. *Journal of Experimental Psychology: Human Perception and Performance*, 1976, *2*, 599–608.

Padgett, J. F. Bounded rationality in budgetary research. *American Political Science Review*, 1980a, *74*, 354–372.

Padgett, J. F. Managing garbage can hierarchies. *Administrative Science Quarterly*, 1980b, *25*, 583-604.

Parsons, T. *Structure and Process in Modern Society*. Glencoe, Ill.: The Free Press, 1960.

Pauly, M. Over insurance and public provision of insurance: The roles of moral hazard and adverse selection. *Quarterly Journal of Economics*, 1974, *88*, 44–62.

Payne, J. W. Task complexity and contingent processing in decision making: An information search and protocol analysis. *Organizational Behavior and Human Performance*, 1976, *26*, 102–115.

Payne, J. W., & Braunstein, M. L. Contingent processing in risky choice: A process tracing investigation. Working Paper, University of Chicago, 1977.

Payne, J. W., Braunstein, M. L., & Carroll, J. S. Exploring predecisional behavior: An alternative approach to decision research. *Organizational Behavior and Human Performance*, 1978, *22*, 17–44.

Payne, J. W., Laughhunn, D. J., & Crum, R. *Levels of Aspiration and Preference Reversals in Risky Choice*. Duke University Graduate School of Business, 1979.

Payne, J. W., Laughhunn, D. J., & Crum, R. Translation of gambles and aspiration level effects in risky choice behavior. *Management Science*, 1980, *26*, 1039–1060.

Pearson, K. On the scientific measure of variability. *National Scientist*, 1897, *11*, 115–118.

Perrow, C. A framework for the comparative analyses of organizations. *American Sociological Review*, 1967, *32*, 194–208.

Perrow, C. *Complex Organizations, A Critical Essay* (2nd ed.). Glenview, Ill.: Scott, Foresman, 1972.

Peters, J. T. Symbols, patterns, and settings: An optimistic case for getting things done. *Organizational Dynamics*, Autumn 1978, 3–23.

Peters, J. T., Hammond, K. R., & Summers, D. A. A note on intuitive vs. analytic thinking. *Organizational Behavior and Human Performance*, 1974, *17*, 125–131.

Pettigrew, A. M. Information control as a power resource. *Sociology,* 1972, *6*(2), 187–204.

Pettigrew, A. M. *The politics of organizational decision-making.* London: Tavistock, 1973.

Pfeffer, J. Management as symbolic action: The creation and maintenance of organizational paradigms. In L. L. Cummings & B. M. Staw (Eds.), *Research in Organizational Behavior* (Vol. 3). Greenwich, Conn.: JAI Press, 1981a.

Pfeffer, J. *Power in Organizations.* Marshfield, Mass.: Pitman Publishing, 1981b.

Pfeffer, J. Organizations and organization theory. In G. Lindzey and E. Aronson (Eds.), *Handbook of Social Psychology,* 3rd ed. Reading, Mass.: Addison-Wesley, 1981c.

Pfeffer, J. & Salancik, G. R. *The External Control of Organizations.* New York: Harper & Row, 1978.

Pfeffer, J., Salancik, G. R., & Leblebici, H. The effect of uncertainty on the use of social influence in organizational decision making. *Administrative Science Quarterly,* 1976, *21*(2), 227–245.

Phelps, R. H. & Shanteau, J. Livestock judges: How much information can an expert use? *Organizational Behavior and Human Performance,* 1978, *21,* 209–219.

Phillips, L. D. Organization structure and decision technology. *Acta Psychologica,* 1980, *45,* 247–264.

Plott, C. R. Axiomatic social choice theory: An overview and interpretation. *American Journal of Political Science,* 1976, *20,* 511–596.

Plott, C. R. & Levine, M. E. A model of agenda influence on committee decisions. *American Economic Review,* 1978, *68,* 146–160.

Polya, G. Heuristic reasoning and the theory of probability. *American Mathematical Monthly,* 1941, *48,* 450–465.

Polya, G. *Patterns of Plausible Inference* (Vol. II). Princeton: Princeton University Press, 1954.

Pondy, L. R. & Mitroff, I. I. Beyond open systems models of organizations. In B. Staw (Ed.), *Research in Organizational Behavior* (Vol. I). Greenwich, Conn.: JAI Press, 1979.

Pople, H. E. The formation of composite hypotheses in diagnostic problem solving; an exercise in synthetic reasoning. *Proceedings of the Fifth International Joint Conference on Artificial Intelligence,* 1977.

Popper, K. R. *The Logic of Scientific Discovery.* London: Hutchinson, 1959.

Posner, M. I. Orienting of attention. The VIIth Sir Frederic Bartlett Lecture. *Quarterly Journal of Experimental Psychology,* 1980, *32,* 3–25.

Pounds, W. F. The process of problem finding. *Industrial Management Review,* Fall 1969, 1–19.

Powers, W. T. Feedback: Beyond behaviorism. *Science,* 1973, *179,* 352–356.

Preston, J. C., Moore, D. E., & Cornick, T. Community response to the flood disaster act of 1973. *Ithaca: Community and Resource Development Series,* Bulletin 10, 1975.

Rachlin, H. & Burkhard, B. The temporal triangle: Response substitution in instrumental conditioning. *Psychological Review,* 1978, *85,* 22–47.

Radner, R. Satisficing. *Journal of Mathematical Economics,* 1975, *2,* 253–262.

Rados, D. L. Selection and evaluation of alternatives in repetitive decision making. *Administrative Science Quarterly,* 1972, *17,* 196-206.

Raffee, H., Jacoby, J., Hefner, M., Scholer, M., & Grabicke, K. Informationsentscheidungen bei unterschiedlichen entscheidungsobjekten. In H. Meffert, H. Steffenhager, & H. Freter (Eds.), *Konsumentenverhalten und information.* Wiesbaden: Gabler Verlag, 1979.

Raphael, B. *The Thinking Computer.* San Francisco: Freeman, 1976.

Rapoport, A. & Wallsten, T. S. Individual decision behavior. *Annual Review of Psychology,* 1972, *23,* 131–175.

Rappoport, L. & Summers, D. A. (Eds.). *Human Judgment and Social Interaction.* New York: Holt, Rinehart and Winston, 1973.

Reitman, W. R. Heuristic decision procedures, open constraints, and the structure of ill-defined problems. In M. Shelly and G. Bryan (Eds.), *Human Judgment and Optimality.* New York: Wiley, 1964.

Rimoldi, H. J. A. The test of diagnostic skills. *Journal of Medical Education*, 1961, *36*, 73–79.

Rogers, E. & Shoemaker, F. F. *Communication of Innovations*. New York: The Free Press, 1971.

Rokeach, M. *The Open and Closed Mind*. New York: Basic Books, 1960.

Rosch, E. R. & Lloyd, B. B. *Cognition and Categorization*. Hillsdale, N.J.: Erlbaum, 1978.

Rosen, S. & Tesser, A. On reluctance to communicate undesirable information: The MUM effect. *Sociometry*, 1970, *33*, 253–263.

Ross, L. & Lepper, M. The perseverance of beliefs: Empirical and normative considerations. In R. A. Shweder (Ed.), *Fallible judgment in behavioral research. New Directions for Methodology of Social and Behavioral Science*, 1980, *4*, 17–36.

Rothbart, M. Memory processes and social beliefs. In D. Hamilton (Ed.), *Cognitive Processes in Stereotyping and Intergroup Perception*. Hillsdale, N.J.: Erlbaum, 1980.

Rothschild, M. & Stiglitz, J. Equilibrium in competitive insurance markets: An essay in the economics of imperfect information. *Quarterly Journal of Economics*, 1976, *90*, 629–649.

Russell, B. *Human Knowledge: Its Scope and Limits*. New York: Simon & Schuster, 1948.

Russo, J. E. More information is better: A reevaluation of Jacoby, Speller, and Kohn. *Journal of Consumer Research*, 1974, *1*, 68–72.

Russo, J. E. The value of unit price information. *Journal of Marketing Research*, 1977, *14*, 193–201.

Russo, J. E. Comments on behavioral and economic approaches to studying market behavior. In A. A. Mitchell (Ed.), *The Effect of Information on Consumer and Market Behavior*. Chicago: American Marketing Association, 1978a.

Russo, J. E. Eye fixations can save the world: A critical evaluation and a comparison between eye fixations and other information processing methodologies. *Advances in Consumer Research*, 1978b, *5*, 561–570.

Russo, J. E. & Rosen, L. D. An eye fixation analysis of multialternative choice. *Memory and Cognition*, 1975, *3*, 267–276.

Saaty, T. L. Modeling unstructured decision problems: The theory of analytic hierarchies. *Mathematics and Computers in Simulations* XX. Amsterdam: North-Holland, 1978.

Sackett, G. P. *Observing Behavior*. Baltimore: University Park Press, 1978.

Sagan, C. *The Dragons of Eden*. New York: Random House, 1977.

Samuelson, P. A. *Economics, an Introductory Analysis*. New York: McGraw-Hill, 1948.

Sapolsky, H. *The Polaris System Development*. Cambridge, Mass.: Harvard University Press, 1972.

Savage, L. J. *The Foundations of Statistics*. New York: Wiley, 1954.

Schaeffer, G. *A Mathematical Theory of Evidence*. Princeton, N.J.: Princeton University Press, 1976.

Schaninger, C. M. & Sciglimpaglia, D. The identification of specific information acquisition patterns in information display board tasks, and their relation to demographics. *Advances in Consumer Research*, 1980, *7*, 513–518.

Schelling, T. C. *Micromotives and Macrobehavior*. New York: Norton, 1978.

Schmidt, S. M. & Kochan, T. A. Conflict: Toward conceptual clarity. *Administrative Science Quarterly*, 1972, *17*(3), 359–370.

Schmitt, N. & Levine, R. L. Statistical and subjective weights: Some problems and proposals. *Organization Behavior and Human Performance*, 1977, *20*, 15–30.

Schneider, W. & Shiffrin, R. M. Controlled and automatic human information processing: I. Detection, search and attention. *Psychological Review*, 1977, *84*, 1–66.

Schoemaker, P. J. H. *Experiments on decisions under risk: The expected utility hypothesis*. Boston: Martinus Nijhoff, 1980a.

Schoemaker, P. J. H. Strategic behavior: Its meaning and determinants. Working paper, Center for Decision Research, University of Chicago Graduate School of Business, 1980b.

Schoemaker, P. J. H. & Kunreuther, H. An experimental study of insurance decisions. *The Journal of Risk and Insurance,* 1979, *46*(4), 603–618.

Schum, D. A. A review of a case against Blaise Pascal and his heirs. *University of Michigan Law Review,* 1979, *77*, 446–483.

Schum, D. A. Current developments in research on cascaded inference processes. In T. S. Wallsten (Ed.), *Cognitive Processes in Choice and Decision Behavior.* Hillsdale, N.J.: Erlbaum, 1980.

Scott, W. R. *Organizations: Rational, Natural and Open Systems.* Englewood Cliffs, N.J.: Prentice-Hall, 1981.

Seligman, M. E. P. On the generality of the laws of learning. *Psychological Review,* 1970, *77*, 406–418.

Shanker, R., Turner, R., & Zoltners, A. Sales territory design: An integrated approach. *Management Science,* 1975, 22, 309–320.

Shanteau, J. & Nagy, G. F. Probability of acceptance in dating choice. *Journal of Personnel and Social Psychology,* 1979, *37*, 522–523.

Shapero, A. What MANAGEMENT says and what managers do. *Interfaces,* February 1977, 106–108.

Shapira, Z. Making tradeoffs between job attributes. *Organizational Behavior and Human Performance,* in press, 1982.

Shavell, S. On moral hazard and insurance. *Quarterly Journal of Economics,* 1979, *92*, 540–562.

Sheluga, D. A. The relationship of product preference, information search, and choice. Unpublished masters thesis, Purdue University, 1978.

Sheluga, D. A., Jaccard, J. J., & Jacoby, J. Process-descriptive methods and the estimation of preference: An integrative approach. *Journal of Consumer Research,* 1979, *6*, 166–176.

Sheluga, D. A. & Jacoby, J. Do comparative claims encourage comparison shopping? — The impact of comparative claims on consumer's acquisition of product information. *Current Issues and Research in Advertising,* 1978, *1*, 23–28.

Shepard, R. N. On subjectively optimum selections among multi-attribute alternatives. In M. W. Shelly & G. L. Bryan (Eds.), *Human Judgments and Optimality.* New York: Wiley, 1964.

Sheridan, J., Slocum, J., & Richards, M. A comparative analysis of expectancy and heuristic models of decision behavior. *Journal of Applied Psychology,* 1975, *60*, 361–368.

Shugan, S. M. The cost of thinking. *Journal of Consumer Research,* 1980, *7*, 99–111.

Shumway, C. R., Maher, P. M., Baker, M. R., Souder, W. E., Rubenstein, A. H., & Gallant, A. R. Diffuse decision-making in hierarchical organizations: An empirical examination. *Management Science,* 1975, *21*(6), 697–707.

Shweder, R. A. Likeness and likelihood in everyday thought: Magical thinking in judgments about personality. *Current Anthropology,* 1977, *18*, 637–658.

Simon, D. P. & Simon, H. A. Individual differences in solving physics problems. Working paper 342, Carnegie-Mellon University, 1977.

Simon, H. A. *Administrative Behavior.* New York: Macmillan, 1947.

Simon, H. A. A behavioral model of rational choice. *Quarterly Journal of Economics,* 1955, *59*, 99–118.

Simon, H. A. Rational choice and the structure of the environment. *Psychological Review,* 1956, *63*, 129–138.

Simon, H. A. *Models of Man.* New York: Wiley, 1957.

Simon, H. A. Theories of decision making in economics and behavioral science. *The American Economic Review,* 1959, *49*, 253–283.

Simon, H. A. The architecture of complexity. *Proceedings of the American Philosophical Society,* 1962, *106*, 467–482.

Simon, H. A. *The Shape of Automation for Men and Management.* New York: Harper & Row, 1965.

Simon, H. A. *The Sciences of the Artificial.* Cambridge, Mass.: M.I.T. Press, 1969.

Simon, H. A. Applying information technology to organization design. *Public Administration Review,* May/June 1973, 268–278.

Simon, H. A. How big is a chunk? *Science,* 1974, *183*, 482–488.

Simon, H. A. *Administrative Behavior: A Study of Decision-Making Processes in Administrative Organizations* (3rd ed.). New York: The Free Press, 1976.

Simon, H. A. Rationality as process and as product of thought. *The American Economic Review,* 1978a, *68,* 1–16.

Simon, H. A. On how to decide what to do. *The Bell Journal of Economics,* 1978b, *9,* 494–507.

Simon, H. A. Information-processing theory of human problem solving. In W. K. Estes (Ed.), *Handbook of Learning and Cognitive Processes.* Hillsdale, N.J.: Erlbaum, 1978c.

Simon, H. A. Information processing models of cognition. *Annual Review of Psychology,* 1979a, *30,* 363–396.

Simon, H. A. Rational decision making in business organizations. *American Economic Review,* 1979b, *64*(4), 493–513.

Simon, H. A. & Barenfeld, M. Information-processing analysis of perceptual processes in problem solving. *Psychological Review,* 1969, *76,* 473–483.

Simon, H. A. & Hayes, J. R. Understanding complex task instructions. In D. Klahr (Ed.), *Cognition and Instruction.* Hillsdale, N.J.: Erlbaum, 1976a.

Simon, H. A. & Hayes, J. R. The understanding process: Problem isomorphs. *Cognitive Psychology,* 1976b, *8,* 165–190.

Skinner, B. F. "Superstition" in the pigeon. *Journal of Experimental Psychology,* 1948, *38,* 168–172.

Skinner, B. F. The phylogeny and ontogeny of behavior. *Science,* 1966, *153,* 1205–1213.

Slovic, P. Information processing, situation specificity, and the generality of risk-taking behavior. *Journal of Personality and Social Psychology,* 1972, *22,* 128–134.

Slovic, P. The psychology of protective behavior. *Journal of Safety Research,* 1978, *10,* 58–68.

Slovic, P. & Fischhoff, B. On the psychology of experimental surprises. *Journal of Experimental Psychology: Human Perception and Performance,* 1977, *3,* 544–551.

Slovic, P., Fischhoff, B., & Lichtenstein, S. Behavioral decision theory. *Annual Review of Psychology,* 1977, *28,* 1–39.

Slovic, P., Fischhoff, B., Lichtenstein, S., Corrigan, B., & Combs, B. Preferences for insuring against probable small losses: Insurance implications. *The Journal of Risk and Insurance,* 1977, *44,* 237.

Slovic, P., Fleissner, D., & Bauman, W. S. Analyzing the use of information in investment decision making: A methodological proposal. *Journal of Business,* 1972, *45,* 283–301.

Slovic, P., Kunreuther, H., & White, G. F. Decision processes, rationality and adjustment to natural hazards. In G. F. White (Ed.), *Natural Hazards, Local, National, and Global.* New York: Oxford University Press, 1974.

Slovic, P. & Lichtenstein, S. Comparison of Bayesian and regression approaches to the study of information processing in judgment. *Organizational Behavior and Human Performance,* 1971, *6,* 649–744.

Slovic, P. & MacPhillamy, D. J. Dimensional commensurability and cue utilization in comparative judgment. *Organizational Behavior and Human Performance,* 1974, *11,* 172–194.

Slovic, P. & Tversky, A. Who accepts Savage's axiom? *Behavioral Science,* 1974, *19,* 368–373.

Smart, C. & Vertinsky, I. Designs for crisis decision units. *Administrative Science Quarterly,* 1977, *22*(4), 640–657.

Smith, E. R. & Miller, F. D. Limits on perception of cognitive processes: A reply to Nisbett and Wilson. *Psychological Review,* 1978, *85,* 355–362.

Smith, R. D. Heuristic simulation of psychological decision processes. *Journal of Applied Psychology,* 1968, *52*(4), 325–330.

Smith, R. D. & Greenlaw, P. S. Simulation of a psychological decision process in personnel selection. *Management Science,* 1967, *18,* B-409–419.

Smullyan, R. *This Book Needs No Title.* Englewood Cliffs, N.J.: Prentice-Hall, 1980.

Snyder, R. C. & Paige, G. D. The U.S. decision to resist aggression in Korea: The application of an analytical scheme. *Administrative Science Quarterly,* December 1958, 343–378.

Spence, M. Product differentiation and consumer choice in insurance markets.

Journal of Public Economics, 1978, *10,* 427–447.

Sprague, R. H., Jr. A framework for research on decision support systems. In G. Fick & R. H. Sprague, Jr. (Eds.), *Decision Support Systems: Issues and Challenges.* Oxford, England: Pergamon Press, 1981.

Sproull, L., Weiner, S., & Wolf, D. *Organizing an Anarchy.* Chicago: University of Chicago Press, 1978.

Staddon, J. E. R. & Motheral, S. On matching and maximizing in operant choice experiments. *Psychological Review,* 1978, *78,* 436–444.

Staddon, J. E. R. & Simmelhag, V. L. The "superstitious" experiment: A reexamination of its implications for the principles of adaptive behavior. *Psychological Review,* 1971, *78,* 3–43.

Stanford Research Institute. *The Role of Risk Classifications in Property and Casualty Insurance: A Study of the Risk Assessment Process.* Menlo Park, Calif.: Stanford Research Institute, 1976.

Starbuck, W. H. & Hedberg, B. L. T. Saving an organization from a stagnating environment. Unpublished manuscript, University of Wisconsin School of Business Administration, 1976.

Staw, B. Rationality and justification in organizational life. In B. M. Staw & L. L. Cummings (Eds.), *Research in Organizational Behavior* (Vol. 2). Greenwich, Conn.: JAI Press, 1980a.

Staw, B. Rationality in organizations. In B. Staw & L. Cummings (Eds.), *Research in Organizational Behavior* (Vol. 2). Greenwich, Conn.: JAI Press, 1980b.

Staw, B. & Ross, J. Commitment to a policy decision: A multi-theoretical perspective. *Administrative Science Quarterly,* 1978, *23,* 40–64.

Steckroth, R., Slocum, J., & Sims, H. Organizational roles, cognitive roles, and problem-solving styles. *Journal of Experimental Learning and Simulation,* 1980, *2,* 77–87.

Steinbruner, J. D. *The Cybernetiheory of Decision.* Princeton: Princeton University Press, 1974.

Summers, J. O. Less information is better? *Journal of Marketing Research,* 1974, *11,* 467–468.

Suppes, P. Probabilistic inference and the concept of total evidence. In J. Hintikka & P. Suppes (Eds.), *Aspects of Inductive Logic.* Amsterdam: North-Holland, 1966.

Svenson, O. Process descriptions of decision making. *Organizational Behavior and Human Performance,* 1979, *23,* 86–112.

Taylor, R. N. & Benbasat, I. A critique of cognitive styles theory and research. *Proceedings of the First International Conference on Information Systems,* Philadelphia, 1980.

Thaler, R. Toward a positive theory of consumer choice. *Journal of Economic Behavioral Organization,* 1980, *1,* 39–60.

Thaler, R. & Shiffrin, H. M. *An Economic Theory of Self-Control.* Cornell University Graduate School of Business, 1980.

Thompson, J. D. *Organizations in Action.* New York: McGraw-Hill, 1967.

Thorngate, W. Must we always think before we act? *Personality and Social Psychology Bulletin,* 1976a, *2,* 31–35.

Thorngate, W. "In general" vs. "it depends"; some comments on the Gergen–Schlenker debate. *Personality and Social Psychology Bulletin,* 1976b, *2,* 404–410.

Thorngate, W. Efficient decision heuristics. *Behavioral Science,* 1980, *25,* 219–225.

Tichomirov, O. K. & Poznyanskaya, E. D. An investigation of visual search as a means of analyzing heuristics. *Soviet Psychology,* 1966, *5,* 2–15.

Toda, M. The design of a fungus-eater: A model of human behavior in an unsophisticated environment. *Behavioral Science,* 1962, *7,* 164–183.

Toda, M. What happens at the moment of decision? Meta decision, emotions and volitions. In L. Sjöberg, T. Tyszka, & J. A. Wise (Eds.), *Human Decision Making* (Vol. 11). Bodafors, Sweden: Doxa, 1980a.

Toda, M. Emotion and decision making. *Acta Psychologica,* 1980b, *45,* 133–155.

Toffler, A. *The Third Wave.* New York: Bantam, 1980.

Tribe, L. H. Technology assessment and the fourth discontinuity: The limits of instrumental rationality. *Southern California Law Review,* 1973, *46,* 617–660.

Tuggle, F. D. & Gerwin, D. An information processing model of organizational perception, strategy, and choice. *Management Science,* 1980, 26, 575–592.

Turoff, M. Delphi conferencing: Computer-based conferencing with anonymity. *Technological Forecasting and Social Change,* 1972, 3, 159–204.

Tversky, A. Intransitivity of preferences. *Psychological Review,* 1969, 76, 31–48.

Tversky, A. Elimination by aspects: A theory of choice. *Psychological Review,* 1972, 79, 281–299.

Tversky, A. Features of similarity. *Psychological Review,* 1977, 84, 327–352.

Tversky, A. & Kahneman, D. Availability: A heuristic for judging frequency and probability. *Cognitive Psychology,* 1973, 4, 207–232.

Tversky, A. & Kahneman, D. Judgment under uncertainty: Heuristics and biases. *Science,* 1974, 185, 1124–1131.

Tversky, A. & Kahneman, D. Causal schemata in judgments under uncertainty. In M. Fishbein (Ed.), *Progress in Social Psychology.* Hillsdale, N.J.: Erlbaum, 1980a.

Tversky, A. & Kahneman, D. The framing of decisions and the rationality of choice. *Science,* in press, 1980b.

Tversky, A., & Kahneman, D. The framing of decisions and the psychology of choice. *Science,* 1981, 211, 453–458.

Tversky, A. & Sattath, S. Preference trees. *Psychological Review,* 1979, 86, 542–573.

Tweney, R. D., Doherty, M. E., Worner, W. J., Pliske, D. B., Mynatt, C. R., Gross, K. A., & Arkkelin, D. L. Strategies of rule discovery in an inference task. *Quarterly Journal of Experimental Psychology,* 1980, 32, 109–123.

Ungson, G., Braunstein, D., & Hall, P. Managerial information processing: A research review. *Administrative Science Quarterly,* 1981, 26, 116–134.

Van de Ven, A. H. A framework of organizational assessment. *Academy of Management Review,* 1976, 1, 64–78.

Van de Ven, A. H. & Ferry, D. *Measuring and Assessing Organizations.* New York: Wiley, 1980.

Van Raaij, W. F. Direct monitoring of consumer information processing by eye movement recorders. Working paper, Tilburg University, The Netherlands, 1976.

Vlek, C. & Stallen, P. Rational and personal aspects of risk. *Acta Psychologica,* 1980, 45, 273–300.

Von Neumann, J. & Morgenstern, O. *Theory of Games and Economic Behavior.* Princeton: Princeton University Press, 1947.

Wallsten, T. S. Processes and models to describe choice and inference. In T. S. Wallsten (Ed.), *Cognitive Processes in Choice and Decision Behavior.* Hillsdale, N.J.: Erlbaum, 1980.

Walton, R. E., Dutton, J. M., & Cafferty, T. P. Organizational context and interdepartmental conflict. *Administrative Science Quarterly,* 1969, 14(4), 522–543.

Wason, P. C. & Joynson-Laird, P. N. *Psychology of Reasoning: Structure and Content.* London: Batsford, 1972.

Weber, C. E. Intraorganizational decision processes influencing the EDP staff budget. *Management Science,* 1965, 12(4), 1369–1393.

Weick, K. E. *The Social Psychology of Organizing.* Reading, Mass.: Addison-Wesley, 1969.

Weick, K. E. Enactment processes in organizations. In B. M. Staw & G. R. Salancik (Eds.), *New Directions in Organizational Behavior.* Chicago: St. Clair, 1977.

Weick, K. E. *The Social Psychology of Organizing* (2nd ed.). Reading, Mass.: Addison-Wesley, 1979.

Weick, K. E. Systematic observational methods. In G. Lindzey & E. Aronson (Eds.), *Handbook of Social Psychology* (3rd ed.). Reading, Mass.: Addison-Wesley, 1980.

Weizkrantz, L. Trying to bridge some neuropsychological gaps between monkey and man. *British Journal of Psychology,* 1977, 68, 431–445.

White, G. F. *Choice of Adjustment to Floods.* Chicago: University of Chicago Press, 1964.

Wickelgren, W. A. Chunking and consolidation: A theoretical synthesis of semantic networks, configuring in conditioning, S-R versus cognitive learning, normal forgetting, the amnesic syndrome, and the hippocampal arousal system. *Psychological Review,* 1979, *86,* 44–60.

Wilkie, W. L. The information display board research technique. *Journal of Consumer Policy,* 1979, *3,* 246–251.

Williamson, O. *Markets and Hierarchies.* New York: The Free Press, 1975.

Wilson, E. O. *On Human Nature.* Cambridge, Mass.: Harvard University Press, 1978.

Wimsatt, W. C. Reductionist research strategies and their biases in the units of selection controversy. In T. Nickles (Ed.), *Scientific Discovery* (Vol. II). Dordrecht, Holland: Reidel, 1980.

Winikoff, A. Eye movements as an aid to protocol analysis in problem solving. Unpublished doctoral dissertation, Carnegie-Mellon University, 1966.

Winter, S. G. Satisficing, selection and the innovating remnant. *Quarterly Journal of Economics,* 1971, *85,* 237–261.

Winter, S. G. Optimization and evolution in the theory of the firm. In R. H. Day & T. Groves (Eds.), *Adaptive Economic Models.* New York: Academic Press, 1975.

Woods, D. H. Improving estimates that involve uncertainty. *Harvard Business Review,* 1966, *44,* 91–98.

Wortman, P. M. Medical diagnosis: An information processing approach. *Computers and Biomedical Research,* 1972, *5,* 315–328.

Wright, P. L. Research orientations for analysing consumer judgment processes. *Advances in Consumer Research,* 1974, *1,* 268–279.

Wright, P. L. Consumer choice strategies: Simplifying vs. optimizing. *Journal of Marketing Research,* 1975, *12,* 60–67.

Yates, J. F. & Zukowski, L. G. Characterization of ambiguity in decision making. *Behavioral Science,* 1976, *21,* 19–25.

Zieve, L. Misinterpretation and abuse of laboratory tests by clinicians. *Annals of the New York Academy of Sciences,* 1966, *134,* 563–572.

Zimbardo, P. G. *The Cognitive Control of Motivation.* Glenview, Ill.: Scott, Foresman, 1969.

Zoltners, A. Integer programming models for sales territory alignment to maximize profit. *Journal of Marketing Research,* 1976, *13,* 426–430.

About the Authors

MARINUS J. BOUWMAN ("The Use of Accounting Information: Expert Versus Novice Behavior" (pp. 134–167)) is an Assistant Professor of Accounting at the University of Oregon, Eugene, OR 97403. His current interests include the uses of accounting information and financial decision-making processes. Two current working papers include "The Use of Accounting Information: Expert Versus Novice Behavior," and "Computer Simulation of Human Decision Making in Accounting: The Analysis of Financial Statements." He received his Ph.D. from Carnegie-Mellon University.

ROBERT W. CHESTNUT (coauthor, "Behavioral Process Research: Concept and Application in Consumer Decision Making" (pp. 232–248)) is a Visiting Professor of Psychology, Tilburg University, The Netherlands. He is on leave (1981–1982) from the Columbia University Graduate School of Business, New York, NY 10027. His current research interests include persuasion and comprehension processes in complex decision environments, and cognitive style and information processing. Recent publications are "Persuasive Effects in Marketing," *Persuasion*, 1980; "Product Comprehension: The Case of Permanent vs. Term Life Insurance," *Advances in Consumer Research*, 1980. He received his Ph.D. from the Department of Psychological Sciences, Purdue University.

TERRY CONNOLLY ("On Taking Action Seriously: Cognitive Fixation in Behavioral Decision Theory" (pp. 42–47)) is an Associate Professor at the School of Industrial and Systems Engineering, and at the College of Management, Georgia Institute of Technology, Atlanta, GA 30332. His current research interests include information-processing/decision-making interface, and organizational decision-making and public-policy decisions. His work has been in *Academy of Management Proceedings, Academy of Management Review, Sociology of the Sciences Yearbook, Decision Sciences*, and others. He received his Ph.D. from Northwestern University.

LARRY CUMMINGS ("A Framework for Decision Analysis and Critique" (pp. 298–308)) was a Slichter Research Professor at the University of Wisconsin Graduate School of Business, Madison, WI 53706 until September 1981, when he became a J. L. Kellogg Distinguished Research Professor of Organizational Behavior at the Kellogg Graduate School of Management, Northwestern University. His current interests include job design, feedback-seeking behavior, and organizational and reward system design. His recent publications include *Introduction to Organizational Behavior*, with R. B. Dunham; "Enhancing Human Productivity," with G. Latham and T. Mitchell; and *Research in Organizational Behavior*, Vol. 3, with B. M. Staw. He received his D.B.A. from Indiana University.

WARD EDWARDS ("A View from a Barefoot Decision Analyst" (pp. 317–320)) is a Professor of Psychology and Industrial and Systems Engineering, and is the Director of the Social Science Research Institute at the University of Southern California, Los Angeles, CA 90007. He has published extensively in the area of decision analysis. He received his Ph.D. from Harvard University.

HILLEL J. EINHORN (coauthor, "Behavioral Decision Theory: Processes of Judgment and Choice" (pp. 15–41)) is a Professor of Behavioral Science and the Director of the Center for Decision Research at the University of Chicago, Chicago, IL 60637. His current research interests include causality and inference, and creativity and imagination in decision making. His work has been published in *Annual Review of Psychology, Psychological Review,* and *Psychological Bulletin.* He received his Ph.D. from Wayne State University.

BARUCH FISCHHOFF ("Latitude and Platitudes: How Much Credit Do People Deserve?" (pp. 116–120)) is a Research Associate at Decision Research — A Branch of Perceptronics, 1201 Oak St., Eugene, OR 97401. His current research interests include hazard management, personal and societal decision making, historical judgment, and cost benefit analysis. His recent book, *Acceptable Risk: A Critical Guide,* with S. Lichtenstein, P. Slovic, S. Derby, and R. Keeney, will be published by the Cambridge University Press, N. Y., N. Y. this year. He is a recipient of the Early Career Development Award from the American Psychological Association in 1980. He received his Ph.D. from Hebrew University at Jerusalem.

DONALD GERWIN (coauthor, "An Information-Processing Model of Intrafirm Dynamics and Their Effects upon Organizational Perceptions, Strategies, and Choices" (pp. 168–194)) is a Professor of Business Administration at the University of Wisconsin at Milwaukee, Milwaukee, WI 53201. His current research interests include the process of strategic decision making in business firms and the innovation process for computerized manufacturing systems. Recent publications include "Information Processing Model of Organizational Perception, Strategy, and Choice," *Management Science,* June 1980, with F. D. Tuggle; and "The Organizational Impacts of Flexible Manufacturing Systems: Some Initial Findings," *Human Systems Management,* November 1980, with S. T. Leung. He received his Ph.D. from Carnegie-Mellon University.

JOHN R. HAYES ("Issues in Protocol Analysis" (pp. 61–77)) is Professor at the Department of Psychology, Carnegie-Mellon University, Pittsburgh, PA 15213. His current interests are problem solving, cognitive processes in writing, and differences between expert and novice writers. His recent book is *The Complete Problem Solver,* to be published soon by The Franklin Institute Press.

ROBIN M. HOGARTH (coauthor, "Behavioral Decision Theory: Processes of Judgment and Choice" (pp. 15–41)) is an Associate Professor of Behavioral Science at the University of Chicago Graduate School of Business, Chicago, IL 60637. His current research interests include psychology of judgment and processes of decision making and theories of rationality and inference. His most recent book is *Judgment and Choice: The Psychology of Decision,* Wiley, 1980. He received his Ph.D. from the University of Chicago.

GEORGE P. HUBER ("Decision Support Systems: Their Present Nature and Future Applications" (pp. 249–262)) is a Professor of Business and Industrial Engineering at the University of Wisconsin Graduate School of Business, Madison, WI 53706. His current research interests include decision support systems, organizational information systems, and organizational decision making. His most recent book is *Managerial Decision Making,* Scott, Foresman, 1980. He received his Ph.D. from Purdue University.

JACOB JACOBY (coauthor, "Behavioral Process Research: Concept and Application in Consumer Decision Making" (pp. 232–248)) was Professor of Psychology in the Department of Psychological Sciences at Purdue University, West Lafayette, IN 47907 until September 1981, when he became the Merchant's Council Professor of Marketing and Director of the Institute of Retail Management, New York University. His current interests include consumer information processing and decision making, advertising, and questionnaire construction. His work has appeared in the *American Psychologist, Journal of Applied Psychology, Journal of Marketing Research, Journal of Marketing, Journal of Consumer Research, Annual Review of Psychology,* and *Handbook of Industrial/Organizational Psychology.* His recent books are *Brank Loyalty: Measurement and Management,* with R. C. Chestnut, and *The Miscomprehension of Televised Communication,* with W. D. Hoyer and D. A. Sheluga. He received his Ph.D. from Michigan State University.

DANIEL KAHNEMAN ("Bureaucracies, Minds, and the Human Engineering of Decisions" (pp. 121–125)) is a Professor at the Faculty of Commerce and Business Administration, University of British Columbia, Vancouver, BC V651W5. He is currently interested in decision making and judgment under uncertainty. Recent publications include "Prospect Theory," with A. Tversky, *Econometrica*, Vol. 47, 1979, and "Framing of Decision and the Psychology of Choice," *Science*, 1981. He received his Ph.D. from the University of California.

HOWARD KUNREUTHER ("The Economics of Protection Against Low Probability Events," (pp. 195–215) and coauthor, "Decision Analysis for Complex Systems: Integrating Descriptive and Prescriptive Components" (pp. 263–279)) is a Professor of Decision Sciences at the Wharton School, University of Pennsylvania, Philadelphia, PA 19174. His current research interests include decision making for low-probability events with an interest in integrating descriptive models of choice with prescriptive analysis (for example, role of market mechanisms, regulation, and incentive systems). His most recent book is *Disaster Insurance Protection: Public Policy Lessons*, with R. Ginsber, L. Miller, P. Sagi, P. Slovic, B. B. Borkan, and N. Katz, Wiley, 1978. He received his Ph.D. in economics from the Massachusetts Institute of Technology.

ARIE Y. LEWIN ("The State of the Art in Decision Making: An Integration of the Issues" (pp. 312–316)) is a Professor of Business Administration at the Fuqua School of Business, Duke University, Durham, NC 27706. His current research involves information processing of leadership attribution, evaluating the efficiency and effectiveness of organization, and social control of state-owned enterprises. His recent papers include "An Information Processing Approach to the Study of Leadership Attribution," with S. S. Layman, *Management Science* (forthcoming); "Information Processing Models of Peer Nominations," with S. S. Layman, *Personnel Psychology*, 32, pages 63–82, 1979; "Measuring the Relative Efficiency and Output Potential of Public Sector Organizations: An Application of Fractional Linear Programming," with R. C. Morey, *Policy Analysis and Information System*, Special Issue on Organization Systems, September 1981. Professor Lewin is departmental editor for organization analysis, performance, and design of *Management Science*. He received his Ph.D. from Carnegie-Mellon University.

SARAH LICHTENSTEIN ("Commentary on Hayes's Paper" (pp. 83–84)) is a Research Associate at Decision Research — A Branch of Perceptronics, 1201 Oak St., Eugene, OR 97401. Her current research interests include judgment, decision making, and the perception of risk. Her recent book, *Acceptable Risk*, with B. Fischhoff, P. Slovic, S. Derby, and R. Keeney, was published by the Cambridge University Press. She received her Ph.D. from the University of Michigan.

KENNETH R. MacCRIMMON ("On Lincoln's Doctor's Dog: Or Where Are We in Behavioral Decision Theory?" (pp. 48–52) is a Professor at the Faculty of Commerce and Business Administration, University of British Columbia; and J. L. Kellogg Distinguished Professor of Strategy and Decision, Kellogg Graduate School of Management, Northwestern University, Evanston, IL 60201. His current research interests include utility theory axioms, models of collective decisions, risk perceptions and assessments, corporate strategic decisions, social motives, and strategies of problem solving. Recent publications include "Utility Theory: Axioms vs. Paradoxes," with S. Larsson, in M. Allais and O. Hagen (Eds.), *Expected Utility and the Allais Paradox*, Holland: Riedel, 1979, pages 333–409; "Real Money Lotteries: A Study of Ideal Risk, Context Effects, and Simple Processes," with W. T. Stanbury and D. A. Wehrung, in T. S. Wallsten (Ed.), *Cognitive Processes in Choice and Decision Behavior*, Hillsdale, N.J.: Erlbaum, 1980, pages 155–177; and "Studying Team Performance: A Decision Theory Perspective," in S. E. Golding and P. Thorndyke (Eds.), *Improving Team Performance*, Santa Monica, Calif.: Rand Corp. (R2606), 1980, pages 144–158. He received his Ph.D. from the University of California at Los Angeles.

JAMES G. MARCH (coauthor, "Behavioral Decision Theory and Organizational Decision Theory" (pp. 92–115)) is Fred H. Merrill Professor of Management at the Graduate School of Business, and Professor of Political Science and of Sociology at Stanford University, Stanford, CA 94305. He has published in the area of organizational decision making. He received his Ph.D. from Yale University.

HENRY MINTZBERG ("Comments on the Huber, Kunreuther and Schoemaker, and Chestnut and Jacoby Papers" (pp. 280–287)) is a Professor of Management, 1001 Sherbrooke St. West, Montreal, Quebec, Canada H3A 1G5. He is currently studying patterns in strategy formation and completing a book on power in and around organizations. His recent publications include *The Structuring of Organizations*, Prentice-Hall, 1979; and "Tracking Strategy in an Entrepreneurial Firm," with James A. Waters, forthcoming in the *Academy of Management Journal*. He received his Ph.D. from the Sloan School of Management, Massachusetts Institute of Technology.

JOHN W. PAYNE ("Applications of Information-Processing and Decision Theories: A Discussion" (pp. 221–225)) is an Associate Professor at the Fuqua School of Business, Duke University, Durham, NC 27706. His current research interest is concerned with how task variables affect the cognitive processes involved in decision making under risk. His most recent articles include "Translation of Gambles and Aspiration Level Effects in Risky Choice Behavior," *Management Science*, 1980, 26, 1039–1060; and "Managerial Risk Preferences for Below-Target Returns," *Management Science*, 1980. He received his Ph.D. from the University of California at Irvine.

LOUIS R. PONDY ("On Real Decisions" (pp. 309–311)) is a Professor and Associate Head at the Department of Business Administration, University of Illinois, Urbana, IL 61801. He has recently received a grant from the National Institute of Education to study strategic decision making by school superintendents in three Chicago area school districts. His recent publications include *Organizational Symbolism*, an anthology of papers forthcoming from JAI Press; and "General Systems Theory and Organizational Development: A Dialectical Inquiry," in T. G. Cummings (Ed.), *Systems Theory for Organizational Development*, Wiley, 1980. He received his Ph.D. from Carnegie-Mellon University.

MICHAEL I. POSNER ("Protocol Analysis and Human Cognition" (pp. 78–82)) is a Professor of Psychology at the Department of Psychology, University of Oregon, Eugene OR 97403. He has received numerous awards for his work in cognitive psychology, including the Distinguished Scientific Contribution Award, given by the American Psychological Association in 1980. He received his Ph.D. from the University of Michigan.

PAUL J. H. SCHOEMAKER (coauthor, "Decision Analysis for Complex Systems: Integrating Descriptive and Prescriptive Components" (pp. 263–279)) is an Assistant Professor of Decision Sciences at the Graduate School of Business, University of Chicago, Chicago, IL 60637. His current research interests include decision making under risk, multiattribute utility theory, and the psychology of judgment and choice. He recently published a book titled *Experiments on Decisions Under Risk: The Expected Utility Hypothesis*, Martinus Nijhoff Publishers, 1980. He received his Ph.D. in decision sciences from the Wharton School, University of Pennsylvania.

ZUR SHAPIRA (coauthor, "Behavioral Decision Theory and Organizational Decision Theory" (pp. 92–115)) is a Lecturer of Organizational Behavior at the Jerusalem School of Business Administration, Hebrew University, Jerusalem, Israel. His recent publications include "Optional Stopping on Non-Stationary Series," with I. Venezia, *Organizational Behavior and Human Performance*, February 1981, and "Making Trade-offs Between Job Attributes," *Organizational Behavior and Human Performance*, 1982, in press. He received his Ph.D. from the University of Rochester.

JOHN W. SLOCUM, JR. ("Decision Making: An Interdisciplinary Focus" (pp. 288–292)) is a Distinguished Professor of Organizational Behavior and Administration at the Edwin L. Cox School of Business, Southern Methodist University, Dallas, TX 75275, and currently the editor of *Academy of Management Journal*. His current interests include the examination of the relationship between organizational climates and job performance and satisfaction. His works have been in *Human Relations, Administrative Science*

Journal, Academy of Management Journal, Journal of Applied Psychology, Organizational Behavior and Human Performance, Management Science, Decision Sciences, Academy of Management Review, Business Horizons, and others. He received his Ph.D. from the University of Washington.

RONALD N. TAYLOR ("On Improving Applied Decision Making: Comments on the Bouwman, Tuggle and Gerwin, and Kunreuther Papers" (pp. 216–220)) is an Associate Professor at the Faculty of Commerce and Business Administration, University of British Columbia, Vancouver, BC V651W5. His current research interests include the behavioral aspects of decision making, human resource decisions, and behavioral research methodology. His latest publications include "Experimenting with Organizational Behavior," with I. Vertinsky, in W. Starbuck and P. Nystrom (Eds.), *Handbook of Organizational Design,* Oxford University Press, 1981; "Organizational and Behavior Aspects of Forecasting," in S. Makridikis and S. C. Wheelwright (Eds.), *The Handbook of Forecasting,* Wiley, 1981; and "Planning and Decision Making in Managing Organizations," in H. Meltzer and W. Nord (eds.), *Making Organizations Humane and Productive,* Wiley, 1981. He received his Ph.D. from the University of Minnesota.

FRANCIS D. TUGGLE (coauthor, "An Information-Processing Model of Intrafirm Dynamics and Their Effects upon Organizational Perceptions, Strategies, and Choices" (pp. 168–194)) is Jesse H. Jones Professor of Management and Dean at the Jesse H. Jones Graduate School of Administration, Rice University, Houston, TX 77001. His current research interest is on the strategic management of academic institutions. His most recent article, "On the Validation of Descriptive Models Decision Making," with F. H. Barron, was published in *Acta Psychologica,* Vol. 45, #1–3, August 1980, pages 197–210. He received his Ph.D. from Carnegie-Mellon University.

AMOS TVERSKY ("Remarks on the Study of Decision Making" (pp. 321–324)) is a Professor of Psychology at the Department of Psychology, Stanford University, Stanford, CA 94305. His current research interests include decision making, inductive inferences, similarity, and measurement theory. His most recent article, "The Framing of Decisions and the Psychology of Choice," with Daniel Kahneman, will be published in *Science.* He received his Ph.D. in psychology from the University of Michigan.

KARL E. WEICK ("Rethinking Research on Decision Making" (pp. 325–333)) is the Nicholas H. Noyes Professor of Psychology at Cornell University, Ithaca, NY 14853, and currently the editor of *Administrative Science Quarterly.* He has recently completed a revision of his book, *Social Psychology of Organizing.* His current research interests include observational methods, loosely coupled systems, and the amplification of small events. He received his Ph.D. from Ohio State University.

About the Editors

GERARDO R. UNGSON (Conference Director) is an Assistant Professor of Management at the Graduate School of Management, University of Oregon, Eugene, OR 97403. His research interests include strategic decision making, government regulations, and organizational adaptation. He has recently completed a study on the organizational impact of government regulations, subcontracted with the Department of Economic Development of Oregon and the Pacific Northwest Regional Commission. His latest publication is "Managerial Information Processing: A Research Review," with Daniel Braunstein and Phillip Hall, *Administrative Science Quarterly,* 1981, *26,* pages 116–134. He received his Ph.D. from Pennsylvania State University.

DANIEL N. BRAUNSTEIN (Conference Director) is a Professor of Management and Psychology at the School of Management and Economics at Oakland University, Rochester, MI 48063. His research interests cover managerial decision making and the organizational impact of computers, which have been the subject of a field study recently completed at a large utility. For five years, he wrote a behavioral science column for *Interfaces,* published by the Institute of Management Science. He received his Ph.D. from Purdue University.

Conference Attendees*

"New Directions in Decision Making" Conference

March 1–3, 1981
Eugene, Oregon

Dennis M. Baker
University of Alberta

Van Ballew
University of Oregon

F. Hutton Barron
University of Kansas

Roger Best
University of Oregon

Ruth Beyth-Marom
Decision Research

Michael Laurie Bishow
University of Oregon

Bill Bordas
Decision Research

Phillip Bromiley
Carnegie-Mellon University

John S. Carroll
Loyola University

Cynthia Cloyd
University of Oregon

Ruth M. Corbin
Trans-Canada Telephone System

Jerome Dasso
University of Oregon

David Dilts
University of Oregon

Dale Duhan
University of Oregon

Tibor Englander
Hungarian Academy of Sciences

Andreas W. Falkenberg
University of Oregon

Joyce E. S. Falkenberg
University of Oregon

Klara Farago
Hungarian Academy of Sciences

Peter H. Farquhar
University of California, Davis

Eduord Fidler
University of British Columbia

Tom Gilpatrick
University of Oregon

Eugene Gloye
Office of Naval Research

Robin Gregory
University of British Columbia

Nina Hatvany
Management Analysis Centre

James Helgeson
University of Oregon

Robert E. Hoskin
Duke University

Edward Howard
Tektronix, Inc.

Eric Johnson
Stanford University

Larry Jones
University of Oregon

Zoltan Kovacs
Hungarian Academy of Sciences

Jerry La Cava
University of Oregon

Patrick D. Larkey
Carnegie-Mellon University

John Lawler
University of Minnesota

Thomas W. Lee
University of Oregon

Angeline W. McArthur
University of Oregon

Don MacGregor
Decision Research

Steve Maurer
University of Oregon

Richard T. Mowday
University of Oregon

Lynda Paule
University of Oregon

Kim R. Robinson
University of Oregon

Philip J. Runkel
University of Oregon

Sarah Rynes
University of Minnesota

James Shanteau
Kansas State University

Paul Slovic
Decision Research

Richard M. Steers
University of Oregon

David Stonner
Office of Naval Research

Ola Svenson
University of Stockholm

Paul Swadener
University of Oregon

Thomas Swenson
University of Oregon

James R. Terborg
University of Oregon

Martin A. Tolcott
Office of Naval Research

Don Tull
University of Oregon

Harry Waters, Jr.
University of Oregon

Jerzy Wilczynski
Decision Research

Van R. Wood
University of Oregon

William Wright
Stanford University

Spencer H. Wyant
University of Oregon

*Does not include conference speakers and conference directors.

Author Index

Subject Index